A Guide to Theatre Study

A Guide to Theatre Study

Second Edition

Kenneth M. Cameron

Theodore J. C. Hoffman

Macmillan Publishing Co., Inc.
New York

Copyright © 1974, Macmillan Publishing Co., Inc.

Printed in the United States of America

Earlier edition, entitled *The Theatrical Response*, copyright © 1969 by Macmillan Publishing Co., Inc.

Macmillan Publishing Co., Inc.
866 Third Avenue, New York, New York 10022

Collier-Macmillan Canada, Ltd.

Library of Congress Cataloging in Publication Data

A guide to theatre study.

First ed. published in 1969 under title: The theatrical response.
Bibliography: p.
   1. Theatre. 2. Drama. I. Hoffman, Theodore J. C., joint author. II. Title.
ISBN 0–02–318350–0
PN1655.B34 1974   792   73–6490

Printing: 1 2 3 4 5 6 7 8   Year: 4 5 6 7 8 9 0

As the title of this book indicates, it is a basic guide for students in the nonmajor introductory course in theatre. As a revision of an existing work, it incorporates much of the first edition, but it has been widely changed and added to for the specific needs of the nonmajor theatre student.

As in the first edition, this version is built around discussions, within a historical context, of a selected handful of plays that represent major periods and types. In response to comments from readers of the first edition, we have found it wise to reduce our emphasis on the medieval period, which is not of primary importance to the introductory course. Because of their greater relevance, therefore, we have added plays of the eighteenth and nineteenth centuries. In addition, developments in the American theatre since the writing of the first edition have resulted in the inclusion of a very recent play, Arthur Kopit's *Indians,* and with it a discussion of the many trends in contemporary theatre.

The second edition offers a new organization of materials. Acting and directing are now considered separately. The chapter on design is virtually new in its entirety, and the descriptive discussions of technical matters (including makeup) have been incorporated into the appropriate chapters. As with the plays, it has been found desirable to add new material concerning trends in theatre in the 1960s and 1970s. Finally, an entirely new chapter on career possibilities has been added in response to readers' requests.

Readers of *A Guide to Theatre Study* need not be bound, of course, to the book's organization. The placement of historical material in Chapter Two, for example, is neither a statement of priority nor a suggestion for a course sequence; many readers will find it preferable to begin with a study of the performance areas or the nature of theatre and go immediately to directing, acting, or design. In such an organization, the historical data in Chapter Two may well serve as a resource, to be read selectively in connection with specific sections of the other chapters.

Nor need any reader be bound by the plays discussed and illustrated in the present edition. We must confess to a certain amount of personal preference in our selection; the same kind of preference will lead many users to other plays—*The Oresteia* or *The Bacchae* instead of *Oedipus Rex; A Doll's House* or *Miss Julie* instead of *Three Sisters;* and so on. This possibility has been kept in mind in preparing this edition; we intend that there be enough supporting material with the discussion of each play so that a substitute play can still be studied in its own context.

More than ever, we want to point out that this is not a how-to-do-it book; it is a how-it-is-done book. We hope that it will stimulate some students to think of a career in the theatre; we hope that it will stimulate many students to make a closer study of theatre; but most of all, we hope that it will stimulate all students to love the theatre.

Our indebtedness for help in preparing this second edition is far greater than we can express. Students and colleagues have provided constant inspiration and encouragement. Our friends and families have given help in everything from providing peace and quiet to checking galleys. To our editors at Macmillan, Lloyd Chilton and J. Edward Neve, we owe a special debt; and for their suggestions for revision, we must thank Jerry Blunt, Los Angeles City College; Stanley A. Waren, The City College of the City University of New York; Farley Richmond, Michigan State University; and Alfred G. Brooks, State University of New York at Binghamton.

Most of all, for his insight and his perceptive comments on both the first and second editions, we want to thank Arthur Wilmurt of Carnegie-Mellon University.

K. M. C.
T. J. C. H.

Contents

"Is this a theatre?" asks a bewildered character in an early Dickens novel, coming in on a rehearsal and seeing the actors without their makeup and fine costumes, the stage bare, the house empty; and he adds plaintively, "I thought it was a blaze of light and finery."

"Why so it is," replies his companion, "but not by day . . . not by day."

There are many such fictional incidents and stories. They all have the same apparently grim moral: Don't look at the theatre too closely. Don't poke around backstage. Don't let the chilly light of reality in on it; you'll find that the makeup is only colored grease, the lace is only cheap gauze, the ornate stonework is only cardboard, the charismatic actor is a sweaty young man who works very long hours. Don't look, or you'll be disenchanted; don't look, or the magic will go away.

The moral is a fine one—for the bedazzled. But it isn't necessarily good advice for everyone.

For those who will look with wiser eyes, the fact that the garish makeup can be made to seem like living flesh *is* enchantment; the means by which the gauze is changed to lace *is* bedazzling; the artistry that can turn cardboard to stone and hard work to dynamic perform-

Figure 1–1. The interior of the Stratford Shakespearean Festival Theater in Stratford, Canada. This design, with its close audience-performer relationship and its formalized stairs and levels was an important influence on the many theatres built in the United States and Canada since the mid-1950s. (*Courtesy of the Stratford Shakespearean Festival. Peter Smith photo.*)

ance *is* the magic. That final product, the performance, is the goal, true. It has unique qualities: the coincidence of illusion and reality, the thrill of spectacle, the suspense of great events unfolding. But those qualities are only enhanced for the viewer who has discovered the arts that were necessary to create them; and the deeper one goes into their discovery, the more fascinating they become. To sit in a theatre and watch a great performance is wonderful. To watch a great performance, and know how it came into being, is to understand why the theatre is the most wonderful of all the arts.

THE THEATRE AS COMMUNICATION

The theatre is a very broad term; it can comfortably include a three-ring circus, light shows, *Hamlet* at The Public Theatre, or a rock show. Of late, it has been rendered a little elastic, and has been made to cover everything—life itself. But such usage makes the word *theatre* unnecessary—better terms already exist to cover "everything." If one wants to argue the inclusiveness or exclusiveness of what is, or is not, *theatre*, one might better start with a study of the normal meaning of the term, and expand that when knowledge is firmly in hand.

So *the theatre*, within the limits of this book, will be a wide area of human experience, to be sure, but one that is firmly supported on three points: *performance* (including such performance elements as plays, scripts, directions, and so on); *performers;* and *audience.* As Eric Bentley put it, in *The Life of the Drama,* "The theatrical situation, reduced to a minimum, is that A impersonates B while C looks on." Performer, performance, audience.

What happens in the theatre, then, must happen among these three elements—it is not a single, hard-edged event, but an on-going transaction. What is involved is a process, the interaction among the performance, performers, and audience, a form of communication. In the modern sense, however, *communication* refers to a great deal more than the mechanical transmission of verbal messages. In the theatre, wiseacres advise, "If you've got a message, send a telegram." We can address ourselves to (1) the thing communicated; (2) the means of communication; and (3) the thing received. Now, much traditional theatre study has assumed that the *thing communicated* is the text, that performance is the *means of communication,* and that the text is the *thing received.* If this assumption were true, two other assumptions would have to be accepted: (1) that the text is a constant that can be communicated exactly by effective performance, and (2) that the audience is also a constant that will always receive the same text if it is effectively communicated by performance.

In this study, however, we are going to assume that the "meaning" of the text is one thing, that of the performance another, and that received by the audience yet another. We must build our methods of study on the process of communication within which these three variable kinds of meaning operate. Before doing so, consider for a moment some of the methods of criticism usually used.

Reviewers write as if they and the audience were "exposed to the text" through a performance. To read the text itself when the reviewer has not, as is the common experience of theatre practitioners, is to realize that the reviewer takes the performance for the play and does not construct the text itself in his mind. He may incidentally damn the text (the play) and praise the performers who have made it public. He may praise a bad play and ignore the performances that have enhanced it. Reviewers also often fail to assess the director's role in a production, perhaps because some theatre reviewers lack practical knowledge of performance techniques. This does not mean that they do their jobs incompetently.

The reviewer is part of the commercial apparatus of theatre. His job is to describe a production so that his readers can decide whether it is worth their while to become its audience. The reviewer, whatever his own understanding of his job, actually describes or predicts audience response. He is most successful when his own perception, knowledge, values, and response are those of his own particular audience. In terms of communication, the producer relies on the reviewers' descriptions of the *thing received* to decide whether to keep his production of the text running.

On the other hand, much criticism and scholarship assume either that performance can effectively communicate the text to *any* audience,

Figure 1–2. *Hamlet* at the University of Missouri, Columbia. Directed by Kirk Mee and Robin Humphrey; setting designed by Lewis Stoerker. (*Courtesy of the University of Missouri, Columbia. Donovan Rhynsburger, Executive Producer.*)

or else ignore the operation of theatre as a process altogether by concentrating on the text. Criticism that deals with the text is really treating the text as literature and may actually be involved with the communication process of literature, which could be described as: *thing communicated*, meaning of text; *means of communication*, audience reading of text; *thing received*, audience's version of meaning of text.

If we want to describe criticism that is good theatre study, we must use a theatre concept of communication: *thing communicated*, performers' production of text; *means of communication*, conditions of performance; *thing received*, audience response to its perception (the meaning an audience finds in performance).

If we propose to study theatre seriously and thoroughly, this concept of "conditions of performance" as the means of communication will be a tremendous burden. We must determine not only the physical conditions of theatre architecture (for example) for any given audience, but also the social and cultural conditions of the audience, its attitudes, values, and tastes, its habits of perception—an almost impossible task, particularly as we move farther away from our own age.

We can begin this attempt in some small way by further considering what is involved when a performance is communicated to an audience through the conditions of performance. We have been suggesting that performance creates a language of its own and we have also suggested that communication involves more than verbal messages. There has been a progressive tendency in critical theory to agree that art communicates "meaning," and to recognize that criticism expresses the "meaning" it finds in art, but in a different way from the work of art itself. Criticism is verbal, of course, and what we are confronted with is the tyranny of words. Words, by a kind of agreement among groups of people, stand for things or concepts and are joined together in an accepted syntax to express relationships among many existing things or concepts in the world. We know that, in society, words and their use vary from place to place, and also vary in time in any place. We also know that although we may in daily life constantly employ words, we add meaning to them by the way we speak them, through sound emphasis, through physical gestures, and through our personal relationships with each other. (In passing, we should note that this added paraphernalia of gesture is one of the things a playwright tries to catch and imply and is also one of the principal components of performance.)

For purposes of precise written and spoken statement, especially for purposes of description, or exact reproduction, the gestural devices of casual life, with their unspoken and nonrepeatable implications, are insufficient. We have, therefore, developed a more formal use of words, based on man's habits of reasoning, which is commonly called logical discourse. Linguistic scholars have discovered both the possibilities

Figure 1–3. *Oedipus Rex* at the Hilberry Classic Theatre, Wayne State University. Directed by Richard D. Spear; setting by Richard D. Spear. Costumes designed by Robert Pusilo. Lighting by Gary M. Witt.

and limitations of logical discourse. Modern philosophy (especially logical positivism) has also explored the kinds of material that logical reasoning cannot handle. And science has expanded mathematics, which was originally a notation of logical discourse, so that it is now another form of discourse, even another kind of language.

But criticism operates through logical discourse, as indeed do all the methods of all the academic disciplines. In the study of the arts, so long as it was believed that meaning was self-contained in texts and remained constant through time and was based on logical discourse, criticism had no problems. But social scientists and humanists over the centuries have learned to recognize that the gestures that accompany spoken language, the nonverbal gestures through which we communicate, the ways in which we perceive and comprehend life, the set of values or common instinctive vision of life that is the property of individual cultures, and, finally, the arts all represent a kind of meaning separate in itself, not based on logical discourse, not communicated through logical discourse, and in fact not readily convertible into logical discourse.

This order of meaning has been variously defined in relation to many forms of thought and behavior. In relation to the arts, if we must make a choice in naming it, we might best treat it as *symbolic* discourse. A symbol is a *perceived pattern of some sort that has a parallel meaning to something in our experience*. It evokes that something as an emotion or a feeling in the individual who encounters the symbol. It is not a sign. Signs stand for something definite, something readily expressed by logical discourse. A red traffic light means stop. A red patch may mean warmth, passion, or fear, depending on its composition and the individual who responds to it. If a man holds up his first two fingers as a sign, it stands for 2 ($2, two beers, whatever is being discussed). As a symbol it may mean *victory* or *courage*, it may mean *World War II*, it may mean an insult.

Theatre can be said to operate as a kind of symbolic discourse. It communicates experience symbolically. The work of art (text or performance) is a complex symbol (or unified groups of symbols). It is a symbol of experience, a "more or less adequate means of representing man as we know him here below" (Francis Fergusson, *The Idea of a Theatre*). Its audiences respond to it as a symbol that stimulates feelings in them—feelings that are dependent on the conditions under which the audience has responded. Of course, if we accept this theory we are obliged to assume that a pattern of human feeling—an image of life, a perception of experience, whatever we choose to call the configuration of meaning that an artist is trying to realize—actually can be made to exist in a symbolic form. We have to see a symbol as a state of meaning, or a container of meaning. We have to agree that works of art made out of various media (animate, inanimate; deliberate, accidental; visual, auditory; verbal, instrumental) constitute self-contained symbols. And we have to assume that when theatre operates successfully, audiences respond to symbols that awaken in the audiences' experiences and perceptions of life an order of meaning of the same kind that the artists try to communicate.

THE MYTHOS OF THEATRE

Two things should now be evident. First, the theatre is an intensely social institution—social because it involves human beings in distinct relationships (artist to artist, artist to audience, audience to critic, and so on); because it is a willing coming-together of people whose only common link may be the theatrical process itself; and because it tries to share symbolic discourse among those gathered, and not to drive them into individual, even isolated, searches for personal symbols and personal solutions. Second, it is an intensely meaningful institution, in the sense that it radiates many meanings in offering its reflection of experience.

To take up the second point first, we must note that as soon as we narrow our idea of theatre, as we have, to symbolic discourse, we have entered an area of profound meaning whose outer limits can be stretched to deal with the entire condition of man. Such a term does not mean merely his social condition (although it may) or his physical environment (although it may), but his own perception of the nature of existence within that environment: what it is like to be alive, to suffer, and to know joy—the realm of what previous (and perhaps more open-minded) ages called the spirit. The matter of perception is itself important, and many, if not all, of the plays discussed in this book are deeply concerned with perception. The theatre process is itself a perceptual one, and many of the changes that theatre history shows in "style" or "convention" are attempts to create for each age and each society new images of the perceptual problem that lies at the heart of any consideration of man's condition, of his place in the universe. For this reason, theatre at our own point in history seems to contain many existential ideas—ideas that were not formulated until very recently but that can retrospectively be seen in any institution that explores the nature of existence. For this reason too the areas of meaning of theatre and religion seem to overlap (although they may not exactly correspond, except in such rare instances as the early medieval period).

One might suggest, as a loose principle of theatre study, that the symbolic meaning of a play in performance is always of an order beyond the one the play seems to deal with; beyond the character is someone else (a type, at least); beyond the plot and the action is something else (a myth).

In our pragmatic, logical way of thinking today, *myth* has come to stand commonly for something that is untrue (the myth of racial superiority, the myth of the divine right of royalty). Behind this meaning, however, is a more profound one, the same one used in speaking of classical mythology—that of myth as an archetypal pattern of human fear or desire or the risky contact with superhuman force: the myth of Prometheus, in which is epitomized the double-edged gains of man's striving to overcome the environment; or the myth of Cupid and Psyche, the uneasy and finally disastrous union of emotion and intellect. In this sense, then, myth making is man's symbolic expression of the meaning of his own experience as it can be expressed by his imagination.

If we see an awareness on Aristotle's part of symbolic action in theatre in his phrase the "imitation of an action," we also find implications of the mythic potential of the theatre. For the Greek word that is

Figure 1–4. Sam Shepard's *Operation Sidewinder* at Lincoln Center, New York. Directed by Michael A. Schultz, with sets by Douglas W. Schmidt, costumes by Willa Kim, and lighting by John Gleason. (*Martha Swope photo.*)

usually translated as *play* is *muthos*, from which *myth* also derives. (We might note the Greek etymology of *poet* as *maker*.) The playwright is a myth maker; the other artists in the theatre process are also myth makers, and the changes of performance enrich or change the myths they make. Individual plays and individual performances may lay bare or obscure a mythic content, and different cultures—different periods —will not tolerate the same degree of mythos or even the same myths. However, when we hear someone say disgustedly that some play is the "old story about . . . ," we are likely to hear a mythlike summary of the play's action—given with contempt, in this case, because the myth is no longer apt. "Boy meets girl" is a very brief summary of a simple myth pattern, although only a more detailed knowledge of the particular action would let us in on which version of that myth we had— Cupid and Psyche, Zeus and Semele, or Actaen and Diana.

Classical and primitive myths allow for superhuman figures with superhuman powers and may tend to strip away details of both character and situation to present the myth clearly. Myth is characterized by much formalism. When it is clothed in the trappings of less formal, even of naturalistic media (being acted out rather than narrated, endowed with the immediacy of the audience's own society, environment, and problems), it may merge with the medium and even almost disappear. It becomes *intrinsic* rather than *extrinsic*, yet it remains. Even in the most shopworn hack work, the kind of thing that closes out of town or posts its closing notice before the first-night curtain goes up, a myth lurks. The trouble with the hack work—all questions of artistic ineptitude aside—is that its myth is no longer relevant.

Classics remain with us for only a few reasons. One of these is certainly their profound mythic content. *Oedipus Rex* and *Hamlet* are such classics, containing at their very hearts stories of man's aspirations beyond those conditions of life he can normally perceive. The elucidation of such classics, when it is not merely self-serving pedantry, is the attempt to bring those myths to life in all their depth and complexity.

Thus, the social nature of the theatre is not founded in the desire to be entertained or diverted or hypnotized, nor in the mere tendency toward gregariousness (although these things may be present), but in the same common urge to perceive important myths, presented within the conventions of one's own time. The theatre may, indeed, be the last truly social, mythic medium available to us in an organized, sophisticated society. If it metamorphoses into a noticeably different medium in the future, it will do so only when the sense of "society" can be maintained by some new, perhaps electronic, matrix. Marshall McLuhan's new tribalism, supposedly to be brought about by the instantaneous electronic exchange of information, may hint at such a development. (But we should find it no accident that myth and tribalism are compatible, tribalism being a social organization that allows for the dissemination of myths more readily than American or European society of the first half of the twentieth century.)

So long, then, as the three essentials—performer, performance, audience—remain, the theatre will remain. Some characteristics of the performance and of the performer's methods may change (and we try to suggest some of these changes in the second chapter). The way in which the audience is organized physically may change. But the activity that we identify as theatre will continue.

THEATRE AND COMMUNITY

The theatre is a group form. In some instances, it is a group art; in others, it is a group game or a group exploration; in still others, it is a group ceremony. The important fact of its dependence on the group lies not in its great power to *create* groups, to pull people together, but rather in its ability to express the feelings of a group—social belonging, adhesion. It is the very expression of group-ness, of community. And the sense of "community" that is meant here is not a casual or a frivolous one, but the most profound social feeling of which humans are capable, the very dynamism of their interpersonal lives.

Like other group arts (music and dance, most obviously) the theatre is communal in both its form and its expression. However, the theatre is unique in incorporating into its form and its expression the very substance of human social and communal existence, the mythic stories and emotions that lie at the center of communal life. The theatre does not merely retell these stories; it relives them.

In some communities, this reliving may involve the entire community, so that the audience and the performers merge, reenacting for each other and with each other. In other communities, a temporary separation may take place, with some participating while others watch, joining in songs and chants, providing rhythmic accompaniment. In still other communities, a permanent separation between performers and audience may take place, and even the lives of the performers away from the theatrical event may be separate from the life of the community (most noticably in those societies where actors have a priestly function.)

Whatever the organization of the theatrical event, however, one fact remains: the theatre, because it is a vitally important expression of man's communal life, must keep itself at the center of communal life if it is to maintain itself. Thus, the theatre performance can be an occasion of celebration (as in Athens in the fifth century B.C., for example, when the performance of plays was the climax of days of religious activity). It celebrates the joy and the importance of community itself—man joining with other men, to create, to protect, to live. It is not contradictory that this feeling of joy can be aroused by solemn or tragic theatrical events; the seriousness of such an event is itself a reason for the joyful recognition of it.

To explain this, we must again move into the area of myth and look at the analogy of individual dreams. (However, we must remember that it is only an analogy, for the theatre is never an individual's event.) Dreams touch deep levels of consciousness. In the past, they have been thought to be magical, prophetic—and for good reason. In dreams, the consciousness is speaking to itself clearly and without repression. So, too, in the communal dream of the theatre, the group consciousness speaks. Lionel Trilling has said of *Oedipus Rex* that it causes its audience to "think the unthinkable"—literally, to perform the same act as the individual dream by forcing the community (in this case, the ancient Athenian audience) to confront a communal event of the utmost seriousness (in this case, the violation of an incest taboo). And, as in the individual's dream, the enactment of this "unthinkable" event progresses through level after level of nonrational horror, forcing the group consciousness to see the communal consequences of a violation of its taboo: the collapse of a ruling house, the near-death of the society, and widespread suffering.

From where, however, do such value systems as taboos come? They derive, of course, from the needs of the group; they are the group's values—not merely those values that the group accepts as its laws in a formal sense, but, rather, those values that make it a group to begin with, those ideals, fears, practices, habits, and communal forms that make continuing social interaction possible. It is, thus, no accident that a tragedy of towering importance is centered around incest; incest is one of the central concerns of most societies, and in most it is forbidden because of its potential effect on the perpetuation of the society. The same is true of male-female sexual relationships, of marriage, of child-parent relationships, of the mutual responsibilities of subject and king, of citizen and society.

Yet, the examination and celebration of vital social values is not a simple, conscious matter, any more than an individual's dream is a simple, conscious matter. Neither the performers nor the audience submits the community to a rational scrutiny and then extracts its subject matter. On the contrary, it is from a communal unconscious ("the unthinkable") that theatre arises, drawing for its events on social values and for its characters on communal heroes, mythic

Figure 1–5. Arthur Kopit's *Indians* in its New York production. Directed by Gene Frankel, with settings by Oliver Smith, costumes by Marjorie Slaiman, and lighting by Thomas Skelton. (*Martha Swope photo.*)

13 / THE NATURE OF THEATRE

archetypes. The myths, as we have already pointed out, are capable of manipulation, reinterpretation, and variety, while the archetype can be given superficial characteristics that will give him individual identity.

The theatre is, then, the art form that demonstrates and celebrates the vital ties of a community. It is not a casual enterprise—"just entertainment," or "pure show-biz," or "only play acting." It can certainly lend its external form to these things, but if it does so, and cuts its ties to the central life of the community, it is deeply troubled. Its passing pleasures can lie in casual frivolity, but its greatness lies in communal celebration.

Theatre As Industry

Yet, looking objectively at the contemporary theatre, one has to say that there is very little communal celebration going around, and a great deal of what looks remarkably like very serious business enterprise. Contemporary theatre, with some exceptions, is vastly different from a purely communal theatre—but contemporary society is vastly different from a simple communal society. What seems like an almost infinite complexity has been interposed between the religious celebration of the fifth century B.C., and the stratified theatre of modern America, with its apparent center in New York City, its links into television and films, and its nearly unending quest for profits.

The theatre today seems to be big business. It is not always a profitable business, to be sure, but profit-making is not a criterion. Consider, for example, the professional and commercial organizations that surround the theatre in New York: the League of New York Theatres; Actors Equity Association; the Dramatists Guild; the United Scenic Artists of America; the Society of Stage Directors and Choreographers; The Association of Theatrical Press Agents; the American Federation of Musicians; the Legitimate Theatrical Employees; the Theatrical Protective Union; the Treasurers and Ticket Sellers. Or consider the network of press agents, reviewers, and media reporters that surround the New York theatre, all concerned solely with the accessibility of information about the theatrical "product" to consumers all over the United States.

For much of our theatre is, by and large, a consumer industry devoted to making a consumer product. As such, it is neither better nor worse than any other consumer industry, and its values are largely the same—to create a desirable (or desired) product and to make a profit. The values of desirability and profit, however, are not necessarily the crucial values of the life of the community; it has never been true that there was money to be made by causing a community to "think the unthinkable." On the other hand, there is nothing in the nature of commercial theatre that causes it *necessarily* to exclude communal values. European and American society have known a mostly commercial theatre since the Renaissance, after all; the last communal, mass theatre of the West was the medieval religious theatre that ended in the sixteenth century. The theatre of Shakespeare, the theatre of Molière, the theatre of Racine and Sheridan and Chekhov, all were "commercial" theatres. Yet, sound arguments can be made that these theatres were more integral to their societies than the theatre of the 1970s—that they somehow managed to be both commercial *and* communal. The difference, perhaps, lies not in the theatre alone, but in the society.

When a society fragments, for whatever reason, its modes of celebration must necessarily fragment, or fail, or change. We hear a great deal today of subcultures and countercultures, and these signs of fragmentation in the larger society are reflected in changes in the theatre. It may seem that its place is shifting from somewhere near the center of a circle to some point on or near the edge. Unable to celebrate the values of the entire society, the commercial theatre (which, after all, has, as one of its goals, its own self-perpetuation) is inclined to concentrate on the values of that segment that can or will buy tickets. It is at this point that genuine danger appears, that the mainstream theatre becomes threatened, for it is an expensive enterprise and seems always in the process of going under financially (the situation of the New York theatre today). To save itself, to sell tickets, to hold on to its financially stable segment of ticket-buying society, it may try to second-guess the

Figure 1–6. Chekhov's *Three Sisters* at the Trinity Square Repertory Company, Providence, Rhode Island. Directed by Adrian Hall. (*Mark III photo.*)

values of that segment, repeating last year's success, rejecting apparent innovation, turning its back on anything that will unsettle or disturb that segment (including causing it to think the unthinkable).

Such a process sounds grim, but it is, in fact, always going on in any commercial theatre. It is emphasized in today's theatre because our social fragmentation is emphasized. Fortunately, it is usually balanced by the appearance of other theatres in other parts of society.

Underground and Avant-Garde Theatre

In a word, an overcautious or alienated commercial theatre creates its own opposite. Where a sense of community exists in the segments of society not being served, a theatre may come into being.

But what constitutes a community? Ten people of similar ideas? A hundred? Two hundred million? The answers differ widely from place to place and from time to time. For the theatre, obviously, a community exists where cohesive values exist; the actual organization of the people need not be formal, either economically or politically. Such a community can exist within other structures. (Many American colleges and universities are communities.) Within our large cities, small communities exist, sometimes made up of people who live geographically apart but share profound similarities of values. (Sectarian churches in America have traditionally been true communities, drawing their members from fairly broad geographical areas to a common celebration.)

Thus, there need not be universal, mass community for theatre to become possible. On the contrary, the theatres that are presently being created in the shadow of the commercial theatre are very small; in fact, one of the puzzling aspects of them (to the commercial theatre) is their miniscule audience. They are often, in fact, economically unstable; but economic stability (especially profit taking) is typically distasteful to them, anyway. An antipathy may exist, therefore, between the commercial and the fractional communal theatre (although the antipathy may actually be less violent than either side admits).

Traditionally, such fractional communal theatre has been dubbed "avant-garde," a movement in advance of the main body. Of late, another term has come into vogue, "underground." *Avant-garde* has typically implied a conscious, artistic breaking away, an intellectual effort, and avant-garde theatre has typically flouted popular taste, reveled in its own differences, and aimed at dismaying or shocking the middle class. It has published manifestoes, ridiculed the artists of the commercial theatre, and, its work done and its goals accomplished, has been quietly absorbed into that very mainstream that was so recently its enemy.

Underground theatre, especially in the United States, seems to have evolved less as an attempt to change the mainstream than as an al-

Figure 1–7. Beckett's *Endgame* at the Dallas Theater Center, directed by Ken Latimer. Setting by Allen Hibbard, costumes by Yoichi Aoki, lighting by Sam Nance. (*Linda Blase photo.*)

ternative to it. Like underground newspapers and underground films, it seeks to be an artifact of an alternative community. There are many such theatres in existence, the best known being those in New York City, largely because of their accessibility to the media there. However, notoriety is hardly the sign of an underground theatre's viability (it may be just the opposite), and alternative theatres exist that no one but their own small communities have ever heard of.

Today, as with the avant-garde theatres of the past, the alternative theatres sometimes are guilty of overstating their own cases. They see themselves as very small voices crying in a very large wilderness, and they tend at times to bellow. Nonetheless, as the psychologist Rollo May has pointed out, artists are the prophets of the future, and much of the potency of the current underground theatres may come from their prefiguration of widespread values to come.

No one kind or level of theatre—neither commercial nor underground, mainstream nor alternative—is by its very nature preferable to any other. Individuals will have very strong preferences, but these will arise from individual needs, not from anything innately better or worse about one kind of theatre. Theatre people will have particularly strong preferences, for their lives are bound up with their beliefs. Absolute judgments, however, are best avoided; in a varied society, a varied theatre is probably a healthy theatre.

2 Classics and Their Theatres

In passing now from an examination of the theatre to the history of plays and theatres, it should be pointed out that the following brief analyses are intended both as examples of approaches to drama and as detailed studies of historical high points. The plays, therefore, were selected to cover a broad historical range as well as a formal range from classical tragedy through Renaissance comedy to the modern mixed mode. The opportunities for varied methods of dealing with the plays, therefore, are many. It should be clear that no single method of play analysis will work for all plays, just as no single method of acting will work for all actors and all roles. In general, each analysis attempts to arrive finally at an evaluation of the plays that will make them meaningful for a contemporary audience.

The inclusion of historical background concerning the nature of each play's theatre, and wherever relevant, its controlling critical theory, should rule out any free-floating interpretation of the plays based on the bare text alone. The recommendation should be obvious: no play of the past can be adequately dealt with unless its historical environment is understood; no play of the present can be translated into full stage life without giving some attention to its sources. Each of the plays, therefore, should be seen as a great theatre work on the one hand, and as a representative of particular kinds of staging and particular critical theories on the other: *Oedipus Rex* as both an example of the Greek theatre and as a vital drama; *Phaedra* as a quintessential piece of neoclassic writing and as a play of continuing importance; *Endgame* as a product of the theatrical theories of Antonin Artaud and as a great existential statement.

The plays form the discussion material of this book. Further discussion of them will be found in the other chapters, where they may be used as examples in describing aspects of acting, directing, design, and so on. Although the selection of these plays makes no pretense of offering a comprehensive survey of all styles or all periods of theatre it should be broad enough to allow a student to move on to other styles and other periods, using this chapter as an example for his working method.

OEDIPUS REX: TRAGEDY IN ANCIENT GREECE

The first great Western theatre was that of Athens in the fifth century B.C. It will be discussed again in Chapter Three, both because it gave us the operative generic terms of criticism (*comedy* and *tragedy*) and because Aristotle's commentary on it gave us the first, probably the greatest, example of dramatic criticism. The origins of this theatre are the subject of much theorizing. The facts surrounding it are detailed enough to let us recreate much of its physical and intellectual environment, yet they are vague enough to leave room for continued argument. The plays were the outstanding literary expression of Athenian culture

in its prime, as Homer's epics were of an earlier age and Plato's dialogues of a slightly later one. They survive as both historical documents
and works of art, and of those that survive, *Oedipus Rex* is without
doubt the most important.

A few terms should be made clear: *fifth-century Greece,* in the
theatrical sense, means Athens in the period generally from the accepted date of the oldest tragedy we possess, Aeschylus' *Persians*
(about 472 B.C.) to the deaths of Sophocles and Euripides (406 B.C.);
Roman refers to the period after the cultural subjugation of Greece by
Rome (about 50 B.C.); *Hellenistic* refers to the period from Alexander
the Great (about 350 B.C.) to the Roman period. These terms are essential to any examination of the Greek theatre because our evidence is
only partly from the fifth century itself, the rest being either Hellenistic
(commentaries, such as that of Pollux, and archaeological remains of
many theatres) or Roman (the reconstruction of certain theatres, including that at Athens, and commentaries that discuss the earlier
period, such as that of Vitruvius in the first century B.C.).

In general, four kinds of evidence are available: the plays themselves,
of which we have only a small sample; dramatic records of the period,
listing dates, plays, and authors (the *didaskalia*); commentaries, such
as those of Aristotle, Pollux, and Vitruvius; and the remains of the
theatre buildings, frequently reconstructed so that the fifth-century
building was obscured or even destroyed. The reasons for controversy
surrounding both the plays and the theatre, then, should be clear, for
our evidence is neither complete, contemporary, nor all of equal reliability. Where the controversy is marked, it will be noted.

We are dealing, then, with a highly organized, sophisticated theatre
of a society at its peak—Athens between 472 and 406 B.C. We shall have
to note that such a theatre necessarily had a lengthy past, about which
we can mainly conjecture. We must point out that it also had a lengthy
continuation into the Hellenistic period, in which we will not be directly
interested because its tragedies have not survived and because our
evidence suggests that its quality declined.

Fifth-Century Production

Underlying the production conditions of both the Greek tragic and
comic theatres was the fact that, almost without exception, theatrical
activity took place within a religious context. Both the physical and the
intellectual environments were religious: the theatres were sited within
the precincts of the cult of the god Dionysus (as, for example, the
tragic theatre at Athens was located on the grounds of the Temple of
Dionysus on the slope of the Acropolis), and the occasions for presenting drama were religious celebrations associated with the worship of
Dionysus. The seating of priests immediately adjacent to the playing
area and the inclusion of a permanent altar within the playing area

were further indications of the overriding religious significance of the presentation.

Given such religious associations, then, it is easy to see why such production aspects as financing, choice of plays, and selection of actors were a combination of state and individual responsibility, for in Athens the citizens were united by both a political and a religious community that were not really separable. Although *state religion* may be too strong (or too modern) a term for the worship of the Olympian gods and their post-Homeric additions, such as Dionysus, the fact remains that the intimate connection between political philosophy, social organization, and religion was natural and necessary. Religious holidays were state occasions; political allies or subject states were expected to send gifts or tribute on Athens' principal religious festivals. Similarly, the involvement of the Athenian government in financing aspects of worship was taken for granted, whether it was the building and repair of temples or the paying of actors.

In general, the large costs of each production were divided between the state (which paid individual actors) and a single wealthy citizen who underwrote the costs of the large choruses used in the plays (between fifteen and fifty men per chorus). A number of such individuals were selected each year to support as many playwrights as had been chosen for production. Although a few may have considered it a financial burden, it appears that the honor of being a *choregus* (supporter

Figure 2–1. The remains of the Greek theatre at Syracuse, Sicily, as modified by Hellenistic and Roman work. Note the semi-circular (Roman) *orkestra*, the massive stone construction beyond the parodos, and the remains of Roman construction joining the skene and the audience area into a single architectural unit. (*Courtesy of the Italian State Tourist Office. Photo ENIT.*)

of a chorus) and the satisfaction of fulfilling a religious duty at the same time assured generous backing for the theatre throughout the fifth century.

The second point to be noted concerning theatre production is that it was carried on only within the limitations of specific competition. Thus, the casual production of plays on an organized urban level was unknown; all new tragedies were staged during competitions held on religious festival days. Such a combination of competition and worship is not surprising in a culture that had a long tradition of the union of the two—evident, for example, in the games organized by Achilles to commemorate the death of Patroklas in the *Iliad* and in the pan-Hellenic Olympic games dedicated to Zeus.

To a modern theatregoer, the idea of a competitive religious art may be confusing. An analogy might be a yearly competition for requiem masses, to be held in St. Peter's in Rome and supported jointly by the Vatican and wealthy Italian citizens; of course, we have no such competition. However, as we shall see, the idea of the contest is central to Greek tragedy (and comedy as well) and the judging of contests is part of the tragic action. Therefore, the creation of works of art for competitive display was natural to the Greek scheme.

Three tragic playwrights were chosen yearly to present plays in competition at the Great (or City) Dionysia, a festival dedicated to Dionysus that involved the entire city. (A lesser competition was held at the Dionysian festival called the Lenaea.) The atmosphere was both festive and serious—processions to the Dionysian precinct on the slope of the Acropolis, a display of gifts and tributes from the Empire, competition in other poetic and quasidramatic forms, sacrifice, and ritual all took place within the five days of the celebration. Preparation for staging the three playwrights' tragedies would have occupied the months before the Great Dionysia. First, the playwrights were selected by the ruling archon (magisterial governor); his selection was supposed to be based on the merits of past works of the known playwrights in the city or on the recommendations for the unproduced work of new, younger men. In actual fact, the system seems to have been something less than impartial, and accusations of political conniving, use of influence, and nepotism were not uncommon. Yet the fact remains that out of this system of selection came great playwrights and great plays, and although the archon's choice among younger or lesser artists may have been open to influence, it is doubtful that playwrights of real merit could be prevented from writing for the Great Dionysia. Certainly, the plays that have come down to us suggest that the system could produce works of colossal stature.

This selection of playwrights dates back to at least 534 B.C., beyond which tragic production cannot be traced. Records of competition at the City Dionysia suggest, however, that the selection of only three playwrights and the formalized competitive system of the fifth century began in about 501 B.C., and lasted well into the Hellenistic period.

After the archon's selection of three playwrights came the selection of *choregoi* (the financial backers) and of actors, who were either assigned to the playwrights or, as must often have been the case, were instrumental in bringing about his selection and so were already associated with him. In the early period of the fifth century, playwrights acted in their own plays and staged them as well. After the middle of the century, it became unlikely that the playwright would also appear as actor. However, it is evident that playwrights would have certain favorite actors, and the competition for the most gifted actors must have been intense.

Actors and Acting

The concept of acting as a separate activity was probably much older than the tragic competitions themselves, having its roots in oratory, in the public narration of Homeric epic, and possibly in certain aspects of Dionysian ritual (See p. 36.) Nevertheless, the emergence of actors as individual artists capable of winning widespread recognition was slower than that of the tragedians, the first competition in acting not having been begun until 449 B.C. In addition, tragic actors did not form themselves into professional and religious guilds until a good deal later, in the Hellenistic period.

One reason for this relative lateness in emphasis on the Greek actor as artist was the gradual development of his function in the presentation of the tragedies. According to Aristotle, only one actor (other than the chorus) was used in tragedy before the time of Aeschylus (before, that is, sometime in the 480s or possibly the 490s), and only two were used until the time of Sophocles (about the first third of the century). The tradition, repeated by Aristotle, that these two playwrights introduced the second and third actor into tragedy may be incorrect in its specifics, but it surely reflects the period at which the number of actors was increased, whether Aeschylus and Sophocles were personally responsible or not. As we shall try to point out (p. 40), there were probably sound dramaturgical reasons for increasing the number of actors. The fact remains that *before about 490 B.C. only one tragic actor was used in each play, and throughout the period there were never more than three.*

To a modern audience, the use of only three actors and a chorus in a play having many roles would be very difficult to accept. However, the restriction seems to have been very rigid, and each actor seems to have "typed" himself virtually for life as one of the three: the *protagonist* (first actor, or, perhaps more correctly, first contestant), who played the most important role and who probably doubled in smaller roles when that character was not onstage; the *deuteragonist*, the second in importance, who played a number of supporting roles throughout the play; and the *tritagonist*, the third, who appeared only in small roles that neither allowed much scope for displays of acting pyrotechnics nor attracted much audience attention. The protagonist would have needed great control of his instrument and the imagination to bring life and variety to a number of demanding roles; the deuteragonist was also challenged by such roles as Jocasta or Creon in *Oedipus Rex*, and probably Teiresias and the Second Messenger in addition; whereas the tritagonist would *normally* have been cast only in the smaller, less active roles of the Priest and the Herdsman.

However, much of the strength of *Oedipus Rex* derives from its great concentration on Oedipus himself, who is onstage through the great proportion of the play; as a result, there is no other role in the play that the protagonist could have played. Therefore, either the role of Creon or the role of Jocasta would have had to be played by the tritagonist, for both characters are involved in scenes with Oedipus and a third speaking character, as well as in scenes with each other. The progression of scenes is as follows: Oedipus–Priest; Oedipus–Priest–Creon; Oedipus–Teiresias; Oedipus–Creon; Oedipus–Creon–Jocasta; Oedipus–Jocasta; First Messenger–Jocasta; First Messenger–Jocasta–Oedipus; First Messenger–Oedipus–Herdsman; Second Messenger; Oedipus–Creon. Many of these scenes are separated by the responsive choral odes, during which ample time existed for any of the actors to make the changes necessary for appearing as a new character. Nevertheless, the rapid sequence of changes and the importance of both Creon and Jocasta suggest that both the deuteragonist and the tritagonist had important large roles, as well as smaller ones, to play. Thus, if consistency of roles was maintained throughout the performance, it is clear that the protagonist could have played only Oedipus; that one of the other actors (probably the deuteragonist, because of the greater importance of the role) played Creon, the First Messenger, and possibly Teiresias and the Second Messenger (whose climactic description of the death of Jocasta and the blinding of Oedipus requires great power); and that the tritagonist probably played the Priest, Jocasta, and the Herdsman.

It should not be assumed that the acting area was bare of other figures because of this limitation, however. First, of course, there was the chorus. In addition, mute actors, apparently without limitation, could be used—the children of Oedipus in *Oedipus Rex;* a royal retinue or a military guard for such plays as Aeschylus' *Agamemnon*. In short, the spectacle made possible through costume, movement, and masses of figures was readily created; the exploitation of scenes having more than three speaking characters was not.

The art of acting that such character change demands must have been challenging. Highly trained instruments, especially the voice, were required. Although the realistic presentation of given circumstances, such as age, social position, or state of health was certainly not as necessary as in the modern realistic theatre, some physical impersonation was undoubtedly necessary. And although the language of each

Figure 2–2. A Roman tragic mask, patterned on Hellenistic and, ultimately, fifth-century models. This example, from a wall-painting in Pompeii, suggests the general structure of the tragic mask, with distorted mouth opening, enlarged eyes, and the hair rising high above the forehead. As painted, however, it is more realistic than the fifth-century mask would have been. (*Courtesy of the Metropolitan Museum of Art, Rogers Fund, 1903.*)

character does not distinguish him as clearly from the others as the language of a naturalistic playwright might, it is still apparent that changes of voice were necessary.

The greatest external aid to the actor making such a change was the mask. All tragic actors wore masks (although the chorus probably did not). The mask conveyed both the given circumstances of the character —age and sex—and the emotional quality of his tragic role. In addition, costumes, although formalized far beyond the actual clothing of the period, maintained enough recognizable features to give the audience information concerning the character's identity, even to his nationality and his social status.

All tragic actors were men. Thus, underlying their art was a degree of stylized formalization that could be carried into playing female roles. Such acting had its own concept of "truth," no doubt, but one far removed from that of our own stage. *Truth of one's own tragic function* might describe it—not inner truth, but adherence to a larger line created by a tragic action.

Playwrights and Plays

The limitations imposed on Greek tragic playwrights by the small number of actors were important in controlling the kinds of scenes such plays could present. Much of their apparent economy and compression springs from this very restriction. Furthermore, the use of a chorus—a partly lyric, partly dramatic group of performers who sang, danced, and still had a direct relationship to the play's action—imposed another condition on the playwright's work. Finally, the nature of the Dionysian tragic competition, which required that each playwright supply four plays (three tragedies and a "satyr" play, a kind of after-piece using a chorus of goat-men or satyrs and, generally, a humorous tone), meant that the fifth-century playwrights who were selected for the City Dionysia had to be men who could produce several plays, on subjects of their own choosing, in any given year.

A brief glance at the statistics of this situation may be helpful. In the years from 501 to 401 B.C., three playwrights should have written three tragedies each for every year of the City Dionysia. The total number of plays, then, is 900 (not counting satyr plays or comedies) for the City Dionysia alone, although certain exceptions that allowed for occasional revivals of old plays indicate that the number could be slightly lower. (See A. E. Haigh, *The Attic Theatre*, 3rd ed., pp. 71–73.) But of this considerable number, *we now possess only thirty-one tragedies,* and those are the work of only three playwrights. We know of other authors from the didaskalia and from other contemporary records (Plato's *Symposium,* for example), but we do not have their plays.

Such a small statistical sample might suggest that we cannot properly judge Greek tragedy by the plays we have. On the other hand, we must remember that the three playwrights whose work we know were all of the first rank in their own day. Two of them were frequent winners in the competitions, whereas the third (Euripides), although not regularly the winner of the first prize, was a frequent competitor and was presented satirically by Aristophanes as the rival to Aeschylus for the tragic crown in *The Frogs.* Finally, the plays we do possess are not an accidental collection, but appear to be a careful compilation of outstanding plays by a later dramatic scholar.

Our three playwrights are Aeschylus (c. 525–456 B.C.), Sophocles (496–406 B.C.), and Euripides (484–406 B.C.). To these three the name of at least Thespis should be added, for it is the semilegendary Thespis who, according to tradition, was invited to take part in the first Athenian tragic celebration in 534 B.C. Thespis represents a firm early date beyond which we cannot go in discussing tragedy, and although we cannot say exactly what his contribution to the form was, modern scholars have been able to make exciting speculations about his work. (See, for example, Gerald F. Else's *The Origin and Early Form of Greek Tragedy,* discussed on p. 39 *ff.*)

Our principal concern here is with the work of Sophocles and, of course, with *Oedipus Rex* in particular. Very generally, the progress of tragedy through the fifth century, as it seems to have developed from the early plays of Aeschylus through the last plays of Euripides, shows three important movements: first, a decrease in the size of the chorus and a growing discomfort with the chorus itself, especially in Euripi-

Figure 2–3. *Oedipus Rex* at the Stratford Shakespearean Festival, 1955. The costumes and masks did not seek to be archaeological reconstructions of the Greek, but modern evocations of it. Some observers have objected to the masks, particularly those of the chorus, as lowering rather than raising the attempt at tragic stature. The highly formalized gestures required by even these modern masks, however, are evident. (*Courtesy of the Stratford Shakespearean Festival.*)

des; secondly, a change from the religious assertiveness and confidence of Aeschylus (notably in the *Oresteia*, 458 B.C.) to a questioning and even skepticism in Euripides; and, finally, a tendency toward realism of character psychology, language, and setting toward the end of the century. We have already noted the progressive changes in the number of actors used by Aeschylus and Sophocles.

In presenting their three tragedies for the City Dionysia, these playwrights had a choice between offering three plays connected by a common story line or three plays of different plot and character, united probably by their tone and their themes. The first possibility was exploited more rarely, although the single instance that we have of three plays written around a central story (Aeschylus' *Oresteia*) is a magnificent accomplishment. The opportunity for development in three connected plays (now called a *trilogy*) could be very great, and in the case of the Aeschylean trilogy it is exploited in terms of a large design that is nothing less than an affirmative presentation of the joint creation of human and divine justice. However, the writing of three quite different plays was far more common, and *Oedipus Rex* was one of such a group. Thus, although Sophocles wrote two other plays on the Oedipus legend that we still possess (*Antigone* and *Oedipus at Colonus*), these three plays do not properly constitute a trilogy, having been written years apart for different competitions.

The subjects available to the tragic playwrights, although fairly broad, were limited by both tradition and formal necessities (number of actors, use of the chorus, tone of the tragedy itself) to heroic stories, especially those drawn from the area of Homeric legend. It was prin-

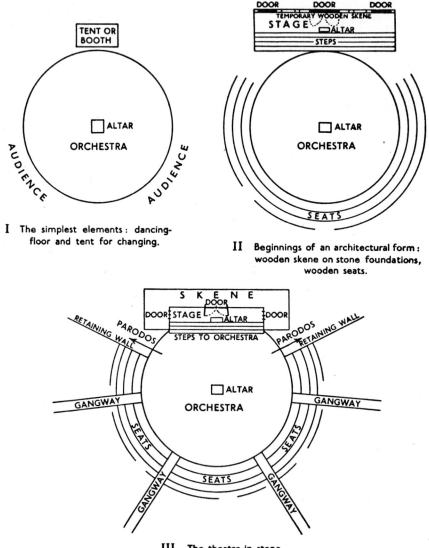

I The simplest elements: dancing-floor and tent for changing.

II Beginnings of an architectural form: wooden skene on stone foundations, wooden seats.

III The theatre in stone.

Figure 2–4. Schematic drawings of three stages in the development of the Greek theatre structure. (*From Peter D. Arnott,* An Introduction to the Greek Theatre, *Macmillan and Co., Ltd., London, 1959.*)

cipally to stories of prehistory that the playwrights addressed themselves. Many such stories involved the Olympian gods directly, whereas others operated within a universe of divine intervention—curses, judgments, orders to act, and reconciliation. *Oedipus Rex*, for example, is one story from a lengthy series involving a divine curse on a human family. Euripides' *The Bacchae*, on the other hand, presents the god Dionysus as an active character as it traces the entry of the Dionysian cult into Greek culture. Only rarely would a playwright devote himself to a story that was not derived from heroic legend; the one example available to us is Aeschylus' *The Persians*, which deals with an incident in the Persian War at the beginning of the fifth century. We know of a small number of similar plays having to do with contemporary or historical incidents. In the main, however, it was to prehistoric myth that the playwrights turned, and over the course of the fifth century the Greek audience saw many versions of such rich legends as that of Oedipus and his children (Sophocles' *Oedipus Rex, Antigone,* and *Oedipus at Colonus;* Aeschylus' *Seven Against Thebes*) or that of the house of Agamemnon (Aeschylus' *Oresteia;* Sophocles' *Electra;* Euripides' *Electra* and *Iphigenia*, and so on). We should not assume that this was a mere catering to the audience's liking for certain stories, or even that use of a given story or a given central character meant that the same plot would be repeated. On the contrary, the treatment of stories common to several playwrights could be so different that the plots would be effectively changed (Euripides particularly was given to changing the myths or combining variant forms of myths). Furthermore, the choral odes within the plays could place the stories in entirely new thematic contexts.

The playwrights, then, saw their plays performed by the state-supported actors, under the sponsorship of a choregus, at the Dionysian competition. It remains for us to examine theories concerning the theatre in which the plays were staged.

The Theatre of Dionysus at Athens

Considerable controversy still exists over the details of the fifth-century theatre at Athens. Despite existing remains of the theatre itself (altered in Hellenistic and Roman times), and of similar theaters elsewhere in the Mediterranean, it is difficult to pin down precisely what the nature of the theatre was. The principal points of difference to be noted are the nature of a hypothetical acting area for the actors, as distinct from that of the chorus; the nature of the structure in front of which both actors and chorus performed; the extent to which theatrical machinery was used; and the function, if any, of scenery. Differences on these points generally fall into a consistent pattern of agreement on all four questions, and the conclusions about them seem to have been conditioned by the extent to which a given scholar has looked at the Greek theatre as if it were a proscenium theatre, or some variant of it. Thus, at the extreme of the proscenium-theater similarity, some scholars have seen the Greek acting area as unified (both actors and chorus); surrounded on three sides by buildings that created a topless frame; backed by painted and three-dimensional, rather realistic scenery; and equipped with complex machinery for spectacular effects. The other extreme, of course, sees the actors as separate from the chorus, denies the existence of frame or scenery, and sees the machinery as relatively unimportant in the fifth century, although admittedly common in the Hellenistic period.

To begin with those points on which there is general agreement, we can note that Greek theaters in general were created with the performance space at the bottom of a slope, preferably in a natural bowl, on whose sides the audience could sit. By the fifth century, wooden stands were being constructed at Athens on the hillside, but the suggestion is strong that an earlier period had used merely the bare slope itself for the audience. At no point, evidently, did the Greeks build free-standing theatres of the Roman type, in which an artificial slope was built up architecturally (as in a modern stadium, for example).

The performance space at the bottom of the slope was circular when the natural shape allowed it, although asymmetrical shapes were known. (See Peter Arnott, *Scenic Conventions of the Greek Theatre in the Fifth Century* B.C.) At Athens, the Theatre of Dionysus had a circular area, surrounded on slightly more than a 180-degree arc by the audience. This performance space—called the *orkestra*—was analogous to the stage of a modern theatre in the round, although it was not raised and was not completely surrounded by the audience. Entrances into it were made by two *parodoi*, corridors located symmetrically at each end of the audience arc. Although the parodoi were used principally by the chorus, there are many clear examples of both entrances and exits through them by the actors.

The Athenian *orkestra* was made smaller during the course of the fifth century, shrinking from about 85 feet in diameter to about 65 midway through the century. (See Margarete Bieber, *The Theatre of Greece and Rome.*) If we remember the decrease in the size of the chorus during the same period, we can see that the smaller *orkestra* could have accommodated the later performances, because its size had to be large enough for the chorus' dancing. At the *orkestra's* center was an altar, the *thymele*, a permanent structural element that cannot be considered so much a theatrical property as a religious object.

Midway between the *parodoi* and perpendicular to the centerline of the audience and the *thymele* was a structure around which much scholarly controversy still revolves. Everyone admits that such a structure, called the *skene*, existed, but just what it was and when it came into existence are not clear. Peter Arnott sees it as having existed from a much earlier period; Margarete Bieber, on the other hand, suggests that no definite form was given to it until the last quarter of the fifth century. Although everyone agrees that the *skene,* like the audience stands, was made of wood at first, there is no agreement as to when it was built permanently of stone: Bieber and Arnott believe that the stone structure was put up in the last quarter of the fifth century. Pickard-Cambridge (*The Theatre of Dionysus at Athens*) believes that it was not begun until the middle of the fourth century.

For our purpose, hard dates are not so important as an idea of what the line of development was. The word *skene* derives from the same Greek word as *tent,* suggesting that its origin may lie in some very simple masking element or dressing room made of cloth. Comparison with the almost universally known booth stage of fairs and traveling performers shows that such a primitive use is theatrically sound. By the middle of the fifth century (and almost certainly before) this booth had become a wooden building, fairly long and possibly only one story high, running between the *parodoi.* By the Hellenistic period, the *skene* was more than 100 feet long and built of stone; in the fifth century, it was probably shorter. Its façade was pierced with doors (almost certainly three of them) that were used by the actors. The *skene,* then—from which our word *scene* comes—was not in the classical period either a scene or a scenery building. It was a structure for the actors, used undoubtedly for changes of mask and costume, for storage of properties, for entrances and exits, and, of course, for acoustical support for actors who had to intone lengthy speeches across the 65-foot orkestra to the audience.

Two other terms associated with the skene must be noted, because the meaning of both is still unclear: *paraskenia* and *proskenion.* The first apparently indicates something "beside the *skene,*" and its normally plural usage suggests symmetrical structures. It is these *paraskenia* that proscenium-oriented scholars have seen as the framing elements of the Greek acting area, interpreting them as wings jutting forward toward the *orkestra* from the ends of the *skene.* The word itself, however, is Hellenistic. The existence of such structures in the fifth century cannot be proved and, of course, was not necessary to the production of the plays.

The proskenion (from which our *proscenium* comes) is, literally, the "front of the *skene,*" and some interpreters have so used it—as meaning a flat surface for scenery on the skene wall facing the audience. Early uses of the word, however, indicate that it was probably a structure, not merely the face of the *skene;* and the only logical structure to be located between the *skene* and the audience is, of course, an acting area or stage. Clearly, *proskenion* and *orkestra* are not the same, so that the *proskenion* would have been a raised stage tangent to the *orkestra* and connected to it. There is no agreement here. Margarete Bieber states flatly that the raised stage did not exist; Arnott, on the other hand, sees its fifth-century existence as obvious—a low platform with central steps leading to the *orkestra*. Examined in terms of the plays and theatre practice, it seems more likely that the low stage did, indeed, exist, for the actors and chorus are so different, their kinds of action so distinct, and their focal requirements so opposed (single figure as compared to choreographic mass) that the separation of their performance spaces seems inevitable. As Richard Southern has pointed out (*Seven Ages of the Theatre*) the rise of acting as an art is accompanied by the raising of a stage to give the actor focus and vocal command. The rise of the actor in the fifth century suggests just such a theatrical development.

In sum, then, we can say of the fifth-century theatre at the time of *Oedipus Rex* (c. 427 B.C.) that it had probably reached a plateau in its development, out of which it would grow again in the Hellenistic period. Still built of wood, it was permanent in the sense that its shape was consistent year after year and in that it was always in the same location, although parts of the theatre may have been taken down between Dionysia. Its principal focus was the *proskenion*, both because of the visual and acoustical support of the *skene* and because the most important seats in the theatre—those of the priests of Dionysus—were directly across the *orkestra* from the *skene*. The audience surrounded the choral area and viewed the *proskenion* from three sides, much as in a thrust-stage theatre, although separated from it by a greater distance. Formal as this plan of *orkestra-parodoi-proskenion* may seem, it created a very flexible theatre with multiple entrances and useful differences of level.

Scenery and Machinery

Without question, some elements of the *skene* were "scenic" in the sense that they provided localizing background for dramatic action. The doorways, for example, could be used consistently throughout a given performance to represent the same building or buildings. (The most common example cited is the use of the central doorway for a palace, as in *Oedipus Rex*.) Less obviously, the *parodoi* at least provided opportunities for localizing; in the Roman theatre, a convention was established that entrances analogous to the *parodoi* always represented the same places, at least in comedy: one led to the center of the city in which the play took place, the other to the harbor or the country. Such a convention is not indicated in fifth-century tragedy, however.

Beyond these few basic scenic functions, there is little certainty about the use of scenery in the classical Greek theater. The use of painted scenes showing the place of the play's action is particularly debatable, because the earliest evidence for their use is Hellenistic. In general, two devices for introducing painted scenes have been suggested, one a painted panel or cloth, called *scaena ductilis* by the

Romans; the other, a three-sided prism that rotated around a central shaft so that each of three painted faces could be presented to the audience in turn, called a *periaktos*. Theories about these devices are ingenious but lack hard proof, and the poles of the debate over their use can be represented by Margarete Bieber, who stated that both "certainly belong to the classical period" and by Peter Arnott, who found them "superfluous in the fifth century."

Both devices were imitated in the Renaissance and are of some importance for their use there, but it must be admitted that neither is essential to the production of a play like *Oedipus Rex*. No change of scene is required, and the primary function of both devices *is* to allow for change, the *scaena ductilis* by unrolling a painted canvas horizontally across the front of the skene or by allowing for new panels to be dropped into prepared holders on the *skene* wall, the *periaktoi* by presenting a new face. If the simplest solution to the problems presented by the plays is sought, then one must agree with Arnott that such devices were superfluous, and the conventional masks, costumes, and style of acting suggest that conventional settings (the architectural façade of the skene) were all that was necessary. By the Hellenistic period, of course, we must accept the use of complicated scenic effects that appear to have been exploited largely for their own sake.

Two other mechanical devices are often mentioned in connection with the fifth-century theatre. Both appear to have been in use by the end of the century. The first, the *mechane,* was a cranelike machine used for flying actors into or out of the playing area. Its design is uncertain, but the many appearances of gods from on high, and the parody of just such a device by Aristophanes (as in *The Clouds*), make its use almost a certainty. Again, it would appear that a powerful convention allowed much of the machine itself to be visible, the "flying" of the actor being accepted by the audience within a limited perceptual reality. (The expression *deus ex machina*—"the god from the machine" —that is used to describe abrupt and contrived dramatic endings probably comes from the use of this machine.)

The second device, the *ekkyklema,* was simply a means for bringing acting forward from the interior of the *skene* on to the *proskenion*. Bieber suggests that it was used for interior scenes (p. 16); certainly, it was used to bring some kind of offstage event within the audience's sightlines. The many scenes in tragedy involving the display of bodies (victims of murder or suicide within the *skene*) probably used the *ekkyklema*. A turntable centered within the *skene* could not possibly bring anything on it more than a foot or two into the acting area when rotated. The simpler suggestion of a low wagon on tracks or grooves is much better. In theory, the doors of the *skene* would be opened, and the ekkyklema wagon—already set up within the *skene*—would be rolled out on the *proskenion*.

Scenery and machinery in the fifth-century theatre, although interesting subjects for speculation, are probably among its least important elements. This was a theatre of strong convention and of spectacle involving choreography, costume, and stylized gesture. The location of the audience around the *orkestra* would make the *skene* wall unimportant scenically to a great many spectators, whereas the scale of the acting area—a 65-foot *orkestra* and a *proskenion* at least as long—would dwarf any practical *periaktos*. We must postulate a good deal of architectural decoration on the *skene* itself, but we need not postulate the use of any specific scenery until after the classical period.

The Origins of Tragedy

So far we have discussed the Greek theatre only as a developed institution, tracing its history only as far back as the historical figure Thespis in the late sixth century. We have left one large area open: the source of tragic form, even of theatre itself in Greece. The reasons for delaying this important question are clear: the fifth-century institution can be described without reference to its primitive sources; and the nature of those sources is purely speculative.

Such has not always been the case. A generation ago, virtually absolute certainty regarding the origin of tragedy was common. As summarized by the English scholar Gilbert Murray and repeated in various forms ever since, it supposed that Greek tragedy was a late reflection of fertility-cult ritual of the kind described in Frazer's *Golden Bough*, exploited in T. S. Eliot's "Wasteland," and fictionalized in such novels as Mary Renault's *The King Must Die*. It will be described in more detail later; for the moment we might note merely that the theory is now looked on as just that—a theory—and that others have been proposed that are equally convincing and a good deal simpler.

The important question in looking at any hypothesis about the origins of tragedy is not, "What is the most primitive analog to tragedy that can be uncovered?" but rather, "How far back in time can one reasonably go without losing the elements that the fifth-century audiences found to distinguish tragedy?"

THE RITUAL THEORY. Ritual is a repeated action aimed at producing the same effect again and again. It is basically irrational, but it is also basically insistent: the effect can be gained only when the process is repeated exactly in all its details. Ritual has no dogma (that is, of itself it makes neither judgments nor demands), but it has a rigid form.

Fertility ritual in primitive societies appears to be almost universal, and its form is strikingly similar in societies thousands of miles apart. Essentially, fertility ritual tries to assure the continuation of seasonal change: winter must give way to spring. The world will be made fertile again by a repeated (religious) action. Behind the ritual is a cult, the worship of a god of spring or fertility or life. The ritual that guarantees his rebirth seeks, of course, to enforce a process of rejuvenation in a god who is born (spring), grows (summer), ages (autumn), dies (winter), and is reborn each spring.

In Greece, the cult of Dionysus was an important fertility cult, much elaborated by the fifth century into separate cults for different locations and separate festivals for different times of the year (the Great Dionysia, the Lenea, the Anthesterion, and so on). The tendency, then, to see the tragic form associated with the Dionysian festival as somehow connected with the fertility ritual is understandable. In addition, we have Aristotle's suggestion in the *Poetics* that tragedy had grown out of *dithyramb*, a lyric form, using large choruses of dancer-singers, that was also performed in the Dionysian competitions. On the surface, the connection with tragedy is fairly convincing, especially when one sees so frequently in fifth-century tragedies an action that can be compared to the fertility god's career: the tragic hero begins his action, lives through its progressive stages, suffers or dies, and is symbolically reborn in either his *anagnorisis* (tragic perception) or the rejuvenation of his society. (Oedipus both gains tragic perception and cures Thebes of the plague.) Connected with such an action is a view of the tragic

Figure 2–5. Two terracotta statuettes, c. 375–350 B.C., of comic actors. In their stylization, the comic masks shown here are probably closer to their fifth-century models than is the tragic mask in Figure 2–2. As well, the simplified comic costumes and the phallus are further signs of theatrical convention. In their grotesqueness and their abstraction from reality, these two statuettes should be compared to the masked *commedia dell'arte* actors in Figures 2–31 and 2–32. (*Courtesy of the Metropolitan Museum of Art, Rogers Fund, 1913.*)

Figure 2–6. *Oedipus Rex* at the Hilberry Classic Theatre, Wayne State University, directed by Richard D. Spear with a setting by Mister Spear. Costumes by Robert Pusilo, lighting by Gary M. Witt.

hero-fertility god as scapegoat: he who dies so that the society can be reborn.

Margarete Bieber has listed four principal reasons for the development of tragic drama out of Dionysian cult: first, the entry of the cults into mainland Greece at a time when Greek language and literature were highly developed, especially in the epic and lyric; second, the rich number of stories connected with Dionysus himself; third, the Dionysian belief in ecstatic possession of the worshipper by the god, allowing for transfer of self, or acting; fourth, the commitment of the individual to the large movement of the ritual (translated artistically into participation in a chorus and the acting out of stories).

In opposition to these suggestions, however, we must cite several obvious problems. For one thing, the Dionysian cult became widespread in Greece in the eighth or seventh century. Why should a literary aspect of it preserve unconscious vestiges in the fifth century? Moreover, all fertility ritual serves the needs of an agrarian society; fifth-century Athens was urban, mercantile, even industrial. Finally, the artistic conventions represented in fifth-century acting, staging, and playwriting indicate so much conscious control on the part of each artist that primitive ecstasy, possession, or loss of self are in direct opposition to what we know of the developed form. In short, there *was* a vigorous cult of Dionysus in fifth-century Athens, but its relevance to fertility ritual in general and to tragic form in particular is very hard to find, its original character having been virtually lost in a mass of state formalities (the processions, the highly organized competitions).

This is not to say that the connection between dramatic competition and the festivals of Dionysus were merely accidental. There may, however, be other explanations for the link.

ELSE'S ARTISTIC THEORY. In *The Origin and Early Form of Greek Tragedy,* certainly one of the most important books to appear on the subject, Gerald F. Else has proposed a different development. He begins with a very obvious but often overlooked point: no matter what conclusions can be made about fertility rituals, about primitive societies in general, or about comparative anthropology, the "cardinal fact remains that Athens in the sixth century B.C. is the only place in the world that has ever given birth to tragedy." In short, we might do better to look for specifically Athenian causes rather than for cross-cultural irrationalities that happen to be present in the cult of Dionysus.

An equally obvious but equally overlooked element of Else's theory is the nature of the stories and characters represented by tragedy. Very, very few of the fifth-century plays dealt with Dionysus himself, and few others with figures like him or associated with him. On the other hand, it is evident that most of the great characters and their stories come from Homeric (pre-Dionysian) myth. Furthermore, these characters are not gods or even godlike, nor do they present an image of divinity. On the contrary, they present an image, even an ideal, of human heroism. For Else, their relevance to sixth- and fifth-century Athens is clear: the Homeric epics and the myths that surrounded them were the great social exemplars for the developing Athens. Their idealistic concept of heroism could be transmitted directly to the entire society through two forms: the older recitation of the epics themselves, and, late in the sixth century, the protodramatic, a new form.

In brief, the new form as it may have been created by Thespis in the last third of the sixth century was simple but revolutionary—"*self-presentation* of the hero [to a chorus] and his *pathos* [suffering]." As yet not fully dramatic, consisting only of narrative and choral response, this protodrama was transformed by Aeschylus in a single great leap by introducing the deuteragonist—"not a hero, or even a person at all, but an instrument for extending the play in time and space." Such projection was possible only after the introduction of the second actor, because only then could the cause of the *pathos* be shown, both directly (as in the many messengers' speeches) and historically as the inter-action of protagonist and deuteragonist showed the *development toward the pathos*, and not merely the *pathos* itself. The addition of the tritagonist (whether by Aeschylus or Sophocles does not really matter) further enlarged the scope of tragedy and allowed for much more complex scenes and more complex actions. However, it was the addition of the deuteragonist that transformed the protodrama into tragedy. After Aeschylus, Else believes, tragic form needed no further large changes. It contained all the possibilities of great drama: the story of one character, heroically conceived, developed in time to include all the causes of the climactic *pathos*, with choral reaction to each step in the development.

Such a brief review hardly suffices for a work as original and as scholarly as Else's book. It shows, however, the bare bones of a workable, nonritual theory of tragedy that seems to go to the heart of the matter, relating tragedy specifically to Athens and to the period of greatness. It does not deny or conflict with the Dionysian links of tragedy, nor does it deny that both tragedy and fertility ritual share in an archetypal movement that is so basic that it may underlie our very concept of suffering, of heroic isolation, and of social behavior.

ARROWSMITH'S JUDICIAL METAPHOR. One further suggestion concerning tragedy deserves our attention. In an essay called "The Criticism of Greek Tragedy," William F. Arrowsmith has pointed, almost casually, to the repeated use of judicial situations and judicial references in the plays. He points out not only the formal atmosphere of the plays, with their legalistic *agons* (contests between two characters, like those between Teiresias and Oedipus and between Oedipus and Creon), but also the direct appeals for judgment that occur again and again: "Over and over again . . . the late fifth-century theatre seems to suggest as its informing image a theatre shaped more by the law-court than by the altar. In this theatre, the *agon* is viewed essentially as a trial. . . . The audience in this theatre sits as jurors. . . ."

To find a possible application of this judging action, we have to look briefly at the Athenian judicial system. At its fullest, the *dykastery*, or court of the whole city consisted of as many as 500 citizen jurors, each of whom voted after testimony was heard. The system is satirized in Aristophanes' early comedy *The Wasps;* a serious treatment of it is contained in the Platonic dialogue *The Apology*, which recounts the trial of Socrates. Here we see the Dykastery assembled; Socrates, on trial for his life, confronts his accusers. The cross-examinations are little agons, with Socrates always the protagonist. The agons are separated by the reactions of the dykasts themselves—outrage, anger, confusion—that may quite reasonably be compared with the choral reactions of tragedy. Finally, Socrates is cast in the role of heroic scapegoat; tried for impiety, he morally saves Athens by allowing himself to be sacrificed. Like the tragic hero, he is a moral exemplar; like the tragic hero, he suffers a pathos of his own making.

It should not be assumed that tragedy was created quite consciously in imitation of the judicial action. It is not contradictory, however, to suggest that the judicial system and the tragic form grew out of the same impulse. In this sense, it is hardly accidental that the goal toward which the great Aeschylean trilogy *The Oresteia* heads is the creation of the Athenian court by Athena herself. Tragedy may have been created, as Else contends, by Thespis and Aeschylus as an exemplary public form. It may also, as the ritualists would have us believe, have gained some of its visceral, irrational power by tracing patterns known to primitive men; but it may have found a final metaphor and even an example for its personal conflicts and its choral judgment in the Athenian public court. What better imperative could the great tragedies put upon their audiences than the same one put upon the Athenian *dykast:* you will be given all the evidence; you must judge what it means.

Oedipus Rex

By the middle of the fifth century, of course, tragedy had evolved from its sources into a distinctive form. Much of the credit, as we have seen, must go to Aeschylus. Conversely, by the end of the century one must admit that Euripides was already finding the form too strict. One gets the feeling that many of Aeschylus' plays were in part experiments and that much artistic energy must have been dissipated in bringing the form into being. With Euripides, on the other hand, too much energy went into struggling against the form. Sophocles at his best seemed to stand between the two extremes, secure, relatively content with tragic form and structure as he knew it.

Nowhere is his confidence in his medium more apparent than in *Oedipus Rex. Oedipus at Colonus* (written at almost the end of his life) may be more profound, more mysterious; *Antigone* may present a personal struggle in easier terms; but *Oedipus Rex* is the near perfect work of an artist working within a form that pleases him.

STRUCTURE. Typical of this form, Oedipus Rex has a rigid structure determined by the interplay of actors' scenes (*episodes*) and choral responses (*odes*). It is not merely the alternation of these elements that creates the very limiting and distinctive structure of Greek tragedy; it is the deeper demands of the kinds of subjects, the kinds of language, and the kinds of theatrical appeal that they make. Not all of the tragedies of the fifth century followed this structure precisely, for reasons we have already cited (as in the great differences between Aeschylus and Euripides), but all were oriented to it, controlled by the playwright's reaction to it. Certainly the most distinctive single feature of Greek tragedy is this structure, and when the chorus is taken away (as in some modern adaptations of Greek plays) a completely different kind of drama results. A modern audience may tend to look upon the actors' scenes *as the play,* and the chorus as a rich commentary at best, an interruption at worst. Still, it must be remembered that *the play,* in the fifth century B.C. was the combination of the two.

Two minor features of the choral songs satisfy a theatrical need—to bring the chorus into the *orkestra* and to take it out at the end of the play. This theatre without lights or curtain could, of course, begin with a silent entrance of the chorus into the *orkestra,* after which the drama could begin. However, such a practice is untheatrical and fails to exploit the exciting possibilities of processional entrances, of voices heard at a distance beyond the *parodoi.* Therefore, the choral entrance, called the *parados,* and the exit at the end of the play, the *exodos,* are important theatrical devices in their own right, as well as being meaningful lyrics about the play.

Before the *parodos*—before, that is, the chorus is in the theatre—there is a short scene among the actors called the *prologos.* Usually expository, this scene may be limited to a single character's monologue or may, as in *Oedipus Rex,* involve all three actors in important roles. Here Oedipus, the Priest of Apollo, and later Creon give an exposition of past action and set the play in motion. This *prologos* is a rather lengthy one; after it, the chorus enters singing a moving but conventional hymn for relief from the plague that is destroying Thebes.

The pattern of episode-ode that follows is quite typical. Four choral odes follow the *parodos,* separating the play's action into five major episodes (the basis for Roman structure and, in turn, the neoclassic five-act play). Within the odes, the chorus is frequently separated into two sections for the responsive lyric form of strophes and antistrophes, parallel stanzas that are normally very regular. The episodes, on the other hand, are rather variable in both length and form, ranging from the two-person confrontations of Oedipus and Teiresias in the first episode to concentrated monologues like the Messenger's speech in the last episode. Throughout, of course, the chorus is included in the episodes and frequently questions, discusses, or advises as the action progresses.

If we review Else's theory of the development of tragedy, we see how far *Oedipus Rex* is from Thespian protodrama. The "self-presentation" of Oedipus is spread over several episodes, dramatized, and given historical scope and focus; his pathos comes in the last episode, broken actually into two parts—the Second Messenger's description of his physical suffering, and his own spiritual and emotional experience. Insofar as it is a typical tragedy, we can say that the developed tragic structure was as follows: *prologos*—exposition (one, two, or three actors); *parodos*—choral entrance; *four episodes* and four *odes*—development of the heroic action, with responsive choral lyrics; *fifth episode*—pathos, anagnorisis, and resolution (if any); *exodos*—choral exit.

PLOT AND ACTION. *Oedipus Rex* appears at first glance to be a play based heavily on suspense. It is frequently, in fact, compared with the modern detective story, the pure plot-suspense narrative, and it does indeed set out almost immediately to answer a detective's question: "Who killed Laius, former king of Thebes?" Many of the devices exploited by Sophocles in answering the question are, to be sure, those of the detective story: the unwilling witness, the possessors of special knowledge, even the questioner (Oedipus) who finds ultimately that he is more involved than he suspected.

Viewed within the context of tragic form, however, the play will

Figure 2–7. *Oedipus Rex* at the Stratford Shakespearean Festival, 1955. Jocasta and Creon are the background figures. The Jocasta mask and costume would seem to be rather too literal as an interpretation of fifth-century practice. (*Courtesy of the Stratford Shakespearean Festival.*)

not stand up as one depending primarily on plot suspense. Whatever one may think of the choral odes as poetic commentary, it must be clear that they destroy suspense, not enhance it; they are both antiplot and anti-involvement. In the modern sense they force the audience to objectify the experience of the play—to suppress, in fact, any direct involvement in the suspense. This is not to say that the impact of the pathos, the profound understanding of human character or the compassionate feelings of pity, even grief, are suppressed; they are not primary responses to suspense of plot. What *is* suppressed is the superficial interest in story alone.

The plot is a rather simple one, made complex by the characters of the people working through it: Oedipus, in seeking to rid Thebes of the plague, learns from the oracle of Apollo that the plague will end only when the murderer of Laius is discovered. He rejects the evidence of Teiresias, the seer, and the advice of Creon, his brother-in-law, thinking that they want to put him off the scent because they seek power for themselves. When he learns that Laius was killed while on a journey, and by one attacker, Oedipus is reminded that he once killed a man under similar circumstances. He is reminded too of an earlier oracle that prophesied that he would kill his father and marry his mother. Because of this oracle he had left his home as a young man. Now he learns that he was an adopted child, that the father he had been afraid of killing was a foster parent. When, then, he is identified by the marks on his feet as the child abandoned in infancy by Laius and Jocasta, he learns the horrifying truth that he is the murderer of Laius. Jocasta kills herself; Oedipus blinds himself, and, victim of his own inexorable search for the polluter of Thebes, goes into exile.

This plot is worked out carefully across the entire play, with special emphasis and unusual length given to the pathos and its consequences. In the prologos, Oedipus learns of the oracle of Apollo and hears the circumstances of Laius' murder. In the first episode, Teiresias tells Oedipus that he is the source of the pollution, but the details that would prove such an accusation are missing, and Teiresias refuses to elaborate. In the second episode, Oedipus accuses Creon of plotting against him with Teiresias; Jocasta mediates between the two and tells Oedipus of an old oracle that Laius would be killed by his own son. As a result, Laius had had his infant son, his feet bound, abandoned in the hills. Oedipus suspects the truth, remembering his own past. In the third episode, a Messenger comes to tell Oedipus that Polybus, his supposed father, is dead. Oedipus' brief joy at learning, as he thinks, that he has not killed his father, is dispelled when the Messenger informs him that he was adopted. Jocasta now senses the truth, while Oedipus, confused, determines to pursue his search. In the fourth episode, the old Herdsman who had saved the infant Oedipus and given him to the servant of Polybus tells the truth of Oedipus' birth, and Oedipus recognizes that he is both the murderer of Laius and the husband of his mother. In the fifth episode, the Second Messenger tells of Jocasta's suicide and Oedipus' self-blinding. Oedipus sees the justice of Creon's assumption of power in Thebes, and, self-exiled, takes the first steps away from the city where he had ruled.

In brief, then, the play traces a search for the truth that is already known. Teiresias' flat statement that Oedipus is the polluter is not a dramatic foreshadowing; it is fact. The three oracles work together to produce another version of the same fact. Oedipus sees the fact dimly in the second episode, but retreats from it. Jocasta sees it clearly in the third episode. The play's plot, then, is suspenseful for Oedipus, but it is a puzzle that is, as it were, cut into pieces only *after* the audience has seen it whole.

IDEA AND IRONY.　At its heart, the play is ironic. Simple irony arises from the comparison of two states of knowledge, one truer than the other. As audience, we have the truth of Oedipus' story; his search for the truth is made ironic by our knowledge. More profoundly, the irony is intensified by our perception that his search is self-destructive. When Oedipus determines to carry on the search even if he is the murderer of Laius, that irony becomes a severe indictment of experience itself, for we see an action that is essentially heroic (Oedipus' attempt to save Thebes) in a totally ironic light. All human action appears ironic, trapped in a fatal paradox: the more one attempts, the more one destroys himself.

Some of this can be attributed to the special character of Oedipus. It has been said that he is overproud, that he commits a kind of sin (*hybris*) in even attempting to penetrate to the truth. He is an angry man, it is true, an abrupt and decisive one. He accuses Creon without foundation; he tortures the old Herdsman when he is afraid to speak. Yet we see that he is a man drawn on (or driven) by an imperative that is not of his own making. The imperative has several aspects— the oracle of Apollo, his position as ruler, the suffering of his people. In being the good ruler he must destroy himself; he is both king and scapegoat. Apollo has decreed that the polluter be found; as ruler, Oedipus must find him. In a sense, then, he has no choice—*unless he is to abandon his very identity* and cease to be Oedipus, King of Thebes.

The oracles provide a key to the play's basic question. They are part of a complex of images and themes that point toward the central irony. What, after all, is an oracle? It is a partial clue to truth. It is sought by a human, given by a god. It is the outward sign of human questioning. It is part of the paradox: the more one seeks to know, the less he can know, until he arrives at the rare, ultimate knowledge that follows pathos. In trying to *act* on the information of an oracle (Laius' abandoning of the infant Oedipus; Oedpius' flight from the home of his supposed parents; Oedipus' pursuit of the polluter) the human being destroys himself.

Figure 2–8. Laurence Olivier as Oedipus in the 1946 production by the Old Vic, probably the most famous modern interpretation of the role. (*Culver Pictures.*)

One cannot overemphasize the word *act*. To *act* is almost equated with to *suffer;* we hardly even need speak of tragic action, but only of action. Perhaps it was for this reason that Aristotle stressed the importance of the action, for it is in this purposeful movement that pathos, tragedy, is born.

There is a great tension in *Oedipus Rex* between action and inaction. Teiresias counsels inaction: "Seek no further." The Herdsman has lived a life of inaction, away from Thebes, trying to escape the consequences of his single act, the giving of Oedipus to the servant of Polybus. Throughout the play, the chorus remains inactive and advises finally against action. Here, of course, *to act* means *to seek the truth,* at least for Oedipus. We have already pointed out that his only other choice could be to surrender his identity: thus, the heroism of Oedipus is his commitment to action and his commitment to his heroic self. The alternative, although not cowardly, would be nonheroic—in fact, would reduce him to the level of the chorus.

Gerald F. Else has said that the second and third actors did not play characters, but "instruments." In one sense this is very true, especially for *Oedipus Rex*, for although Teiresias, Jocasta, and Creon have human attributes and are acceptable as human characters, they are not presented as *active*. Greek tragedy is the study of the man who acts. There is only one such man in this play.

But what of other kinds of men? What, for example, of Oedipus after the pathos? Who is this blind, tortured exile?

Perhaps there is a third mode of existence, different from action and inaction—not an alternative to them, but the product of one. After pathos, what? Merely suffering, resolution of the play, exile? No, something more—the revelation that Aristotle called *anagnorisis*, tragic wisdom. If we look elsewhere in the play for it, we find Teiresias, the blind seer, the old man led by a child, the man who has also been woman for part of his life. Out of his blindness comes the truth; it remains truth despite Oedipus' inability to understand it. Closer to the gods (Apollo, here) closer to the facts of the oracles, Teiresias is wise. He counsels inaction, true, but for quite a different reason from the chorus or the Herdsman: he anticipates the pathos.

Oedipus, after the pathos, takes the first steps toward this condition. It is obviously no artistic accident that he blinds himself. Knowledge of the myth surrounding the play tells us that he will live to grow old, will be blessed by the gods at his death and carried to Olympus (as in Sophocles' *Oedipus at Colonus*), and that the last city to give him sanctuary (Athens) will have special favor from the gods. Out of his tragic pathos, therefore, has come a mode of existence that is substantively different from action or inaction: wisdom. It is mystical, beyond rational understanding. It is knowledge beyond intellect, as it were, earned at great expense. It is possible only for the heroic individual who will pursue the human paradox to its limit: the search for truth is self-destructive, but out of heroic self-destruction comes knowledge of the truth.

Oedipus Rex is both the quintessential fifth-century tragedy and a great rarity. It typifies the structure, the subject matter, and the character of the form. Its final statement is a mystery because Sophocles was operating in the religious area of the mysterious. There is no other tragedy like it, although all others can be measured by it.

TRANSITION: THE THEATRE OF ROME

The dramas of ancient Rome, like many of its institutions and its customs, were adaptations of the Greek, and often showed a curious sense of inferiority to the Greek model (the playwright Plautus, for example, apologized for writing in his own "barbaric" language instead of in Greek); ironically, however, it was Roman drama and the Roman theatre building (adapted from the Greek) that were to have the greatest influence on European theatre in the Renaissance (see pp. 89–97). It is, of course, unfair to say that all of Roman theatre was inferior to all of Greek theatre. It is true that the theatre occupied a different (and probably less important) spot in Roman life than it had in Greek life, at least if the highest historical moments of those two civilizations are compared.

In looking at Roman drama and the Roman theatre, we encounter the same sorts of difficulty that we did with the Greek. None of the dramatic manuscripts that survive were contemporary with the playwrights, and all may have been corrupted by later alterations; much of the visual evidence concerning performances (vase paintings and frescoes, for example) are of debatable relevance to the theatre; and the archaeological remains of theatre buildings are the grandiose monuments of the Roman Empire, not the more modest wooden structures of the formative period before the first century B.C. And it may be that the form of drama about which we know the least—the native Oscan or Attellan farce—was the most successful theatrically and (in Rome) the most influential of all. And, most importantly, we must remember that in talking about "Rome," we are discussing a period of nine hundred years—roughly the same amount of time that elapsed from the crudest beginnings of religious drama in the Middle Ages until the most recent Broadway hit. Thus, "the theatre of ancient Greece" usually means the theatre of the fifth century B.C.; and "the theatre of ancient Rome" usually means the theatre of the second and first centuries B.C. However, both Greece and Rome had very active, very popular theatres for centuries before and after these brief periods that the accident of history has chosen to emphasize.

Sources: Greece and Italy

The formative period of Roman theatre (roughly from about 350–150 B.C.) saw an interaction of native and imported elements. Although the acknowledged crest of Greek theatre had been passed (c. 400 B.C.), the Greek theatre was still vital, and criticism and the art of acting

Figure 2–9. An artist's reconstruction of a Roman theatre, distinguishable from the fifth-century Greek theatre by the free-standing architectural shell, the elevated stage, and the complex façade behind the stage. (*Bettman Archive.*)

were more highly developed in the later years. It was probably natural, then, that the expanding Roman culture should absorb and copy much of the Greek theatre, both in its form and in the content of its plays, as well as in its mode of production.

In tragedy, direct translations of Greek plays were staged in Rome as early as 240 B.C. However, despite the nominal respect given to tragedy as a literary accomplishment, it never attained the religious or the theatrical status that it had in Greece, and after the middle of the first century B.C., it declined drastically in popularity. When its best-remembered author, Seneca (4 B.C.–A.D. 65) wrote, it is doubtful that he even intended his plays for public performance, and his tragedies—which were to exert such an important influence on English drama—may well have been meant only for reading. Bombastic, sensational, larded with poetic figures of speech and conceits, they have been called radio plays—dramas for the ear, not the eye. To be sure, the unique characteristics of Roman society may explain the relative unimportance of tragedy as a living form; of equal importance, at the least, is the absence of any native antecedent for a serious dramatic genre.

The same cannot be said of comedy. A vigorous native farce, *The Attellan*, is known from 350 B.C., a partly improvised low comedy with a stock group of characters, which, according to W. Beare, (*The Roman Stage*) "have a certain family resemblance as coarse, greedy clowns, whose animal characteristics were such as might amuse a primitive and rustic audience, ever ready to laugh at gluttony and drunkeness, at horseplay and obscene jest." Primitive though such theatre may be made to sound, it was evidently no less viable as the root of a native form than the Attic farce had been for Greek comedy, and, when the society was ready for a native Italian comedy, the Attellan farce was there to be drawn upon. (One can note in passing, as well, the similarities between Attellan farce and the Renaissance *commedia dell'arte* of the same region of Italy, also improvised, physical, often obscene, and based on a small group of stock characters. For further discussion of it, see pp. 110–116.)

Fabula Palliata and Fabula Togata

As already noted, there was a Roman cultural insecurity toward Greek models before the Imperial period; it expressed itself as a cleavage between plays based on Greek originals and performed in Greek costumes (the pallium), called *fabula palliata*, and plays in Roman dress (toga) based on Roman life, *fabula togata*. Only with the ascendancy of the Empire after the middle of the first century B.C. were the *togata* the more influential—only, that is, after Roman life had become a model for the world could its theatrical presentation also become a model. A natural development of the concentration on Roman themes and Roman manners was the more "realistic" quality of *fabula togata* for its Roman audience, which could see its own world in such plays.

The more important line of development of the *fabula togata* was in comedy, which, despite certain Greek literary origins, drew heavily on native farce. The Greek models were the plays of the so-called Greek "New" Comedy—plays from about 330 B.C. and later—whose most noted playwright was Menander (c. 343–292 B.C.). The designation "Old" is applied to Greek comedy before about 390 B.C., and includes most of the plays of Aristophanes (c. 448–380 B.C.), plays that were satirical and political, using a large chorus, with plots that were more properly sequences of comic incidents than linked, causal actions. So-called "Middle" Comedy, from about 390 to 330 B.C., was a transition from Aristophanes to Menander, with a de-emphasis of the comic chorus (noticeable in Aristophanes' *Plutus*, 388 B.C.), its suppression of political themes and satire, and its increasing exploitation of plots with domestic and romantic subject matter. The three stages, then— Old, Middle, and New Comedy—were closely linked, marking evolutionary changes in a form, with certain elements retained throughout: the use of characterizing masks and of typed characters (fathers, two types of young men, the courtesan, the virgin, and so on) most significantly.

Two Roman comic playwrights adapted Greek comedy to the Roman theatre. Plautus (254–184 B.C.) was a prolific comic dramatist of whom twenty-one plays survive, all copied or adapted from plays by Menander and his Greek contemporaries, but all crossed with native farce. The most important theatrical element of the Plautine comedies was the use of music; although there was no chorus, the plays were filled with songs and with chanted or intoned set pieces, with musical accompaniment, and with dancing. Usually romantic (boy-meets-girl is a Plautine staple), the performances were apparently joyous and musical, aiming toward the happy resolution of all entanglements and the final request for "plaudite," the audience's approval. Plautus' durability can be seen from his great popularity in Roman times and in his early revival on the Renaissance stage, as well as from the adaptation of his plays to such widely different works as Shakespeare's *Two Gentlemen of Verona* and the recent Broadway musical, *A Funny Thing Happened on the Way to the Forum*.

Terence (185–159 B.C.) copied Menander even more closely than Plautus had. His literary reputation was greater than Plautus', perhaps because of his greater fidelity to the Greek model, or perhaps because he was judged the better poet. Margarete Bieber, for example, finds Terence "not . . . a strong and jocose humorist, but a refined, subtle, cultured and morally eminent poet." Like Plautus, he was popular not only in his own period, but also in the Renaissance. Although only six Terentian plays have survived, they have served as the base for such works as Wycherley's *The Country Wife* (1675) and Thornton Wilder's novel, *The Woman of Andros*.

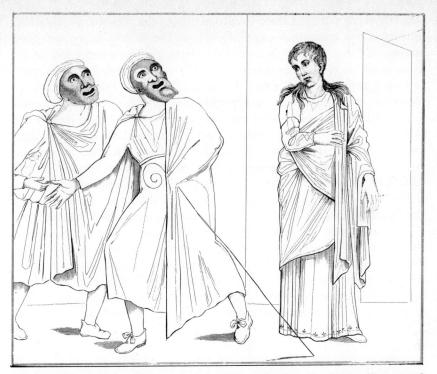

Figure 2–10. A nineteenth-century artist's rendering of a Pompeiian mural. The designation of "comic scene" is highly questionable; what is shown is probably a Roman theatrical version of a Greek theme. Whether this is actually a depiction of a performance, or merely of a Greek story in the conventions of the theatre, is debatable. (*Culver Pictures.*)

Later Forms

The Roman drama that has traditionally been prized—that is, the literary drama—seems to have reached the height of its theatre life in the latter part of the first century B.C. Plautus and Terence, although dead for well over a century, were still being imitated and their plays kept in the repertory; the temporary (usually wooden) theatre buildings of that earlier day were being replaced with permanent structures in stone; the art of acting reached its highest level, and one actor, Roscius, has left us his name (thanks to one of Cicero's orations) as the epitome of the Roman actor—a freed slave who, through his art, passed beyond many of the barriers of Roman society.

Two works of major importance to the theatre appeared in the same early Imperial era: the *De Architectura* of Vitruvius Pollio (first century B.C.), and the *Ars Poetica* of Horace (65–8 B.C.).

Vitrivius' multivolume work contained descriptions of all kinds of buildings, public and private, but Book V was devoted particularly to a discussion of theatre architecture. Setting aside the highly technical geometry of Vitruvius, we can say that his theatre was based on the

Greek theatre, with the difference that the Greek theatre of Vitruvius' time was not quite the same as that of the fifth century B.C. Two important things had happened to it: the actors' area had been raised to as much as twelve feet above the *orkestra*, and the *orkestra* itself had been reduced from a full circle to little more than a semicircle (accomplished by pushing the *proskenion* forward). In the Roman theatre, the *orkestra* was cut to a semicircle and was used mostly for audience seating, not for choral performance; the stage, although lower than the Hellenistic Greek, was at least five feet above the orchestra. Again unlike the fifth-century Athenian stage, provision was made by Vitruvius for scene changing by using *periaktoi* at each side of the stage. Finally, the three entrances to the stage were architecturally embellished, with particular emphasis given to the central door.

In actual construction Roman theatres showed two other important differences from the Greek. Besides seating more people (up to 40,000), they were unified structures, with the audience area and the playing area joined by arches over what, in the early Greek theatre, would have been the *paradoi*. Finally, they were complete architectural constructions, not structures adapted to the existing terrain. Where the

Figure 2–11. An artist's interpretation of the Theatre of Dionysus at Athens, but after its modifications in the Hellenistic period. Much of the detail is purely speculative, and the artist has obviously been influenced by the proscenium theatres of the nineteenth century. (*Bettman Archive.*)

early Greeks had built on a hillside, using its contours for the theatre shape, the Romans built complete structures on flat terrain, with a perfectly semicircular audience area flowing smoothly into a roofed, elevated stage and scene area. (Simple logic will suggest that no society erects complex stone structures capable of seating 40,000 people if there is no vital theatre form to be seen in such buildings. The very existence of these monumental Imperial theatres shows that the Roman theatre was in vigorous good health. However, through a historical accident that springs from the evanescent nature of theatre performance, we have come to believe that this theatre was somehow not worth our attention. In part, this is because of a lack of historical evidence, and particularly of dramatic texts; in part, it is because the Roman theatre of the Empire was a mass, even low-class pastime, and so not thought worth being noted; and in part, it is because of the intense hatred of the theatre by early Christian writers in the late Roman period.)

What Vitruvius did for theatre architecture, Horace accomplished for dramatic theory, with the rather different end that he was writing of a practice (dramaturgy) that was becoming merely the elegant pastime of Augustan court poets. Vitruvius was writing of the burgeoning field of architecture. Horace's criticism is a Romanizing of Aristotle's *Poetics*, a conversion of Aristotle's pragmatic observations into authoritarian rules. He dealt principally with the differences between comedy and tragedy, with the propriety of character and language, and with unity—but in a much stricter sense than Aristotle can ever have intended. The product of an increasingly aristocratic and authoritarian literary scene, Horace's critical principles for drama were not of much relevance to the popular theatre, but they were to prove attractive to the erudite dramatists of a later age, who could use them to make the ordered, proper, and unified plays of neoclassic theatre (see pp. 93–97).

After the first century B.C.—after the century of Roscius, of Vitruvius and Horace, and of the birth of Seneca—the theatre of Rome underwent those changes that saw its literary drama and its Greek influences decline. Although literary tragedy and comedy maintained critical respectability, and were played on occasion, they were increasingly treated like "classics"—respected but not loved; in their places, several already existing, but theretofor minor forms of theatre became popular. One was *mime*, a highly realistic, mundane form, played without masks and in contemporary costume. It allowed for highly mimetic acting, including detailed and varied facial expression. Gone were the conventionalized types of New Comedy that had been represented by rigid masks; in their places were the shifting, specific, real-life characters of the Roman populace. *Pantomime* in many cases replaced the performance of literary drama, especially tragedy; in pantomime, a single actor performed while the text of the play was read. (Some early

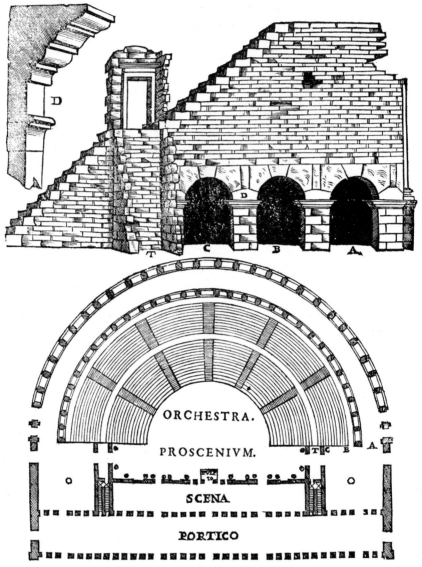

Figure 2–12. An early Renaissance interpretation of a classical theatre upon which, in part, both the Elizabethan and the neoclassic theatres were based. From the 1569 edition of Sebastiano Serlio's *De Architectura*. (*Courtesy of the New York Public Library.*)

Renaissance editions of the plays of Terence show an understanding of this practice when they depict a reader with the play's script and a number of comedians performing.) In some cases, both mime and pantomime earned the reproof of early Christians because of their incorporation of sensational elements—violence and bloodshed (including at least one actual crucifixion) into the realistic mime, and overt sexuality into pantomime.

At the distance of almost two millenia, it is difficult to sum up the Roman theatre easily. That it was a vital theatre throughout its centuries of life is clear, yet it did not leave a large body of plays. Except for the playwrights already named, and some others of lesser stature, it was a theatre that found much of its popularity in spectacle and sensationalism. Perhaps it is not unfair to compare it with the theatre of early nineteenth-century England. It is certainly possible that the very things that made it successful with its audience were those that could least easily be recorded and handed on. As well, the two forces that ended Rome's political life, Christianity and the barbarian influx, were both deeply antitheatrical, and much of what we know of the Roman theatre is harshly negative as a result. Its legacy, therefore, was not to be passed on to the period immediately following the collapse of the Empire, but to a much more distant one, the Renaissance, which would use Rome as its model, just as Rome had used the theatre of Greece.

MEDIEVAL AND ELIZABETHAN THEATRE

The Rome of politics and culture died in the middle of the sixth century A.D. Institutionalized theater died with it, but individual actors appear to have gone on, working out into the barbarian world where their practiced and professional routines were unknown. Certainly their art, however debased, was passed on to the *jongleurs* and other traveling entertainers of later centuries. Its later incorporation into the dominant religious drama of the high Middle Ages is clear from numerous references in town and city records to payments for professional players, actors, and musicians who appeared in the completely developed religious drama. By that time, of course, professional entertainers were fairly common, and most English towns employed several *waits* (musicians) for public ceremonies, important visits, and civic-religious plays. Thus, although the most important medieval drama was never secular or professional, it was able to use secular and professional performers whose craft had its antecedents in Rome.

Major Medieval Drama: The Introit Trope

The beginnings of the spectacular religious dramas that were to dominate European theatre in the fifteenth century were so meager that their final development could hardly have been apparent in their modest start. In essence, those beginnings were nothing more than a slight elaboration of one section of the mass (the introit, the first part of the mass) sung antiphonally by the choir. Although this elaboration appears to have been carried out in many parts of Europe at about the same time, the most important record of it is contained in the *Concordia Regularis* of the Bishop of Winchester, England, a catalogue of rules and customs of religious ceremonies set down in about 975 A.D. Among many other matters, it deals briefly with the following proto-dramatic Easter ceremony, a choral elaboration of part of the introit:

> While the third lesson is being sung, let four brothers vest [costume] themselves. . . . Let [one] without being seen approach the sepulchre and sit down there, holding a palm. . . . Let the other three follow . . . slowly, in the manner of seeking something, and come to the sepulchre. *These things are done in imitation of the angel at the monument, and of the women coming with spices to annoint the body of Christ.* [our italics] When [the angel] sees the others, as if . . . looking for something, approach him, let him . . . sing:

> *Quem quaeritis in sepulchro, O Christicolae?* [Whom are you looking for, oh followers of Christ?]

> After J. Q. Adams, *Chief Pre-Shakespearean Dramas*

The ensuing dialogue is brief, highly formalized, and sung throughout, with the three representing the three Maries singing always in unison. The dialogue, which is very short, ends with a cue for the choir to sing a *Te deum*, the traditional hymn of praise to God that would end most religious plays for the next three centuries.

On the surface, this *Quem quaeritis* dialogue, or trope (a variation or elaboration of a choral passage), is not very promising as drama. The sepulchre it mentions, however, has the basic localizing function of a theatrical setting. The primitive elements of costume (special robes for the four participants) and of emblematic hand properties (the palm for the angel) are also present. Finally, the idea of impersonation is at least suggested by the "in the manner of seeking" and "in imitation of" that describe how the choir members will behave. The special characters of this tenth-century protodrama should be noted: it was sung, not spoken; it was in Latin, not in the vernacular; it took place in the sanctuary, that part of a medieval church reserved for the clergy; it was performed by men only; its subject matter was strictly scriptural; and it took place on a particular occasion (Easter). Each of these characteristics maintained an important influence, despite some changes, through the entire medieval period.

The *Quem quaeritis* form—question and answer between seeker and adviser—could be used in more than one way, and there are actually several scriptural scenes that can begin in exactly that fashion. Following no particular order, either historical or geographic, simple choral scenes were sung at Christmas and Easter around a number of subjects: the Three Maries, already noted; the *Hortolanus* (gardener), the appearance of Christ to Mary Magdalene as a gardener; the *Pastores* (shepherds), the Christmas trope of the shepherds' search for Christ;

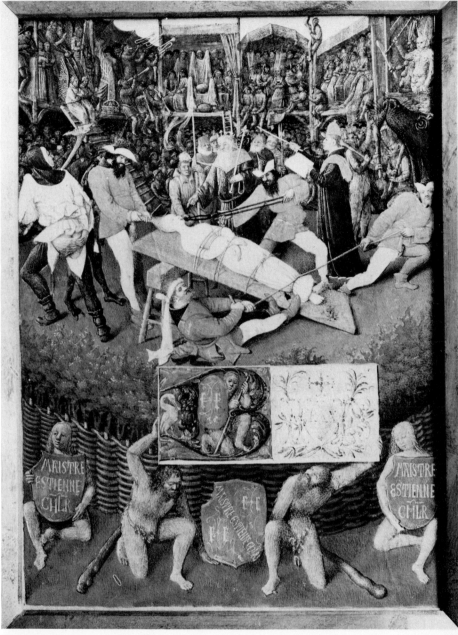

Figure 2–13. A late fifteenth-century miniature of an outdoor theatre and a performance. The artist, Jean Fouquet, is known to have worked on theatrical spectacles for the French court, and it seems likely that the painting is authentic in its details. Particular note should be taken of the scaffolds, with their ladders, curtains and costumed occupants; of the devils' costumes and the hell-mouth; of the extreme realism of the tortures of the central figure; and of the simultaneity of the settings. (*Courtesy of the Musée Condé, Chantilly. Photo Giraudon.*)

the *Magi,* the same action involving the gift-bearing kings; and, some- what later the *Stella* (star), another Christmas trope in which the Magi meet and follow the star; and the *Herodes,* the brief encounter between Herod and the Magi. Each of these can be self-sufficient if it is kept simple enough, and the same choir could present a number of Christ- mas scenes at *different* services during the same season. Each can be- gin *quem quaeritis* and each can lead to *Te deum laudamus* or a similar choral work; no further complication is needed. If, however, the evi- dent didactic potential of dramatized scripture is to be exploited, and if a priest-artist senses the possibilities of complication and develop- ment in these primitive protodramas, then the brief scenes can hardly stay static, but must grow. In many places, it must be realized, they never did grow, and the tropes remained tropes and nothing more. However, in other places, a rapid flowering of sung drama occurred after the very slow beginnings of the tenth and eleventh centuries.

Crude though the early liturgical drama may be, its theatrical con- sciousness is great, and in its staging one can see the great principle that was to dominate European staging until the Renaissance: multi- plicity, or simultaneity, of setting. Real distance was ignored; symbolic distance was substituted. Thus, even as the real dimensions of figures, buildings, and cities are ignored in medieval painting and sculpture, and a symbolic dimension based on doctrinal emphasis is used, so in these dramas staged inside the church, Herod's throne and the shep- herd's hill could be actually located side by side, but dramatically lo- cated miles apart. If the purpose of procession was theatrical (for ex- ample, to display the commitment and generosity of the Magi in the gifts they brought—often the church's own treasury put on display), then the procession could move through the nave, displaying its spec- tacular jewels and gold and cloth, although the shortest distance from Herod's palace to the nativity scene might be a thirty-foot stroll across the transept of the church. This was genuine theatricality in a doc- trinal mode, the "in imitation of" of the *Concordia Regularis* elevated to an exciting art.

Doctrine and Drama

In reading medieval drama, there is a danger of confusing its religious piety with naivete. The danger is increased by early critical and histori- cal treatments, which intentionally misrepresented medieval religious plays as the didactic products of rural bigots. Protestant attacks on the English religious cycles, as Glynn Wickham has shown in *Early English Stages,* were politically motivated in the sixteenth century as part of the anti-Roman Catholic movement of the period. Looking beyond such bias, however, should allow us to see that the relative simplicity of the pious message in these plays is *not* reflected in simplicity of either dramaturgy or staging. At its height, medieval religious drama commanded the talents of playwrights and theatre men of imposing talent.

The doctrinal content of the plays was relatively stable throughout the period—from the early eleventh-century plays of the Continent to the lengthy cycles of the sixteenth century in England and even later in the rest of Catholic Europe—although emphasis on particular points of doctrine sometimes varied. In general, the plays fell into three rough categories: stories of the life of Christ; stories from the Old Testament; and stories from the lives of the saints, historical or legendary. Primarily, then, the plays represented didactic examples; a Christian code is implicit in their plots, and imitation of that code in the behavior of the audience is their goal.

More importantly, however, the plays came to represent a specific idea within medieval theology, the "doctrine of repentance" (Eleonor Prosser, *Drama and Religion in the English Mystery Plays*). Although some form of this doctrine was implicit in Christianity from its beginning, it was in the late thirteenth and early fourteenth centuries that it was formulated in a number of papal and episcopal statements. Not accidentally, the emergence of this doctrine coincided with the most rapid flowering of religious drama, for it was easily seen that the plays themselves were the ideal vehicle for this doctrine of repentance.

The doctrine is a reminder to the Christian that he is sinful and that he must acknowledge sin in the present, now, not in some unspecified future when a deathbed confession will absolve him. It has three important stages: repentance for sinfulness, confession of sins, and atonement or penance. Any form that puts this doctrine forward as message must also put forward a number of allied ideas: the lure and power of sin, the greatness and compassion of God, and the ultimate punishment that awaits unrepentant sin. The most vivid dramatic action that could contain an idea of such scope was nothing less than the entire history of mankind, past, present, and ultimate future: Creation to Doomsday.

The characters of such ultimate drama was evident representatives of the idea. Two great types stand out, the perfect Christian (Christ) and the perfect sinner (Antichrist and Satan). Christ himself is an important figure in many medieval dramas, but not the only important protagonist. Man himself, in many guises, is also exemplary of many positive Christian actions. Satan, too, is an important figure and one who appears as a power in many plays, just as he appears in the scriptures upon which many of the plays are based. The Antichrist, on the other hand, is seldom so named, but he has many human guises, of whom the most important early example is certainly the Herod of the Nativity story. He is Antichrist because, although he does not understand the infant Christ's significance, he is opposed to the idea of any divine or human power greater than his own. Typically, he swears by Mohammed or by Allah, because the great non-Christian enemy of the period (as in the Crusades) was Islam. The Antichrist figure is not Satan himself, but he is frequently motivated by Satan and he is meant to remind his audience, through his actions and his personal characteristics, of that primal Antichrist who tried a military overthrow of Heaven itself—Satan. The constellation of characters in any medieval religious play, then, will involve four basic characters—Christ, Christian Man, Satan, and Antichrist Man—in an action based on the doctrine of repentance.

The structure of that dramatic action aims for repetition and reminiscence. We have already seen that human characters in such plays represented two extremes, Christian and Antichristian behavior (although the variations within those extremes can be very great). We must now add that, to the medieval view, existence itself was patterned on reminiscence and on at least symbolic repetition: existence was itself didactic. Thus, history was meant by God to be a lesson for man, and any drama based on history would teach by showing the reminders that God had already caused to happen. Certain great incidents were patterns of great importance (the Virgin Birth, the Resurrection). They were anticipated in history by analogous events called "types" that man can examine to learn God's power and compassion. (For example, the burning bush seen by Moses was thought to be a type of the Virgin Birth, because it represented the same degree of impossibility—that which burns but goes on living; the raising of Lazarus by Christ is a direct type of the resurrection of Christ himself.) Even as Christ himself is the great *type* of Christian man, so the story of his life will be the great lesson to Christian man; anything that anticipated his life (all of his types) will reinforce that lesson. Both the content and the structure of the cycle plays are clear, then: They will focus on the life of Christ as history, but will do so within the larger context of the history of man, with all its types, and of the *future* history of man, for which the life of Christ is itself a type (Christ's resurrection and his descent into Hell to free many Old Testament figures being an anticipation of Doomsday, when a universal judging will be held and some will rise and the rest descend).

The message of this doctrine may seem simple. The number of essential character types may seem small. But the design is enormous, the artistic end very noble.

The presentation of such plays in *outdoor* religious precincts was by no means universal; throughout Europe, there were instances of plays being presented in the open air in certain places, even though others maintained their in-church staging for centuries more.

Although a general episcopal dissatisfaction with the presentation of plays in the churches can be seen as early as the eleventh and twelfth centuries, there is little real evidence that plays were ever *forced* to leave the churches. It should be assumed, therefore, that the tendency for religious plays to appear outside European churches in the thirteenth century and after is far more a function of the changing needs of the plays themselves than of any clerical bias against the plays. Indeed,

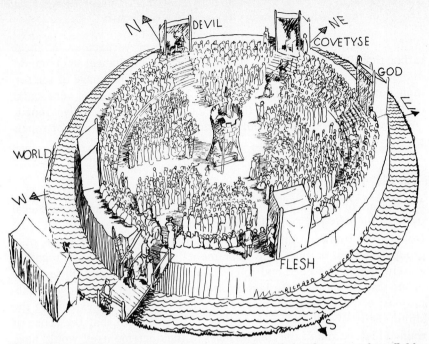

Figure 2–14. Richard Southern's reconstruction of the theatre and scaffolds for the medieval morality play, *The Castle of Perseverance*. It should be compared with Figure 2–13, upon which some of the reconstruction is based. Again, the multiplicity of locations, the central "castle" with its open legs through which the audience can see, and the location of the audience in and around the playing-area should be noted. (*From Richard Southern,* The Medieval Theatre in the Round, *Faber and Faber, Ltd., London, 1957.*)

because control of the play scripts and of production remained, almost without exception, in clerical hands through the end of the fifteenth century, it seems unlikely that there was any real dissatisfaction with the plays.

The first production of a full-fledged passion play (Christ's life from the entry into Jerusalem through the resurrection) appears to have been given in Italy at the very beginning of the thirteenth century. The date, however, is not representative; at least a century more would be needed to include even the beginnings of a general movement from the church interior. As Glynn Wickham has pointed out in *Early English Stages*,

> During a span of some six hundred years (after 975 A.D.) . . . the stages of growth are reasonably clear. If gradual expansion of narrative content eventually obliged performance of liturgical plays outside the house of God, the performances remained attached to an ecclesiastical festival. By virtue of this the ecclesiastical festival

came to be transformed into a civic event. . . . This was occurring as the fourteenth century replaced the thirteenth.

With the movement outdoors came the use of vernacular language rather than Latin. Again, this was not a matter of chance; doctrine demanded that the language of didactic drama be the language of the sermon, not the language of the sacrament. Earlier examples of vernacular drama exist, but in general the use of the audience's native tongue comes with the fourteenth-century emphasis on the doctrine of repentance.

Outdoor Theatre: Pageant, Scaffold, Place

At the time of the evolution into outdoor vernacular staging, medieval dramaturgy was not fully developed, and many characteristics of the trope protodramas remained. Particularly, the individual plays of a group (passion, nativity, Old Testament) were rarely woven together closely, but were joined end to end. As a result, two possibilities were open: staging individual plays in sequence, like the end-to-end protodramas; or presenting the plays as a unified whole, thus exploiting the simultaneity of the in-church setting. It would seem that the sense of unified history and of the timelessness of the doctrine itself would have demanded simultaneity; nevertheless, a considerable proportion of medieval producers chose the other mode. Sequential, rather than simultaneous, staging became common in many European cities (and particularly in England) and even persisted, in cities like York, England, through the final suppression of the plays in the late sixteenth century. However, as a very general rule one may say that after the move outside the church, sequential staging preceded, and developed into, simultaneous staging. This statement would seem to suggest a circular development—from simultaneous staging in the nave, to sequential staging outdoors, to simultaneous staging outdoors—but the introduction of other production factors demanded a change from in-church staging. In essence, these new factors were the introduction of nonclerical producers into the theater.

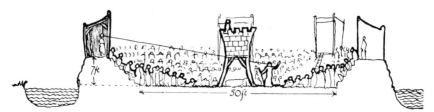

Figure 2–15. A cross-section of a small medieval theatre of the type shown in Figure 2–14. (*From Richard Southern*, The Medieval Theatre in the Round, *Faber and Faber, Ltd., London, 1957.*)

Nonclerical does not mean secular. It most emphatically does not mean *anticlerical*. It does mean devout, interested, and lay. These lay producers were Christian communicants united into *guilds*, groups that were originally religious and later technological. It is hardly an accident, for example, that the religious guild of a specific parish in an English city should include men of one technological craft (arrow-makers or tailors or armorers or sailors). The medieval city placed men of like crafts in the same streets and in the same small neighbor-hoods, and they quite naturally were members of the same parish. Thus, their church rector and their guild chaplain might well be the same, and we cannot distinguish (at least during the medieval period) be-tween a religious guild and a craft guild, except to say that in some cities men of all crafts joined a municipal, or citywide, religious guild *as well as* their own parish or technological guild, thus connecting the town as a whole (the corporation, in English terminology) with the church. When we say, therefore, that a certain guild in Coventry, Eng-land, presented the nativity plays (as the Guild of Shearmen and Tailors are known to have done), what we mean is that a *religious* group, with a clergyman as its spiritual head, organized around a physical commu-nity and nominal dedication to a certain patron saint, took over the pro-duction of the nativity plays as a religious duty. The reasons for their doing so are obvious: in guild records, we read again and again of a guild that "processes to the cathedral" each year, or of a guild that "shows forth statues of its patron and the Virgin" annually. These guilds made it their business to express their dedication through an annual, communal effort to be seen by the entire city. When, therefore, didactic drama became a vital, exciting, growing element in the life of the medieval city, it was natural that the guilds should take part in its production.

The guilds, however, were separate, as cathedral or church clergy were not. There was rivalry among guilds; part of their dedication was a desire to excel. Often, a guild took a play it could best handle: sailors or shipbuilders took the Noah play; in at least one case, leather work-ers took the Creation play, because full-length leather tights were needed for the nude Adam and Eve. The result of such individual selec-tion of incidents is the fragmentation of plotted history, if the entire historical sweep is the subject; as a result, sequence rather than simul-taneity was necessary. The clergy controlled and supervised; they could not force interaction. Simultaneous settings became unlikely, particu-larly because each guild had its own day for procession and playing.

Where sequential staging was maintained, the use of pageant wagons became common, the word *pageant* being used variously for the play itself, for the spectacle of the play's presentation, and even for the ve-hicle on which the play was staged. The use of vehicles became neces-sary, because sequence demanded that the plays be brought one by one before the audience. It became necessary for the audience area to be broken up, and finally as many as twelve *stations* (viewing points) were established. Each pageant thus played twelve times. Beginning shortly after dawn, the Creation play would be performed at the first station; when it moved on to the second station, the next play (the Fall of Man) would perform at station one. For most of the day, twelve plays would be performing simultaneously; it would be almost night before Doomsday played its last performance at station twelve. The disadvantages of such a system are fairly clear: a different actor was required for the same character each time he appeared in a different play (God or Christ, for example, had many interpreters), and the interaction among locations was impossible. Such drama was self-limiting; if it could not develop out of the rigid limits of mere sequence, it would miss the complex interrelationships that the subject itself (man's entire history) promised.

The use of a more unified scheme was a possible alternative. A theatre that would allow many locations to be shown at once, with actors moving from one to another and back again would provide exactly the interaction that sequential staging lacked. In fact, the difference between sequential and simultaneous staging is not so marked as it might seem, except at the extremes of each method. If, for example, several pageant wagons are drawn up around the same playing area, a simultaneous stage has been created. As we have seen, simultaneity had already been exploited in church drama, and it may always have been used to some degree in the outdoor cycles. However, there are suggestions in the English mystery plays that simultaneity was reached after considerable experimentation with sequential staging. Some of the cycles, indeed (most noticeably that at York), seem to have found their final development in the sequential method. Other cycles (that of Lincoln, England, for example) show a mixture of movable wagons and permanent, simultaneous settings, whereas on the Continent, particularly, completely simultaneous settings with many locations were common (as in the great *Mystères de la Passion* of the French playwrights of the fifteenth and sixteenth centuries).

Richard Southern's *Medieval Theatre in the Round* is the clearest and most original discussion of this kind of staging in its extreme form. The title itself is misleading as a description of simultaneous staging, however, for the "roundness" of such theaters was probably rare, the actual shape having been determined by local conditions (as with the Greek orkestra). Town squares, open spaces near a church or cathedral, even large interiors such as guildhalls or refectories, could all be adapted to this method. What is important is not either symmetry or geometrical shape, but the presentation of all necessary locations at one time and the inclusion of the audience within the acting-scenic area. The "sedes" of the church dramas became "mansions" or "scaffolds"; real distances between locations was irrelevant, the structures being sited in and around the most important acting area, the "platea" or place. The center of the place, as primary visual focus, was the most important acting area and could sometimes be used for an important structure (although, as Southern has shown, such a structure had to be constructed so that spectators could see through or over it to action on the other side). The mansions or scaffolds sited around such a place provided localizing settings for individual characters (God, Herod) and elevated stages for important actions (the Last Supper, Pilate's Judgment). Particularly in a drama of the cycle type, long journeys could be effectively shown as movements around the place, whereas direct speeches and sermons to the audience could be made by a character moving among the audience in the place (John the Baptist).

Use of the simultaneous theatre was not confined, however, to the production of large cycle dramas. Effective as it was in allowing the presentation of epic actions lasting several days (as many as seven in some Continental cycles), it proved to be equally effective as a theatre for a newer kind of didactic drama, the morality play. Such plays, based not on scriptural sources but on allegorized doctrine, were shorter and less complex than the cycles; they maintained, however, the cycles' need for simultaneity and spectacle.

The Morality Play

Allegory—the symbolic presentation of concepts as people and places —is a very ancient literary form. In Christian use it anticipated medieval drama by centuries; its poetic uses, as in *Piers Plowman* and Spen-

Figure 2–16. A modern interpretation of one of the most common movable pageants of the cycles, Noah's ship, seen here in the Grantham, England production of the "N–Town Plays." The ship is pushed from inside. The medieval pageant at Grantham, England would probably have been built by shipwrights with the same materials and the same care as a full-sized ship. (*Courtesy of Margaret Birkett. Chris Windows photo.*)

ser's *Faerie Queen,* were many. Until the end of the fifteenth century, however, it was not often applied in drama, but in the last half of the fifteenth and the first half of the sixteenth centuries, dramatic allegories became increasingly common. Called moralities, they were symbolic theatrical versions of important doctrine; to the prose or poetic allegory they added an important visual element that cannot be forgotten. Costume and setting assumed tremendous significance because they are outward signs of abstract meaning, and if the abstraction itself is sufficiently complex, the settings and costumes can present rich possibilities.

It is probably to the sermon that the morality can best be compared. Allegory had frequently been used in medieval sermons; the moralities linked the sermon directly with the theatre, passing over the mystery cycles' reliance on historical (scriptural) action. Certain morality techniques appear to have worked back into the English cycles in the late fifteenth century, although their influence on later English drama is evident in the emblematic names and characters of Ben Jonson (c. 1573–1637) and in such characters in Shakespeare as Rumour and Time.

With the Reformation, the morality play did not disappear (as the cycle did, in England), but was adapted to secular or to Protestant purposes. Purely secular moralities like *The Marriage of Wit and Science* were popular between about 1520 and 1570; anti-Catholic moralities became a propaganda device of the Protestant monarchs. All of these had their formal origins in the didactic religious moralities of the fifteenth century.

THE THEATRE OF SHAKESPEARE

Before fairly recent scholarship on medieval theatre suggested that the Middle Ages were neither naive nor primitive, it was popular to see the theatre of Shakespeare's day as having sprung up, virtually without antecedents, in the middle of the sixteenth century, living for two or three glorious decades around the turn of the seventeenth century, and then expiring from malnutrition before the Puritans could cut off its head in 1642. Shakespeare's theatre needs no such invented uniqueness; its quality was so high that we can acknowledge its medieval antecedents without tarnishing its reputation.

The English theatre did reach a high point around 1590–1630, and it did disappear during the Puritan revolution and the Cromwellian dictatorship (1642–1660). Its secular side did become easily noticeable in the 1560s, just at the time when the medieval cycles and moralities were experiencing their enforced decline. However, it is hardly true that the secular theatre rose without debt to the declining medieval and religious theatre. Even if we can note the beginnings of Renaissance critical consciousness in the secular imitations of the Roman playwright Seneca, we can still see a vigorous holdover from the Middle

Ages in methods of staging, in theories of dramatic character, and in the creation of a drama with epic scope in time and space.

The Elizabethan theatre is neither wholly of the Renaissance nor wholly of the Middle Ages. Much of its greatness and some of its problems spring from the tension between Renaissance and medieval, and Shakespeare himself most frequently seems to be a late medieval man struggling with a newborn Renaissance environment. Nowhere is this conflict more evident than in *Hamlet*, whose protagonist finds himself in very much the same world.

Production in London, c. 1600

If we begin by looking at this theatre in its developed form (that is, at about 1600, or within a few years of the first production of *Hamlet*), we find a situation markedly different from that of the medieval period. By 1600, to speak of the English theatre is to speak of London. Whatever took place outside of London was either a pallid imitation of London production and London plays, or a dying vestige of the medieval religious theatre. The difference is significant; instead of finding a regional center in each major city, with regional or local plays and widespread civic involvement, we find a theatre restricted to the capital and to a small group of professional theater men. Guild production and clerical or scholastic authorship are gone. In their place are a new group of businessmen, some artists and some hacks, all of whom are dedicated to making the theatre work because it means their livelihoods. Some, like Philip Henslowe (d. 1616), were as practical, even as cynical, as modern New York producers, striking that happy blend of the promoter and the real estate man who builds theatres, gives actors jobs, and only occasionally turns down a good play for the wrong reason. Others, like Shakespeare himself, adapted a high artistry to popular demand and produced plays that attracted wide audiences to the theatres and brought wealth to their authors.

There were a number of theatres. The first one, aptly named The Theater, had gone up in 1576, to be followed a few months later by The Curtain (named apparently for an old title of the land on which it stood, not for any theatrical connotation of the word). By 1600, at least seven theatre buildings had been put up in London, and at least two other existing spaces had been adapted for theatrical use. In addition, there are indications that a number of inns were used from time to time for productions, and there was, of course, a quite separate erudite theatre for the staging of masques at court. A number of these theatres continued in use until the Puritan suppression in 1642, and one or two of them even survived into the Restoration period. (For a fuller description of the theatres themselves, see p. 75 "Shakespeare's Globe.")

The primary producing organization was the company. Made up of several "sharers," it was a business organization whose members—ac-

Figure 2–17. After the "Swan" drawing (c. 1596) of de Witt, with the Latin labels translated. Presumably the original Latin was an attempt to adapt classical terminology to the English structure. Of particular interest here is the lack of any "inner" space between the doors of the *actors' house;* the apparent separation between the gallery over the stage and the *benches* or *nobles' seats* (audience areas), and the *plain* or *arena*, normally used as an audience area.

tors and playwrights—shared the profits. A leading actor or an important playwright would own a full share; lesser figures held half or quarter shares. In addition, the company hired a variable number of actors, backstage personnel, and so on, to be paid out of income but to take no regular share of the profits (the so-called hirelings). Plays not written by shareholding playwrights could be bought outright from unattached dramatists, or staged, as in the Restoration custom, with one night's profits going to the author.

Not all companies were regularly associated with one theatre building. Lesser companies might use any of several theatres for a brief time; the important ones, on the other hand, leased or even built theaters of their own. Two eminent companies of Shakespeare's day stand out from all the rest: Shakespeare's own, the Lord Chamberlain's (so called after its nominal patron), and the Lord Admiral's. After 1603, the Lord Chamberlain's company became the King's Men, coming under the patronage of James I.

As we deduce from the players in *Hamlet*, the make-up of the acting companies was rather different from either that of the medieval period or of later troupes. Probably most significantly, the companies were all male; boys (up to late adolescence) played women's roles. Behind the great leading actors were many secondary ones, who undertook supporting roles according to the same general categories of types that still prevail. Unlike many other theatres, however, the Elizabethan distinguished rather sharply between actors who played straight or serious roles and the so-called clowns, those who played comic (often lower-class) roles. In *Hamlet*, too, the gravediggers' scene can be analyzed for its evidence concerning the acting company. The gravediggers are both called clowns, and it has been suggested that much of their dialogue is not Shakespeare's, but that of his company's leading clowns. Hamlet and Horatio, on the other hand, are clearly the roles of a leading and a straight supporting actor. The great clowns of the period—Richard Tarleton, William Kemp, and Robert Armin—were as famous as any of the tragedians and distinguished themselves not only for their performances onstage, but also for such feats as Kemp's "dance" from London to Norwich (later unsuccessfully enlarged into a dance to Rome).

All companies, except for the scruffiest touring troupes of "three men and a boy" (the latter to play women's roles), were nominal servants of a noble and carried his name and his written authorization wherever they played. The reason for this was twofold: (1) a powerful noble who took an interest in the company could lend it great status and help it in the frequent conflicts with authority, and (2) an early law declaring all unattached actors as social undesirables made it necessary for every actor to be officially connected with a household. Thus, actors and writers wore their patron's livery on special occasions, just as other servants did.

Such nominal servant status, however, did not inhibit the professionalism of the theatre men, nor did it prevent many of them from having sizable incomes. A few became truly wealthy; many were able to live decently; and some never rose above the hand-to-mouth existence that had marked the very beginnings of the theatres as a profession.

The Rise of Professionalism

As was pointed out earlier, the published moralities often became part of the repertoire of simple traveling acting companies. There are reasons for believing that in certain cases such companies were made up of pious amateurs, but these cases are not typical. Rather, from the beginning of the sixteenth century on, small companies of professionals were working in England. They lacked the association with a permanent theatre of the later London companies, but they frequently carried the name of a noble household. Even before 1500, the smaller towns and cities were paying for performances by such groups as Norfolk's Men (a company belonging to the Duke of Norfolk), and a few actors, along with the more established musicians, were attached to the royal household itself.

The crudest of these troupes, often working without a license, were

in frequent danger of arrest as "rogues and vagabonds"; their repertoire was a mangled assortment of moralities, interludes (short secular
comedies, frequently with allegorical elements), and religious plays, all
cut and rearranged for four players only. Crazy-quilt doubling, rapid
costume changes, reliance on gross effects of role interpretation, and
the novelty of their performance made such troupes possible. They persisted until the Puritan revolution, and even after the Restoration
(1660) there are frequent contemptuous references to "strollers," the
small companies with no fixed home. The best temporary theatre they
could hope for was a nobleman's hall (like Hamlet's players); the most
common was an inn at a small town or a booth at a fair.

By the 1560s, however, some of the strollers had moved far beyond
the "rogue and vagabond" class; while their lesser fellows worked the
countryside, they began to act more and more in London itself. For at
least a decade before The Theatre and The Curtain were built in 1576–
1577, performances at London inns were very common and very popular—so much so, in fact, that the city government had serious misgiv-
ings about the morality and the propriety of theatre in any form. Thus,
when the first theatres went up, they went up outside the jurisdictional
limits of London, in the suburbs of Shoreditch and Southwark: the
theatre had become a profitable profession, and actors had become
noble servants, but every form of immorality from simple time-wasting
to sedition would be suspected of them throughout the period.

A few actors rose above such accusations. It has been said that not
until the nineteenth-century actor Henry Irving was knighted did actors really become respectable in England; nevertheless, respectability
was the prize that some Elizabethan actors aimed for. Shakespeare
himself is often cited as the *parvenu* theatre man who, after his success
in London, retired to his native Stratford, bought himself a coat of
arms and a big house, and lived out his remaining years as a rather self-
conscious gentleman. Richard Burbage (d. 1619), probably the greatest
actor of the age (and the leading member of Shakespeare's company),
was admired for his art and his intelligence; Edward Alleyn (1566–
1626), in a sense Burbage's chief rival in tragic roles, earned a small
fortune, established himself, and ultimately founded Dulwych College
outside London. Few actors, of course, ever rose to their eminence, but
the fact that men like Shakespeare, Burbage, Alleyn, and others were
able to build solid careers in the theatre indicates how far the profession had come since the end of the fifteenth century.

Acting and Hamlet's Players

Like all historical acting methods, the Elizabethan is impossible to
gauge exactly. There is very little iconographic evidence (unlike, for
example, the situation with Greek or neoclassic acting); interpretive or
didactic works suggest that oratory and rhetoric were so closely allied

with the theatre that the two must be seen at best as branches of the same art; and the plays of the period provide a very wide range of acting approaches.

Nevertheless, certain conclusions can be drawn. The connection between oratory and acting is the first, and the plays (*Hamlet* is an excellent example) offer one opportunity after another for displays of vocal skill. The extended phrase, the symmetrical expression, the progressive paragraph made up of complicated figures of speech, and the "set speech" are verbal structures that demand vocal control of a very high order (lengthy soliloquies such as Hamlet's "Oh what a rogue and peasant slave" or Claudius' "Oh my offense is rank"; or the extended perorations such as Hamlet's advice to his mother, "Look here upon this picture, and on this," or Polonius' parting advice to Laertes; or descriptive speeches such as Gertrude's account of the death of Ophelia, and so on). The Elizabethan interest in oratory as an art, in the sense learned from Roman models, was very great. Despite the development of printing and a high rate of literacy, vocal communication was still dominant, and the Shakespearean theatre was certainly a hearing place as much as it was a seeing place. The great actor needed a great voice and all the devices of the great speaker. Perhaps oratorical interpretation of the lines even preceded psychological interpretation of the role.

Glynn Wickham (*Early English Stages*) has outlined two approaches to the role, which he calls "the Image and the Emblem," analogous to the Inner and Outer, or the Truthful and the Technical of more recent actors. In brief, the actor could present his audience with a true image of the character, or with certain emblematic clues to it; the first is closer to identification with the role, the second to an objective demonstration of its outward signs. It must be realized, of course, that both approaches were made within the demands of the elevated vocal technique and the expanded gesture required by the scale of the stage; still, varying approaches were possible. Edward Alleyn, for example, was known for his effects—the convincing wildness of his scenes of insanity, the bloodthirsty excesses of his scenes of revenge. Richard Burbage, on the other hand, was evidently more restrained; his vocal technique aside, he seems to have aimed at a communicable and highly selective representation of the characters he played.

Hamlet itself includes one of the more revealing keys to Shakespearean acting. The inclusion of a play within a play was far from original with Shakespeare; indeed, by 1600 it was a very overused device (although it continued to be popular until the end of the period). The major action of the play does not require that the audience come to know the actors who present the "thing wherein I'll catch the conscience of the king" (although one of the subjects of the play's examination—surface appearance—is greatly extended by Hamlet's discussion with them). In part, then, Hamlet's scenes with the players are digressions from the main action, interesting for what they have to say about the theatre and important for their metaphorical comparison between Hamlet's behavior and an actor's. In fact, it is through this comparison, made by Hamlet himself, that we can learn something of the actor's techniques:

> What would he [the First Player] do
> Had he the motive and the cue for passion
> That I have?

The First Player has just given a lengthy set speech about the death of Priam; Polonius notes that at the speech's passionate ending, the Player "has turned his color and has tears in's eyes." Hamlet echoes him:

> . . . this player here
> But in a fiction, in a dream of passion,
> Could force his soul so to his own conceit
> That from her working all his visage wanned,
> Tears in his eyes, distraction in's aspect,
> A broken voice, and his whole function suiting
> With forms to his conceit. . . .

The actor's art, then (and we must assume that the First Player is at least a competent actor), results in an effective reproduction of truth— "his whole function" expressing outwardly what his "conceit" has created. The conceit in this sense is probably best understood as *imaginative creation*, not merely as imagination in the Stanislavskian sense (see Chapter Four) or as mere inventiveness. It is both an intellectual, conscious activity and one that lies beyond consciousness, for to Hamlet it springs ultimately from the "dream of passion's" work on the soul (part of the human essence distinct from the conscious mind). The source of the soul's creative act (its subject matter, as it were) is the dream of passion, the "fiction," the speech itself and its related elements of characterization. That none of these things is "real" is essential to *Hamlet*, for it is through the very fiction of the actor's work that Hamlet approaches his own idea of proper behavior, and it is evident in another of Hamlet's lines that the First Player is controlled and capable of even greater actions:

> What would he do
> Had he the motive and the cue for passion
> That I have? He would drown the stage with tears
> And cleave the general ear with horrid speech,
> Make mad the guilty and appal the free,
> Confound the ignorant, and amaze indeed
> The very faculties of eyes and ears.

THE GLOBE'S STAGE, SEEN FROM THE NORTHEAST (CHEAPER) GALLERY

Figure 2–18. Another interpretation of Shakespeare's theatre, this one based principally on medieval ideas of staging. Note especially the scaffolds along the sides of the stage and the audience members in the galleries above the stage. (*Reprinted with permission of the Macmillan Company from* Shakespeare's Wooden O *by Leslie Hotson. First published in the United States in 1960. Courtesy also of Rupert Hart-Davis, London.*)

The point is not that the First Player would drown the stage *if he were Hamlet,* but *if he had Hamlet's cue;* that is, he would go to such extremes if he were to *play* Hamlet, not *be* Hamlet. (And it must be remembered that, in reciting his speech, the First Player was interpreting the character of Aeneas, not of any relative of Priam's; in other words, the cue for passion was considerably less than Hamlet's own.)

Thus, the Elizabethan actor used the text (the "dream of passion") as the key to his most profound emotional and intellectual self (the "soul"), so that his own imaginative creation (his "conceit") could find outward expression. Although the actor's emotions and actions were founded in a fiction, they yet had reality for him (real tears, the broken voice), which he controlled in terms of the intensity of the *character's,* not his own, emotions (the "cue for passion"). Fictional although the source may have been, however, the outward presentation by the actor had to be convincing and had to be very close to reality. Hamlet used the play within a play because it was truthful:

> . . . I have heard
> That guilty creatures sitting at a play
> Have by the very cunning of the scene
> Been struck so to the soul that presently
> They have proclaimed their malefactions

The audience was deeply involved in such acting, not merely engaged by techniques of oratory, movement, and impersonation: it could be deeply moved ("struck to the soul") by the convincing actuality of the actor's behavior (the "cunning of the scene").

It remains only to examine the famous lines spoken to all the players by Hamlet, that "Advice to the Actor" that every theatre student must inevitably encounter. One may first wonder where Hamlet gained such theatrical experience, but on a second reading the speech seems to be that of a sensitive audience member, not of a director. Nevertheless, it is to the point and very revealing:

Speak the speech, I pray you, as I pronounced it to you, trippingly on the tongue. But if you mouth it, as many of your players do, I had as lief the town crier spoke my lines. Nor do not saw the air too much with your hands, thus, but use all gently. . . . It offends me to the soul to hear a robustious periwig-pated fellow tear a passion to tatters, to very rags. . . . Be not too tame neither, but let your own discretion be your tutor. Suit the action to the word, the word to the action, with this special observance, that you o'erstep not the modesty of nature. For anything so overdone is from the purpose of playing, whose end, both at the first and now, was and is to hold as 'twere the mirror up to Nature . . . to show . . . the very age and body of the time his form and pressure.

Hamlet has earlier warned Polonius that actors are the "abstract and brief chronicle of the time." They are, in short, truthful. Their truth may be compressed, epitomized, intensified, but it remains truth all the same. Certain conventions of the theatre may prevent the actor's truth from seeming perfectly convincing (the stage, for example, can never be a perfect Elsinore), but ideally the actor strives "to hold as 'twere the mirror up to Nature." Bad actors, in Hamlet's view, may do otherwise, and may be admired for so doing, but they are not satisfying the "purpose of playing"; they are crowd-pleasing. In brief, the ideal of acting that Shakespeare seems here to be offering is one of moderation, with the actor's instrument (reduced by Hamlet to speech and simple gesture) fully developed, but controlled by his conceit so that it always conforms to the actor's concept of reality (Nature). Especially in psychology, of course, this concept of Nature has changed radically from Shakespeare's period, but within the Elizabethan concept a sincere adherence to truthfulness was apparently desired. If compared to the acting of classical Greece, English acting in 1600 would probably have seemed far less conventionalized, less limited by the mask and by traditional gesture. The goal was, it seems, a convincing representation of the character and his action. The governing idea of psychology and of behavior turned such representation toward oratory and toward actions and gestures (drowning the stage in tears; changing color) that the twentieth century might not accept as truly reflective of Nature. However, the natural was an ideal. As we shall see, it had, in turn, to be mirrored within the conventions of a very special theatre.

Shakespeare's Globe

Evidence concerning the Elizabethan theatre structures is tantalizingly scanty. Other than the plays themselves, there is only the Swan drawing (see Figure 2–17), a sketch by a Dutch visitor in his "commonplace book"; the builder's contract for the Fortune, another theatre; diaries, letters, and accounts by audience members; and, slightly later, illustrations, in published plays, of real or imaginary stages that may or may not resemble Shakespeare's. Thus, as with the Greek theatre, there is enough evidence to permit extensive theorizing and not quite enough to allow for proof. Several theories exist, a number of which are plausible. (See Figures 2–18 through 2–20.)

To begin with the plays, we are able to find a number of terms that indicate parts of the theatre. Clearly, at least two acting levels existed, called variously "above" and "below," or "on the top" and "on the stage"; and context indicated that such directions as "at a window" (as in Kyd's 1586 play *The Spanish Tragedy*) are above the principal acting area. The *stage* was the main level, but another existed *above*. In addition, as we can see from *Hamlet*, the area below the stage was used ("The Ghost cries under the stage"), at least for sound effects, whereas at least part of the audience was on a level lower than the stage itself, the "ground" ("tear a passion to tatters, to very rags, to split the ears of the *Groundlings*"). On the principal level or stage, the use of the words *in* or *within* clearly indicated what we now mean by *offstage* ("Exit Hamlet tugging in Polonius"), so that *to come out* was to enter the acting area, *to go in* was to leave it. Thus, we have such directions as "Hamlet within" before the closet scene.

If we try to apply these terms to the Swan drawing (Figure 2–17), at least a general idea of the theatre begins to take shape. Clearly, the *stage* is the large platform occupying the center of the "plain or arena" in the drawing. The only *above* that is visible is the gallery running the length of the "actors' house" (although we cannot accept this as the only possibility for its location). The two doors in the same wall may help to explain the term *in* and *out*, for, seen from the actor's point of view, to leave the stage through them is to enter his house—presumably the location of his dressing room, green room (a common room for actors' use) and so on. The use of two doors may be clarified by such juxtaposed stage directions in *Hamlet* as: "Exit Hamlet tugging

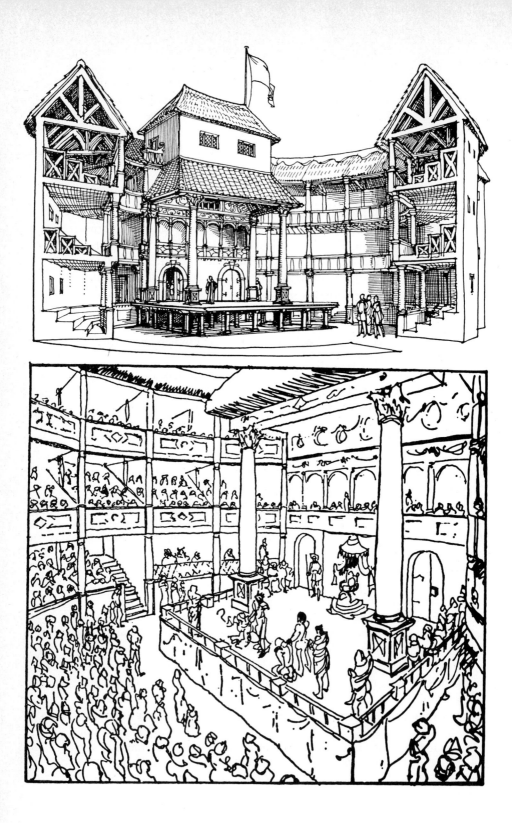

in Polonius. Enter King." Presumably, the exit is made through one door, the entrance through another; another direction in *The Spanish Tragedy* is, "He goes in at one door and comes out at another."

The Swan drawing suggests further structural details that may not be immediately evident in the plays. Most obvious is the roof over the stage and its supporting pillars, which rest on the stage itself. In the drawing, this roof seems to project out only about half way. Contemporary usage indicates that this roof was called the heavens, that its underside was decorated, and that from it gods and suitable properties could descend, the machinery presumably being housed in the structure rising over the actor's house and from which the flag is flying. Ben Jonson, in the Prologue to *Every Man in His Humour*, for example, lists as one of the evils of the popular theatre those effects in which "creaking throne comes down, the boys to please." *Hamlet* may contain at least an oblique description of the decorated heavens in Hamlet's "most excellent Canopy the Ayre, look you, this brave orehanging, this majestical Roof, fretted with golden fire."

A further detail to be drawn from the Swan drawing is the shape of the audience area itself, shown here apparently as circular. Hamlet's "ground" is the circular "plain or arena," whereas the three tiers or floors are so labeled that a descending scale of social position seems to run from lowest to highest. The labeled entrances appear to be stairways from the lowest tier into the "plain or arena," and we must conclude that if the lowest tier did, indeed, contain the most desirable locations, then the stairway entrances must have been reached directly from the street, thus preventing the groundlings from going through the expensive section.

To put these theatre elements in to Elizabethan terminology, we need only cite the use of the words *pit* and *yard* for the *plain or arena*; of *tiring house* (the place where actors were attired) for *actors' house*; and of *lords' room* for the *nobles' seats*.

The picture of the theatre that we have formed, then, is of a freestanding, circular structure whose center is open to the sky, with a large stage, backed by the tiring house, in its center. The audience sur-

Figure 2–19. (*Top*) A modern interpretation of Shakespeare's theatre as it may have appeared in about 1595, showing cross-section details of the audience galleries. Note the fidelity to the "Swan" drawing in the arrangement of doors and gallery, and the very solid "heavens" over the stage for machinery. (*From C. Walter Hodges*, The Globe Restored, *Ernest Benn, Ltd., London, 1953.*)

Figure 2–20. (*Bottom*) Richard Southern's reconstruction of an Elizabethan theatre, showing the use of a curtained pavilion between the doors in the actors' house or tiring house. (*A line drawing by Richard Southern, which appears in his book*, The Seven Ages of the Theatre. *Copyright © 1961 by Richard Southern. Used with the permission of Hill and Wang and of Faber and Faber, Ltd.*)

rounded it on three sides, both standing in the pit around it and sitting in the tiers of lords' rooms, benches, and "gallery."

Problem: Renaissance or Medieval?

The alternate theories concerning this theatre show how much mystery still surrounds the details of the Shakespearean theatre. Part of the mystery springs from conflicts of evidence; for example, although the Swan drawing seems to show a stage projecting far out into the pit, the Fortune contract specifies a stage that projects only about half way across the pit (28 feet from the tiring-house façade and 43 feet wide). The Swan drawing seems to show a circular theatre, but exterior views of the period show octagonal, hexagonal, and even square buildings (although Shakespeare's *Henry V* calls the theatre a "Wooden O"). The Swan drawing clearly shows the façade of the tiring house to be blank except for the colonnaded upper gallery and the two doors, but for generations scholars have been insisting on something else—a space of some sort that is distinct from the stage, somehow contained and suggesting an interior, and probably curtained. Their reasons are found in the confusing stage directions and references in the plays: Polonius offers to hide himself "behind the Arras" (what arras?), and in the closet scene he "hides me here" (where?). Many characters are "discovered," and even beds and tables are "discovered." It is hard to see how the audience could "discover" an actor or an object that had to be carried on through one of the Swan drawing's doors, and so a "discovery space" has been postulated. Where it is and what it is remains a mystery.

Hypotheses abound, however. Until recently the almost universally accepted solution was the "inner" space, even doubled by some scholars into an "inner above" and an "inner below." What is necessary for it, of course, is to pierce the façade of the tiring house between the Swan drawing's doors, thus creating a curtained recess within which Polonius could hide, and which, by drawing open a curtain, could reveal actors or objects within. The principal objection to the "inner below" theory is the appalling sight lines of such a space. It is, in effect, a little proscenium stage, and it offers only a restricted segment of the audience any decent view of the action within.

The best alternative offered to this idea is the "pavilion" theory, which sees a structure set up between the Swan drawing's doors and jutting out into the stage. Curtained like a medieval scaffold, it would be opened on three sides to let the audience see what was within. Closed, it could be used for such purposes as Polonius' concealment, and its top has been suggested as a possibility for the "above" location. Again, however, a sight-line problem is created by such a structure, for when closed, it would hide one or the other of the doors (and part of the stage) to two considerable chunks of the audience. It can be argued that it was usually open and that, in fact, no sight-line problem existed because the areas on each side of such a pavilion were unimportant, that the action inevitably moved downstage below any shallow pavilion and out on the unroofed forestage.

To oversimplify only slightly, it can be suggested that the problem can be looked at a bit differently—that, in effect, one must first decide whether the staging is basically medieval or basically Continental Renaissance—and the space question comes into perspective. Things are not all that easy, of course; the one scholar who has given a completely medieval interpretation of this stage (see Leslie Hotson's hypothesis, Figure 2–18) has gone to such an extreme that his theory is frequently thrown out *in toto* without giving attention to some of its ingenious details. Even if we do not go so far as Hotson, however, we can see the medieval reminiscences of both the Swan drawing and the other evidence. The yard is comparable to the medieval place (and "plain or arena" suggests that the medieval usage may have been in mind when it was so labeled), although many historians will stoutly defend their belief that it derives directly from the inn yard. The large raised stage has a medieval precedent in the shallow forestages of the scaffolds and in such large raised stages in a few medieval illustrations. Apparently the audience both surrounds the action and presses close against the acting area, and we cannot reject the suggestion that even the yard itself was used for some scenes (Fortinbras' army, for example) much as the medieval place was used. On the raised stage, then, we might expect to see structures analogous to scaffolds or to the central castle of Southern's reconstruction of *The Castle of Perseverance* (Figure 2–8). The "pavilion" is such a structure, curtained as we should expect it to be.

Other details of certain plays give further evidence of medieval practice. To go again to Kyd's *The Spanish Tragedy*, we might note that it calls for at least two large set pieces to remain onstage throughout the play (an arbor and a scaffold) in the tradition of simultaneous staging. Other plays suggest the same practice, and one of Henslowe's records—a list of stage properties—mentions such medieval items as a hell and other set pieces that apparently could be used in the medieval fashion. We do not have to admit that Sakespeare's stage *was* a medieval stage, but we cannot deny that it would have allowed extensive use of medieval staging.

No such case can be made for fully developed Renaissance staging, particularly with its use of perspective scenery, movable scenery, and a limiting frame (see pp. 92 *ff*). On the contrary, we know that such staging did not come into English practice until the designer Inigo Jones (1573–1652) began to exploit it in the court masque theatre after about 1603. Thus, no "inner stage" can be justified in terms of major influences on the development of the theatre itself.

To date, the most workable solutions to the problems of the Shakespearean stage seem to be those of C. W. Hodges and Richard Southern (see Figures 2–19 and 2–20). Objections have been raised to them, of

Figure 2–21. *Hamlet* at the Hilberry Classic Theatre, Wayne State University, 1968. Directed by Leonard Leone, with setting by William Rowe, costumes by Stephanie Schoelzel, and lighting by Gary M. Witt. Note the use of wire mesh to effect the appearance of the Ghost.

course, but they remain the most consistently successful theories. The theatre that they offer us is one of medieval freedom in time and space, with few localizing elements and a highly presentational acting area. Unlike most medieval acting spaces, however, the Shakespearean is highly focused, and the real development seems to be in the concentration on the individual actor (and his character) instead of on a diffuse and constantly shifting group.

Performance

The performance of such a play as *Hamlet* in this kind of theatre was evidently a far cry from the rather elaborately polite, formal performances of the modern London or New York theatres. Instead of the darkened auditorium and the artistically lighted stage, there was bright sunlight or silver-gray overcast; instead of carpeted aisles and tea between the acts there were the paved yard and hawkers selling food; instead of the clean separation of actor and audience there was sometimes the intimacy of privileged spectators sitting on the stage itself and others in the pit crowding to its very edge.

The idea of a rowdy, jostling, richly varied crowd at such a performance may now seem a bit sentimental and dated. There is no evidence that the Elizabethan audience was either more or less aware than the modern one, nor that its social make-up was markedly different. However, the theatrical occasion was certainly less formal and more robust. The theatre was a social place. The physical shape lent itself to seeing and being seen, to audience cohesion rather than to audience fragmentation. When one arrived, in the middle of the afternoon, he paid a general admission fee; then, by paying more inside the theatre, he could go to whatever audience level he could afford. The flag flew over the stage house to indicate that a performance was being given; just before it was to begin, a trumpeter appeared, probably from a door high up over the stage (as in the Swan drawing), and blew the call that signaled the start of the performance.

Until after Shakespeare began writing, but clearly before *Hamlet*, it was a common practice to begin many performances with a pantomime, or dumb-show, that foretold all the action. Some of the companies were still following this custom after 1600, but Hamlet's sardonic comment on the practice indicates that the Lord Chamberlain's Men were not:

O, it offends me to the soul, to see a robustious periwig-pated fellow tear a Passion to tatters, to very rags, to split the ears of the groundlings, who, for the most part, are capable of nothing but inexplicable dumb-shows and noise. . . .

Nevertheless, the company of players that present Hamlet's "mouse-trap" use the introductory dumb-show, and the stage directions describing it are worth examining for what they have to say about stage custom:

Hautboy play. The dumb show enters.

Enter a King and Queen, very lovingly; the Queen embraces him. She kneels and makes show of Protestation unto him. He takes her up, and declines his head upon her neck. Lays down upon a bank of flowers. She, seeing him asleep, leaves him. Anon comes in a fellow, takes off his [the King's] crown, kisses it, and pours poison in the King's ears, and exits. The Queen returns, finds the King dead, and makes passionate action. The poisoner, with some two or three mutes comes in again, seeming to lament with her. The dead body is carried away. The poisoner woos the Queen with gifts: she seems loathe and unwilling a while, but in the end accepts his love.

Exeunt

Thus, the performance is introduced with music (hautboys) and begins with a pantomime of a very obvious and formal kind: the Queen "makes a show of protestation"; the King "declines his head upon her neck," and so on. The dumb-show is a very close foretelling of what is to follow; and although the play within the play never gets as far in its plot as the pantomime does, it is clear from Hamlet's description of it that, except for Claudius' interruption, it would have.

A further detail of the performance, the use of a prologue, can be seen in the play within the play. Although *Hamlet* itself has no prologue, it is far from certain that it would never have had one in performance; that of the Players' performance, for example, is very simple and very general.

> Enter prologue.
> For us, and for our tragedy,
> Here stooping to your clemency,
> We beg your hearing patiently.

More specific prologues were frequently used to comment on contemporary events, to explain peculiarities of the play, or to apologize for supposed faults, and in rare cases an "induction" was used even more elaborately—a staged scene between two or more people, not characters in the play, to introduce the play itself.

Following the prologue, the action of the play itself could begin. Cruder productions and an earlier period used signs to indicate the locale. As in *Hamlet*, more sophisticated productions could probably do without them after a statement of the general location ("Denmark") because of the nonspecific nature of Shakespeare's scenes and the inclusion of all really necessary information in the scene itself.

Although we customarily see Elizabethan plays printed in acts and scenes, we can hardly conclude that they were so staged in their original performances. The scene, particularly, is a concept rather foreign to such a fluid theater; without curtain or lighting change, it could move from group to group, subaction to subaction, without any sense of changing dramatic units at all. Act divisions were usually used for the double purpose of relieving actors and audience and of providing time for brief entertainments between acts. Music was the simplest; the more popular was the jig (as in Hamlet's dismissal of Polonius, "He's for a jig or a tale of bawdry, or he sleeps"). Jigs took a number of forms, including the dance still called by that name. Songs, bawdy or not, with a dance accompaniment, and brief plays, with more than one character, with sung dialogue, narration, and danced (jigged) action were brief *intermedi*, entertainment between the acts. They had no relation to the principal play at all.

The performance frequently concluded with an epilogue. Such an ending is almost obligatory in comedy, where the requests for "plaudite" are part of the comic relationship with the audience. In tragedy, unless a moral was being pointed, no formal epilogue was necessary. Nevertheless, as in *Hamlet*, an internal speech that closes the action functions clearly as an epilogue, summing up its effects, if not its moral, for both characters and audience:

FORTINBRAS. Let four Captains
  Bear Hamlet like a soldier to the stage,
  For he was likely, had he been put on,
  To have prov'd most royally;

And for his passage,
The soldier's music and the rites of war
Speak loudly for him.
Take up the body; such a fight as this
Becomes the field, but here shows much amiss.
Go, bid the soldiers shoot.

> (*Exeunt marching, after the which a
> peal of ordnance is shot off.*)

Shakespeare and Hamlet

Hamlet was first staged shortly after 1600, probably in 1602. Its first production was at the Globe, the theatre put up by the Lord Chamberlain's Men in 1599. (It burned down in 1613 and was replaced with a new and enlarged Globe.) At the time of the *Hamlet* production, Shakespeare was a sharer in the company, one of London's leading playwrights, and an actor who appeared, apparently in minor roles, in both his own plays and in those of other dramatists.

Shakespeare had been born in 1564 in Stratford, the small town that is now the site of the Memorial Theatre, a shrine, and various commercial enterprises centering around Shakespeariana. Of his marriage,

Figure 2–22. The closet scene from *Hamlet* in the 1957 production at the Stratford Shakespearean Festival in Stratford, Ontario. (*Courtesy of the Stratford Shakespearean Festival.*)

his education, and his personal life little need be said, because they form the largely irrelevant subject of many biographies of varying degrees of authenticity. His real professional career began when he came to London, probably in the late 1580s, and started to work with the company then playing at The Theatre. His earliest efforts as a playwright were, typically, revisions and additions to old plays. His earliest works (*Love's Labours Lost*, the three parts of *Henry VI*, and others) show both the influence of such leading writers of the time as Kyd, Christopher Marlowe (1564–1593), and Robert Greene (c. 1560–1592), and passages taken directly from older plays or written by other playwrights. In the late 1590s and in the early years of the seventeenth century, he produced the body of great tragedies and romantic comedies for which he is best known. In 1611, he more or less retired, spending the greater part of his time at New Place, a Stratford property he had purchased as his earnings increased at the turn of the century. Until his death in 1616, he maintained an interest in the professional theatre, but his direct involvement in production seems to have ended with *Henry VIII* in 1613.

A number of influences were at work on his writing throughout this period, not the least of them his work with, or revision of, the other playwrights already mentioned. Kyd certainly epitomizes the pre-Shakespearean tragedian—bombastic, rather mannered, clearly trying to break new ground in the theatre and showing the effort. The First Player's speech in *Hamlet* is not unlike Kyd, and the rather crude dramaturgy of the dumb-show is reminiscent of some of the work in *The Spanish Tragedy*. However, Kyd's sense of a postmedieval English tragedy continues in Shakespeare and accounts for much of his contemporary success; both were the "abstract and brief chronicle of the times" in that both caught the tragic mood of an age that was swinging between a new sense of individual responsibility and individual action, on the one hand, and the older distrust of action, of individuality, on the other. Simplified, the literary counterparts of these two poles are medieval drama and the plays of Seneca, the first religious and transcendental, the second secular and immediate. Kyd was vastly Shakespeare's inferior, but in expressing the tension between the two extremes, he brought the so-called *revenge play* to a new level, a level from which Marlowe, and later Shakespeare, could work. By the time of *Hamlet*, the revenge plot was successfully submerged in complexities of character, language, and idea, but it remained as the outward expression of the late medieval playwright's deepest concerns.

In encountering any of these writers, the Elizabethan concern with language (both rhetoric and oratory) must be kept in mind. The carefully worked conceits of such writers as John Lyly (c. 1554–1606) were more mannered than any but the very earliest writing of Shakespeare, but even Shakespeare's language is cast in a mold of inventiveness, of elaborate decoration and of sheer verbal pyrotechnics. Along with the nature of his theatre, perhaps the greatest operative convention of Shakespeare's dramaturgy is the verbal expressiveness of his lines. George Bernard Shaw once observed that his own characters, if encountered in life, would seem "monsters of genius" for their intellectual expressiveness; it is fair to say that Shakespeare's would seem monsters of lyricism. Their speech should not be looked at as merely the real speech of real people; it is the poetic speech of real people who inhabit a world of gaudy imagery and joyful poetry.

Hamlet

PLOT AND STRUCTURE. *Hamlet* is a play in which plot *can* be discussed, for it progresses along a line, from beginning to end, that does demand fairly strict sequence. It has a few important subplots (the story of Ophelia; the story of Laertes) and what has been called an overplot— the political involvement of Norway and Denmark—whose outcome depends on the outcome of the principal plot.

In its bare outlines, the plot of *Hamlet* is that of the "revenge play." The revenge code, at least as it appeared on the Elizabethan stage, had a typical shape that both determined the protagonist's course and constantly questioned the nature of tragedy in the period: because of the murder or violation of a member of his immediate family, the protagonist had to assure the death and the damnation of the guilty party and often of *his* immediate family as well. Frequently, the protagonist was informed or egged on by a ghost. Most often he was opposed by a "Machiavellian" intriguer, a trickster whose outward appearance was respectable and whose inward character was without scruple. Thus, one of the protagonist's tasks was to pierce the Machiavellian's appearance in order to get at the truth; this could be accomplished only by tricking the trickster. A second task was to dispose of the Machiavellian villain in such a way that he suffered both physically and spiritually, assuring that his soul would be damned. Finally, the revenging protagonist (at least in those plays that were not merely sensation-seeking) had to come to terms with his own perceptual doubts about the proof of the villain's guilt.

If we try to find what is tragic in such a plot, we ultimately do best to set Aristotle aside and suspect that the tragedy of the revenger lies in the fact that he is cast in a role from which there is no proper escape: the revenge code demands that he act (kill); the Christian code demands that he leave judgment to God ("leave her to Heaven," as the Ghost tells Hamlet). Caught between these two irreconcilable choices, the revenger destroys himself in trying to satisfy both, and although his death is usually prepared for in the plot, we are frequently led to feel that the playwright, perhaps unconsciously, sought to punish his own protagonist for taking matters into his own hands.

Hamlet fits the revenge plot on all counts. Setting aside the five-act structure of published editions, which, as we have seen, was imposed by editors or publishers after the performance, we can break the plot into four major sections. In the first one, Hamlet is given the order to revenge (by the Ghost) and tests its validity with the play within the play. In the second, Claudius, alarmed by Hamlet's discovery, resolves to kill him by sending him to England; Hamlet rejects the opportunity of murdering Claudius while he is at prayers lest the villain go to Heaven, not to Hell, and he then confronts his mother with his own crimes. In the third section, Hamlet is absent from the court, but the plot is complicated by the madness of Ophelia and the return of Laertes, seeking his own revenge for the death of his father, Polonius. In the last section, the returned Hamlet faces Laertes in the rigged duel; the King is exposed to all as the trickster ("The King! The King's to blame!"), and Hamlet kills him, finally succumbing himself to the poison that has been prepared for him. At the end of the play, neither the Machiavellian Claudius nor the revenging Hamlet is alive, and the new power figure who emerges to save the kingdom is Fortinbras, the man of action who has been more talked about than present throughout the play.

CHARACTER. It was fashionable in the nineteenth century to speak of Hamlet's "problem," as if some romantic quirk of character was the cause of his lengthy delay in killing Claudius. Even Laurence Oliver's film version began with the solemn statement that this was the story of a "man who could not make up his mind." The problem theory of Hamlet's character may gain some little support from the question of Hamlet's madness ("That he is mad, 'tis true; 'Tis true 'tis pity/ And pity it is true"), and at least one actor-director has solved the problem very simply by making Hamlet very little else but mad.

Figure 2–23. George Grizzard as Hamlet, Jessica Tandy as Gertrude, in the 1963 production of The Guthrie Theatre Company. Directed by Tyrone Guthrie, designed by Tanya Moiseiwitsch. (*Courtesy of The Guthrie Theatre Company.*)

Understanding Hamlet's character—insofar as that is possible—is necessary to understanding the play. Therefore, two points of Elizabethan psychology—melancholy and madness— must be examined, and then Hamlet must be looked at in the light of two people with whom he compares himself, Fortinbras and the First Player.

Melancholy, or the melancholic humor, was both a fashionable and a real concern of psychology (or medicine) in the period. Although there were degrees and types of melancholy, the sort shown by Hamlet was the most compelling. Hamlet wears the costume of the melancholy man (black); he has the melancholy's intense introspection (the soliloquies, his isolation from the court); he is sardonic, satirical, suspicious of the motives of others and of his environment; he is self-destructive ("O what a rogue and peasant slave am I" is the melancholic's self-criticism; "To be or not to be" is his despairing, and unresolved, question). The melancholy, as a humor, or psychological state, was used to explain certain kinds of behavior; on the stage, as in Hamlet's case, those patterns of behavior were used to express problems that ran deeper than psychology. In brief, it is the introspection, the questioning of *everything*, that is externalized as stage melancholy, and we may say that Hamlet is a melancholic humor because he suspects the truth about his father's death *even before* he encounters his father's ghost. He is literally driven into melancholy by his intelligence, his own perception. Everything that he learns after that point "feeds his humor" (to use Jonson's phrase) and drives him still deeper into himself. We may speculate that such behavior was considered odd because suspicion, introspection, and the deep questioning of one's entire environment had been disallowed for centuries by the medieval habit of pious acceptance.

But is he mad? The question is not easily answered. An excessive humor (such as melancholy) was a form of madness; yet we know that on several occasions Hamlet admits to feigning madness ("It is not madness/ That I have uttered; bring me to the test; And I the matter will reword, that madness/ Would gambol from." "I am but mad North-North-West . . ."). That he is near to collapse we must believe from the very extremes of his behavior, from frenetic activity to melancholy sloth; that he may sometimes allow the pressure of his situation to contort his view of reality, as in the murder of Polonius, we must accept; but out-and-out madness does not gibe with either his over-all action or his words. Like a number of other revengers, he comes close to mental breakdown when the imperative of revenge comes into direct conflict with the teachings of religion (and some early revengers, like Hieronomo in *The Spanish Tragedy*, do go temporarily insane). Yet at the end he is sane and clearheaded, or his final action would be merely compulsory. His final sanity, and his final sane action, reveal the torment of the introspective man faced with the need to countermand universal law.

This struggle is expressed by Hamlet himself in his comparison with

Fortinbras and with the First Player. Each represents an important quality to him—Fortinbras ("strength of arms") the easy activity of the man who does not think, and the First Player the outward manifestations of an emotion he does not feel. It is probably ironic that Fortinbras assumes command at the end of the play, his way having been cleared by the melancholy Hamlet; surely, neither can function without the other. Fortinbras should not be looked on as an ideal in any sense; for all of Hamlet's soliloquizing about him, it is hardly even suggested that Hamlet would like to be Fortinbras (although he is certainly aware that life would be easier that way). Rather, Fortinbras is one of the "new men"—opportunistic, decisive, ambitious, and without profound conscience. He can sacrifice vast numbers of lives for a land he has never seen; the idea of the deed does not frighten him. Hamlet finds it almost impossible to tick off one man for a crime he knows has been committed.

The First Player gives us a clue to Hamlet's own concern about penetrating outward appearance (see p. 72). On the one hand, Hamlet must penetrate the disguise of Claudius; on the other, he must wonder why he cannot put on the face that his own offended consciousness (his cue for passion) would seem to require. There is a kind of envy here: in a good world, the sane man would let his outward self be consonant with the inward. But Hamlet does not live in a good world; only the actor, and he through an artifice, can be truthful. Hamlet exists within a paradox.

In its most developed form, the melancholy worrier of Hamlet's sort becomes a type known on the post-Elizabethan stage as the "malcontent," best seen in John Marston's play of that name (1604). Unlike Hamlet, the malcontent is innately ill at ease in the world; there is no place for him. Hamlet has not reached that state. "Something is rotten in the state of Denmark"; his world is "an unweeded garden." Only the imperative that forces him to play the active revenger, the gardener, drives him into melancholy and the appearance of madness.

IDEA.   Ultimately, *Hamlet* remains a mystery. The play is fluid enough so that minor characters can be cut, scenes can be transposed, and lines can be rearranged to make a new play called *Hamlet*. Montage *Hamlets* and improvised *Hamlets* have recently been performed on the assumption that everyone knows the old one all too well. The suggestion is clear that Shakespeare's play has almost passed out of the realm of theatrical literature and into that of myth.

The mystery is there, as it is in *Oedipus Rex*, because Shakespeare touches so many profound and finally unanswerable questions. Metaphysical problems are only a hair's breadth away, when they are not brought outright upon the stage. Death, responsibility to an outdated ethical code, filial piety, existential doubt, perceptual proof—these matters and many more are examined closely in the soliloquies, played out in the scenes, and made active in the plot. There is no simple single idea behind the play.

What was suggested at the beginning of this section is, perhaps, the most important idea for a modern audience: *Hamlet* is a play about the Renaissance crisis (which is a modern crisis). One can play games with Hamlet's supposed love for his mother, or his supposed hallucinations about the ghost, or his supposedly real madness, or his political acumen, or any of a number of imposed interpretations, but in historical perspective the play remains the greatest of late medieval plays about the collapse of Christian passivity. Hamlet, like Oedipus, is distinguished because he is the man who acts; he is significantly different because action is such torment for him. The tragedy, then, comes not from the knowledge that *action* is doomed but that *conscience* is doomed. In Shakespeare's tragic universe, the active men at arms like Fortinbras take charge; the conscience-stricken men of spirit are destroyed by their own engines.

RACINE AND CONTINENTAL NEOCLASSICISM

The appearance of a "new" drama in England, one created according to Renaissance rather than medieval principles, cannot be noted with any confidence before the death of Shakespeare, but in Italy, and in France, attempts to follow a new line of theatre practice dated well back into the sixteenth century. As might be expected, the writing of new plays with new ideas and new critical thinking was paralleled by new theatres and new ways of producing theatrical spectacle.

The history of the Renaissance theatre, from its beginnings in Italy in the late fifteenth century to such high points as Racine's *Phaedra* in 1677, is essentially the history of a belated interpretation (and imitation), from very scanty evidence, of the theatre of Rome. In discussing the Renaissance theatre, therefore, we must speak of it as neoclassic—

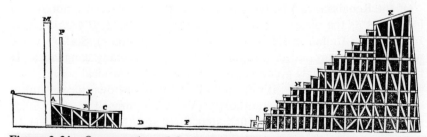

Figure 2–24. Cross-section of Serlio's reconstruction, in wood, of a Roman theatre, from the 1569 edition of his *Dell'Architectura*. Note particularly the sloping stage (AB) for scenery in false perspective; the flat playing-area, C, analogous to the playing-area in front of the Greek skene; and the stands for spectators, G-K. This illustration should be compared with Figures 2–12 and 2–25. (*Courtesy of the New York Public Library.*)

quite consciously imitative of a past that may never have existed except in the minds of its imitators. For critical principles, there had been Horace; for plays, there had been the comedies of Terence and Plautus, and the tragedies of Seneca; for theatre architecture there had been Vitruvius. Each of these Romans was studied, reproduced, and imitated. The new products were not exactly like the models because, first, there was inadequate information about the models themselves and, secondly, the men who imitated them were creative—that is, original in their own right.

The failure to use Greek sources was largely due to the greater scarcity of Greek manuscripts and the prevalence of Latin as a language. In addition, the concept of classical Rome as the foundation of Roman Catholic temporal power (as in Dante's *Divine Comedy*, for example) explains the much greater reliance on Latin materials until well into the seventeenth century.

In looking at the antecedents of Racine, then, it will be impossible to overlook Roman practice entirely. If Racine stands at a pinnacle in the development of neoclassical theatre, he can best be understood in terms of the development that preceded him, with its early productions of Latin plays, its elaboration of Roman "rules" of dramaturgy, and its construction of a spectacular new theatre structure on the skeleton of the Roman.

Building the Renaissance Theatre

Vitruvius' *De Architectura* was first printed (in Latin) in Rome in about 1486; many later editions and translations followed. None contained illustrations drawn from the original manuscripts, so that a good deal of interpretation went into each edition. Like the illustrations for the fifteenth- and sixteenth-century Terence collections, both the text and the diagrams of the Vitruvius editions reflected Renaissance practice as much as they expressed Vitruvius.

Of the Renaissance Vitruvius editions and commentaries, none is so important as the massive work of Sebastiano Serlio, *Dell'Archittetura*. Published in Italian in 1559–1562 (in separate volumes), Serlio's work was quickly reproduced throughout Europe in many languages. It represented the single greatest interpretation of a classical source by a contemporary authority; it reflected all of Vitruvius' own ideas—imitation of an earlier model as authority (Vitruvius himself in this case); symmetrical construction; unified structure; and the use of scenery to parallel generic categories of drama (comic, tragic, and pastoral) already derived from Latin critical sources. This seminal work set down the guidelines for every subsequent designer and architect in the erudite theatre for the next century and a half. Its interpretation of Vitruvius' Roman theatre (however mistaken it was) set the model for the great Renaissance theatres of Europe. Serlio added one pre-eminent design scheme of his own: the use of linear perspective. Taken from contemporary painting, this illusory reproduction of three-dimensional space was adapted to fit Vitruvius' structure, and it, in turn, altered that structure to its own needs. The final result was a theatre whose

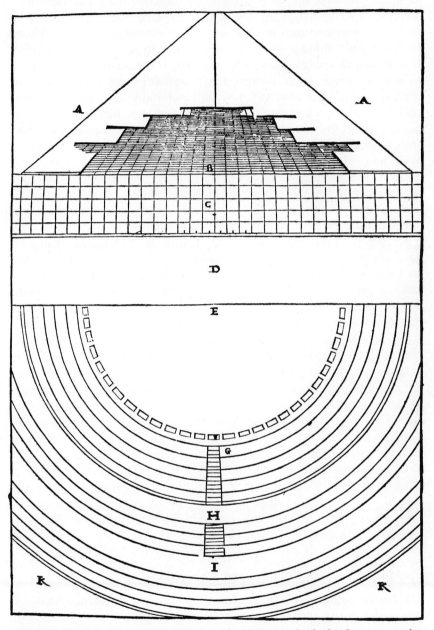

Figure 2–25. The plan of Serlio's theatre. Note particularly the perspective effect created on the sloping stage, AB. (*Courtesy of the New York Public Library.*)

use of scenery—especially scenery designed around the rules of linear perspective—fitted the very vague terms of the Roman example, but which was actually an entirely new idea in scenic design. Serlio's comic, tragic, and pastoral scenes were generally derived from Vitruvius; their reliance on linear perspective matched the social scheme of the erudite Renaissance theatre. It was a spatial break from medieval concepts; it symbolized an individual perception of external reality. Its great disadvantage—that all perception in a perspective theatre was limited to a single viewpoint—was answered, at least temporarily, by another Renaissance theatre, the *Teatro Olimpico* of Vicenza. The tension created between the new sense of individualism and the increasingly aristocratic politics of the period was nowhere expressed better than in the theatre erected for the Olympic Academy of Vicenza, Italy (an intellectual organization of wealthy men). Designed originally by Andrea Palladio, whose own commentary on Vitruvius had appeared in 1570, the building was actually finished by Palladio's colleague Scamozzi after Palladio's death in 1580. Completed in 1584, the theatre still stands.

The unique importance of the *Teatro Olimpico* is its attempt to solve a perspective problem with several viewing points, rather than only one, within the architectural limitations of Roman example. A quick glance at Serlio's design for his theatre of the mid 1550s shows that it was temporary, being built of wood scaffolding, with its Roman shape actually adapted to a rectangle, probably an outdoor courtyard. The Palladio-Scamozzi theatre, on the other hand, is a completely unified stone building, roofed, ornately decorated, and permanent. The solution to the perspective problem was the conversion of Vitruvius' five stage openings (the three doors in the stage wall and the side openings for periaktoi) to frames for street scenes constructed in the manner of Serlio's built-up scenes. In the *Teatro Olimpico*, however, these streets receded in false perspective to five different vanishing points. The benefit gained was the multiplicity of focal audience locations; one could sit virtually anywhere in the semicircular audience and enjoy the glories of at least one perspective setting. Like Serlio's setting, those of Scamozzi could not be changed; they were part of the permanent furniture of the theatre. The stage in front of the five openings was still the playing area, with the actors seen against the background of the five framed scenes.

Theatre As Motion: Niccolo Sabattini and Changeable Scenery

The Serlian system, phenomenal as it had seemed in the middle of the sixteenth century, was nevertheless self-limiting. Days were required to change the heavy constructions. The basic scene unit, the "Serlian wing," could not be shifted easily because it had two important faces— a flat surface parallel to the front of the stage and a "return" set at an angle to it—and both would have to be moved. The great heaviness of construction, too, with built-up detail and much wood and plaster ornament, made the job still more difficult.

It was almost eighty years before a work as important as Serlio's *Architettura* could appear with a new system that would overcome the Serlian disadvantages. Published in 1638, Niccolo Sabattini's *Prattica de Fabricar Scene e Machine ne'Teatri* effectively completed the Renaissance revolution in theatre design. Its title (*Scenes and Machines in Theatres*) indicates its improvement on Serlio; the *moving* of scenery was its real thesis. Essentially what Sabattini had done was to set down the developments of an entire generation, developments based on the substitution of a single light wing for the Serlian wing-with-return, and the substitution of painted detail for constructed detail. Perspective painting had been greatly improved, and it was now possible to paint the illusion of a Serlian return (the dimension receding to the vanishing point) on a single flat surface parallel to the stage front. In addition, Sabattini's *Prattica* contained the inventions of his own time and its improvements on medieval methods of flying both men and large set pieces, of bringing "machines"—clouds with actors riding on them, thrones with gods—out of the painted "heavens" over the stage and down into the playing area. Not only movable scenery, but the spectacular effects of all the tricks that were to fill the stage until the late nineteenth century were now possible.

Another designer-architect of the period, Joseph Furttenbach, whose *Architectura Recreationis* appeared in 1640, used a variation of Sabattini's flat wing to change scenes before the audience's eyes. By combining three such wings into a three-sided prism, he built a Renaissance version of the Hellenistic and Roman *periaktos*. With a different scene on each side, and only one side visible to the audience at a time, he could completely change his perspective settings by rotating his prisms 120 degrees. Pairs of Furttenbach's *periaktoi* were placed opposite each other on the stage like Serlio's wings, with members of each pair closer together as they receded from the audience. The perspective effect was successful.

By the time of Racine, methods of painting, building, and changing scenery had reached such a point that the Italian designer Giacomo Torelli (1608–1678) was accused of witchcraft because his settings were so convincing and his changes so swift. He took his art to Paris, where Italian settings and spectacular effects were immensely successful at the French court. By the beginning of the eighteenth century, the Italian-dominated school of stage design was universally powerful in both opera and drama, and families like the Bibienas held that power by passing on their knowledge from generation to generation.

Dramaturgy and Criticism

The theatrical changes were, as we have seen, based on a quite sincere belief that classical practice was being revived. The movable back

Figure 2–26. A sixteenth-century interpretation of a Roman stage, from a 1563 edition of the collected works of Terence. Clearly, established scenic practice has been an influence, as seen in the three Serlian buildings in constructed perspective on each side of the stage, and in the apparently painted backscene. The elevated stage, the framed action, and the disposition of the spectators should be noted. (*Courtesy of the New York Public Library.*)

scene was *scaena ductilis;* the grooved machine was the Greek *ek-kyklema;* changeable wings were analgous to *periaktoi;* and so on. The same re-creative force was at work in criticism.

In France, sixteenth-century criticism had already begun to explore the ideas of propriety, unity, and symmetry, but it was in the mid- and late seventeenth century that these ideas were brought to their full development. Racine's older contemporary and rival, Pierre Corneille (1606–1684), had reflected much of the neoclassical theorizing in the prefaces to his tragedies, and in *Le Cid* (1636) he had produced an outstanding early example of these theories put into practice. The play has a strictly controlled and limited time scheme; all the scenes are linked by having at least one character remain onstage from each scene to the following one, so that the stage is never empty. Corneille practiced a linguistic and ethical propriety that dictated which characters could do or say what things; and the characters, notably the protagonist, pursue an ideal of *gloire* that is at least analogous to Aristotle's moral heroism.

It should not be assumed, of course, that Pierre Corneille was a theatrical purist. In tragedy, indeed, he pursued the ideal of neoclassical purity, but in his other works he was quite capable of writing farces and spectacular "machine" plays (those that would exploit, for example, the new movable scenery of someone like Torrelli). The real drive toward purist tragedy came from critics and academicians, of whom Nicolas Boileau (1636–1711) was perhaps the outstanding example. Henry Carrington Lancaster has summarized Boileau's ideas in

Figure 2–27. Serlio's comic scene. It should be compared with Figure 2–28 for changes in the degree of formalism, the types of buildings, and the movement from classical Roman décor to middle-class Renaissance. (*Courtesy of the New York Public Library.*)

French Dramatic Literature in the Seventeenth Century: "[According to Boileau] a tragedy must please the spectator and rouse his emotions. Terror and pity should be inspired. . . . There should be but one place, one day, one action. Verisimilitude rather than historical truth should be the author's aim. . . . The author should rework his production, discarding much and following the instructions of a good critic." (The last statement is especially revealing; it should be compared to the *commedia dell'arte*-based work of someone like Molière.)

In English, the greatest statement of the conflict between this perfected neoclassicism and older practices is John Dryden's "Essay of Dramatic Poesy" (1666). In a fictional dialogue among a group of friends with such classical names as Crites and Lisideius, Dryden analyzed Corneille, the contrasting epic drama of the Elizabethans, and the contemporary theories of England. The essay is itself very humane;

its neoclassical bias is evident, but not insistent. The discussion is balanced. The defender of neoclassicism defines the three neoclassical Unities:

> The Unity of Time they comprehend in twenty-four hours, the compass of a natural day, or as near it as it can be contrived. . . . The second Unity, which is that of Place . . . [means] that the scene ought to be continued throughout the play, in the same place where it was laid in the beginning: for, the stage being but one and the same place, it is unnatural to conceive it many. . . . As for the third Unity, which is that of Action . . . the poet is to aim at one great and complete action. . . .

Of tragedy, the neoclassic spokesman has this to say: "Ovid . . . had a way of writing so fit to stir up *a pleasing admiration and concernment*, which are the objects of a tragedy." This essay contains a lengthy discussion of the proper verse for drama, especially for tragedy, but it reaches its humane climax in Dryden's concept of the "hand of art"— a rejection of anything that is intentionally artificial. Thus, his ultimate standard for testing all neoclassic principles is the believability of the work of art, its proximity to nature. We are apparently back to the problem of relative perception in the theatre, for neither Dryden nor Boileau could legislate the means by which their audiences could perceive a theatrical event as being "real." Dryden's sense of this is the finest point of the *Essay*. Regrettably, a number of playwrights chose to follow the neoclassic rules slavishly, creating, as a result, plays of dumbfounding artificiality.

To be sure, there was a good deal of wrestling with the rules. The twenty-four-hour unity of time was frequently, and with utter seriousness, expanded to thirty-six. The unity of place was expanded to include "several rooms of a palace," or even several locations within the same city. The medieval disregard for either place or time was, on the other hand, rejected outright, and with it was lost the freedom and the scope of Shakespearean drama. And, especially in the question of unity of place, neoclassical criticism was unconsciously in opposition to neoclassical scenic practice; one was demanding a single location while the other was inventing ever more sensational movable scenery. The frequent result was the play that moved from one awe-inspiring palatial interior to another for each of five acts. Movable scenery was ultimately to win the battle. In the Romantic theatre of the early nineteenth century, a multiplicity of scenes became the imperative principle of much playwriting.

Unity of action and unity of plot, on the other hand, have remained as practicable ideas. Unity of action was really the only one that Aristotle had talked about, and unity of action may, in fact, be basic to our understanding of drama itself. Even in the narrower sense of unity of plot, the neoclassic theatre followed this principle, and the large casts, the subplots, and overplots of Shakespearean theatre were not exploited. In addition, propriety of language and of character were strictly followed, and the unifying Corneillian practice of scene linkage was followed as much as possible. At its best, a theatre based on such critical ideas could produce works of genius within the narrow range allowed it—and *Phaedra* was one of these. At its worst it could produce plays as bad as those of any other age, for no amount of critical principle will prevent bad plays. The neoclassic theatre is probably rare, in fact, in being one in which a direct connection can be seen between its critical principles and its great plays.

Acting

Application of these principles created a kind of drama that in turn demanded a special kind of acting. The upper-class orientation of such plays, of course, limited the given circumstances of the characters. More importantly, the sense of propriety and the "high language" used in the plays required an acting attack that was already abstracted from a mere representation of everyday life.

As in the Elizabethan theatre, a highly developed vocal technique was required. The same interest in oratory that influenced Elizabethan acting was at work in France; however, the poetic line to which it was applied was more formalized than the English. Where blank verse seems the best compromise between poetic rhythm and natural speech in English, the *alexandrine*—a couplet of two twelve-syllable lines— became the dominant one in France. It is the poetic base of *Phaedra*. It lends itself to the long, developed speech that proceeds from rhyme to rhyme and has the great advantage of allowing the playwright to leap over rational connections with a poetic connection. On the other hand, it requires of the actor great control in avoiding a jingling emphasis on end-rhymes and an excessive metrical emphasis of the six-foot line. As an imitation of real speech, of course, the alexandrine is very abstract indeed, and it is easy to see that neither the actor nor the playwright can approach a rhymed couplet as if it were mere conversation. A convention of poetic diction must rule; the result, for the French actor, was concentration on the verbal elements of his part and a spare, limited use of physical resources.

Two further devices were exploited by playwrights, the *récit* and the *tirade*. The first is a lengthy recitation of past, or offstage, action similar to the messengers' speeches of Greek tragedy. (The account of Hippolytus' meeting with the monster from the sea is an example.) The second is a detailed examination of a character's emotional state. Both kinds of speeches are formal; their very length demands that the actor develop them rather as a rhetorical argument is developed, with progressive emphases and a careful attention to introduction, develop-

Figure 2–28. Serlio's tragic scene of formal buildings in constructed perspective wings. The abundance of three-dimensional detail, the use of such Roman elements as statues and obelisks, and the stairs down to the orchestra should be noted. (*Courtesy of the New York Public Library.*)

ment, and climax. In performance, they seem to have been done for the audience, rather like an aria in opera, with the actor putting all his work into his voice, the body kept almost rigid. Again, the extreme abstraction of such an approach must be appreciated. If one can speak of a neoclassic acting style, it must be in terms of highly selective, large gesture, of physical control that would place the body in "proper" (that is, stately and graceful) postures, and of the most careful cultivation of the vocal techniques of oratory.

Gesture in the performance of tragedy was not merely limited, but virtually symbolic. Acting books of the period indicate that a system of gestures appropriate to given emotions had been worked out, and that many actors used such a set of gestures for every role they played. In untalented hands, such a system could obviously lead to the worst kind of clichés. Nevertheless, with actors of great subtlety and sensitivity, selection from among systematized poses, movements, and actions could be used to focus attention on the carefully selected high points of the character and the scene.

By the time of Racine, acting was an organized profession with its own hierarchy. Molière, in *The Versailles Impromptu*, ticked off the personalities of a number of the leading tragic actors of the day, and what is immediately apparent from his parody is the great difference between the relatively realistic approach of comedy and the often bombastic, pompous, highly artificial approach of tragedy. Nevertheless, such tragic acting was very popular, and in at least two Parisian theatres—the *Marais* and the *Hôtel de Bourgogne*—troupes of actors, organized on a sharing plan much like that of Shakespeare's theatre, regularly performed in the tragic high style.

It was to such a theatre that Racine brought his *Phaedra*. The play is still performed in European repertoires, frequently in a manner that attempts to reproduce that of the seventeenth century. At its best, such acting gives its audience the auditory pleasure of the alexandrine, well vocalized; the intricacies of the *récit* and the *tirade;* and the very real complexity of the tragic action, performed with absolute clarity and simplicity.

Racine's Theatre

Although Racine's first tragedy was performed by Molière's troupe, Racine moved immediately after to the company of the *Hôtel de Bourgogne*, where his major tragedies were then to be staged. This theatre, already in use for over a century by the time of *Phaedra*, was abandoned in 1680 because of its severe limitations in presenting "machine" plays and its small size. Nevertheless, it was at this theatre that many of the greatest plays of the age were performed, and under conditions, significantly, that encouraged the very limitations that Racine himself practiced, especially in the unity of place.

One of the most interesting documents available to the student of theatre history is the record kept by the designer-technicians of the *Hôtel de Bourgogne*, the so-called *Mémoire de Mahelot*. Begun by Laurent Mahelot in the 1630s, and continued into the 1680s by his successor, Michel Laurent (and others), it offers a fairly detailed picture of the *Hôtel de Bourgogne's* development of neoclassical staging techniques. As Henry Carrington Lancaster has pointed out in his introduction to the modern edition of the *Mémoire*, the contrast between Mahelot and Laurent is the contrast between the simultaneity of the Middle Ages and the unity of the neoclassic period—and all on the same stage. Mahelot's description of his simultaneous setting for a typical drama of the 1630s, for example (Hardy's *La Folie de Clidamant*) is

> There must be, in the middle of the stage, a handsome palace; and, at one side, an ocean, with a ship having masts and sails, where a woman appears who throws herself into the ocean; and, on the

other side, a handsome room that can be opened and closed, where there is a decorated bed with sheets.

(Le Mémoire de Mahelot)

A later hand has added the property note, "some blood." Frequently the *Mémoire* has such items that the designer-technician had to furnish.

By contrast, Michel Laurent's note concerning the setting for *Phaedra* is terse to the point of inadequacy, but it epitomizes the great change: "The stage is a vaulted palace. A chair for the opening." In short, Mahelot's three locations (sometimes as many as seven) all in view throughout the performance, have become a single interior. The note concerning the chair is, again, revealing. Contrary to modern illusionistic practice, which dictates that interior settings will be "dressed" with furniture so that the illusion of a real room will be maintained, both Mahelot and Laurent limited themselves strictly to articles of furniture that were needed in the play. Thus, *Phaedra* requires only one chair, and only for the first act, in which occurs the only staging note inserted into the play by Racine: "She sits." This remarkable economy may have been dictated at the *Hôtel de Bourgogne* by limited space, especially in the period of multiple, simultaneous settings; it also explains in part the modern French style, described as "spare" or "clean" by many designers because of its similar economy of space and its lack of clutter.

As we have seen from the Mahelot note, the theatre's designer-technician was expected to furnish unusual properties, such as blood, and such ordinary items as chairs, tables, candles, and so on, which must have come from the theatre's collection of stock pieces. In the area of costumes, however, the practice was rather different, for the actors typically supplied their own, even to such articles as fans and swords when such items were merely part of the costume and were not given unusual use as properties. Practice in the area of costume varied considerably, because there are many indications that nobles frequently gave their own clothes to actors for use as costumes, especially for great occasions. Although the archaeological tendency of a later age had not yet started, and there was little attempt to imitate historical clothes precisely, there was still a conventional tragic or heroic dressing of stage costumes that was different from everyday wear. The desire to "Romanize" a hero's costume with a highly decorated breastplate and a helmet, or to costume the actors *à la Turque* for the production of Racine's *Bajazet*, which has a Turkish setting, demanded that the theatre itself collaborated with the actor in creating his costume.

In general, the practice continued of dressing classical Greek and Roman heroes and heroines as seventeenth-century men and women; certainly the typical costume outline was evidently Louis XIV. To this basic look, however, could be added accessories or minor changes that suggested Greece or Rome. In the case of spectacles, machine plays, and performances for special occasions, of course, entire sets of un-usual costumes might occasionally be created—when the money was made available.

Racine

Jean Racine (1639–1699) produced a number of very successful and highly praised tragedies between 1667 and 1677, and then, with appar-ent abruptness, ceased writing for the theatre to become royal histori-ographer for Louis XIV. Toward the end of his life, he wrote two more dramas, both religious, neither intended primarily for professional production. This apparent contradiction in his life, suggesting a rejec-tion of the very theatre he had helped to bring to its high point, is the subject of both argument and speculation. It must suffice here to say that he was a most complex man, and perhaps a tormented one. His early education within the Jansenist atmosphere of the religious colony at Port-Royal, where a doctrine of the most severe moral deter-minism and moral austerity was taught, may account for both his per-sonal shifts of interest and the extraordinary quality of his plays. *Phaedra* has even been seen as a form of Jansenist demonstration (that is, Phaedra is a human being without free will, doomed to moral depravity and without hope of divine grace), although such a view of the play hardly seems necessary to its theatrical impact. It may be, however, that the underlying assumptions of Jansenism—the tendency toward austerity, denial, and purity; the division of human beings into rigid classes—are also Racine's.

Unlike Shakespeare (and, as we shall see, Molière), Racine was not a man of the theatre. He had unquestioned genius for the theatre, and he had evident knowledge of the theatre, but he never actively worked in it as an actor or in any capacity but playwright. To be sure, the play-wright's function in the period was broader than it now generally is, and often the casting of roles, much coaching, and some of what we would call direction were expected from the playwright. Indeed, both legend and history have left stories of Racine's detailed coaching of actresses in the roles that he created, but because such coaching seems inevitably to have been part of a more intimate relationship in each case, we must be led finally to question just how theatrical its goal was. In short, then, Racine brought certain great gifts to the French theatre at the exact moment when they were needed; that those gifts derived more from classical knowledge and literary genius than from any total involvement in the theatre itself will explain some of Racine's unique qualities.

There is in Racine, more than in any of his contemporaries, except perhaps Louis XIV himself, a drive toward "purity." In part, the moral purity of a character like Hippolytus in *Phaedra* can be explained by Racine's Jansenist background, and his Jansenism can be seen as at least a metaphor for his admiration of purity in form and in language. The tendency toward unification is part of this. The cutting away of all excess fat—the trimming down to the barest essentials of plot, character, and diction—is uniquely neoclassical and Racinian. He wrote only one comedy, and no machine plays or mixed-genre plays. On the contrary, his was a drive toward theatrical purity that had to reject the very sensationalism on which the machine play thrived. There is, then, a certain aloofness to Racine's approach to the theatre, a cool zeal for improving, for rescuing—in short, for purifying. In this tendency Racine is most like his Latin models of the age of Augustus Caesar, those men like Horace and Vergil who welcomed imperial patronage both because it freed them of the need to write "impurely" for profit, and because it represented in itself an identification with the embodiment of unity and power. So with Racine: Louis XIV was his Augustus, and when, after *Phaedra*, he was offered the position of royal historiographer, why should he not have put aside the theatre—of which he was never an integral part in the sense that Molière and Mahelot were, for example—and move even closer to the pure center? Louis was, after all, the great unifier of the seventeenth century, in politics, in religion, and in state affairs. To move from writing tragedies in the neoclassic mold to writing history for the Sun King should not be seen as either inconsistent or opportunistic; on the contrary, it shows a remarkable consistency and a certain kind of idealism.

In his secular tragedies, however, and most of all in *Phaedra*, Racine created worlds that suggested the world of Louis XIV's court and that then stripped that world bare. He seems to have been able to do this by working in a paradox: within the mold of civilized, formalized behavior, his people are passional compulsives. Martin Turnell, in *The Classical Moment*, has pointed out the very real anarchy that Racine explores. "The morality of Racine's world is the morality of the jungle, but the violence is intensified and not diminished by the characters' exceptional powers of insight . . ." To Turnell, the purity and control of Racinian society is mere veneer, a "surface elegance which does nothing to mitigate the violence of the tumult which goes on beneath." The order that society would impose is an invention, a pretense, and Racinian man is really a moral and emotional primitive, suffering impulses that are "anterior to all civilization and which a supreme degree of civilization covers but cannot extinguish."

Racine's *Phaedra*

Based on the *Hippolytus* of Euripides and the play of Seneca, Racine's five-act tragedy is a highly compressed examination—even a dissection —of the problems raised by a very simple situation: Phaedra's struggle with her love for her stepson, Hippolytus. In terms of the seventeenth-century theatre, the play is significant for its easy adherence to neo-

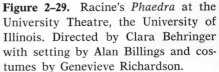

Figure 2–29. Racine's *Phaedra* at the University Theatre, the University of Illinois. Directed by Clara Behringer with setting by Alan Billings and costumes by Genevieve Richardson.

classic rules—unity, linking of scenes, propriety—without ever revealing the "hand of art." It is, in many ways, a very natural play despite its artifices; the action grows clearly out of the situation and the characters are entirely consistent. Finally, the language in which Racine has couched the play is elegant, a rare use of a compressed French vocabulary that charges the words themselves with poetic excitement.

PLOT AND CHARACTER.   Racine rejected the use of gods as characters (as in Euripides' play) and the direct, bombastic clash of antagonists (as in Seneca's). He added one important character not found in his antecedents, that of Aricia, with whom Hippolytus falls reluctantly and dangerously in love (thus relieving the militant chastity of Euripides' character and avoiding the romanticized purity found in Seneca). In addition, he gave a new quality to the story by keeping Theseus, father of Hippolytus and husband of Phaedra, out of the action until well into the play. The further addition of a false report of Theseus' death, not found in either of the earlier plays, allowed Racine to show how his characters would behave if they were freed of the moral imperative represented by Theseus. (That is, if the guilt of overt adultery were removed from Phaedra, and the guilt of overt disobedience removed from Hippolytus' love for Aricia, the political enemy of his father.)

With Theseus' return, however, none of the personal desires of the principal characters (Phaedra, Hippolytus, and Aricia) can be reconciled with this moral imperative; Phaedra, who has confessed her passion for Hippolytus, is guilty—in will, which to Racine is as bad as in act—of adultery and even incest. Hippolytus and Aricia cannot marry. It remains only for Oenone, Phaedra's servant, to accuse Hippolytus of attempting to rape Phaedra. The play's action is resolved when Theseus, the only one whose character allows him to act selfishly, without regard to a moral imperative, begs Neptune to destroy his son. Hippolytus, guiltless, is butchered in the battle with the monster cast up from the sea by Neptune. Phaedra, dying of self-administered poison, absolves Hippolytus and dies, leaving the shattered Theseus with Aricia.

The basic story is a very old one, reflected in myths like that of Joseph and Potiphar's wife. In Racine's hands, however, it takes on a new quality and becomes the means by which he examines two important questions: the relationship between private desire and public duty, and the internal struggle between supposedly rational judgments and wildly irrational, animal impulses.

EXTRINSIC IDEAS. By introducing the supposed death of Theseus into the early part of the play, Racine extended its concern out of the merely personal conflicts of the characters and into the much larger area of public responsibility. The power struggle for the supposedly vacant throne of Athens opened up an overplot that would have been rather foreign to Euripides, but one that reinforced an essential problem in neoclassic tragedy: the struggle to reach a balance between individual motive (love, revenge, lust) and social duty (wifely fidelity, filial piety, the search for honor). This question is central to Corneille's *Le Cid*, and to many of the plays of the period. Racine went beyond it, but it remains as at least the extrinsic subject of the play.

Several aspects of public morality are revealed by the report of Theseus' death: a wife cannot betray her husband, but widowhood frees her to love; a prince cannot marry one of his father's political enemies, but the death of the father removes the enmity. In both cases, private desire—here, as so often, expressed as romantic and sexual love—can be brought into harmony with a moral imperative (Theseus' law) only when the source of the imperative is removed. The "tragedy" of the situation becomes apparent, then, with Theseus' appearance, for we then discover that the imperative is still in force. However, private desires have already been expressed and have been allowed to indulge themselves. (Phaedra has announced her love for Hippolytus, whereas he has confessed his own love to Aricia.) Ultimately, the conflict is between private and public imperatives, and the play seems to

Figure 2–30. James Pritchett and Mildred Dunnock in *Phaedra*, at the Institute for Advanced Study in Theatre Arts, New York. (*Zodiac Photographers, Ltd.*)

suggest that the conflict cannot be resolved, for love is set up as the enemy of honor (seen both as *gloire*—Hippolytus' desire to win reputation by killing monsters—and as piety or fidelity).

Phaedra cannot very easily be approached from the point of view of Greek tragedy. Despite the titular emphasis on Phaedra herself, the *pathos* of the play would seem to belong to Hippolytus; the *anagnorisis*, on the other hand, belongs to Theseus. Phaedra remains the pivotal character, the one who forces the action. Unlike Oedipus, she does so in the knowledge that she is wrong; nor does she gain any important wisdom, as he does. She suffers, but to no apparent end. No chorus interprets her suffering, or that of Hippolytus or Theseus, for us. The play, therefore, is not one that rests with a presentation of the outward conflict between private and public desire. At a further level, it explores the nature of the human being itself in order to explain the outward conflict.

INTRINSIC IDEAS. It is in Racine's involved use of a symbol—the monster—that *Phaedra* finds its ultimate meaning, for he creates each of his principal characters (except Theseus) as a potentially monstrous human whose pairing with a servant makes monstrous behavior possible.[1] Phaedra is encouraged and stimulated by Oenone; Hippolytus tests his extreme rationalism against Theramanes; Aricia needs Ismene as confidante. For each, the servant creates the possibility of behavior motivated by personal impulse, and the servant externalizes the otherwise hidden dialogue between moral self and indulgent self. Theseus is exempted from this pairing; he has no other self. On the contrary, his very position as power center—legendary hero and king of Athens—is founded on his independence. Ultimately, his *gloire* is the killing of the monsters that have endangered mankind. When, then, Phaedra becomes a monster of passion (which she recognizes as the heritage of her mother, who bore the Minotaur), and Hippolytus is called a monster by Theseus and a monster of dispassion by Phaedra, Theseus must pursue his *gloire* and destroy them both. Significantly, he is left at the end of the play, contrite, with a new confidante, Aricia. The hero of personal impulse and public glory has become a guilty monster himself, divided, potentially evil, and penitent.

Racine's final view of man is bleak. *Phaedra* was his last secular tragedy; he seemed content with it as an ultimate statement. Within the neoclassic mold, that statement implies that even in an age of reason the human animal is divided internally, doomed to improper action by a split self that will always seek both private impulse and public glory, and never with complete success.

The play has remained in the French classical repertoire since its first performance, and just as Hamlet is one of the touchstones of his talent for the English-speaking actor, so the role of Phaedra is a touchstone for the French actress. It has been subject to very diverse interpretations; indeed, it shows as well as any discussed in this book how "conditions of performance" (in this case, the actress's interpretation of the role) change that thing communicated, the performance:

> Such is the role of Phaedra, in which can be seen so well the difficulty, the complexity, that have caused its diverse interpretations. The religious Phaedra . . . this was [the actress] Rachel, as well as that of [the director] Gaston Baty. The poetic, musical, harmonious Phaedra, this was [the actress] Sarah Bernhardt. Phaedra and her furies, Raucourt. The voluptuous Phaedra, Clairon; the touching Phaedra, Duchesnois. And each of these facets was still that of the Phaedra of Racine.
> Maurice Descotes, *Les Grands Rôles du Théâtre de Jean Racine*, p. 165.

RELUCTANT CLASSICISM: MOLIERE

If Racine's purpose was accomplished in the pure form of Renaissance tragedy, the goal of the greatest of comic playwrights was reached

[1] This discussion is based on Robert J. Nelson's essay in *Phaedra*, Chandler Editions in Drama (San Francisco: Chandler Publishing Co., 1961).

by way of the Italian *commedia dell'arte* and the rejection of rigid form for its own sake. The young actor-playwright who called himself Molière (Jean Baptiste Pocquelin) came to Paris in 1658 with a small, unknown troupe that he had led through the provinces for a decade. When he died in 1673, he left behind a body of comedies, matched for consistency and quality only by those of Ben Jonson and Aristophanes, and an established urban theatre that survives as the *Comédie Française*, the "House of Molière."

Molière's Theatre

Molière was primarily an actor. He created roles and actions; his plays are not especially witty and his language lacks the elegance and the distinction of Racine's and the creative inventiveness of Shakespeare's. Yet his plays exist as great theatrical experiences. Most of them are centered around a protagonist whose peculiarly distorted vision of reality creates social chaos around him. In the typical Molièresque action, the protagonist's wrong perception causes families to disintegrate, money to be lost, marriages to be almost wrecked, and love affairs to be endangered. When these actions end, they end happily for everyone but the protagonist: balance is restored, often by an outside force, but the protagonist is usually as rigidly wrong as he was in the beginning. Comedy demands the happy ending, but it need not alter character.

The Molièresque idea of character is derived from the *commedia dell'arte* and certainly is similar to the late medieval concept of a character of *humors* (four fluids analogous to the four elements). One scholar (W. G. Moore) has called this idea of character the *mask*, the peculiarly distorted sense of reality that *drives* the character into situations where he must become ridiculous. Just as Pantalone (see p. 114) is identified by, and cannot deviate from, his emblematic mask, so the Molièresque character cannot deviate from the mask of his own rigid sense of reality. Thus, Harpagon, in *The Miser*, has a single-minded sense of values that redefines all experience in terms of money. What is valuable to him *must*, in his view, be valuable to everybody else, and therefore he is in constant danger from a world that he sees as a mass of thieves. In his climactic paroxysm of greedy fear, Harpagon finds that even his *own* hand in his pocket is the hand of a thief, and he turns on the audience to accuse them, his family, and the world of trying to steal from him.

Without exception Molière's field was social. This is not to say that he was interested in social problems, but, rather, that he dealt with a world whose concerns were for social realities like family structure, marriage, and money, rather than one whose people underwent the metaphysical tortures of Racine's people. And, in this sphere, Molière was very unsparing: Harpagon comes close to destroying his own son; Orgon, in *Tartuffe*, almost wrecks his family and disinherits his son; Alceste, in *The Misanthrope*, attacks the whole of contemporary society with his bared fangs, and for all that Alceste is finally a self-deluding fool, his attacks are viciously accurate.

However, Molière was not merely a social satirist. He was a comedian who happened to find funny matters in social relationships. He wrote no criticism, but in three works—the preface to *Les Facheux*, the short play, *The Critique of the School for Wives*, and *The Versailles Impromptu*—he stated very simply that he wrote plays about types of behavior that amused him. He sternly denied ever having used a single individual as the object of his comedy, and he defended all of his plays on the basis of a single fact: that he had made people laugh. Only one play was really written according to the neoclassic rules (*The Misanthrope*), and that was done largely to prove that he could use the proper form if necessary. His was normative comedy, seeking to mend social mistakes with as little pain as possible.

Formally, Molière was responsible for an important innovation, the *comédie-ballet*. With the composer Lully, he wrote several of these plays using music and dance, masquelike entertainments that used the new Italianate staging to great effect and that usually ended in colossal production numbers. The best known is probably *The Bourgeois Gentleman*, although *The Imaginary Invalid* and *Monsieur de Pourceaugnac* are also excellent examples of the form. *Pourceaugnac*, particularly, is a very happy combination of Molière's mask character, of *commedia dell'arte* scenes of trickery, beatings, and ridicule, and of Lully's music.

When Molière died in 1673, his theatre was continued by his wife and one of his leading actors. His influence on subsequent comedy was very important. In Italy, Carlo Goldoni (1707–1793) acknowledged Molière as his great example in creating a new written Italian comedy out of the declining improvised theatre, whereas in France the whole comic tradition looked back to Molière. In the eighteenth century, Beaumarchais' excellent *Marriage of Figaro* (1784) was a late flowering of Molièresque comedy.

Molière and Neoclassicism

Tragedy, as it had attained its popularity at the *Marais* and the *Hôtel de Bourgogne*, was an established and successful form when Molière attempted Paris in 1658. However much Molière might satirize its practitioners and their style, he could not deny his own nagging desire to succeed in their established form. Not until the failure of his serious play *Dom Garcie de Navarre* (1661) was he firmly committed to pulling comedy by its very bootstraps into critical and artistic acceptance.

The work was not all uphill, nor was it work he had to do alone. He had a first-rate collaborator in his public. If he was ready for Paris, history suggests that Paris was ready for him. Thus, whereas the tragedian reaches high, attaining a critical approval traditionally denied to comedy, the comedian has the advantage of working directly with his audience: they laugh or they do not laugh. If he touches that nerve that so wants to be touched, but that so coyly hides itself, he will produce a reaction that the tragedian seldom can. His public will help him.

Although Molière was not given to critical statements, the few that he made, however they may smack of special pleading or of propaganda, are supremely aware of the comic end of comedy. His aim was "to depict behavior without touching on personalities," "to show common foibles entertainingly on the stage," "to make decent men laugh."

Most importantly, the end of comedy was laughter, and that end justified a dramatic practice that defied neoclassic principles:

> I should like to know if the great rule of rules is not to please. For, if the plays that are written according to the rules do not please, and those do please that are not written according to the rules, then it must be that the rules are badly made.

The first rule is to please. Thus, Molière's collaborator, the public, could be either a genial giant who dwarfed Aristotle and the rules, or an ugly monster acting from what the French critic René Bray calls the "primordial need."

Pleasing the audience and seeking applause are the rigorous aims of both the hack and the genius, and in his own time the genius cannot hope to be called other than hack. Regrettably, for Molière, that insistence on the rules that is the caste mark of Corneille and Racine meant that the comedian had to prove his genius on grounds other than the accepted ones.

The aim was to please the multitude, rules or no rules. However, pleasing implies a suppression of the personal desire and a subservience to an external imperative. This imperative (the primordial need) is satisfied not by overt satire or overt thesis plays, but by recourse to a more basic, and at the same time more dangerous, kind of comedy. Its sources are free in space and in time, but, having to exist in space and time, it particularizes those sources to the satisfaction of the primordial need. As a result, the kind of comedy that is often popular is, as in Molière's case, immediate, timely, and apparently satirical.

The result of this progress from popular comedy to apparent satire, however, was that Molière succeeded in raising French comedy to a dangerously high level, where, in both moral and ideological terms, it could compete with tragedy. As Roman Fernandez has pointed out, "*Tartuffe* and *Don Juan* mean that comedy knows no privileged vices, and *Le Misanthrope* means that comedy knows no privileged virtues."

This is success of a kind. Molière knew other successes as well: royal patronage, public applause, the satisfactions of both the accepted actor and the accepted author. His career was bound up inextricably with the march of comedy; his success was the success of comedy; and the process by which he raised the *Illustre Théâtre* of 1658 into the troupe of the *Palais Royal* of 1673 is the process by which comedy itself rose from knockabout farce to the comedy of those who know "neither privileged vices nor privileged virtues."

The *Commedia dell'Arte*

It is not accidental that both Molière and Molièresque comedy came to Paris by way of Lyons. During the years of Molière's residence there, Lyons was a city of great theatrical sophistication, with a history of almost 150 years of exposure to Italian comedy. It was Molière's great good fortune to have this *commedia dell'arte*-oriented audience as his early collaborator, to be able to satisfy its primordial need with a strong mixture of *commedia* and French farce.

In order to understand the kind of theatre that Molière found in Lyons, it will be necessary to describe the *commedia dell'arte* briefly, to look at its theatrical practice, and most importantly, to discuss its outstanding element, the emblematic mask.

Commedia dell'arte ("theatre of skill" or "theatre of professionals") can be opposed to *commedia erudita* ("erudite theatre") in at least one way, for as its name implies, it was a theatre whose practitioners were dedicated to it. These were professionals, not capable amateurs. They performed for the general audience, not for the smaller audience of the educated or the aristocratic. Their performances were based on the world around them, presenting at least a reflection of the audience's world, whereas the *commedia erudita* was based on plays of the classic past or imitations of them. Nevertheless, it is wrong to see *commedia dell'arte* as the enemy of erudite theatre, for in actuality the professional performers learned many techniques and took over a number of characters and actions from the erudite performances they encountered.

Commedia dell'arte was an Italian phenomenon, appearing first as a distinct theatrical form in the middle of the sixteenth century. Other than its professionalism, it was distinguished by two primary characteristics: the use of masked actors playing typed characters and the improvising of scenes within a set, outlined plot. Many troupes came into existence to carry on this kind of theatre, a considerable number of them made up of families who stayed together for many years, even handing their characters and routines down from one generation to the next. One of the earliest commedia troupes was led by Alberto da Ganassa, in the latter half of the sixteenth century. It had a limited number of character types as compared to such later troupes as the one, probably the most famous, led by the Andreini family. Named simply *I Gelosi*, the company formed around Isabella Andreini and her brother Francesco was a brilliant group that traveled widely in both France and Italy, doing much to make *commedia dell'arte* famous and

Figure 2–31. The combined companies of Molière and Tiberio Fiorilli (Scaramuccio) on the stage they shared. Molière is at the far left; Fiorilli is in the right foreground, in black. Other *commedia dell'arte* masks—Arlecchino, Capitano, a Dottore and others—can be seen. The practical buildings in artificial perspective and the use of candelabra for illumination should be noted. (*Collection of the Comédie Française. Photo Laniepce.*)

to raise it from the popular entertainment of fairs and one-day stands into one of the most respected forms of theatre entertainment in seventeenth-century Europe. Before the decline of the form in the eighteenth century, *commedia dell'arte* troupes had been seen widely throughout the Continent, in England, and as far east as Poland and even Russia. For many years the French court supported a company, so that along with the surviving *Comédie Française* there was a *Comédie Italienne* playing in Paris. From the 1650s through the 1680s (through the entire period of Molière's work in Paris), the "Old Troupe of the Italian Comedy" enjoyed royal patronage and played on a stage supplied by the king—a stage that was shared for several years with Molière's French company. (See Figure 2–31.) It is little wonder, then, that distinct Italian elements can be seen in Molière's plays, or that during his lifetime he was accused of having learned all his comic techniques from Tiberio Fiorilli, with whom he shared a theatre and who led the Italian company.

The *commedia dell'arte* began to lose its popularity in the eighteenth century, although certain of its characters have remained as stage types. Harlequin, for example (the Italian *Arlecchino*), became a stock figure on the English stage, and the harlequinade was a popular nineteenth-century farce form. In addition, playwrights like Carlo Goldoni and Carlo Gozzi (1720–1806) were responsible for a literary revival of the *commedia dell'arte* characters late in the eighteenth century, when they wrote plays incorporating the mask types, such as Goldoni's *Servant of Two Masters* and Gozzi's *King Stag*. Vestiges of the *commedia* can still be seen in such local theatre forms as the neighborhood Pulcinellas of Naples and many plays of the French and Italian puppet theatres.

THE COMMEDIA DELL'ARTE PERFORMANCE. One cannot really speak of *commedia dell'arte* plays, although at their height the more important troupes hired playwrights and in the eighteenth-century theatre plays were written about the stock characters. Rather, it is usual to speak of

Figure 2–32. A seventeenth-century French drawing of a *commedia dell'arte* troupe, probably showing a number of *lazzi* simultaneously. Although the artist may seem to have exaggerated gestures and body positions, other evidence indicates that performances were this vigorous. The central, kneeling figure is a Pantalone, the man leaning over him probably a Brighella. Evidently, the artist has taken some license in showing the running figures upstage in the same perspective as the scenery; if that area immediately below the back-scene were so used, the actors would dwarf the buildings. (*Copyright © the Fitzwilliam Museum, Cambridge.*)

commedia improvisation, although it must hastily be added that neither the over-all plot nor the content of individual scenes was made up on the spot by the performers, and any confusion with the modern use of improvisation by actors is most unfortunate. The leader of a troupe, or a playwright hired by him, would present the company with a *scenario*—the narrative description of a dramatic plot, often with detailed description of what would happen in each scene. In addition, songs, music, and lyric poems to be recited by young lovers could well be created especially for a performance and set beforehand. (Isabella Andreini, for example, was famous as a poetess; some of her poetry she supposedly made up extempore, but much of it was certainly composed with great care.)

Within even a detailed outline, however, much was left to the artistic judgment of individual performers. Each member of a company would have many *lazzi* (from *l'azione,* "actions") or memorized and rehearsed actions that could be inserted into a performance without reference to a specific plot. A good performer might have as many as eighty *lazzi,* and because he usually played the same character all his life, he would have them ready to perform in a highly developed manner. Many of these have come down to us in the memoirs of outstanding actors as detailed descriptions of what they did and what they said in each *lazzo.* At one extreme, they prove to be the age-old routines of the circus clown, the vaudeville comedian, and the comic pantomimist. At the other, they are either the bombastic, ornate speeches of boasters such as Shakespeare's Falstaff or the lyrical outpourings of ecstatic young lovers. Each *lazzo* was carefully geared to the character type who was to enact it, and it can readily be seen that a company of eight to ten performers, each with fifty to eighty *lazzi,* could create very complicated and almost endlessly varied performances within similar plots.

No two performances were quite the same. Some genuine improvising probably went on (that is, the invention of new business on the spot to please a given audience), and the length of the same *lazzo* would vary from performance to performance as it did, or did not, entertain different audiences. For such variations each performer would prepare closing cues, known to the rest of the company, so that he could indicate that he was about to close a *lazzo* and toss the ball to another actor. Nonetheless, it should never be thought that the *commedia dell'arte* performances were truly improvisatory. Much rehearsal, much preparation, even years of developing certain routines went into the best performances. What was improvisatory was the *order* of the *lazzi* within the plot outline, the timing, and the playing directly to the reactions of each audience.

Commedia dell'arte was a very physical kind of theatre; drawings of it, like those by Jacques Callot, suggest that it may sometimes have had an almost balletic quality. This is not to say, however, that it was non-verbal. Many of the *lazzi* were primarily verbal, both the comic ones and the noncomic, lyrical exchanges of the many young lovers. Verbal wit, poetry, song, social comment, and character revelation through soliloquies typified it just as much as did the many pantomimes, grotesque actions, and balletic patterns.

TYPES AND MASKS. In its heyday during the seventeenth century, the *commedia dell'arte* saw a great proliferation of its character types as new actors tried to create new characters and new troupes tried to satisfy the demand for performances. Still, the creation of new characters took place within the general limits of types already established, types that go back as far as Terence, at least, and probably even farther into primitive farce.

The reason for the similarities to Terence and Plautus can be seen in the contact between *commedia dell'arte* and *commedia erudita.* Many professional troupes wintered in ducal or royal households, often taking part in staging classic or neoclassic plays. Many performers came into direct contact with erudite audiences at places like the French and English courts. As a result, the romantic plots of Terence, the zany slaves of Plautus, and the easy reliance on coincidence found in both are common in much of *commedia dell'arte.* Classical drama is far from being the only source, but it was a very important one. Perhaps the greatest similarity (possibly because of a common ancestor) is in the character types: old men; lovers; braggarts and parasites; and clever male and female servants. As performed by the *commedia dell'arte* actors, these types became unchanging characters, recognized immediately by their individualized masks, their special costumes, and their unchanging behavior. In brief, the important character masks are described subsequently.

Old Men: Pantalone was one of the earliest characters. Usually old, miserly, and lecherous, he functioned in the plays as a cuckold husband or a demanding father. His costume, supposedly founded on that of a sixteenth-century Venetian merchant, consisted of red tights (pantaloons), a black robe and cap, and a purse and dagger worn on a belt around his waist (frequently as a very obvious phallic symbol over the groin). His half mask was brown, with a hooked nose, letting his mouth and white beard show. The *Dottore* (doctor) was also an early character, analogous to the pedant of classical comedy. He was sententious, pompous, and his speeches were filled with ridiculous Latin and Greek quotes. Often a husband or a father, he was in frequent conflict with Pantalone. His costume was a variation of academic regalia, his half mask brown or flesh-colored.

Braggarts and Parasites: The *Capitano,* a somewhat late addition to the group (possibly created by Francesco Andreini) was a parody of the mercenary soldier, a ridiculous boaster and usually a coward. He frequently vied with the young lover for the daughter or the wife of

Pantalone or the *Dottore*. His mask, if he wore one, had a grotesque nose; his costume was a parody of military dress, with a very long sword and an overdecorated hat. *Brighella*, although usually functioning as a servant, had many of the characteristics of the braggart or the Roman parasite. Boastful, sly, often a thug, he was capable of violence and often posed a genuine physical threat to other characters. His olive-brown half mask was menacing, and his dagger and purse, unlike Pantalone's, were indicative of his penchant for violence and theft.

Tricksters and Clever Servants: The *zanni* (similar to the English *zany*) made up a group of comic figures, some shrewd and full of tricks, some stupid and ridiculous, who functioned as servants to Pantalone and the *Dottore* or as go-betweens for the young lovers. Both male and female, they frequently played out love affairs that lacked the lyricism of the young lovers' scenes. Brighella is sometimes included among the *zanni*, as are his artistic descendants like *Scapino*, *Mezzetino*, *Sbrigani*, and others. Probably the most important representative of the type, however, is *Arlecchino*, whose badly patched suit of tights of the sixteenth century became the stylized diamond pattern of the late seventeenth and eighteenth centuries. Physically supple but often stupid, he was in and out of trouble constantly; his black half mask, phallic club, and patterned tights are still seen in the character Harlequin. A later female equivalent, *Arlecchina*, was an extension of the type. He has many imitators, especially *Truffaldino, Pedrolino* and, in a more intelligent guise, *Coviello*. The most common female servant was *Franceschina*—clever, outspoken, physically attractive, and experienced. Like virtually all the women in the *commedia dell'arte*, she was unmasked. She has an analog in the French Colombine, and many imitators.

Lovers: The *inamoratti*, both male and female, were unmasked. Their roles demanded that they be physically attractive, and they frequently appeared as the children of Pantalone or the *Dottore;* the *prima donna*, or female lover, was inevitably sought after by more than one man. Typically, actors playing the *inamoratti* gave their own names to the roles, and the names given by outstanding actors were continued by others; as a result, there were many Leandros and Lelios among male lovers, many Isabellas and Cintias among the females. As already discussed, in the hand of performers like the Andreinis, these characters carried a considerable burden of the musical and lyrical part of the performance. Attractive, graceful, and articulate, they could poke gentle fun at romantic love, but it was they who carried the romantic actions around which so many *scenarii* revolved.

Such a brief survey should at least suggest the strict limits of type put on each character. It is perhaps paradoxical that such a limited kind of dramatic characterization could ever have produced an interesting theatrical form. Yet we must face the fact that *commedia dell'arte* has attracted more attention than most other forms of Western theatre. Ultimately, its attraction seems to have been the result of an interaction between (1) the choice of universal character types, so created that the actor could perform many *lazzi* and many actions with the character as a kind of springboard; and (2) the open structure of the performance itself. In a sense, these can be seen as symbolized by the masks, the outward marks of the types and the sign of the convention within which the actor could perform. Such a mask is a useful tool. It limits the actors, but, like so many other human limitations, it frees him as well; the face, that "interpreter of the passions" as Goldoni called it, is hidden, for which the body compensates. The result is peculiarly comic, for, as the burden of recognizable human passion slips from the shoulders of both actor and audience, a new relationship is established between spectator and dehumanized and masked comedian. Empathy is discouraged; the audience is allowed to watch, rather than to experience; comedy *is* alienation. The actor approaches the marionette or the puppet, and when his acrobatics and his buffooneries support this impression of the puppet unhindered by clinging humanity, the audience can indulge in the luxury of inhuman laughter.

After the *Commedia*

Here, however, *commedia dell'arte* stopped, and Molière began. He very soon abandoned the real mask; and it might be said that at the moment when the tangible black leather mask was laid aside, and intangible masks of character and language were assumed, that Molièresque comedy came into being. Into the mold of an acting technique that assumed the mask, Molière poured a new mixture of character and language. The new form was a comedy whose characters, although physically unmasked, sought still to free themselves and their audience from the restrictions of being merely semihuman. The comic effect is bound up inextricably with a new conflict between the rather abstract behavior of one of the *commedia* masks and the very real behavior of a dramatic character. Pantalone is Pantalone and no one else because he exists only in the theatre, and he exists only to entertain. Harpagon, on the other hand, exists in part in a world we recognize as our own, and he exists only in part to entertain us. The physical mask that the actor playing Pantalone wears symbolizes the elements of Pantalone's character that make him distinctly unlike any other mask; those elements are unchangeable. Pantalone is often gullible, but we do not expect him to learn from being gulled or to grow out of his shortsightedness, his illusions about himself, or his ridiculous pretensions. If he did, he would cease to be Pantalone and he would cease to exist.

Figure 2–33. *The Miser* at the Bonstelle Theatre of Wayne State University, 1969, directed by Joseph Calarco, with setting by Norman Hamlin, costumes by Michael L. Seiser, and lighting by Tom Bryant.

A character like Harpagon, on the other hand, has many of Pantalone's qualities (especially his self-delusion, verging on self-hypnosis), but he is not absolutely unchangeable. His mask is more subtle and less stable. He can, as it were, be "unmasked"—not to reveal the actor inside the mask, but to reveal the truth of his own character, without illusion. In fact, the action of a Molière comedy can be generalized as the "process of revealing his illusions to the protagonist," a process that is carried forward by the attempts of saner characters to persuade, shock, or trick the protagonist into reality. Thus, Harpagon is subjected to the trickery of Monsieur Jacques and Frosine, to the persuasions of Elise and Valère, and so on. None of these things do any good, of course, because the "mask"—the personal obsession, the self-hypnosis—is not susceptible to any but the most severe attacks. Harpagon cannot be unmasked until his dearest possession, the casket, is stolen from him, and then not so much because the theft of the casket is shocking as because his recovery of it depends on his admitting that he cannot possess the entire universe. The *admission* is the unmasking. Thus, the mask must be seen as a psychological state, a pathologically held belief that he, Harpagon, can possess the world. It is the *fantasy of ownership.* The play's action, then, is the *process by which Harpagon's ownership is denied.*

The series of crises by which this final unmasking is reached are important steps in a comic progression (Cléante's refusal to be a dutiful son; the theft of the casket; La Flèche's trickery). At each point, we see the mask endangered, as it appears that the truth must become evident to Harpagon. However, he resumes his self-delusion after each crisis with greater and greater desperation, thus preparing the way for his final disastrous revelation, when the demand of absolute fact (the bargaining for the casket) cannot be denied. Thus, Molière's protagonist is a mask; he wears a mode of behavior (miserliness) that is almost as obvious as the *commedia* leather mask. Being unstable, however, the mask must fall under the assault of comic action—an action that has the removal of the mask, however briefly, as its goal.

The Miser

The Miser was first staged in Paris in 1668, with Molière in the title role. Although not an especially popular play in the first years of its life, it remained in the repertoire and has become, along with *Tartuffe, The Bourgeois Gentleman,* and one or two others, the most often staged of Molière's comedies.

PLOT. The extreme simplicity of the incidents in *The Miser* makes it difficult to discuss its plot at much length. Many aspects of the story are considerably older than Molière's play (the revelation of Anselme, for example, as the father of Mariane and Valère, goes back at least to Terence). In brief, Harpagon, the miser, has two children (Elise and Cléante) for whom he has arranged advantageous marriages. Both are in love with someone else: Elise with Valère, a young man posing as a trusted servant in Harpagon's house; Cléante with Mariane, a young woman who lives nearby. Harpagon himself, however, plans to marry Mariane, because she has been represented to him as an extremely thrifty woman by Frosine, a matchmaker (*femme d'intrigue* is Molière's expression). Throughout the play, Harpagon's concern for his money, and especially for a casket containing many valuables, blinds him to the emotional ties of his children. He insists on Elise's marriage to old Anselme and even finds that he is himself the usurer to whom his own son must go to borrow enough money to court Mariane. Ultimately, the theft of the prized casket by Cléante and his servant, La Flèche, makes possible the happy resolution of the love affairs: Mariane can love Cléante; Elise can love Valère; and old Anselme can be happy in the discovery that Valère and Mariane are his lost children. Harpagon, nearly destroyed by his inability to find the casket, recovers it and takes it with the same fervor that the lovers take each other.

Clearly, loss of property is destruction for Harpagon. Reality is represented by need of the other characters to possess the thing that Harpagon himself wants: Cléante can marry Mariane only if he gets some of the father's money; Elise can marry Valère only if she denies her father the money he would gain from a marriage to old Anselme. Harpagon would marry Mariane himself, but only for her thrift. Inevitably, he loses on all counts. That we, the audience, *want* him to lose is important to an understanding of the comic qualities of the play.

The ending of *The Miser* seems less black and less bitter than the endings of many Molière comedies largely because Harpagon's obsession is directed toward material things and not toward human beings. Thus, Harpagon is not crushed when Mariane and Cléante are united; he is more concerned about his casket. He cannot love a girl, he loves money. In this play it is possible for Molière to bring off the archetypal happy ending (the union of the lovers and the defeat of the father-figure miser) without driving his protagonist completely out of the play. The ending does not imply the complete destruction of Harpagon, but only a temporary setback, and there is a distinct air of rapture in his final recovery of the casket. He cannot be converted, of course; he remains a miser. Thus, although the plot of *The Miser* leads to an ending that is, in almost all respects, happy, it cannot be said to lead to one that is morally uplifting. Molière was too honest for that.

STRUCTURE.   Like a *commedia dell'arte* scenario, *The Miser* is written in a farcical mode. Farcical though it may be, however, it is not struc-

Figure 2–34. *The Miser* at the Front Street Theatre, Memphis, in a distinctly Brechtian production directed by Carl Weber. (*Courtesy of the Front Street Theatre.*)

tured on a linear development of either character or plot; the plot outline just given, for example, ignores the scenes that actually occupy the bulk of the play. These scenes, it is easily noted, do not build sequentially to the final resolution; on the conrtary, they are often horizontal developments *away* from the simple story line of the play. Thus, instead of linear plot, we have a succession of incidents—unmaskings, tricks, *lazzi*—arranged sequentially in time to replace linear plot. This development can best be described as *contextual;* that is, it is based on the presentation of different facets of the same situation, progression being seen in the increasing tensions around Harpagon's character as that situation becomes more acute.

It must be pointed out that the farce structure of *commedia dell'arte* used the same contextual structure. The aim, however, was somewhat different; farce scenarios were generally successive or serial without necessarily showing any development. Molière comedies, on the other hand, are always progressive. A very real order—based on the increasing comic intensity as the protagonist nears his unmasking—governs Molière's scene sequence. Conversely, the *commedia dell'arte* scenario set up the order of certain scenes along a simple plot, but left the order of specific *lazzi* to the performers. In *The Miser,* to take only one example, the first scene of Act II is one in which almost nothing essential to the central plot happens, and one that could easily be an extended *lazzo:* Cléante, with La Flèche, prepares to meet an unknown usurer; La Flèche reads him the extensive list of articles to be offered as collateral; the usurer turns out to be Harpagon; and Cléante and Harpagon become furious with each other. To be sure, the contextual contribution of the scene is very great: it develops Harpagon's real greed; it reveals Cléante's weakness and his spendthrift irresponsibility; it sets the emotional climate for the theft of the casket. But it does very little, if anything, to advance the *plot*. Its placement in the play's structure, on the other hand, is as carefully controlled as if it gave us some essential piece of story information at precisely that point where a well-made play would demand it, for it comes after the opening scene between Elise and Valère, the battle between Harpagon and La Flèche, and the announcement of the proposed marriages.

It might seem to be early in the play for such an intense scene, yet Harpagon's character has far to go on its road toward ultimate revelation. Still in the future are the rejection of Cléante and the theft of the casket. In purely comic terms, this scene, with its balanced insults between Cléante and Harpagon, its comic recognition between father and son, and its laughably long and incongruous list of collateral items, lacks the intensity (and rightly so) of such later scenes as Frosine's gulling of Harpagon, of the Maître Jacques scene, or of the climactic theft *tirade* of Harpagon. Nevertheless, the scene builds internally to its own climax, one that is comic in its structure (parallel speeches, parallel movements, the confrontation of opposites) but devastatingly cruel in its character revelations:

HARPAGON (*recognizing that his own son is the would-be borrower*). What! You gallows-bird! Is it you who has gone to such sinful extremes!

CLÉANTE (*recognizing that his own father is the would-be usurer*). What! My own father! Is it you who has come to such shameful doings!

HARPAGON. It's you who'd ruin himself by these damnable debts?

CLÉANTE. It's you who'd get rich by these damnable loans?

HARPAGON. Can you, after this, dare to face the world?

and, a moment after, Cléante asks the very realistic question that puts the remainder of the entire play into focus:

CLÉANTE. Who is the greater sinner, I ask you—the one who buys money that he desperately needs, or the one who steals money that can do him no good?

Thus, the placement of the scene in the play is not controlled by plot at all, but by level of comic intensity and by development of contextual progression. Molièresque comedy may seem unordered, and in the linear sense it is little more than a chronological sequence of incidents; but when it is seen contextually, it has the inevitable order of the poetic.

Viewed in this way, the apparent slightness of involvement in *The Miser* is explicable as a different use of dramatic form from that of Racine. Although a superficial view of this play, and several others, would indicate that the incidents could be rearranged without damaging the climax or the *dénouement*, a deeper understanding shows that the development toward character revelation could find no better structure.

LANGUAGE. Such contextual development is closely paralleled by a Molière device, the soliloquy (*tirade*) and the expository monologue (*récit*). Granted that, in certain plays, the soliloquies are in part comic reminders of the Racinian *tirades*, still, the soliloquy and the *récit* are far too widely used, and at far too crucial points in the action, to be merely burlesques. The soliloquy is the linguistic arm of the revelatory process; the *récits* are devices aimed not at skipping incident by summarizing exposition, but at showing the reaction of a character to that incident when he could not possibly have been present. That is, the *récits* allow us to see the protagonist suffering under a fact that he is not supposed to know. In much the same way, the *tirade* (for example, Harpagon's speech accusing the audience of theft) allows the protagonist's entire self-delusion to reach a linguistic high point.

To the extent that Molière's language grows in incoherence as the protagonist's suffering increases, Molière can be said to belong to a truly modern theatre. It is significant that the progress toward incoherence matches the progress of the self toward revelation. The revelation, however, is the climax of the *action*, but does not occur at

Figure 2–35. Valere, Anselme, and Mariane in *The Miser*, at the Charles Playhouse, Boston, 1965.

the same time as the untangling of the plot, a disparity that points up the essential separation of plot and action in Molièresque comedy. Moreover, because the character revelation comes very late, little of importance can follow it; there is no time for conversion. The unmasked Molière protagonist does not leave the stage a better man, or even a changed man; he leaves hurriedly, carrying the burden of his new suffering, and without the benefit of the final, self-appreciative *tirade* that is allowed to his tragic counterpart. The ends of the plot may be gathered up after he is gone, but the action has ended when we see Harpagon depart, reduced to silence or even to incoherence. He goes, still babbling about his casket.

CHARACTER. George Meredith, whose "Essay on Comedy" is a classic in the analysis of comedy, saw Harpagon's self-deception as a denial of middle-class common sense. Such an explanation does not explain adequately the power of Molière's characters to reach an audience. To see Harpagon simply as a man who wilfully deviates from a social norm is to ignore the broader, more interesting areas that involve psychological rather than ethical behavior. Although it is perfectly true that Harpagon can be partly explained as a social deviate, such a merely social or ethical analysis can hardly explain a character whose behavior is compulsive and evidently not caused by circumstances within the context of the play.

A more satisfactory explanation of such behavior is W. G. Moore's antithesis of natural man and rational man—that is, of the operation of the intellect on the subintellectual (natural) psyche, producing deviations from the norm that Moore calls the masks. As we have already noted, these masks are obsessions that literally destroy the character's ability to believe the evidence of his senses and that make him deaf to rational communication. A simple example of such a state is the exchange between Cléante and Harpagon (p. 120) in which Harpagon, although admitting the evils of usury as they apply to his own son, cannot see those evils working in his own behavior.

Ultimately Molière's ideas are contained in characters like Harpagon. The ideas are not simple, perhaps because they are not often stated within the body of the play. *The Miser*, for example, is a play whose extrinsic interest is usury, but the play is about something more. Usury is too easy a target for a comedian like Molière. Beyond usury, beyond any simple situation and any particular kind of behavior, lies Harpagon as a human being—the disinheritor, the self-deceiver, the self-created mask. He is laughable always; we know that he is wrong and we know that he is rendered harmless by his artistic context. Yet we must sense a potent psychology at work in the creation of such a character, a psychology that touches us in a very sensitive area. The Molièresque fantasist is both repulsive and sympathetic; to laugh at him is to laugh finally at oneself. Yet to laugh at oneself for self-delusion, for fantasy, is to laugh at a very deep strain in our make-up. At such a remove, Molière becomes less laughable, and makes existence more comic. His plays are clearly a comic rendition of the same world that Racine saw, in which human beings grope through problem after problem, creating fantasy where they think they exercise reason. (For a further discussion of the ideas in *The Miser*, see Chapter Three, "Extrinsic and Intrinsic Ideas.")

THE DECLINE OF AUTOCRACY: FROM MOLIERE TO *THE SCHOOL FOR SCANDAL*

Racine and Molière, writing for Louis XIV at the height of his splendor, were not unlike other theatre artists in the other major capitals of Europe, particularly in London; they were the creatures of an elegant court. Racine, in his role as royal historiographer, was formally so;

Molière, as the servant of the Sun King and sometime sycophant to his courtiers, was symbolically so.

In England, Charles II had established a little copy of the French court in London. He, too, sought to be authoritarian; he, too, had formal (and state-financed) mistresses, splendid displays of royal pomp, and expensive wars; he, too, was an interested patron of the theatre, as he was of science. In both countries, the preferred manners and morals were those of the court; the manners and morals of the burgeoning middle class were a subject for wry amusement or outright satire. Power still lay with the nobility, although the power of wealth was slipping away into new hands. Reason and wit were the admired mental qualities, but they were still tempered by a Renaissance toleration for the irrational and the wild: Louis XIV agonized through the poison and witchcraft scandals of 1680; Charles II had the Duke of Buckingham confined to the Tower for commissioning the royal horoscope; and in New England, the witchcraft trials of the 1690s were an orgy of nonreason.

Yet, within half a century, the world was much changed. By the 1730s, the merchant class had established itself, especially in England, not only as the new possessor of wealth, but also as the new arbiter of political power. International expansion and international trade had created a new class of moneyed and influential people, and, although the older nobility might smirk behind its fans at the "nabobs" and "city knights," the overt satire of them that had been so amusing in the Restoration theatre was blunted. As well, the professional author had emerged from the sometimes protective, sometimes oppressive shadow of his noble or royal patron, and independent writers could find a livelihood without stipends or pensions. The freedom and the power of the English theatre were acknowledged by parliament in its passing of the Licensing Act of 1737, which strictly regulated the number of London theatres and affirmed the limitations on sensitive (especially political) subject matter. And the theatre itself was changing: John Gay's enormously successful *Beggar's Opera* (1728), a "Newgate pastoral" that put common ballads and low-class characters into the format of aristocratic opera, established a new genre for a new audience. George Lillo's *London Merchant* (1731) was a "domestic tragedy" that celebrated the new virtues of mercantilism and condemned the old Restoration vices of libertinism; the play, which was translated into several languages, was to have an important influence on both English and German drama.

From the 1730s through the 1770s, there came a period of apparent stabilization, a period of bourgeois consolidation. It was, indeed, the Age of Reason, and of common sense; it was also the age of morality and moralizing. To an extent, the critical adherence to neoclassic principles that had marked the seventeenth century was slackened; the plays of Shakespeare, after being more and more neglected at the turn of the century, were revived. The first Shakespearean jubilee, in 1769 (in large part the brain child of the actor-manager David Garrick), marks the impressive revival of interest in Shakespeare, which has not slackened since. Garrick, too, is the finest example of a change to an easier and more realistic style of acting in those years.

Despite the appearance of outer stability, however, several events of the 1770s and early 1780s will show that radical change was at hand: In 1771, the German artist Phillipe de Loutherbourg was brought to London by Garrick to create scenery, ushering in a new period of scenic spectacle; in 1774, Goethe's novel, *Sorrows of Young Werther,* was published and marked an important work in the new Romantic movement; in 1775–1776 the American Revolution began; and, in 1777, Richard Brinsley Sheridan presented *The School for Scandal*—"one of the last important [English] dramas to combine suitability for the stage with literary quality." (James J. Lynch, *Box, Pit and Gallery*). It was a brilliant comedy, perhaps the most brilliant comedy ever written in English, but it marked the end of one period of English theatre

Inside View of the New Theatre, Philadelphia.

Figure 2–36. The New Theatre, Philadelphia (1798). One of the first theatres built in the United States, it should be compared with the theatres of the seventeenth and the nineteenth centuries. Its marked proscenium arch, for example, is similar to those still in use in many theatres; its scenery—wings, borders, and painted back scene—represents a scenic system no longer in wide use, but traceable to the sixteenth century. The arrangement of the audience is a transitional one between that in which the audience surrounded the acting-area on three sides, and the early-twentieth-century one in which audience and acting-area were separated by a proscenium plane. (*Courtesy of the Cooper Union Museum.*)

and the beginning of another. After the 1770s and 1780s, the theatre would begin its change toward spectacle, toward the romantic escapism of Gothic tragedy and melodrama, and, finally, to the romantic realism that was the root of the modern theatre.

The London Theatre, 1660–1777

With the temporary supremacy of the Puritans under Cromwell in 1642, the post-Shakespearean theatres of London had been closed. Already of declining importance because of their failure to appeal to a broad spectrum of society, they were shut down for the same underlying reason that the Roman theatres had been condemned by the early Christians: they were gathering places for those who celebrated earthly pleasure. Less idealistically, and perhaps more importantly, they were potentially dangerous gathering places for political unrest.

The London theatres remained closed throughout the dictatorship of Oliver Cromwell and for two years after his death in 1658, and during those years, most of the theatre buildings were torn down. By the time, then, that Charles II was restored to the English throne in 1660, the theatre had suffered an apparently severe setback; however, the situation had its advantages, in that it cleared the way for new theatrical practices. Although older actors, who had been active before the 1642 closing, made some attempt to organize companies in 1660, two of Charles's courtiers had established a virtual theatrical monopoly by securing exclusive "patents" to run two theatres in London. The first, Sir William D'Avenant (1606–1668) was a playwright whose plays had been staged before the closing of the theatres; even before the Restoration, he had been successful in presenting occasional theatrical performances after 1656. The other patentee was Thomas Killigrew (1612–1683), also a playwright and a loyal companion of the King. Each established and maintained a company of actors, D'Avenant under the nominal patronage of the Duke of York (the King's brother, and, after 1685, himself king as James II) and Killigrew the Theatre Royal, under the patronage of the King. As with the theatres of Shakespeare's time, this patronage meant the protection and licensing of actors (under the Lord Chamberlain) and the wearing of appropriate servants' livery by the actors on occasion.

Although both managements subsequently rebuilt their theatres, and later still put up new buildings, they began production in London (after some minor initial performances) with a significant change in the physical arrangement of the playhouse. Instead of the Elizabethan stage and yard, which had allowed the audience to surround the playing area on three sides, their structure was adapted from the tennis court. It was a rectangular building with the playing area at one end. The result was closer to the theatre of the court masque than to the theatre in the round and allowed for a most important innovation: movable, perspective scenery after the Continental fashion. The audience was arranged in such a way as to face the stage from its broad apron rather than to surround it. In time, a permanent scene space behind the forestage was enclosed in an architectural frame (much like the later proscenium arch) and permanent doors opened on the stage at each side. Despite the over-all movement of the audience to a "pit" at the front of the stage and tiers of boxes above that, some members of the audience were frequently allowed to sit along the sides of the forestage on stools or chairs.

The two new London companies shifted their quarters a number of times and improved and rebuilt their houses; from the tennis-court theatre, Killigrew's Theatre Royal relocated itself in Drury Lane. It suffered a disastrous fire in 1671, but rebuilt in the same location. The Duke of York's theatre moved from Salisbury Court to an old theatre called the Cockpit and finally to a succession of locations in the Lincoln's Inn and Dorset Gardens area. The Theatre Royal's Drury Lane location was to become one of the permanent monopoly theatres after

Figure 2–37. John Drew and Ethel Barrymore in *The School for Scandal*, 1923. This photograph can be compared with Figure 2–38 for differences in costume, gesture, and level of realism in producing the same play. (*Courtesy of the Walter Hampden Memorial Library at The Players, New York City.*)

the 1737 Licensing Act; the other (no longer called the Duke of York's) would ultimately prove to be what is now the Covent Garden Opera House.

Management of the original patent companies became complicated by the deaths of the original patentees (D'Avenant in 1668 and Killigrew in 1683) and by the combining and redividing of the companies. What was ultimately to emerge at the end of the seventeenth century, however, was the growing domination of both theatres by a single man, Christopher Rich. When, as a partial antidote to this domination, a new theatre was built in 1705 in the Haymarket (designed by the playwright-architect Sir John Vanbrugh [1664–1726] and still in use), control of it, as well, passed into Rich's hands within the year. Internal dissatisfaction within the theatre companies led to an eventual slackening of Christopher Rich's power, although, at his death in 1714, he was in the process of building yet another new theatre. This new structure, the theatre in Lincoln's Inn Fields, was completed by his son, John, so that by the time of the Licensing Act, London had four important "new" theatres—Lincoln's Inn, Drury Lane, the Haymarket, and Covent Garden, as well as others that were older. Their intense competition and bitter struggles led to the monopoly clause of the Licensing Act, which brought apparent (or at least relative) peace between 1737 and the last two decades of the century. Thereafter, changes in the audience and the increased popularity of "illegitimate" theatre (particularly such musical forms as melodrama, and such spectacles as pantomime and equestrian drama) increasingly undermined the law (which referred only to "legitimate," or nonmusical, plays), and in the nineteenth century the number of London theatres again increased rapidly. (It should not be forgotten, however, that many of the smaller cities outside London had excellent theatres, many of them splendid examples of Georgian architecture, and that the British touring "circuits" had their foundation in the many provincial Theatres Royal of the period.)

Theatre Production

Three important developments can be traced to the period between the Licensing Act and the production of *The School for Scandal:* (1) the increasing reliance on plays as vehicles for a "star" actor (of whom David Garrick was the great example) surrounded by supporting actors; (2) the increasing necessity that the leading actor function as a director (of whom the great example was David Garrick); and (3) the increasing impatience with stock settings (that is, interior and exterior set pieces that were used interchangeably for all sorts of plays, a practice that went back to the Restoration), which led to an increased emphasis on scene painting and design, a development that was climaxed by the bringing to London of Phillipe de Loutherbourg—by David Garrick, of course.

For Garrick was the first of the great actor-managers of the English theatre. To be sure, he had been preceded by a number of actors who had also led and managed their companies, notably Thomas Betterton (c. 1635–1710), who had first appeared with the Duke of York's company immediately after the Restoration and who had had an important voice in the management of it and of the so-called United Company of the 1690s. Yet, Betterton, for all his genius as an actor and his highly respected reputation as a man, never exercised the kind of artistic control over his productions that Garrick did after he assumed control of Drury Lane in 1747. When Garrick relinquished that control to Sheridan in 1776, he sold his share in the theatre for thirty-five thousand pounds, a fortune for that day.

Garrick was the friend of Samuel Johnson, the companion of the

Figure 2–38. *The School for Scandal* at the Stratford Festival, Canada, 1970, directed by Michael Langham and designed by Leslie Hurry. Mervyn Blake as Sir Oliver (seated), Blair Brown as Maria, Helen Carey as Lady Teazle, Stephen Murray as Sir Peter Teazle, and Robin Gammell as Joseph. (*Douglas Spillane, The Festival Photographer.*)

Figure 2–39. John Gielgud and Gwen Ffrangcon-Davies in *The School for Scandal*, 1963. (*Photo Fred Fehl.*)

most learned and witty men of his day. He was buried in Westminster Abbey. It is often said that the Elizabethan actor Edward Alleyn (1566–1626) was the first actor to bring respectability to his profession, and that Henry Irving (1838–1905) dignified that profession by earning a knighthood from Queen Victoria. Yet, it is doubtful that either Alleyn or Irving accomplished more for the theatre than Garrick did. He was the outstanding actor of his age, and the leading innovator of what then was a newly realistic presentation of the role, "the undisputed monarch of the British stage [in the period] . . . a small man whose behaviour on stage is so natural that one forgets that he is acting," as Frederick A. Pottle said of him. Around him were other, lesser actors—and actresses, who were first introduced to the London stage after the Restoration. Pre-eminent among them were Peg Woffington (c. 1714–1760) and, at the end of the period, Sarah Siddons (1775–1831).

Following Garrick, the way was open for the great actor-managers who dominated the nineteenth-century English stage: John Philip Kemble (1757–1823), Sarah Siddons' brother; Edmund Kean (1787–1833); William Macready (1793–1873); and Henry Irving himself. They, and the theatre, profited from Garrick's genius. Regrettably, they also indulged themselves in one inevitable offshoot of his work: the subordination of the play, and the entire dramatic repertory, to a single, charismatic actor.

The Dramatic Repertory

At the Restoration, the two patent theatres had made a division of existing plays; among them were the works of Shakespeare and of Beaumont and Fletcher, whose plays were frequently performed (often with extreme alterations) until the end of the seventeenth century. Shortly after the two companies were established, new plays were introduced, including many translations, adaptations, and outright plagiarisms of foreign plays (there being nothing like the modern copyright law). With the taste for foreign plays came a taste (but not really an appetite) for the principles of foreign criticism, and especially of the neoclassical critics. (For a discussion of John Dryden's English views of neoclassicism, see pp. 95–96.)

Five-act tragedies with strict unity, linked scenes, and high-sounding heroic couplets were frequently attempted, but Dryden's *All for Love* (1678) stands out in the period as much for lack of any close competitors as for its own excellence. The rhymed couplet, which in French had managed to avoid a jogging rhythm and a ludicrous end rhyme, in English all too often sacrificed sense and sound to the demands of a strict meter and unimaginitive rhyming. As well, the conflict between love and duty, or private and public imperatives, which seemed such a source of inspiration to French tragedians, was often mangled into simple inhumanity in London. Perhaps the Shakespearean tradition was too strong; perhaps the English audience was too earth-bound. For whatever reason, the tragedies of the Restoration, far from becoming the classics by which other serious drama must be measured in English, are almost without exception laughable, or dull, or both. The form reached its rarefied height (or depth, depending on one's tastes) with Joseph Addison's *Cato*, in 1713. Thereafter, exploitation of the neoclassic rules grew less attractive, and the noble periods and well-wrought moralizings of erstwhile tragic heroes would be heard in the mouths of the characters of "sentimental comedy" (see pp. 134–136).

In comedy, the foreign influence was felt, but the native tradition of Jonsonian "comedy of humours" was the principal antecedent. Molière reached the English stage in plays by writers as diverse as the actors John Lacey and Thomas Betterton, and writers like Thomas Shadwell (c. 1642–1692), whose *Sullen Lovers* (1688) was an adaptation of Molière's *Les Facheux*, with a bit of *The Misanthrope* thrown in. Shadwell's vigorous reworking of *The Miser* (1670) is an excellent play in its own right—thoroughly "Englished" by the addition of new characters, subplots, ribaldry, and realistically drawn scenes in such London settings as the streets and a gambling house. This English use of Molière is revealing, for with only rare exceptions, he was found "not witty," insufficiently verbal, and lacking in plot complication. The London audience until well after 1700 wanted to see its own complex, witty, highly verbal, and sometimes licentious upper class in plays with complicated plots and stratagems and many characters (often accomplished by multiplying the same type over and over, so that many plays have two or three friends of the protagonist who are virtually identical to him, except for name and costume).

Restoration comedy was a comedy of sexual involvement and of verbal pyrotechnics; the Restoration comic hero was a gentleman who pursued one woman (partly for her money) while trying to shake off another, often with the help of a third, who might be a former lover with some hopes of getting him back. The women were emancipated, and sometimes as aggressive as the men; marriage was a convenience (money again) or a burden—but a burden easily set down; youth and virility and self-indulgence were prized, but old age and ugliness or impotence and lack of wit were ruthlessly satirized. In William Wycherley's *The Country Wife* (1675), the protagonist, Horner (the emblematic name is typical), pretends to be impotent because of syphilis, thus earning the amused trust of husbands and the amused admiration of wives who are in on the joke. He pursues a rather brainless country girl, the recently married Margery Pinchwife (the name is again emblematic, but of her aging husband). In an important scene, Horner is pursued by several women at once, all of whom want a piece from his china collection—the word *china* having been turned into a synonym for sex, so that there is a wealth of innuendoes about the size, inexhaustability, beauty, and privacy of Mr. Horner's china. The china scene has been called "the vilest in all of English drama" by one critic, but it is an excellent example (perhaps somewhat extreme, but not atypical) of Restoration comedy—verbal inventiveness combined with complex plotting and a slightly self-mocking study of an indulgent upper class.

As a type, the Restoration "comedy of manners" (that is, a comedy that depicts the foibles and the values of an upper class) remains as one of the elegant high points in the history of English literary drama. Despite an apparent overuse of the same characters, situations, and themes (many of the plays being as much repetitions of established successes as modern television shows are copies of other successes), any list of the outstanding comedies between 1660 and 1710 must include some of the most brilliant in the language: Wycherley's *Country Wife;* George Etherege's *The Man of Mode* (1676); Vanbrugh's *The Relapse* (1696); William Congreve's *The Way of the World* (1700), of course; and George Farquhar's *The Beaux' Stratagem* (1707). Although the wit and class consciousness of such plays attracted and held their audience, they could not appeal to any wider community, and the patent theatres of the Restoration were not financially stable. In large part, of course, the problem lay in the separation between the world of these comedies (and their counterparts in heroic tragedy) and the potentially large, and ever-growing, middle-class audience. And, as the seventeenth century was ending, it became clear that the times—and taste—were changing.

In 1688, when the last of the Stuart kings, James II, was replaced on the throne in a constitutional revolution by the rather dour William of Orange (a Hollander married to James's daughter, Mary), the moral atmosphere of England was already changing. In 1698, the Puritan

Figure 2–40. Helen Carey and Stephen Murray in *The School for Scandal* at the Stratford Festival, Canada, directed by Michael Langham, designed by Leslie Hurry. (*Douglas Spillane, The Festival Photographer.*)

pamphleteer Jeremy Collier launched a persuasive and often popular attack on the theatres with his *Short View of the Immorality and Profaneness of the English Stage*, to which he added amendations and defences until 1708. With the accession of Queen Anne in 1702, neither the English court nor the increasingly politicized upper class can be said to have been ready any longer to applaud the manners (and the morals) that had made the Restoration comedy of manners successful. Tragedy, in name, at least, could continue in a rather bloodless way, but comedy would have to undergo an important change. It was to shift its focus from delighting its audience, to instructing it; from offering an amoral and amusing view of an idealized upper class, to presenting a moralistic and sometimes unamusing view of the *morally* best people.

Laughing and Sentimental Comedy

In 1711 and 1712, two men of letters (who were also dramatists) published the so-called *Spectator* papers—well-written, urbane, "common-sensical" essays on matters of taste, politics, behavior, intellect, and literature—papers for a new and instruction-hungry bourgeoisie, papers whose "great and only end . . . [was] to banish vice and ignorance out of the territories of Great Britain. . . ." The men were Joseph Addison, whose *Cato* (whatever one's view of it is today) was a triumph at Drury Lane in 1713, and Richard Steele (1672–1729), whose important theatre work was to lie in the popularizing of a new kind of comedy. The two men were "Augustans"—neo-Romans who espoused the critical principles of Horace and who accepted as a given of literary life that the "ancients" (most particularly the classical Romans) were superior to the "moderns." In comedy, this meant above all paying tribute to Terence (see pp. 49–51), "refined, subtle, cultured . . . morally eminent . . ." Terence. Even the titles of two of Steele's comedies give some idea of the direction that he was taking comedy—*The Tender Husband* (1703) and *The Conscious Lovers* (1722) —and two quotations from *The Spectator* papers will show it even more clearly:

> Our general taste in England is for epigrams, turns of wit, and forced conceits, which have no manner of influence, *either for the bettering or enlarging the mind of him who reads them*, and have been carefully avoided by the greatest writers, both among the ancients and the moderns. (Our italics)

> The talent of turning men into ridicule, and exposing to laughter those one converses with, is the qualification of little ungenerous tempers. . . . If the talent of ridicule were employed to laugh men out of vice and folly, it might be of some use to the world; but instead of this, we find that it is generally made use of to laugh men out of virtue and good sense. . . .

The incorporation of such ideas into comedy led Steele (or Steele led them) to the form now called sentimental comedy. It should not be inferred that this use of "sentiment" necessarily meant tearful or lugubrious or excessively emotional; rather, it was originally associated with an idea of natural goodness, as opposed to artifice and mere superficiality (which expressed themselves through artfully constructed conceits and epigrams). Such natural goodness was pre-rational; it expressed itself in unplanned (untutored, or artless, or not witty) statements of emotion. There is an oversimple association of such behavior with romantic love, both because of the age-old acceptance of love as a convenient literary emotion and because of the popularity of love plots in dramatists as respectable as Menander and Terence. Still, romantic love was not the only emotional state that could be expressed as a *sentiment;* the spectrum of moral virtues could also find such a sentimental outlet.

Clearly, the sentiment, as a literary device, was far different from the witty epigram of Restoration comedy, and the moralizing behind it was far different from Restoration amorality. (Nor can one overlook the importance of *natural* states in the idea of natural goodness. Inherent in this concept of nature—precivilized, pre-educated, presocial—is an interest in primitivism, in rural landscape, and in the "simple" (common) man, that would lead philosophers to celebrate the noble savage, poets and painters to celebrate wild landscape, and political reformers to demand social democracy—even through revolution.)

By the time of Sheridan's *School for Scandal,* in 1777, sentimental comedy had become a dominant form. So many sentiments were being expressed in plays, pamphlets, and novels, that a well-read man could be surfeited with sentiment. Comic drama certainly seemed to have become more sentimental than comic, and Steele's implied goal of instructing *and* delighting appeared to have been sliced in half, leaving mere moral instruction. No work of the period so nicely sums up the situation as an essay titled, *Essay on the Theatre, or, a Comparison Between Sentimental and Laughing Comedy* (1773), by the novelist and playwright, Oliver Goldsmith (c. 1730–1774). In his own plays, *The Good-Natured Man* (1768) and *She Stoops to Conquer* (1773), there is as much natural goodness and emotional expression as any early sentimentalist could have asked for. However, the plays are also genuinely *comic* (*She Stoops to Conquer* has never left the repertory and is still a highly amusing play). It was the increasing loss of the comic, at the expense of sentimentalism, that Goldsmith chose to attack:

> Since the first origin of the stage, tragedy and comedy have run in distinct channels, and never till of late encroached upon the provinces of each other. . . . [Ancient comic writers like Terence] aim only at rendering folly or vice ridiculous, but never exalt their characters into buskined pomp, or make what Voltaire humourously calls a *tradesman's tragedy.*

> Yet . . . a new species of dramatic composition has been introduced under the name of *sentimental* comedy, in which the virtues of private life are exhibited, rather than the vices exposed. . . . In these plays almost all the characters are good . . . and though they want humour, have abundance of sentiment and feeling. . . .

It is of all other [kinds] the most easily written. . . . It is only
sufficient to raise the characters a little; to deck out the hero with
a riband, or give the heroine a title; then to put an insipid dialogue,
without character or humour, into their mouths, give them mighty
good hearts, very fine clothes, furnish a new set of scenes, make a
pathetic scene or two, with a sprinkling of tender melancholy conversation through the whole; and there is no doubt but all the
ladies will cry and all the gentlemen applaud.

Regrettably for his own cause, Goldsmith stated the truth: there was
a large audience for this debased sentimental comedy. He was witness-
ing the destruction of the traditional lines between comic and serious
drama. With gloomy prescience, he said:

Humour at present seems to be departing from the stage. . . . It is
not easy to recover an art when once lost; and it will be a just
punishment, that when, by our being too fastidious, we have ban-
ished humour from the stage, we should ourselves be deprived of
the art of laughing.

Laughter, in fact, did not disappear—but comedy did. Farce and melodrama for a time were to take command; yet, before that, one quintessential comedy was to enjoy an enormous success on the London
stage.

Richard Brinsley Sheridan and *The School for Scandal*

"The author of a play might be a gentleman of leisure . . . or a lady
. . . or a clergyman . . . or an actor . . . or a man of letters, who,
like Johnson and Goldsmith, tried that line as well as others; or a foot-
man who subsequently became a book-seller; or a general like John
Burgoyne, who brought out his first play before he surrendered with
his army to the Americans at Saratoga." So wrote Lewis Gibbs in
Sheridan, His Life and His Theatre, trying to place Sheridan in his
time, and trying as well to show why Sheridan's very brief career as a
playwright was not so very unusual. In fact, the greater part of Sheridan's life was spent in politics; during most of it, he was also the manager of the Theatre Royal; only for a period of less than five years—
1775 through 1779—was he actively writing plays. The fact that he wrote
one of the finest comedies in English during that time should not
obscure the fact that for Sheridan, as for the other playwrights of the
period, the theatre was merely an occasional means for earning money
and fame.

Sheridan was born in 1751 in Dublin, the son of the actor-manager of
the Dublin theatre. Married early and with no real career, Sheridan
was forced to find a way to earn enough to support his rather expensive
tastes. After abortive attempts in several fields, he wrote, in 1774–1775,
his first play, *The Rivals*. Although initially it was a failure, the play

was rewritten and was a success. In the same year, two other plays, *The Duenna* and *St. Patrick's Day*, were also successful; in 1776, he was able to buy (although with largely borrowed funds) Garrick's share in Drury Lane, and he remained active as its manager until 1809. As manager, he presented the rest of his own plays: *The School for Scandal*, 1777; *A Trip to Scarborough*, 1778 (based on Vanbrugh's *The Relapse*); *The Critic*, 1779 (which owes much to the Restoration satire, *The Rehearsal*); and *Pizarro*, 1779, adapted from a play by the notoriously sentimental German writer, August von Kotzebue (1761–1819). Sheridan was now twenty-nine and, for all intents, his career as a dramatist was over.

It has often been said of Sheridan that he did nothing original as a playwright. A glance at the list of his plays shows that a number of them are, indeed, indebted to other works; as well, there are marked similarities between *The School for Scandal* and Congreve's *The Way of the World*. Whether or not this shows a want of originality is neither here nor there; the important thing, both for Sheridan and for his audience, was that by taking his models in part from Restoration comedy, he was able to create a truly laughing comedy. And his audience delighted in it. (Which is not to say that he stemmed the tide of sentimentalism, by any means; as a manager, for example, he produced

Figure 2–41. *The School for Scandal* production of the APA-Phoenix in 1966, one of the outstanding American productions of the play. Left to right, Jennifer Harmon as Maria, Rosemary Harris as Lady Teazle, Ellis Rabb as Joseph Surface, Will Geer as Sir Peter Teazle, Helen Hayes as Mrs. Candour, Dee Victor as Lady Sneerwell, and Richard Woods as Crabtree. (*Photo by Robert Alan Gold.*)

not only his own adaptation of von Kotzebue, but also the same playwright's *The Stranger*, in 1798.) Indeed, to think of Sheridan as an antisentimental playwright is a mistake. He is as much of his age as Goldsmith. Characters like Charles Surface, in *The School for Scandal*, are still naturally good; they still mouth virtuous sentiments (but sparingly); and, happily for them, their virtuous sentiments are overheard by the proper people at the proper time. There is still poetic justice; virtue still triumphs, and vice is still punished. And best of all, the audience is allowed to laugh at the entire process.

PLOT. The plot of *The School for Scandal* can sound complex, and yet its actual working out on the stage seems quite simple. In fact, Sheridan has been accused of poor plotting—meaning, presumably, using insufficient incidents for the amount of time taken up in performance, or insufficient complication and causality. To say this, however, is to assume that the play is ineffective for its audience; yet, it is one of the most easily effective of traditional plays. It is true, of course, that Sheridan sometimes alternates scenes of plot activity with scenes of largely verbal comedy (principally the satire of the genteel practice of gossip mongering), and a line of suspense may sometimes be set aside for these satirical scenes. However, in performance these scenes are intensely active in their own right because of the strong motivations and powerful involvement (largely intellectual, to be sure) of the participants. As well, such scenes are played against the background of plot suspense, and, although they may not seem to contribute greatly to it, they are part of the rhythm of its progression.

The first plot line that is presented to us is the attempt of Lady Sneerwell (a social gossip with the usual emblematic name) to capture the supposedly dissolute Charles Surface, while destroying the affection that exists between Charles and the virtuous young Maria, so that Charles's elder brother, Joseph Surface, can marry Maria (largely for her money). Lady Sneerwell's weapons are gossip and slander, which she spreads with the help of the "scandalous college" that gathers at her house; as well, she has the aid of a plotter and tale-bearer named Snake.

Almost parallel to this line throughout much of the play is the up-and-down course of the marriage of Sir Peter and Lady Teazle. The connections with the other plotline are, admittedly, somewhat fragile: Lady Teazle is a member of the scandalous college, and Sir Peter is "a kind of guardian" to Charles and Joseph Surface, and an actual guardian to Maria. The connection is strengthened by Joseph Surface's burgeoning affair with Lady Teazle, although even he seems somewhat puzzled by his attachment to her. (In a speech to the audience, he confesses that "I wanted, at first, only to ingratiate myself with Lady Teazle . . . and I have, I don't know how, become her serious lover.") Without too much unkindness to Sheridan, one might suggest that the affair is more attractive to the author than it is to the character.

A third, and very important, line in the play is the attempt of Sir Oliver, the Surfaces' wealthy uncle, to determine which brother is worthier—an attempt that is carried to a successful conclusion (his selection of Charles) by using the old comic device of disguise. And finally, of course, there is a plot line concerning the love affair between Maria and Charles Surface, but it is desperately thin.

Charles is the common factor in all these lines—desired by Lady Sneerwell, envied by his brother Joseph, loved by Maria, tested by Sir Oliver. It is a sign of Sheridan's curious genius, therefore, that Charles does not even appear onstage until the final scene of the third (of five) acts, after which, to be sure, he dominates the stage for two long scenes. He never has a scene with Maria (their sole interaction being an exchange of glances in the fifth act), and his only words in the play to a very important character, Lady Teazle, are, "Lady Teazle, by all that's wonderful," when he finds her hiding behind a screen in his brother's house in the final scene of the fourth act. The active interplay that we might expect between highly motivated characters of a multilevel plot is, it would seem, mostly absent from *The School for Scandal*.

In part, this condition exists because of Sheridan's tendency to push action forward in large blocks, settling one matter before taking up another. Again, he is seldom concerned with minute details of plot involvement. For example, important as it is that Lady Teazle be in Joseph Surface's library at the same time as Charles Surface and her husband, Sheridan gives us none of the mechanics (letters, crossed directions, misunderstanding, stopped clocks, or whatever) behind the coincidence; it simply more or less comes about that way. His interest is in the confrontation, the climactic moment. Another playwright—any of the bedroom farce writers of the nineteenth century, for example— might have made an entire play out of the events by which these characters all arrived at this compromising place at the same time. Sheridan does not. He is a brilliant writer of dialogue for a few brilliantly conceived characters, and he needs only to create the opportunities for those qualities to come into play. (Lady Teazle, for example, is not vital to the plot—any woman would have served behind that screen— yet, she is one of the most famous female characters in English comedy, a choice acting role for any actress.)

CHARACTER. Sir Oliver's testing of his two nephews is so clearly echoed in other parts of the play by other characters that we soon understand that the play's over-all question is to find a "worthy" man. It would seem, therefore, that that worthy man should prove to be the play's protagonist; yet, although we suspect all along that Charles Surface is the man, and although we do hear about him from the first scene of the play, he actively appears quite late, and is then almost entirely passive. If we look for active figures, we find Sir Oliver, Lady Sneerwell, and, above all, Joseph Surface. Joseph is shown to be (at least in comparison with Charles) an "unworthy" man—treacherous to his friends.

adulterous (at least in intention, for the play is a determinedly sexless one), vain, greedy, and very falsely sentimental. He oozes moral sentiments; his every public utterance is a hollowly noble thought; his final words in the climatic screen scene, when he has been exposed, are the beginnings of yet another monstrous piety. And yet, like Lady Teazle, he is a memorable character and an actor's joy. Loathesome as he may be in the abstract, on the stage he is a constant comic delight.

And therein lies the success of Sheridan's characterizations. One observer explained the quality as "charm," and charm it well may be, if by that we mean the ability to present character without malice (the characteristic, as Maria says early in the play—and as Addison had said seventy-five years earlier—of true wit). Even those monsters of scandal mongering, the members of the scandalous college—Mrs. Candour, Sir Benjamin Backbite, Mr. Crabtree—are offered to us without malice, however malicious they may be themselves. We laugh at them, to be sure, but we are never made to hate them. Sheridan never allows their malice to have malicious effects within the world of the play, and the creatures about whom they gossip are unreal, offstage confections— Miss Gadabout, Sir Filigree Flirt, Lord Buffalo, and Miss Tattle. The gossips shoot real bullets, but at ghosts.

The same device that distances these unseen figures from malice works also for onstage characters. The emblematic names are again present, some ironically, some specifically. Snake is a snake-in-the-grass who, although he helps the "good" characters in the final scene, begs them not to reveal it, for, "if it were known that I had been betrayed into an honest action, I should lose every friend I have in the world." Mrs. Candour is candid, but ironically so: she villifies her friends by candidly "defending" them against her own charges. Lady Sneerwell sneers; Sir Peter Teazle is as prickly as a teasel; Joseph Surface is superficial.

Yet, such obvious characterizing has a drawback in the case of those characters who are to prove innocent or good or honest—Sir Oliver, Maria, and Charles Surface. Is Charles also superficial? Presumably, Sheridan would not have had us think so, but he is a Surface, nonetheless. The lack of emblematic names among the others hints, perhaps, at a certain vagueness surrounding their virtues: Maria is innocent, yes, but passive; Sir Oliver's confidant is honest Rowley, a *raisonneur*, an author's character.

It is, perhaps, unjust to say of any character in comedy that he seems less than human, and certainly in the cases of those figures who are the objects of the author's wit—Joseph Surface, Mrs. Candour, and Sir Peter Teazle—we do not demand more than that they supply us with a reason to laugh. Yet, goodness, because it is not laughable, may seem vague by comparison, and it is perhaps true that Sheridan's satirical theme undercuts the very characters whose virtues he would seem to be extolling.

IDEA. *The School for Scandal* is primarily a satire—a laughing exposure of the human vices of scandal mongering, pretense, and slavish submission to fashion, with glances along the way at married love, the waste of idleness, the behavior of servants, and many smaller matters. It is a normalizing satire; that is, one that tries to return its audience to a norm of social behavior by asking it to laugh at its own foibles.

Yet, what is the norm of *The School for Scandal?* It seems clear from its early success that the play was a fairly accurate, if comically exaggerated, picture of London society in 1777; but that it suggested a better society, a better kind of behavior, is not clear at all. Like the problems for which it offers a corrective laughter, the play is itself all surface. Such deeper matters as the social changes wrought by the Industrial Revolution, the situation of England's masses, the conditions of streets and prisons shown by Hogarth, and even the fact of the American Revolution are entirely absent. Now, comedy need not, simply because it is comedy, banish all such matters, and Sheridan himself was a man whose later political career proved him capable of considering them. Yet, *The School for Scandal* does not consider them, and, as a result, the satire that is its extrinsic idea seems (but only to a modern viewer) to be undercut by the inconclusiveness of its intrinsic idea.

Extrinsically, the play drives joyously toward the examination of the two aspects of sentimental comedy: the man who is good by nature and given to natural expressions of true goodness (Charles), and the man who is corrupted and who hides his corruption under the sham of noble expression (Joseph). In the world of *The School for Scandal*, corruption and innocence are very real. Maria is still innocent, praying that "heaven grant me a double portion of dullness" rather than corrupt her with the wit of malice. Lady Teazle seems on the very edge of being corrupted from innocence (her country-bred naturalness) to sham (love of fashion), and from fidelity to her older husband to adultery with Joseph Surface. Joseph, at the beginning of the screen scene, argues that her "consciousness of innocence" makes her imprudent; if she were to lose that innocence, she would become prudent. "So, so," says Lady Teazle, "then I perceive your prescription is, that I must sin in my own defense, and part with my virtue to preserve my reputation?" And, upon his agreeing, she observes that this is "the oddest doctrine." When she raises the subject of "honour," Joseph tells her that "the ill-effects of your country education . . . still remain with you," and in this dichotomy of city corruption and country innocence we have the kernel of Sheridan's—and sentimental comedy's—sense of values.

There is a delightful love scene (if one may call such testy badinage, love) between Sir Peter and Lady Teazle in Act II, Scene 1, in which she contemptuously reviews her activities as a country girl, and Sir Peter plaintively, even touchingly muses, without his usual spleen, "Yes, yes ma'am, 'twas so indeed." These two people do love each other; we must believe this, for all their wrangles; and it is the country innocence that Sir Peter loves most of all. It is now hateful to Lady Teazle because it is against "fashion"—the manners of the city. However, having passed so close to corruption with Joseph Surface, and having been saved from it, she is ready at the end of the play to return again to the locus of innocence, the country.

Yet, Sheridan himself was an urbanite, and he was fashionable. His own commitment to London society was evidently too great for him to satirize its very roots; consequently, he satirized its surfaces—sham, verbosity, and gossip. And, consequently, his alternatives, his moral recommendations, are also superficial: wit without malice; generosity (Charles's greatest, if not his only virtue; "While I have, by heaven I'll give," he cries); benevolence (most notable in Sir Oliver, who, like Charles Dickens's Cheeryble Brothers, seems to dispense good feeling as well as money); sexual virtue (clearest in Maria, Lady Teazle, and perhaps, surprisingly, Charles Surface); and the lack of moral cant, or sentiment. But we are faced with the necessity, at the play's end, of accepting as eminently desirable the marriage of Maria to Charles, who, except for his generosity and lack of sentiment, is a dissolute ne'er-do-well; and the restriction of Sir Oliver's benevolence to the small circle of his friends and relatives—a well-meant act that must help, ultimately, to preserve urban fashion and all its ills.

It was Sheridan's extrinsic idea, in creating the two Surfaces, to create a good and a bad example for his audience. It was perhaps his necessary (and unconscious, intrinsic) idea to create two Surfaces of the same coin—two opposite, but closely linked, aspects of the same thing. The age was difficult, and its moral issues were complex, as Sheridan saw. His answer, as a comic writer, was not to perform surgery on the ills of the age, but to offer a comic diagnosis of two aspects of it.

NINETEENTH-CENTURY THEATRE AND *THE THREE SISTERS*

The European Theatre evolved slowly between the last quarter of the eighteenth century and the third quarter of the nineteenth. In those years, there were changes in both dramaturgy and production techniques, but it remained a theatre that might have been recognizable to both Molière and Sheridan. Rather abruptly, in the last twenty-five years of the nineteenth century, the theatre was altered by a very self-conscious revolution; and by 1900, Molière, at least, would not have been able to recognize much that was going on in many important theatres. Before that time it had been highly presentational, full of scenic effects, bombastic acting (especially under the influence of Romanticism), and elevated drama with elevated subject matter. Afterward, it was determinedly representational, its scenery illusionistic (trying to copy the actual, the real), its acting "truthful," its drama typically concerned with social problems and social protest. A second revolution followed, an anti-illusionistic reaction against the mundane and the prosaic, but it did not drive out the new theatre; the two continued to coexist in many guises.

There had been advance symptoms of the illusionistic revolution. Serious plays dealing with lower-class problems can be traced, in English, back through George Lillo's popular success *The London Merchant* (1731) to *Arden of Feversham* (1592), although both of these plays were rarities in their own times. Later playwrights like the German August von Kotzebue were influential in shaping a serious, but sentimental, middle-class drama that was no longer neoclassical in either its structure or its concerns. In addition, the development, especially in England, of melodrama in the early nineteenth century indicated a broad interest in recognizable human problems (however much those problems were couched in an inflated rhetoric and resolved by actions that defied comparison with human behavior).

Since the time of Molière and Racine, the theatre building itself had been changed gradually in the direction of greater scenic realism: the forestage shrank until it was virtually absorbed into the scene space; the proscenium arch not only framed the scenery but contained both it and the action, allowing for some of the strict visual control that the picture frame gives to the painter's composition. An increased antiquarian interest led to use of more and more "correct" costumes and scenes, derived directly from period clothes, paintings, and other evidence. Especially in the English production of Shakespeare, designers such as William Capon (1757–1827) strove for historical accuracy. The gradual adoption of the box set after about 1850 (one, that is, having solid back and side walls instead of the older wings and borders) allowed for a more convincing creation of interiors.

Outside the theatre, but influencing it, were the ideas of language, subject matter, and character developed by the Romantic movement. William Wordsworth's "Preface to *Lyrical Ballads*" (1798) urged that poetry use contemporary language as it was spoken, and not the dated and mannered language that was derived from other literature rather than from life. Victor Hugo's preface to his play *Cromwell* (1827) argued for a poetic departure from the language and rules of neoclassicism and a concentration on the "grotesque" elements of real life—those things that stand out, that have meaning because they are real and are yet unique. (Somewhat oddly, Romantic drama now seems unrealistic in the extreme, for the plays feature the excessive effects, the chiaroscuro extremes, the straining after emotional impact that are typical of Romantic poetry and the Romantic novel.)

The nineteenth-century force that ultimately changed the theatre, however, was not poetic Romanticism, but its opposite: applied science. Walter Kerr, in *The Decline of Pleasure*, has argued that it was a utilitarian, not an aesthetic, imperative that revolutionized all the arts. The theatre, to use George Bernard Shaw's phrase, had to "do its work in the world," and the image that should come to mind when that work is considered is not one of Byronic elegance or Keatsian beauty, but one of a stout little lady who said, "We are not amused"—Queen Victoria.

Emile Zola and Scientific Naturalism

Fundamental to the new idea of the theatre was an opposition of amusement or entertainment, on the one hand, and work or profit or social contribution, on the other. As we have seen in Chapter One, this is a recurring dichotomy in ideas in the theatre as well as in other arts. In the case of the late nineteenth century, the idea of function became bound up with the idea of "science"—that is, the suposedly amoral experimentation of the scientific method replaced the more typical moralizing or didacticism of earlier ages. Instead of the older concept that art should entertain and instruct, art was now to experiment and analyze.

No theorist of the period was more outspoken or more influential than the French novelist and playwright, Emile Zola (1840–1902), whose essay, "Naturalism and the Art of the Theatre" (1880), was both a detailed attack on the playwrights then dominating the French stage and a forceful argument for change. Underlying the entire essay—and others like it—was the clearly stated assumption that the theatre not only can, but *must*, take the example and the techniques of the scientist for its own. "Naturalism, that is, a return to nature . . . to build on experiment and to proceed by analysis. Naturalism in literature is equally the return to nature and to man, direct observation, exact anatomy, the acceptance and depicting of what is." Observation, then, was to replace invention for the artist; exact reproduction of "what is" would drive out the very personal and very private inspiration of the Romantics. In short, the poet's eye would no longer in fine frenzy roll; it would observe objectively, even skeptically.

The debt of such a concept to Darwin's theories of evolution should be clear. *On the Origin of Species by Means of Natural Selection* had appeared in 1859, and, despite intense resistance from many quarters, had been broadly disseminated. "Natural selection" and "survival of the fittest" may have been imperfectly understood, and the theory itself may have been only partially developed, but to people like Zola and his many sympathizers Darwinism suggested at least one idea of gigantic importance: environment conditions behavior. Darwin, of course, was dealing mainly with animals (although the human implications of his work were understood from the beginning), but the extension into human affairs was a very easy step. Animals are the products of their environment; man is an animal; therefore, man is a product of his environment. From this conclusion, it was but one short step to the basic assumption of Zola's scientific naturalism: *exact (artistic) reproduction of human environment will bring exact reproduction of human behavior.*

In applying this idea of the "close affinity of the dramatic formula and the social surroundings," Zola dissected French drama and found it lacking. Molière and Racine, he concluded, were successful and natural because the neoclassical rules and the catering to a courtly audience were the "exact reproduction of contemporaneous society"; but the dramaturgy of the seventeenth century was outdated and had, in fact, been destroyed by Romanticism, itself now (1880) moribund.

Zola looked closely at three contemporary playwrights: Victorien Sardou (1831–1908), Alexandre Dumas the younger (1824–1895) and Emile Augier (1820–1889). He found Sardou to be the "true heir of M. Scribe," the exemplar of the "well-made play" (see Chapter Three) in his manufacture of carefully engineered plots and attractive, but lifeless characters:

> His observation is superficial; the human data which he produces have dragged about everywhere and are only patched up skillfully; the world into which he leads us is a pasteboard world, peopled by puppets. . . . Real life is entirely different.

Of Dumas, he had more complimentary things to say, but he was ultimately negative. Dumas was on the way toward true naturalism, but he had sacrificed that truth for "cleverness," especially in his dialogue:

> M. Dumas has imbued all his characters with wit; the men, the women, even the children in his plays make witty remarks. . . . Nothing can be falser or more fatiguing; it destroys all the truth of the dialogue.

Dumas, then, "never made use of truth but as a springboard into emptiness." Situations, even characters might reflect the truth of real life, but that truth was finally driven out by the need to create witty dialogue and a telling philosophical message. Finally, in Augier he purported to find a playwright working toward naturalism, but one who almost always gave over a naturalistically conceived character at the end of the play to accommodate the needs of a "chic" plot. In brief, Augier indulged himself in quite unnatural changes of heart at the climactic moments of his plays.

> Considered from the point of view of genuine observation, these brusque changes are to be deplored; a temperament is the same to the end or at least is only changed by slowly working causes, apparent only to a very minute analysis.
> In a word, [in Augier] the interesting character predominates; I mean that ideal type of good and beautiful sentiments . . . that mere symbol.

In each of the three dramatists, then, Zola found one compelling vice that militated against true naturalism: the manufacturing of plot at the expense of character; the sacrifice of believable speech to clever dialogue; and the changing of observed character to match a preconceived idea or type.

Scientific naturalism, as the new formula for the theatre, would avoid these three mistakes. It would found itself on observation; its product would be true to life in its action, its language, and its character. In the completely developed form, a play would constitute an experiment in human behavior, from which both artists and audience, in a scientific, analytic frame of mind, would draw conclusions. Zola's favorite terms are *data* and *logic:*

> I am waiting for them [the naturalistic authors] to rid us of fictitious characters, of conventional symbols of virtue and vice, which possess no value as human data. I am waiting for the surroundings to determine the characters, and for characters to act according to the logic of their own temperament.

Objections to such a view are obvious, and they were not long in finding expression. (For discussion of them, see pp. 173 *ff*).

Application of Theory: Saxe-Meiningen, Antoine, and the Free Theatres

Clearly, Zola's essay was the culmination of an anti-Romantic movement that had been building for years—one that had already changed the novel. It should not be surprising that, in the theatre, its first impact was felt in acting, staging, and design rather than in playwriting. Naturalism called as much for a reformation of stage environments as of stage action and language. In fact, the revolution in staging came about before that in dramaturgy and was being prepared before Zola gave a final voice to the movement.

The important innovations in stage illusion came about most clearly in the work of the man who is sometimes also seen as the first modern director, the Duke of Saxe-Meiningen (1826–1914). This German nobleman built a company that became famous for its ensemble (unified) acting, its meticulous attention to visual detail, and its innovating creation of stage pictures. First in the theatre of his small duchy and later in the great theatres of Europe, the Duke of Saxe-Meiningen demonstrated a new concept of totality in theatre production. Between the troupe's first important appearance in Berlin in 1874 and their tours as far away as Russia in 1890, they stimulated the thinking and drastically changed the practice of theatre men all over Europe. Virtually every European innovator of the last quarter of the nineteenth century saw and imitated the famous Meiningers. Only in the United States, where they did not appear, was the effect of their company not immediately felt.

The Duke of Saxe-Meiningen was a tyrant. He demanded discipline; he commanded every aspect of his productions. Individual actors were subordinated to the whole; leading players, in those productions where they did not play large roles, were expected to take part in crowd scenes, to work as extras, both for the help they could give the company and for the discipline it taught them. It was Saxe-Meiningen's (or his assistant's) concept of the production that dominated, and there was probably little of the creative give-and-take between actor and director that one associates with many of today's directors. The Duke of Saxe-Meiningen, however, must be seen against the background of the theatre that preceded him—one in which there was very little attention to detail, very little exploitation of visual values beyond those of the leading players' personal attributes or the sensational, but often irrelevant, scenery. Where there had been boring symmetry, he brought asymmetrical balance and exciting variety. Where there had been monotonous visual emphasis on the star, he brought fluid picturization of the scene. Where there had been often ludicrous conflict between the three-dimensional, living actor and the painted scenery in false perspective, he tried to bring a believable integration of actor and scenery so that the two became part of a total picture. Where, before, the lesser actors of a play might rehearse without ever hearing the leading actors go through their lines, the Meiningers rehearsed in full detail for weeks. Where earlier an actor might supply his own costume without regard to color or line or texture of the others, the Meiningers' director now ruled on every inch of material that appeared on the stage.

The Duke of Saxe-Meiningen, however, was not a scientific naturalist. The plays he did were largely from the established repertoire, including Shakespeare, and so were not the "scientific experiments" that Zola called for. The relationship between settings and action was aesthetic, not scientific. Scenery was still largely painted canvas in false perspective. The Meiningers were not naturalistic; they were, at best, prenaturalistic, supplying the new naturalists with a working method and an example.

The first young revolutionary to act on that example was André Antoine (1858–1943). In 1886, in Paris, he founded the *Théâtre Libre*, the first of the "free theaters" that were to rise shortly all over Europe. In the same year, he saw the Meiningers. The troupe was evidently a revelation to him, pointing the way toward the new theatre. He could now work with his actors (largely amateur) toward an ensemble company (one, that is, in which no single figure would be any more emphasized than he is in real life). As director, he had the example of a man who gave meticulous attention to the environment of the play, and Antoine could go a step farther and make that environment as real, as true to life, as the very bodies of the actors themselves. His was the theatre of the "slice of life," a supposedly convincing rendering of one cross-section through the human situation. It was Antoine who introduced the concept of *fourth-wall realism*, the belief that in the theatre the audience is looking through one transparent wall of a real room at a real situation.

To these ends, Antoine very early tried most of the experiments that were to occur to other scientific naturalists during the next generation: the use of actual objects instead of their imitations as properties (the most famous probably being his reconstruction of a butchershop—including the meat—on the stage); the construction of interior settings to conform to the dimensions and shapes and relationships of an actual house, rather than to the theatrical need of sightlines, effective composition, mood, and style; the blocking of actors into "natural" positions —for example, with their backs to the audience—rather than into the highly presentational attitudes of the Romantic theatre.

However, by 1900, Antoine's revolution was over. He had succeeded so well that there was nothing left to fight. Like a mercenary soldier when the wars end, he was virtually through, and his theatre closed. Later (from 1906–1916), he took charge of one of France's important state-supported theatres, and there tried to expand the practices of naturalism into a largely classical repertoire.

The free theatre movement had, meanwhile, spread throughout Europe. The *Freie Buhne* of Otto Brahm opened in Berlin in 1889; the Independent Theatre opened, under Jacob Grein, in London, in 1891; and in 1898, Konstantin Stanislavski and Vladimir Nemerovich-Danchenko started the Moscow Art Theatre. All three theatres were indebted to both the Meiningers and to Antoine. Only the Moscow Art Theatre persisted as an institution and is still functioning. The others, like Antoine's theatre, succeeded so well that they quickly failed. Otto Brahm went on to a wider success in his national theatre, where the "Brahm style" became dominant: ensemble acting, controlled by the director's sense of the profound needs of the scripts; careful attention to setting, properties, costumes, and acting style, so that all would be "natural"; and integrated and realistic productions, even in classics. The English Independent Theatre did not last long, nor was its founder as successful as Antoine and Brahm Nevertheless, he was the first to produce any of the plays of Henrik Ibsen in England (see p. 150) and the first to stage a play by George Bernard Shaw—through whose voluminous writings a good deal of the Antoine-Brahm-Grein theories were carried on.

Stanislavski's work at the Moscow Art Theatre was of the greatest importance for twentieth-century theatre. Unlike the other directors who worked with the developing theatre of illusion, he created a coherent theory, a vocabulary, and a working method that still dominates much of American and European directing and acting. The specifics of his theory and his method were worked out over virtually his entire lifetime, and were set down at different stages of his life in the several books that Stanislavski wrote. A discussion of his contribution to mod-

Figure 2–42. Chekhov's *Three Sisters* at the Moscow Art Theatre, 1901. (*Courtesy of the Theatre Collection of the New York Public Library.*)

ern theatre will be found in Chapter Four. Of particular importance here were his emphasis on truthfulness in acting, his concentration on both inner and outer techniques in role creation, and his working method as a director in helping his actors to practice their own art, rather than as a director despotically ruling all other theatre artists.

Early Playwrights: Ibsen, Strindberg

Although a number of minor playwrights tried to write according to the strictest formula of scientific naturalism, as it had been set down by Zola (who attempted the genre himself, without notable success), the most influential and probably the most successful dramatist of the period never became a strict scientific naturalist. Henrik Ibsen (1828–1906) was writing before scientific naturalism was dogmatized, and although many of his plays inspired new playwrights, they were not themselves examples of the theory. Ibsen was more honestly interested in conclusions he had already drawn than in the mask of scientific objectivity, and many of his plays are so directed at popular targets as to be satires and not "scientific experiments." Without lessening his stature in the least, it is fair to say that he owed much of his idea of plot to Scribe, and if such a statement appears to violate the theories of Zola, then it may indicate where scientific naturalism was lacking.

Ibsen, a Norwegian, began by writing the epic historical dramas then fashionable in his country and in much of Europe. In the middle of this period of his life, he wrote two plays of broad, poetic scope, *Brand*

(1866) and *Peer Gynt* (1867), whose characters were far larger than life and whose language, action, and scenic demands far exceeded the bonds of any "slice-of-life" realism. In the next decade, Ibsen began the group of realistic, often satirical, plays that were most influential on other dramatists and for which he is usually remembered: *Pillars of Society* (1877), *A Doll's House* (1879), *Ghosts* (1881), *An Enemy of the People* (1882). (We might note that the latter play was a satirical comedy; an adaptation of it by Arthur Miller was serious). Then there are *The Wild Duck* (1884), *Rosmersholm* (1886), *Hedda Gabler* (1890), and *The Master Builder* (1892). Toward the end of his life, Ibsen again began to explore symbolic, nonrealistic means of working in the theatre, and his last plays—especially *When We Dead Awaken* (1899)—are reminiscent of *Brand* and *Peer Gynt* in their extensions beyond the strict theatre of illusion. It may be, in fact, that these nonnaturalistic plays will be the ones for which Ibsen will finally be remembered, rather than for the group of social plays for which he was made famous by those critics and artists who were seeking to promote a realistic, socially concerned theatre (especially Shaw in England and the critic George Jean Nathan in the United States). For the developing naturalistic theatre, however, the middle plays of Ibsen's career were the important ones.

It is difficult to separate the extent to which Ibsen's content (social evils embodied in the lives of individuals) was more important than his use of dramatic form. As we have pointed out, the carefully worked-out plots owe something to Scribe and the well-made play, and his language and his characters, although certainly the product of observation, are subject to the same imaginative control. The plays are surely not "thesis" plays (that is, plays that merely prove a hypothesis about a carefully stated problem). They are, first and last, plays concerned with the lives of their characters far more than with the social problems that affect those lives. *A Doll's House* did make much of its first impact because it involved the very real and widespread social problem of a wife's rights, but it works as a play and is still relevant because it is specifically concerned with one wife, Nora, and her relationship with her husband. It is far too particularized to be a general thesis play about the problem. Similarly, *An Enemy of the People* deals with small-town politics, corruption, and the unstable morality of a democratic society, but its impact in the theatre comes from its comic effectiveness and its particular development of particular actions. In fact, removed from the notoriety of their own day, these social-problem plays of Ibsen's seem to be far less concerned with those problems than they are with human fallibility, as that fallibility appears in certain nineteenth-century situations. If one asks, "What is Ibsen's recommended solution to the social problem of _____?" for these plays, the answer inevitably seems to be that he gives no other answer than the play itself; that is, he does not generalize. Others, it would seem, generalized for him.

Figure 2–43. An American production of Henrik Ibsen's *Ghosts* in 1903. The photograph illustrates the changeable nature of stage realism: the costumes and makeup, for example, would no longer be thought realistic renditions of Ibsen's period; rather they would have to be adapted to contemporary ideas of style, line, and silhouette. As well, the painted paneling, moulding, and backdrop (seen through the center doors) are characteristic of a less rigorous naturalism than that of Antoine or Belasco. (*Culver Pictures, Inc.*)

However, Ibsen's plays (those of his middle years, at any rate) come close to scientific naturalism. In them, character and language are interdependent, especially in terms of social class. The lives of his characters are concerned with the problems of middle-class society—money, respectability, power, and class—and so seemed, to a middle-class audience, to be more pertinent, more "real," than plays that dealt with the neoclassical conflict between love and duty. The settings are the recognizable environments of the same people, described in detail by the playwright in his stage directions (but frequently staged in the period in nonrepresentational scenery, with some furniture painted on the walls, and wings and borders used instead of box sets). Ibsen was not a naturalist; he was of the period, and so showed many of the same tendencies as the naturalists. He anticipated many of their concerns in the theatre and exceeded many of their rules when those rules would not allow him room. Zola had assumed the pose of the objective recorder; Ibsen wrote frankly as a subjective, passionate inventor.

If Ibsen seems more personal and more imaginative than the strictest naturalists, his Swedish contemporary Auguste Strindberg (1849–

1912) must seem positively idiosyncratic. Strindberg's career bears some superficial resemblance to Ibsen's, but in every case where there is a correspondence, Strindberg seems to have gone further, to have grappled with the problems of the theatre more passionately and more privately. His career began, like Ibsen's, with romantic history plays in a loose epic style. Also like Ibsen, he went through periods when he satisfied the external precepts of the naturalists and when he dealt with social and psychological problems, and toward the end of his life there was a greater concentration of symbolic dramas. Yet his symbolism was unlike Ibsen's: it was frequently private and almost impenetrable. His concept of social problems was always colored by his acute sense of the individual's psychological isolation; and his experiments in scientific naturalism—written with full knowledge of the theorizing of Zola and the practice of Antoine—at once stood out as remarkable examples of naturalism in the theatre and as subjective products of an imagination that went beyond simple naturalism. Strindberg's own mental state was not always balanced, and he spent brief periods of his life in mental institutions. Paranoid and misogynistic, he was never the objective observer. All of his plays are informed with his own psychological suffering, and from it they gain their complexity, their vision, their poetic ambiguity.

The most often published and produced, and therefore the best known of Strindberg's plays, is his first important naturalistic work, *Miss Julie* (1888.) In a preface to the play, Strindberg listed the stage conditions that would make of it an effective illusionistic drama: playing in one piece, without a break; angling the scenery and furniture to destroy the customary four-square movements and attitudes; using actual objects for set dressing instead of having things painted on the scenery; natural attitudes and positions for the actors, including turning their backs or shoulders to the audience; and adjusting lighting, make-up, and costumes to give an exact reproduction of real life instead of a glamorous imitation of other dramas. *Miss Julie* conforms to Zola's ideas in its dialogue, its characters, and its action, but it goes beyond Zola in its exploration of pathological mental states, rather than the mere examination of the effects of environment on social behavior. Its protagonist, the young noblewoman, Miss Julie, is a vivid example of the Strindbergian woman: ambivalent toward men and fluctuating between sadism and masochistic surrender; sexually driven and yet sexually blocked; and ultimately isolated, unloved and unloving, going finally to desperate suicide.

Elements of naturalism can be found in most of Strindberg's later plays (especially in the language and the unrelenting use of exact, often sordid detail); but in many of the plays these elements only serve a much larger, often symbolic, end. *The Father* (1887) is, again, a dramatization of the ambivalent and destructive relationship between a man and a woman. *The Dance of Death* (1901) and *There Are Crimes and*

Figure 2–44. Eva Le Gallienne as Masha in *The Three Sisters* at her Civic Repertory Theatre, New York, in 1926. (*Courtesy of the Theatre Collection of the New York Public Library.*)

Crimes (1899) place the same kind of recognizable human behavior in distorted, grotesque, even surrealistic environments. *To Damascus* (1898), *The Dream Play* (1902), and the *Ghost Sonata* (1907) can hardly be related to Zolaesque naturalism, so compressed are they and so full of an often private symbolism, both in the settings and in the preoccupations of the characters. In some instances, character itself is cut off from any realistic limitation, and the presence of the dead, of ghosts and vampires, of gods and invisible figures is needed. There is no clear progression in Strindberg's work from one style to another, from one subject matter to another; rather, all are mixed as his obsessions were mixed in his own mind. As the occasional scientific naturalist that he was, Strindberg was very much of the late nineteenth century, like Ibsen and Antoine. As a nonillusionistic playwright of mixed styles and genres, more interested in his own preoccupations than in those of the society at large, he was already looking far into the twentieth century.

Shaw and Chekhov

The gross (and oversimplified) pattern that has been implied for both Ibsen and Strindberg—from sprawling Romantic drama; to social-problem drama in the naturalistic stream; to symbolic, less illusionistic drama exploring private themes—is really the gross pattern of the drama itself at the end of the nineteenth century and the beginning of the twentieth, viewed from a detail-obscuring distance. Without regard to certain notable exceptions, one can say that naturalism was only a step along the development toward the forms of contemporary theatre. It produced only a few permanent disciples, but a large flock of erstwhile followers who then explored other techniques. Few of the committed naturalists produced plays of lasting interest, although among them Henri Becque (1837–1899) stands out for his *Woman of Paris* and *The Vultures* (1885). In Russia, Maxim Gorki (1868–1936) produced the noteworthy *The Lower Depths* (1906); and among German playwrights Gerhart Hauptmann (1862–1946) is cited for his group-protagonist play *The Weavers* (1892), which dramatized a large area of social injustice through the examination of the mass, rather than of an individual, hero.

The weakness of the theories of naturalism as they applied to the playwright lay in their implied denial of personal attitude and personal creation. Even in Zola, the supposed objectivity of the scientific observer was really a mask for a predetermined attitude that did not so much observe and record human data as it shaped, ordered, and created an idea of that data. Zola's plays—his own adaptation of *Thérèse Racquin*, for example—now seem mannered and artificial for the very reasons that Zola attacked Sardou, Dumas, and Augier: they sought to prove a hypothesis, and by using the same manipulation of character and dialogue. There is a difference, of course; the staging technique of naturalistic theatre *was* a new departure, and in it lay the real revolution. The social concepts of the new playwrights were different, too, for they examined new problems of class and of social responsibility. To many their plays seemed sordid and banal because they tended to examine working-class and lower-class life (*The Weavers* and *The Lower Depths*) instead of the life of the established middle or upper class. To others, they seemed offensive and shocking, because they looked at the human psychology behind such conventionalized stage subjects as love, ambition, and domestic power.

By about 1895, however, the smoke was beginning to clear. Antoine and Brahm were already successes; Ibsen and Strindberg were widely produced. The effects on theatre practice and on dramaturgy were being felt at many levels throughout Europe. Two new playwrights appeared, one in Russia and one in England. Both were, in part, products of the change in the theatre; both wrought further change. One, George Bernard Shaw (1856–1950), had his first play produced at Jacob Grein's Independent Theatre and was a devoted follower of Ibsen. The other, Anton Chekhov (1860–1904) after failing to find established theatres that could properly stage his plays, allied himself with Stanislavski and the Moscow Art Theatre.

In most respects the plays of George Bernard Shaw do not seem to have much in common with those of Chekhov, although Shaw's *Heartbreak House* (written in 1917, but staged in 1919) is described as a "fantasia in the Russian manner," that is, an imitation of Chekhov. The two playwrights are not really susceptible to the same approaches, nor do they find their best theatrical expression in the interpretations of the same actors. Indeed, although Chekhov is certainly one of the playwrights who attract the American proponents of the Stanislavski system, Shaw is definitely not; he may, in fact, be accused from such a quarter of encouraging technique and of lacking truth. To see such a sharp difference in the dramatists, however, is to overlook their very real similarities, which have their roots in a common debt to nineteenth-century realism. Where Chekhov is comic but sad, Shaw is comic and funny. Where Chekhov's social observation is expressed in terms of mood, of symbol, and of the individual futility that is also futility of a class, Shaw's social theory is expressed in direct confrontation between opposing members of different classes and in a highly articulate discussion of social problems. What the two playwrights have in common is a very complex manipulation of language and the shaping of dramatic action within the mold of recognizable settings and believable behavior.

Shaw, however, was a comedian above all else, one who belongs squarely in a tradition of witty comedy that dates back to Ben Jonson. His immediate antecedents are the writers of nineteenth-century farce, and in his use of verbal paradox, insult, and wit play he has much in common with even so nonrealistic a playwright as Oscar Wilde (1854–1900). Both accepted as a given of the theatre that total articulateness is inherent in dramatic character; that is, any character can be completely capable of expressing himself, his ideas, and his attitudes. For this reason it often seems that Shavian characters have no inner life and his plays no subtext; everything is said, nothing is left unsaid. In actuality, however, this is seldom true, for although many of Shaw's characters say everything that can be said *on an extrinsic subject*, they may also refuse or fail to say anything at all on the subject of their own inner lives. Shaw's comedies are frequently called talky or wordy, and it is true that verbal expression is typically Shaws' most useful form of stage gesture (partly because he wrote in a time, and of a society, in which physical action was inhibited or sublimated into language). But it is a drastic mistake to think of Shaw as a playwright who can be read instead of acted. The actor who complains that Shaw's characters are all "technique" may mean merely that his own vocal technique is not up to their verbal virtuosity and that he, the actor, fails to see the human face behind the mask of language.

Shaw came fairly late to playwriting, after careers as music and theatre critic and as novelist. His early plays followed hard on his writing of *The Quintessence of Ibsenism* (1891), an analysis of Ibsen and a passionate defense of the Norwegian's work. Within the established frame of English comedy, Shaw began to write plays that matched Ibsen's in their shocking insistence on dealing with unacceptable subjects in an

unsettling fashion: war, in *Arms and the Man* (1894); social pretensions, in *Mrs. Warren's Profession* (1893); greed and power, in *Major
Barbara* (1905); English snobbery, in *Pygmalion* (1912); sex and the
Life Force, in *Man and Superman* (1903); and many others. Yet to
speak of these plays in terms of their over-all subjects is to do them a
disservice. As with the plays of Ibsen, the further one comes from their
own time the more one is able to see their enduring value, which is not
the transient value of a pertinent subject matter, but the value of human action set forth in an exciting, comic theatrical fashion. Shaw's
later plays—*Heartbreak House, Saint Joan* (1924); and *The Millionairess* (1935)—show him working more deeply into the natures of his
characters and, like Chekhov and Ibsen, extending the scope of the
plays through the development of symbols (evident especially in *Heartbreak House*). From the glittering verbal surface of the early farce-
comedies, he moved to a presentation of the human situation that, in
this last play and in *Saint Joan*, has an inner sadness that is more important, more lasting, than any of the wit play of the first social dramas.

Shaw was a social activist, a critic, and a philosopher as well as a
playwright. Many of the elements of his plays are peculiar to him because of his own interests. Yet he remains the most important playwright in the English language of the first half of the twentieth century,
not only because he wrote an astonishing number of successful comedies, and not only because he effectively used the stage as a platform
from which to preach social change (at a time when the English stage
seemed in danger of giving up any responsibility to its society), but
also because he was the English playwright who was most squarely in
the mainstream of European theatre. His love of Ibsen was both theatrical and philosophical; it showed him to be an exponent of the same
honesty and the same realism. He noted in an essay that a dose of realism was the antidote for decadence in any art, and his plays were the
antidote for decadence in the British theatre. He said at another time
that any playwright could create good plays by taking his characters
from Dickens and his methods from Molière. He might have added that
he, as a playwright, had taken the social consciousness of both.

By contrast with Shaw's, Chekhov's career as a successful playwright
was crowded into a brief seven years at the end of his life. He had
written for the theatre before the Moscow Art Theatre was founded,
but he had enjoyed little success. In a tradition of realistic Russian
farces that went back to Nikolai Gogol (1809–1852), whose *The Inspec-
tor-General* (1836) is still frequently staged, Chekhov wrote short plays
in the early 1880s. In 1895, his full-length play, *The Seagull*, received a
disastrous production in a commercial theatre, and it was not until it
was staged three years later by Stanislavski that Chekhov's unique
style found a proper complement in theatre techniques. After that,
Chekhov and the Moscow Art Theatre were linked, and it is impossible
to say how much each was responsible for the success of the other—or,
in fact, if either could have flourished without the other. The Moscow

Art Theatre still carries on its curtain the symbol of the seagull, the sign of its bond to the dramatist.

Chekhov is remembered for four great plays: *The Seagull, The Three Sisters* (1900), *Uncle Vanya* (the final version of a play written in 1889 as *The Wood Demon*), and *The Cherry Orchard* (1902). The four have many elements in common, including Chekhov's much imitated use of language, his virtual abandonment of plot suspense, and his repeated use of similar social types in doomed situations. He is properly seen as a prophet of the Russian Revolution, for his sense of the futility of aristocratic life in Russia looks directly ahead to the extinction of that class. Although there are precedents in Russian drama—notably Ivan Turgenyev (1818–1883) and Alexander Ostrovsky (1823–1896)—there are no equals. Not only was Chekhov unequalled in his acute historical sense, but he was also unique in his development of a stage action and dialogue that expressed the isolation and the futility of his characters.

In a sense, the apparently realistic action of Chekhov's characters is a sham. His manipulation of language, in fact the very articulateness of his people, is much more the product of imaginative genius than of observation. Yet the illusion of reality is there for two principal reasons: first, Chekhovian dialogue has an internal rhythm, in the pauses and the speech patterns of characters who speak much but who listen little, that is the rhythm of living creatures; and second, the inner psychology of the characters themselves is as compellingly truthful as the more pathological psychology of Strindberg. Added to this is an inner core of symbolism within each of Chekhov's plays, unobstrusive and never asserted by the playwright, but finally extending the meaning of the play far beyond the limits of the action because those symbols exist, often unconsciously, for the characters themselves. This symbolic core is sometimes contained in the titles of the plays themselves: the orchard of *The Cherry Orchard;* the seagull; and the forests of *Uncle Vanya* as they are hinted at in the first title of that play, *The Wood Demon.* In *The Three Sisters* the title is not symbolic, but the recurring *leit-motif* of the three sisters' hopes (going to Moscow) is, and Moscow becomes in that play not merely a city, but a vibrant image of all the unrealistic, foolish hopes of the Russian provincial aristocracy.

Chekhov thought of his plays as comedies. Stanislavski tended to see them as serious dramas. The two men had a now famous correspondence over Stanislavski's serious interpretation of *The Cherry Orchard.* To see this play, or any of the four major plays, as comic, demands a willingness to accept the kind of statement that Beckett's Nell makes in *Endgame:* "Nothing is funnier than unhappiness." One can, indeed, laugh at the futility of Chekhov's people, at their constant rebirth of hope in what we know to be a hopeless situation. Our laughter, however, is always tinged with the knowledge that it is directed at a situation too much like our own. In fact, we are asked to find comic the very existential dilemma that underlies the "black comedies" of the 1950s and 1960s. This is the final greatness of Chekhov, and it explains his distinction from the naturalists: behind a theatrical illusion of cause and effect, of environment and psychology, is a much more important metaphysical idea, informing the entire drama and giving it its shape.

Three Sisters

PLOT. *The Three Sisters,* alone among Chekhov's plays, was called a *drama* by him. It is a little-used term to distinguish an essentially serious play from a comic one. In its final effect, the play may not actually be more serious than *The Seagull* or *The Cherry Orchard,* but its over-all tone is more serious. It lacks the truly funny moments of the latter play, certainly, and it does not have the kind of melodramatic moments found in *The Seagull.*

It is perhaps contradictory, therefore, that the "violent acts and emotional climaxes occur offstage or between the acts," as Robert Brustein has observed. Yet, it is very much Chekhov's method of building a play to keep violent acts and emotional climaxes away from the center of things—probably because such events are not really at the center of the lives of his characters. Their attention is focused on apparent trivia—boring jobs, gambling debts, a baby's mild illness. And it is not as if Chekhov were concerned with people to whom highly charged events never happen; on the contrary. *The Three Sisters* includes a disastrously wrong marriage, two adulterous affairs, the collapse of a family, a fatal duel, and immeasurable amounts of unhappiness. The potential for heart-stopping melodrama is there; Chekhov chooses to use his materials for a different purpose.

The action of the play focuses on the three sisters of the title—Olga, Masha, and Irina Prosorov. Of the three, only Masha is married. In its four acts, it follows the three women and the people around them through a gradual degeneration from hopefulness in the first act to hopelessness in the fourth act. The process covers several years, but it goes forward so delicately that it is all but invisible to the protagonists themselves. Each act of the play takes place in a part of the Prosorov property in a stiflingly mediocre Russian town: acts one and two in a drawing room and a connected reception area; act three in a bedroom; and act four in the garden outside.

At the play's beginning, the three sisters chat, lamenting their boredom and their lack of purpose, and plan to return to Moscow, where they once lived. They are visited by a contingent of officers from a local military garrison, including a new arrival, Colonel Vershinin, who has known the family in Moscow. At the end of the first act, the girls' brother proposes marriage to a local girl, Natasha, whom the sisters think "vulgar and common"; the attachment seems innocent at this point, without implication for the Prozorov family.

At the beginning of Act II, however, we learn immediately that Andrei has married Natasha, that he is now a father, and that Natasha's presence in the household is an abrasive one. She has, as it were, brought the stultifying forces of the town into the Prozorov household; some commentators have called her evil, but this kind of moral judgment is extraneous. Natasha is selfish, defensive, and ambitious, but she is as unconscious of her own motives as the sisters themselves seem to be. Already, however, she has gained enough power in the household to ruin an evening's entertainment that the sisters have planned: she sends away some masked revelers who would visit the house, because she thinks they will wake her baby. Simply by being her own strong and rather unfeeling self, she dampens the spirits of the sisters, each of whom would use the party to escape from her own increasing self-pity.

In the third act, a fire in the town has driven a number of its residents to the Prosorovs' for lodging. The sisters gladly offer their hospitality; Natasha, now the mother of two children, admits grudgingly that it is "the duty of the rich to help the poor," but it is clear that she utterly lacks the sisters' sense of hospitality. In fact, she is trying to move the sisters out of the house to make room for her own growing brood. It becomes clear, as well, that two quite different adulterous love affairs are being carried on by people in the house: one between Natasha and Protopopov, an unseen figure who is made to embody the most bourgeois and philistine aspects of the provincial town, and another between Masha and Colonel Vershinin. At the end of the third act, the sisters are all in distinct states of unsatisfied anticipation, Masha loving Vershinin but dreading the future, because both are married; Olga awaiting an appointment as headmistress of the local high school, a tedious responsibility she does not want; and Irina, the youngest, aware that another of the military officers, Baron Tuzenbach, is in love with her and will probably propose a marriage that she does not welcome.

In the fourth act, it is some months later. The military garrison is being posted to a new location; goodbyes are being said. Masha will probably not see Vershinin again; Olga is already living in a government apartment and is the headmistress of the school; Irina is to marry Tuzenbach the next day. He has resigned his commission, and together they are going off, not to Moscow, but to "the brickyard," he to labor, she to work as a schoolteacher. After tearful goodbyes, set against the unfeeling blindness of Natasha (who is entertaining her lover, Protopopov, in the house while brother Andrei wheels a baby carriage in the garden), word comes that Tuzenbach has been killed in a duel with another admirer of Irina's; she is left to face a life of work alone. And so the play ends with the officers gone, the dream of Moscow shattered, the Prozorov house in the firm possession of Natasha, and the three sisters clinging to each other in desperation.

CHARACTER. As in his other plays, Chekhov employs a number of character types that were common to Russian society and are common

Figure 2–45. *The Three Sisters* at the Long Wharf Theatre, New Haven, Connecticut, 1966. Directed by Arvin Brown, with (left to right) Laurie Hutchinson, Denise Ferguson, and Anna Lindig. (*Courtesy of the Long Wharf Theatre.*)

to his plays: a central aristocratic protagonist (the sisters) who is unable to free himself from his cultured past or mundane present; an idealistic dreamer (Vershinin, very much like Doctor Astrov in *Uncle Vanya*); a foolish nihilist (Chebutykin, a parallel of the Gaev of *The Cherry Orchard*); a faithful servant whose life lies in service to others (Anfisa, very much like the Nurse of *Uncle Vanya* and Firs of *The Cherry Orchard*); a bourgeois vulgarian (Natasha, similar to Lopakhin in *The Cherry Orchard*); and a futile intellectual (Andrei Prosorov, reminiscent of Serebryakov in *Uncle Vanya*). Yet, with all this use of repeated types, Chekhov is not guilty of imitating himself or of merely repeating the same play over and over. Like many good writers, he is able to draw fresh dramatic action from the same sources.

The Three Sisters can be called a play of character. However, it is not really a play of character suspense: there is little interest in the development of anybody. Rather, it is the very lack of development that gives the play its horrifying fascination; the central characters are trapped like flies in glue as disaster overtakes them. It is the very static nature of their characters that creates the dramatic suspense in the play—the inevitable crushing of the three sisters by a world they cannot control.

And their inability to exercise control is a crucial part of their characters. Of all the people in the play, only Natasha, the vulgarian, and Anfisa, the old servant, seem able to bend events to their own desires; the others simply complain and wait. Significantly, the military officers—"the most cultured people in the town"—arrive and leave by someone else's order; they do not control their own destinies. Andrei, the brother, is much respected as an intellect, and yet his kind of intellectualism is impotent—"pouring water from one glass into another," as someone says of his counterpart in *Uncle Vanya*. The sisters themselves lament, grieve, dream of Moscow, work at boring and unprofitable jobs, but never slow for a moment the force that is overtaking them. In the beginning, they are like children who expect a mother or a father to make everything come right. At the end, they are old enough to know that there is no mother and no father, but they cannot exercise any mature self-defense of their own.

IDEA. To suggest that Chekhov was an ideological playwright would be entirely unfair. To say, however, that he was ignorant of the powerful forces at work in the Russia of 1900 would be wildly inaccurate. It is no accident that he is revered in Russia as one who foresaw the Revolution; one cannot read *The Three Sisters* or *The Cherry Orchard* or *Uncle Vanya* without granting him a considerable amount of prophesy.

It could be argued that the external force at work in *The Three Sisters* is the force of history itself. In a very narrow sense, this can be seen as the historical conflict of classes that erupted in the Revolution;

in a larger compass, it is the conflict between any dying but entrenched class and the one that is about to oust it. The embodiments of that force, after all—Natasha and the unseen Protopopov—are not revolutionaries, not exploited members of the working class. They are well-to-do bourgeois, already far above the level of the exploited.

Again and again, the word culture is used by the sisters and by those close to them. It is a favorite Russian term still; to be *nyetkulturnyi* (uncultured) is to be something far worse than bad mannered. But of what does the sisters' culture consist? It consists of speaking French and Italian, playing the piano and the violin, reading Gogol, entertaining friends, and going to Moscow. And of what does anticulture consist? It consists of selfishness, bad taste, lack of hospitality, and the ability to endure tedium and small-mindedness.

Yet, these are not the real polarities of the play. If they were, the sisters would be pathetic, but nothing more; they might easily be comic. Chekhov was enough of a comic observer to know that his sisters were *poseurs* in their way; again and again, he underlines the futility of their position. Thus, their apparent rival, Natasha, is not so much their enemy as an alternative to their impotence.

The polarities of the play lie in the difference of the points of view stated at the beginning and end of the play. Two words rebound, like rubber balls in a closed room—*work* and *culture*. Work is a Chekhovian absolute; it is the absolution of the servant, the answer for the futile aristocrat. It is selfless work that gives the old servants like Anfisa a special status in all of Chekhov's plays. Colonel Vershinin ex-

Figure 2–46. *The Three Sisters* at Wayne State University Theatre, 1959. Directed by Joan Hackett, with settings by Russ Smith, costumes by James R. Essen and lighting by Audley Grossman, Jr.

presses one side of the issue early in the play. He is an idealist who places his faith in time itself, in the gradual evolution of human society through an amalgam of work and culture: everything will be better in a hundred years or so. And even sooner, if "we could add culture to the love of work, and love of work to culture."

But work is tedious and uncultured. The three sisters talk of work almost as much as they talk of Moscow, but the gulf between the two is enormous; indeed, within the understated symbolism of the play, Moscow is the escape from work, just as the provincial town is the grinding subjugation to work as schoolteacher, as telegraph operator, as housewife.

At the end of the play, the three sisters are alone with the nihilist doctor, Chebutykin. Vershinin is gone; Tuzenbach is dead. Irina says, "We must work, only work!" Olga tries to cheer the others. "We shall live! The music is so gay, so joyous, it seems as if just a little more and we shall know why we live, why we suffer. . . . If we knew, if only we knew!" And Chebutykin murmurs gloomily, "It doesn't matter. It doesn't matter." The music of the military band fades; culture is gone. Olga speaks the last words of the play: "If we only knew."

But she does not. The dichotomy in the play's beginning—work and culture—has become a quite different dichotomy of suffering and ignorance. Culture is a dream; tedium and grief are inevitable.

THEATRE OF ILLUSION IN AMERICA AND *DEATH OF A SALESMAN*

Until about the time of World War I, theatre in the United States was very much in the shadow (or perhaps in the belated mirror image) of the theatre of Europe. With little real innovation in either production or dramaturgy, it produced few plays of any consequence until the appearance of the mature work of Eugene O'Neill (1888–1953) after 1920. Before that date, American plays appeared only within a long tradition of imitation of European models, and in almost every case the imitations were inferior to the originals. Most often cited are Bronson Howard (1870–1908), James A. Herne (1839–1901), Owen Davis (1874–1956), and Percy MacKaye (1875–1956). However, nowhere in the works of these men does one find anything like the originality, the vision, or the depth of statement of Ibsen, Strindberg, Chekhov, or Shaw.

This is not to say, of course, that the United States lacked theatres or audiences. A highly organized commercial theatre dominated both New York and regional production, and the presence of professional theatres in most of the West, for example, can be found almost as early in the nineteenth century as the first settlements. Actors of great ability and justified reputation grew up in the American theatre, among them the famous Edwin Booth (1833–1893), son of a prominent actor and brother of John Wilkes Booth. Although there were no contemporary American theatre men to compare with Saxe-Meiningen, Antoine, Brahm, or Stanislavski, such Americans as Steele MacKaye (1842–1894), were innovators in their native theatres who sought to bring the best of European practice to America. Steele MacKaye was interested in virtually every aspect of theatre, from acting to architecture, and it was he who brought (for better or worse) the acting "system" of Delsarte—a rigidly structured collection of positions and gestures keyed to emotions and attitudes—to American audiences. Throughout the late nineteenth century, he experimented with electric stage lighting and sophisticated stage machinery, and it was he who was largely responsible for bringing new theatre technology to the United States.

With the staging of David Belasco (1854–1931), however, American production began to move toward its own version of the then new theatre of illusion. Belasco properly deserves the title of the first important American director, as Helen Krich Chinoy has pointed out in *Directors on Directing*, and it is for his painstaking, meticulous reproduction of illusionistic detail that he is most to be remembered. Perhaps regrettably, Belasco's illusionism served no greater goal than itself; it was a stage effect meant to be as sensational as movable scenery had been in the sixteenth century. Belasco was neither obeying a Zola nor serving a Strindberg; he was seeking commercial success from an audience with a taste for photographic accuracy. The plays that he staged—among them his own *Girl of the Golden West*—were too often mere hack work. Thus, he made strict theatrical illusion effective in America, but no American playwright yet existed who could turn it to account.

At the time of the appearance of Eugene O'Neill, however, several changes in the American theatre indicated that new forces were working and that a belated equality with England and Europe was at hand. In fact, so rapidly did things change after 1920, that by 1930 many dominant forces in the English-speaking theatre were American. Until the mid-1950s American playwrights, American acting methods, American directors, and American scene designers were to overshadow most others. Between George Bernard Shaw's *The Millionairess* and John Osborne's *Look Back in Anger* (1956) the English theatre produced few plays comparable in quality to those of its own past. In the same period, the United States saw the writing of many plays by at least a dozen playwrights that far overshadowed anything before in the American theatre and that were highly valued throughout the world. Of these writers, the first, and to some the most important, was Eugene O'Neill.

The changes that began the O'Neill era are symbolized by the establishment of two production groups whose basic aim was noncommercial. In 1915, the Provincetown Players was formed as a so-called little theatre in Provincetown, Massachusetts. Shortly thereafter, it moved to New York City, where it became the producer of the early O'Neill plays. The rough equivalent of the Off-Broadway movement of the 1950s, it sought out new playwrights and tried to give their plays a worthy start. In 1919, the Theatre Guild was formed out of another such group, and it continued to function until after World War II, working on Broadway and in the more competitive and commercial world of the theatrical mainstream. It, in turn, gave rise to the Group Theatre in 1931.

Eugene O'Neill was a playwright who tried many styles of theatre. In many respects, he is reminiscent of Strindberg in his restless, never-satisfied experimentation with new forms and in his mixing of styles throughout his career. Actually indebted to Strindberg for his symbolic plays, he seems to have sought throughout his life to find a dramatic form in which to couch actions that his contemporaries saw as the first truly American tragedies—but which, in retrospect, too often seem to have been the overstated versions of his own personal pessimism. His first full-length success, *Beyond the Horizon* (1920), has all the humorless solemnity that was to mark his plays (with the exception of *Ah! Wilderness*, a comedy) through the posthumously produced *More Stately Mansions* (1968). Between 1920 and 1968 were works whose very size suggests O'Neill's continuing failure to measure his dramatic experiments against a reasonable sense of his theatre's

Figure 2–47. David Belasco's production of his own play, *The Girl of the Golden West*, 1905. Of particular interest is the contrast between the meticulous naturalism of setting and costume, on the one hand, and the rather exaggerated theatricalism of gesture and expression, on the other. (*Courtesy of the Theatre Collection of the New York Public Library.*)

limits: *Strange Interlude* (1927), which took more than four hours to play; the neo-Greek *Mourning Becomes Electra* (1931), a trilogy based on Aeschylus' *Oresteia; Marco Millions* (1928), a flaccid satire of the American mercantile ethic; and the top-heavy *Lazarus Laughed* (1928), with its superabundance of scenes, settings, characters, and dialogue. Two characteristics seem to typify the O'Neill play—excess (especially of dialogue) and an ultimately impressive serious theme. In the best plays (especially the autobiographical *Long Day's Journey into Night*, staged after O'Neill's death, in 1956) the very weight of dialogue becomes part of the play's most serious impact. In some others, the action will not bear the ponderous, solemn wordiness, and play and characters become almost ludicrous. O'Neill was unquestionably the most respected American playwright of his time; whether that reputation will continue remains to be seen.

The 1930s and After

Continued exploitation of illusionism in the American theatre became increasingly difficult with the growth of anti-illusionistic styles after World War I, and Zolaesque naturalism was already a dead issue in Europe by the time it could have had any influence in the United States. Nevertheless, one of the principal trends in the American theatre through the present day has been a selective, usually psychological, illusionism. It is reflected in playwriting in the use of the language of everyday speech and in characters taken from the mass society. In staging, it is seen in the acting and directing ideas of Stanislavski and in stage settings using considerable fidelity of properties and scenery. In some instances, totally naturalistic settings have been best suited to American plays (for example, Sidney Kingsley's slum drama, *Dead End*, 1935). More commonly, meticulously reproduced details of an actual location have been aesthetically arranged in stage space to serve a nonillusionistic end. As a result, some conflict between dramaturgy, acting, and stage design can be seen, although at their best, American playwrights like Arthur Miller (b. 1915) and Tennessee Williams (b. 1914) have created characters whose realistic psychological development is very well suited to American acting and the highly eclectic American scenic design. In general, these playwrights have their direct antecedent in Eugene O'Neill. The acting method that has best served their plays became dominant in the 1930s. (American stage designers have found inspiring examples in a wide variety of native and European styles; their work will be discussed later in the larger context of the work of Gordon Craig and Adolphe Appia.)

The organization that brought a new focus to acting, directing, and writing after 1931 was the Group Theatre, an offshoot of the Theatre Guild that succeeded in bringing some of the Moscow Art's methods to New York. Those methods had been introduced to the United States both by Russian emigrés like Michael Chekhov, Richard Boleslawski and Maria Ouspenskaya and by the worldwide spread of Stanislavski's reputation and the growing importance of Soviet Russia as an international power. (American audiences had seen Moscow Art Companies in 1923 and 1925.) At academies like the Neighborhood Playhouse School of the Theatre in New York, ex-members of the Moscow Art Theatre were teaching Stanislavski's techniques; others carried them into the professional American theatre and films, and books like Boleslawski's *First Six Lessons of Acting* (1933) made the then new theory even more widely available. When the Group Theatre was founded, therefore, it had a clear aim of creating the ensemble conditions, the artistic honesty and the social relevance of the Russian company's work. By the time it effectively disbanded in 1940, it had proved itself to be vastly more important as a new force than either the Provincetown Players or the Theatre Guild. It was the first important (artistically) revolutionary theatre in America, probably as significant in the future of theatre here as Antoine's had been in France or Brahm's in Germany. Out of its hard work, its sacrifices, and its intense creativity, as they are described in Harold Clurman's memoir of the Group, *The Fervent Years*, came the most influential and gifted theatre artists of the 1940s and 1950s: the teacher-director Lee Strasberg, founder of the Actors Studio; the actress Stella Adler, also an important acting teacher; directors like Clurman himself and Elia Kazan (who directed important premiere productions of many outstanding plays, including *Death of a Salesman*); actors like Lee J. Cobb, Luther Adler, Morris Carnovsky, Aline MacMahon, and many others.

The direct effect of the Group Theater's work lay in its encouragement of new, especially social-activist, playwrights. Probably the most important of these was Clifford Odets (1906–1964), whose *Waiting for Lefty* (1935) sought directly to involve its audience in an unjust labor dispute. Odets' other plays of the Depression period—*Awake and Sing* (1935) and *Golden Boy* (1937)—reflect the same interest in a realistic presentation of a social problem. His later play, *The Country Girl* (1950), is a study more concentrated on a single psychological problem. In addition, the Group was responsible for producing plays by John Howard Lawson (b. 1894), Paul Green (b. 1894), Maxwell Anderson (1888–1959), and Sidney Kingsley (b. 1906). In most of these productions, the Group Theater maintained a consistent acting ensemble, with surprisingly few losses to the more lucrative films and Broadway theatres. The total impact of the Group Theatre's dissemination of Stanislavskian theory was not felt until after World War II. The Group's most important contributions were carried on in the teaching of Lee Strasberg at the Actors Studio (which set up its own production unit in 1965).

It must be remembered, of course, that the Group Theatre was only one of many producing organizations in the 1930s, and that the principal emphasis of the New York theatre continued, throughout that period, to be on less social-activist writers, on an older, more technical acting method, and on the established dramatic staples of musical comedy, farce, and an often sentimental melodrama. The series of plays written by Moss Hart (1908–1963) and George S. Kaufmann (1889–1966) gave the American theatre its happiest farces. George Kelly's (b. 1887) important comedy, *The Show-Off* (1924), and melodramas like Robert E. Sherwood's *The Petrified Forest* (1935) and Lillian Hellman's (b. 1905) *The Little Foxes* (1939) were popular. The latter play is probably the best example of a well-made serious drama in the Ibsen tradition to come from the United States.

The two most important playwrights to emerge after World War II, however, were writing for a theatre whose techniques and whose beliefs were swinging toward those of the Group. Both Arthur Miller and Tennessee Williams had their major plays of the late 1940s directed by Elia Kazan and designed by Jo Mielziner. Both featured actors either trained in the Group Theater or in one of the schools (especially the Actors Studio) that grew out of it. Both showed a combination of psychological and social emphasis that was well served by the Group's approach and that is reminiscent of O'Neill and Strindberg. Williams seemed more concerned with inner psychological stress, and in *A Streetcar Named Desire* (1948) he explored psychosexual conflict and suffering with more shocking honesty, and with more sensitivity, than any other American. Arthur Miller, on the other hand, seemed to share Odets' desire to arouse and move the social conscience to action. However, he cast his greatest play, *Death of a Salesman*, in the form of an internal psychological development.

Arthur Miller: *Death of a Salesman*

Arthur Miller's first New York success, *All My Sons*, had been widely praised in its 1947 production. Although *Death of a Salesman* (1949) remains for many the most effective of Miller's plays—even the greatest of all American plays—it must be pointed out that he has been a fairly prolific playwright whose general level has remained unusually high. After *Death of a Salesman*, his plays, from *The Crucible* (1951) to *The Price* (1968), have spoken strongly on issues that both Miller himself and American society have felt deeply. Yet, in that very depth of feeling may lie some of the reservations felt concerning many of Miller's plays. In some cases, seriousness of purpose has become mere humorlessness, as in the previously mentioned adaptation of Ibsen's *An Enemy of the People*. In others, the apparent need to let his protagonist find moral enlightenment or personal satisfaction has led to unconvincing, contrived endings, a charge sometimes laid to *After the Fall* (1964). Finally, Miller's sense of dedication to an ideal of the "common man" (Miller's own phrase) seems to have led him unintentionally into the sphere of comedy, as in *Death of a Salesman*—a sphere in which he refuses to operate in anything like a comic manner. Nevertheless, he remains as one of the three most important mid-century American playwrights (with Williams and Edward Albee), and there is every indication that his future work will continue on the same high level.

PLOT. Although hardly fitting the well-made play category, *Death of a Salesman* is quite traditional in its plot emphasis, despite a cutting back and forth across time through the use of scenes from the past of its protagonist, Willy Loman. Elia Kazan, in his production notes to the play, emphasized that these scenes of the past are not flashbacks in the conventional sense, but scenes from Willy's memory of the past. We see them always through the filter of Willy's consciousness. There is a slight flaw in the aesthetic consistency of such an idea, because there are scenes in the play in which Willy does not appear or of which has no direct knowledge; therefore, the entire play can never be seen wholly as his inner life. Rather, the *present* of the action with which the play begins represents an objective reality in which Willy plays a part, and it develops with its own consistency throughout the play, even in those scenes in which Willy is absent. The *past* of Willy's memories of events leading up to the present crises are internal and subjective and are consistent within themselves. The blending of these two levels of reality into a single dramatic progression gives the play a unique and poignant air, for we are able to contrast the two realities as Willy cannot, and the result is sad and touching.

Given the existence of two different realities developing at different rates, however, we can still trace a single plot for the play. At the beginning, Willy Loman has returned early from a selling trip to his New York house, huddled as it is among the cold apartment buildings of an urban mass. Willy, growing old, futile, shaken by the wavering of his contact with outer reality and loss of control over it, seeks comfort from his wife, Linda. There can, in fact, be no comfort for him, but she quiets him and he withdraws into a contemplation of the past. In another room, his two grown sons, Biff and Happy, are wakened by his talking to himself, and we learn more of the details of Willy's disintegration. In a fairly lengthy exposition scene we are told that Biff was a promising high school athlete who has gone nowhere, whereas Happy is a blowhard and a wastrel. With Willy's return onstage, the first lengthy interior memory begins, this one of a happy Willy, proud of his teenage sons and in love, for the moment, with the image of himself and of his place in his society: "America is full of beautiful towns and fine, upstanding people. And they know me, boys, they know me. . . ." Willy makes slighting remarks about a neighbor, Charley. "He's liked, but he's not—well liked." The boys make fun of Charley's son, Bernard, the neighborhood nonathlete with glasses who studies hard. As this Willy of the past begins to talk to the Linda of the past, we get the first real implication that something is wrong, even here in memory, for a woman with whom Willy is having an affair in Boston draws his attention away from Linda, and memory wanders to her. Then, in an abrupt return to the present, neighbor Charley appears and tries to calm Willy, but again memory and fantasy intervene and Willy's successful brother Ben appears—"the only man I ever met who knew the answers"—and Willy carries on a bizarre three-way conversation with the real Charley and the remembered Ben. At the end of the first act, after a lengthy wrangle between Willy and his son Biff, the salesman and his two sons talk themselves into an absurd optimism that is itself an echo of the memoried past. Willy assures Linda that, "Everything'll be all right," even as Biff discovers evidence that Willy has been planning to commit suicide by inhaling gas from a water heater.

In Act Two, these conflicts between the remembered past and the critical present are intensified increasingly until Willy's suicide at the end of the act. His optimistic hope of securing a New York job is shattered when he encounters the company's manager. Next, he goes to Charley's office to borrow money, and finds that the kid with glasses

Figure 2–48. The original New York production of Arthur Miller's *Death of a Salesman*. (*Culver Pictures.*)

whom his sons laughed at, Bernard, is now a successful lawyer on his way to argue a case in the Supreme Court. Then what was to have been a triumphant dinner with his grown sons turns to disaster when Happy cannot resist picking up a prostitute in the restaurant, and Biff's own hopes for his future—based on Willy's mad dreams of the night before—have been broken. The climax of the act comes when a question of Bernard's—"What happened in Boston, Willy?"—is answered in another interior memory: we see Willy with The Woman, discovered by the teenage Biff. The encounter, with its disillusionment for the young Biff, explains Willy's shame, explains Biff's mature failure, explains even Willy's own crushing need to find "the answer," as he calls it. Most of Willy's torment centers around Biff, in whom he sees his own fantastic dreams embodied. In the same way, his guilty memories center around Biff and the destruction of Biff in Boston.

Before his suicide Willy has a last encounter with brother Ben, this one not a memory of the past but a present fantasy: the past has caught up with the present. Ben encourages Willy's suicide, in order that Biff may see in Willy's funeral the fact that he was "well liked" and so that Linda will get $20,000—"not another damned-fool appointment, Ben. . . . Guaranteed, gilt-edged. . . ." And Willy goes off, his mind seeking fantasy diamonds in Africa with Ben, and commits suicide by smashing up his automobile.

CHARACTER. Willy Loman, in the decades since Miller created him, has taken on the status of an American myth figure. Whether it was the selection of Willy's profession as a salesman—the man "out there in the blue, riding on a smile and a shoeshine," as Charley puts it at Willy's funeral—or whether it was the compressed dramatic interweave of memory and hard fact, Miller succeeded in making a character who finds a profound response in American audiences. The phrase *the American dream* must come to mind, for that dream is Willy's (to be well liked, to know the answers, to succeed), and the destruction of that dream by circumstance is Willy's, and apparently America's, experience.

Yet, as Hamlet can be understood in part through Horatio and the First Player, so Willy can be understood in part through Biff, Ben, and Charley. He is surrounded by these three: Biff, disillusioned by the dream's underbelly; Ben, the ice-cold embodiment of the dream's accomplishment; Charley, the friendly, not well-liked, fairly successful plugger who sired a boy who argues cases before the Supreme Court, and who denied the dream even while he lived it. Willy is unique, but he is made so for us by the contrasts with these others. Biff seems like Willy in his tendency to dream and in his yearning for a kind of pastoral America, a place of open spaces and "wonderful people." However, the two are not really alike because Biff's dreams are grounded in despair, Willy's in foolish fantasy. Between Ben and Willy there is less resemblance, and one can legitimately ask how the two could spring from the same family (although the same pairing of dissimilar brothers can be seen in Biff and Happy, as well as in the sons of *All My Sons*, and the principal characters of *The Price*). Ben is not a dreamer; he is an adventurer, a pirate, and although pirates may in time become the figures of other people's fantasies (Willy's, for example), they are seldom other than cold-blooded themselves. Ben's language is studded with references to glitter, to hardness, and to savagery—diamonds, the jungle, Alaskan gold. In a brief, shocking scene, Ben mock-playfully fights with the young Biff, and ends by tripping him with his umbrella and standing over the fallen boy, the steel tip of the umbrella pointed at Biff's eye. "Never fight fair with a stranger, boy. You'll never get out of the jungle that way," is his sardonic advice. Willy, one feels, believes in fighting fair, but we see that he has often sacrificed that belief, and the conflict between idealism and pragmatism tears him in two. For brother Ben, there is no such conflict.

Between Willy and Charley, the contrast of professions virtually symbolizes the differences in their modes of approaching life. Willy is a salesman; Charley is a manufacturer. What Willy sells, what Charley makes, is never clear and is irrelevant, but the fact that the salesman—creating nothing of his own, doing no work in the world, trying to peddle his goods with his own smile and his charm—must finally go to the manufacturer for money is significant of the failure of Willy's way. Charley's way is relatively successful; it is the way of the industrious animal—but it renders him a trifle passive and anonymous. It is his son, Bernard, after all, who tells Willy that sometimes it is "better to walk away" from irreconcilable conflict. Yet, the man who walks away would not become the protagonist of so powerful a play, and just as *Hamlet* is not about the passive Horatio, so this play is about the death of Willy Loman and not the death of Charley.

IDEA. Shortly after *Death of a Salesman* opened, Arthur Miller wrote a short essay called "Tragedy and the Common Man." Part of its aim was to defend the attitude that tragedy could present protagonists who lacked social stature, an attitude that it would be pointless to debate here. Of more importance for our purposes was Miller's insistence on the activeness of the tragic protagonist, a characteristic we have already pointed out in Willy Loman. Whether that characteristic alone renders him tragic or not is scarcely the point; what must be seen is that, to Miller, no heroism of any kind can exist passively. In *Oedipus Rex*, as we have already said, to act is to be self-isolated and to become tragic. In *Death of a Salesman*, that statement is true, at least to the extent that Willy's action is isolated, is individual, and is finally and profoundly moving.

It has been suggested, however, that *Death of a Salesman* operates in large part in the world of comedy. This statement is true in that the principal preoccupations of its characters are precisely the preoccupations of comedy—money and sex. Willy's dreams have material success at their end, even as Harpagon's have; Willy's *pathos* in Boston centers on a very tawdry little sexual matter; and Willy's final enlightenment (if it can be dignified with that term) involves the vision of a $20,000 insurance benefit. Occasionally Miller allows this comic subject matter to become truly funny, as The Woman in Boston ("Miss Francis") is funny and as Willy's remarks about his decrepit refrigerator and his decaying car are funny. Nevertheless, most of the play operates in a gray area between the traditional subject matters of tragedy and comedy.

There is nothing inherently wrong with such dramatic practice. The mixture of the subjects of comedy and tragedy has, in fact, become one of the trademarks of contemporary theatre, but with the great difference that the tone is mixed, so that the comic becomes sad and the tragic blackly humorous. In *Death of a Salesman*, the mixture remains merely that, a mixture, and represents the limitations placed (perhaps unconsciously) by Miller on Willy himself: He has the active personality of the tragic hero, and we would allow him his tragedy without high social stature, but he is quite simply without the intellectual, the emotional, or the moral depth to comprehend and to enlighten a tragic situation. The play would seem to castigate American society for giving Willy the materialistic stuff his dreams are made on, but in fact it is the total acceptance of the materialistic (comic) world by the entire play that finally undercuts it. It remains a moving study of a little—socially and morally little—man caught in an impossible crisis, but it never can enlarge our theatrical response as *Hamlet* and *Oedipus Rex* do because it does not give its hero sufficient tragic scope.

REACTIONS AGAINST THE THEATRE OF ILLUSION: BECKETT'S *ENDGAME*

Within ten years of Antoine's founding of the *Théâtre Libre* in Paris, a movement was already under way to counter the representation of actuality on the stage. Its earliest proponents were French and German, just as the inspiring agents of naturalism were. However, in truth these first antinaturalists were part of a much larger movement that had its roots in the personal, emotional obsession of Romanticism and its guiding, early example in the theatre of Richard Wagner (1813–1883). Presentational in its staging, poetic rather than mundane in its language, symbolic rather than psychological in its characters, this new theatre veered away from that of Zola and Antoine, crossed back to join with it in producing many hybrids, and again and again moved away as illusionism seemed to endanger the theatre by restricting its art within excessively narrow limits. Almost from its beginning, however, the nonillusionistic theatre has been dominated by the ideas and reputation of one man, Gordon Craig. Perhaps significantly, he was far less a doer in the theatre than a proselytizer of his own and other men's inventions. At the other end of the historical development—that is, in our time—stands another theorist, another propagandist who only rarely worked in the theatrical mainstream, Antonin Artaud. Between the two men virtually the entire spectrum of presentational or theatrical or symbolist or expressionist theatre (there are many labels) can be envisioned, and with it, the great practitioners, Copeau, Reinhardt, Meyerhold, Piscator, and Barrault; the playwrights, Kaiser, O'Neill, Brecht, Pirandello, Genet, and Beckett; and the designers, Bel Geddes, Simonson, Otto, Neher, Svoboda, Jones, Gorelik, and Mielziner. In general, the labels have been affixed most conveniently to plays and playwrights; by extension, they can be pasted on certain works of directors and designers, but, with one or two exceptions, they cannot easily be made to apply to the work of actors.

Nineteenth-Century Beginnings: Appia and Craig

Although the most outspoken and most widely heard new voice was Gordon Craig's, he was not actually either the first nor the most innovative of the anti-illusionists. The honor probably belongs to Adolphe Appia (1862–1928), a Swiss who built on Richard Wagner's idea of total theatre and combined it with his own highly original perception of the theatrical possibilities of light. In Appia's writings, the mystical and the metaphorical sometimes obscure the practicality of what he said, but his genius cannot be overvalued. Far more than Craig, and before Craig, he sensed that the interaction of three-dimensional forms, including the living actor, with light could produce an entirely new theatrical image.

The use of controlled incandescent light is surely one of the outstanding instances of the effects of technology on theatrical art. Appia grasped the implications of the new means of providing focused, controlled light very early, and in his *Music and the Art of the Theater* (1895) he was already discussing how it could be used as a living element of theatrical production—hence his own term *living light*. Under the "despotic" control of a director, the many elements of the theatre would all be made to serve a similarly living form, plastic in its use of the moving actor, its continuous, controlled alteration of light, and its creation of rhythms, analogous to the rhythms of music, that are the connecting link between the living actor and the static stage environment. It was Appia, too, who most successfully argued for a three-dimensional, or architectural, scenery to replace the much older painted scenery in two dimensions. Real depth, created by the play of changeable light over three-dimensional masses, could replace the unconvincing, uniformly illuminated, painted perspective of the Renaissance. Elements of scenic mass and actors could be isolated in space, as no actor or scenic element could ever have been isolated on the earlier stages, illuminated as they had been with candles, lamps, or even gas. Appia's designs for both operas and plays (many of them never executed) were seminal in their effect on later designers, and the popularity of architectural settings and "space stages" (nonrepresentational masses of levels, ramps, and steps) can be traced back to the published designs of Appia.

Appia was a visionary and a mystic. By comparison, Gordon Craig (1872–1965) seems brash and self-consciously iconoclastic. George Bernard Shaw, with whom he had a lengthy feud, once said that "if ever there was a spoilt child in artistic Europe, that child was Teddy Craig," and he went on, perhaps unfairly, to class Craig as a "literary propagandist of pictorial art on the stage." A propagandist Craig certainly was, but necessarily so; like Appia, he was preaching innovation at a time when most European theatre was making money on something far less adventurous. Yet, he achieved some general success and some aceptance; an actor at first, he became a designer and went to Moscow to design *Hamlet* for Stanislavski (1912) and to Berlin to design for Otto Brahm. However, he seemed always to find practice dragging its feet behind desire, and his books—*The Art of the Theater* (1905), *Towards a New Theater* (1913), *The Theater—Advancing* (1919), and others—and the periodical, *The Mask,* were clarion calls (repeated again and again) for ideal reforms to create an ideal theatre. His drawings frequently show disdain or indifference for practicality; yet they, with Appia's designs, are the foundation of modern scene design. Like Appia, he sensed the value of controlled light, both for its ability to mold three-dimensional forms and for its ability to create mood. One series of drawings, for example, shows the same structure as lighted in four quite different ways, for four different emotional values. His published designs for Shakespeare reveal his great genius for striking pictorially to the heart of the dramatic scene, for creating images of the inner values of the play. Coming as soon as they did after the historically correct Shakespeare popular in England, they are particularly impressive, for they show us a man of the theatre creating each work anew, without relying on comfortable or fashionable modes.

As a theatre practitioner Craig advocated single-artist dominance. That single artist, of course, was Gordon Craig, as director, designer, and interpreter of the text. His objection to "literary men" in the theatre was healthy; his utter rejection of collective creation is questionable. So extreme did his desire for dominance become that he advocated the creation of an *uber marionette* to replace the actor, a carefully articulated, perfectly responsive mechanical man to respond to the director-designer's needs. In his own time such a creature was technologically impossible; it is now becoming possible, and we may yet see it (and, in a sense, the films have already given it to us). Craig's suggestion, inhuman and egocentric as it may seem, is not without parallel among other theatre artists for whom the actor's variable performance, personal mannerisms, and exhibitionism are often disquieting. As always, of course, Craig's attitude was extreme; it was by taking extreme positions, after all, that he made himself heard.

In 1965, when Gordon Craig died, it was hard for many people to believe that the man had lived so long. Like many outspoken innovators, he was finally so successful that he had nothing left to say. In fact, he outlived the general acceptance of his ideas by more than three decades, and if at his death he seemed a man from the distant past, he seemed so only because we now live with theatre that has completely adopted his theories of design, of lighting, and of intense pictorial presentation of dramatic images.

Through Expressionism: Dramatic Symbolism

Before 1900, an existing symbolist tendency in poetry found its theatrical counterpart in the creation, in Paris, of the *Théâtre de l'Oeuvre* by Aurelien Lugne-Poe (1869–1940), in 1892. The first work of this theatre can hardly be said to have shown the influence of Appia or Craig, and the most famous playwright to have work staged there, Maurice Maeterlinck (1862–1949), was hardly a fitting answer to such illusionists as Shaw, Becque, Chekhov, or Ibsen. Still, Maeterlinck's plays enjoyed some reputation during their day, especially *Pelleas and Melisande* (1892), *The Death of Tintagiles* (1894), *The Bluebird* (1909), and *Death* (1912). Their terrible vagueness would seem now to render them irrelevant and dull, but as an antidote to naturalism they were a significant change. Their language is spare and indirect, their characters motivated by symbolic forces beyond their intellectual control, and their settings intentionally unreal. Maeterlinck's plays tend to be inactive, his characters passive; they are attempts to sustain moods, emotional states, portentous situations, and little else.

Of far more significance in the growth of a nonillusionistic drama were the symbolic plays of Strindberg, especially those written and staged toward the end of his life. *The Ghost Sonata, The Dream Play*, and the *Damascus* plays used conscious symbolism, as Maeterlinck's plays did, but in a far more telling matrix of psychological and metaphysical action. Although no significant playwright appeared to carry on Strindberg's kind of symbolism during the years immediately following his death, by 1920 his influence was having great effect on the playwrights of the so-called expressionist movement. In addition, the production in 1913 of Georg Buechner's anachronistic *Woyzzeck* (written in 1836, but not then staged) had a profound influence on German playwrights who found contemporary significance in its nonlinear structure, its cinematic cuts from scene to scene, its symbolism, and its pathological, antiheroic protagonist.

Expressionism in drama was a short-lived movement. Its principal German exponents were Georg Kaiser (1878–1945) and Ernst Toller

Figure 2-49. Lee Simonson's expressionistic setting for the original New York production of Elmer Rice's *The Adding Machine*. The distorted angles, selective use of light and mass, and the dehumanized judge-figure, center, are characteristic of expressionism. (*Courtesy of the Theatre Collection of the New York Public Library.*)

(1893–1939). The titles of their plays are themselves indicative of the movement's beliefs: Toller's *Man and the Masses* (1921) and Kaiser's *Gas I* and *Gas II* (1920). In the United States, Elmer Rice (1892–1966) wrote *The Adding Machine* (1923), and in 1924 George Kaufman and Marc Connelly adapted an expressionist European play into *Beggar on Horseback*, although the placing of its action within a dream undercuts the symbolic impact of the major events. Most important, of course, were Eugene O'Neill's expressionist plays—*Dynamo* (1929), *The Great God Brown* (1926), and *The Hairy Ape* (1922). The common elements of all these plays were the symbolic externalization, in acting, setting, and incident, of the inner emotional content and the inner psychology of the characters and action. Typically, an expressionist play centered on a "little" protagonist, and typically it showed him in conflict with, or at the mercy of, a machinelike government. In *The Hairy Ape*, the protagonist is a stoker on a steamship, so ground down by the economic machine that he is little more than an animal. In one scene, walking down a New York street, he is bumped, pushed aside, and ignored by zombies of the urban mass. In these plays, the symbols emanate from the protagonist; they symbolize his predicament in his own terms. Unlike later existential plays, they do not suggest that individualism is a fiction or that the protagonist is locked into a prison of his own consciousness. Instead, they make the individual the measure of all things, presenting his world to the audience in the heightened symbolic language of dreams.

In its influence on stage design, expressionism is still important. Although it may originally have confined itself to such simplistic devices as altering dimensions or changing the familiar angles of objects (for example, in the setting for Rice's *The Adding Machine*, a courtroom scene had a distorted judge's bench, below which the protagonist cowered, while other skew lines suggested an even greater disorientation), it gave expression to such ideas as Craig's sense of the inner image of a play. Thus, Jo Mielziner's setting for *Death of a Salesman*, although almost naturalistic in its use of such properties as a refrigerator and chairs and beds, exploited the symbolic background of the city and the symbolic projection of sunlit leaves in an expressionistic manner.

As a movement with a manifesto and with partisans, expressionism is dead. As a practicable theory of dramaturgy, it lasted for only a very short time. As a more general expression of distaste for illusionism and a sense that the theatre could deal in nonlogical symbolism, its tendencies can still be seen.

After Craig: Reinhardt, Copeau, and Meyerhold

As we have already noted, a production of Georg Buechner's *Woyzzeck* was an early stimulant to the expressionist movement. It was staged by Max Reinhardt (1873–1943), an eclectic Austrian director and producer whose work ranged from the subtleties of intimate productions of Strindberg's "chamber plays" to such extravaganzas as *The Miracle* (1923–1924) and a film version of Shakespeare's *A Midsummer Night's Dream*. As a director, Reinhardt's artistic control of his productions owed much to the tradition of Saxe-Meiningen and Otto Brahm. (Reinhardt had worked under the latter early in his career.) Hardly a slavish follower of any theory, Reinhardt moved rapidly, even restlessly, from style to style, seeking new means for staging each new drama. For the Strindberg plays he used a small theatre with a close audience-actor relationship. For the New York production of *The Miracle*, his designer, Norman Bel Geddes, sought to transform the interior of the theatre into a replica of a cathedral. Reinhardt's outdoor production of *Everyman*, in Salzburg, Austria, was a spectacle using large portions of an urban square. His production of another Buechner play, *Danton's Death*, moved the action into the audience area to try to give the audience the feeling of taking part in the parliamentary upheavals with which that play is concerned. Reinhardt was not a notable theorist, nor did he leave any body of work upon which a cult or movement could be built; rather, he was a creative, authoritarian director of immense scope, capable of spanning historical periods, social attitudes, and stylistic schools. His place in the development of the practice of directing is an important one, for he set an example—followed generally until the 1950s—of directorial authoritarianism, symbolized in his keeping of meticulous production books (*Regiebuch*).

Where Reinhardt was eclectic, his French contemporary Jacques Copeau (1878–1949) was single-minded and innovative. Reinhardt was interested in visual spectacle and theatrical surprise, and he used a wide range of technical devices—*tricks* might be the word used by a director of the 1960s—to achieve his ends. Copeau, by comparison, was a purist. Personally ascetic and devoutly religious, he carried some of his personal attitudes into his theatre work, putting into effect a theory of theatricalism based on simplicity rather than eclectic complexity. In 1913, he founded *Le Vieux Colombier*, a theatre whose approach to acting and to staging, and especially its creation of a unique stage space, made it a great influence on modern French theatre. Although Copeau himself withdrew from the theatrical world with a few disciples in the 1920s (the religious metaphor is inescapable), the effect of his work was already made, and it persisted in the later work and writing of such men as the great French actor Louis Jouvet (1891–1951), Charles Dullin (1885–1949), such diverse contemporary talents as the mimes Etienne Decroux (b. 1898) and Marcel Marceau (b. 1923), and the actor-director Jean-Louis Barrault (b. 1910). The "clean" or "spare" feeling of French scene design shows the same influence of the reduction of all elements to a *theatrical* (not an illusionistic) minimum, traceable finally to neoclassicism.

At the *Vieux Colombier*, Copeau created an acting area with a permanent but flexible setting consisting of a forward platform backed by a largely symmetrical arrangement of stairs, doors, levels, and an arched central recess. The over-all arrangement is reminiscent of contemporary ideas of the Elizabethan theatre, with its "inner below," its "above," and its forward platform. However, it clearly profited from the three-dimensional designs of Appia (with whom Copeau worked) and of Gordon Craig. Like other directors of the period, Copeau dominated his theatre, not perhaps in such an apparently dictatorial manner as Saxe-Meiningen or Reinhardt, but more as a master teacher controlling very talented students. The *Vieux Colombier* was, in part, a school for the dissemination of Copeau's creative thought. The Copeau ideal was something like the theatre of Molière, led and governed by the genius of the author-actor-producer, moving, as Molière had, to a complete unification of text and movement. The words *life* and *living* are central to many of Copeau's remarks about performance, and are rightfully reminiscent of Appia's "living art." However, for Copeau it was pre-eminently the actor, moving through space to the rhythms of the dramatic text, who was the vital source. On the fixed acting area of his theatre, Copeau sought a revitilization of theatre whose techniques can still be seen: a concept of setting that proclaims, not denies, "This is the theatre"; a reduction of all elements, and especially gesture, to the most potent theatrical essence; and concentration on the dramatic text as dominant. If there is such a thing today as a national style in various countries, one can say that, as Stanislavski created a Russian style and the Group Theater an American style, so Copeau created a French style.

One other major European innovator must be mentioned. Although his contributions to theatre theory have not been as far-reaching as those of the directors already mentioned, Vsevolod Meyerhold (1874–1942?) was an important director in the Russian theatre until the middle 1930s. Finally removed from his post as director of a Moscow theatre because of "aesthetic revisionism," or some similar flouting of the then mandatory social realism, he had been active in the Russian theatre as an innovator since World War I. Although his work went through several stages after his early years at the Moscow Art Theatre, Meyerhold's most significant contribution was his application of two anti-illusionist ideas, "biomechanics" and "constructivism." Both reflected an essential philosophical materialism, the one in relating human behavior to mechanics and the other in representing manmade and natural objects by a structural framework developed by modern technology. As an acting system, bio-mechanics owed something to Stanislavski's psychological gesture and something to Pavlovian response theory. In essence, it required that the actor respond automatically, within a limited range of mechanistic gestures, to stimuli. In practice, the stimulus seems to have been Meyerhold, who exercised rigid control over everything done on the stage. (It has been suggested that he left his actors so little scope for creative work that it was virtually impossible for him to keep actors in his company for long periods.) Meyerhold's theatrical constructivism was an extension of a movement in sculpture and architecture. Many of his settings—designed by him—were constructivist in their abstraction, their frank display of the materials from which they were made, and their total rejection of representation. A constructivist tree might be a jungle-gym of iron pipe; a constructivist mountain might be a corrugated-steel ramp. Meyerhold's actors could be expected to perform on swings, on playground slides, or over and under and around the set's structure. In brief, his was a theatrical theatre so far removed from illusionism that it represented an extreme in the staging of written plays (as opposed, that is, to nontextual theatre).

Meyerhold staged both new and classic texts, notably a now famous production of Gogol's classic, *The Inspector General.* His obvious affinities with expressionism, however, can best be seen in his having produced Vladimir Mayakovsky's *The Bedbug* in 1929, with music by Shostakovitch. The play was a satire of Soviet aspirations and bureaucracy, with an expressionistic use of machinelike characters and a protagonist who is frozen solid for fifty years—to be revived in a Communist Utopia where he, and his resident bedbug, are equally strange. The play was a failure, but it clearly represented to Meyerhold a dramatic embodiment of his own ideas of the theatre, as Patricia Blake has pointed out in the American collection of Mayakovsky's work.

Meyerhold disappeared from Moscow in the late 1930s. Clearly, his theatricalism was not acceptable in Stalinist Russia. Nevertheless, it had gained wide attention around the world and had many imitators. Constructivism is still an important style in design for both drama and dance.

Epic Theatre: Piscator and Brecht

Reinhardt, Copeau, and Meyerhold are representative of movements that were influenced to some degree by Appia and Craig through the 1920s and early 1930s. Even taking into account the materialism of Meyerhold's theories, it cannot be said of any of the three that he was primarily interested in dramatizing social protest or in presenting ideas didactically. However, in the 1930s there was an upsurge of sociopolitical didacticism in the theatre, seen in the United States in some of the plays of the Group Theater and in the "Living Newspaper" productions of the WPA Theater Project. The postwar theatre of Europe saw this tendency even more noticeably, to the extent that playwrights with strong social themes dominated the theatres through much of the 1950s in Germany, Switzerland, Eastern Europe, and England. The "workers' theatres" and the "agit-prop" (activist-propagandist) dramas of the Depression period were continued in more sophisticated forms (except in the United States, where, until the 1960s, social themes were generally subordinated to psychological ones).

Setting the pattern for didactic social drama and establishing its most effective theatrical conventions was the *epic theatre,* both a dramaturgical and a staging theory developed principally by the German director Erwin Piscator (1893–1967) and his early co-worker, Berthold Brecht (1898–1956). As a playwright, Brecht himself is unquestionably the most outstanding in the German-language theatre of the twentieth century. He was a director-manager, after 1949, at the famed Berliner Ensemble (still in vital existence this long after his death), the greatest practitioner of the epic—or Brechtian—style. Piscator's own contribution to the development of epic theatre is very important. It was he who coined the term, and he was able, even until the year of his death, to establish his principles of staging in a broad repertoire of classics and new plays. Piscator was both director and designer, and even carried his concepts into architectural designs. He was perhaps the experimentalist of epic theatre as Brecht was the dogmatist.

Epic theatre seeks to focus rational audience attention on the social and historical questions embodied in the performance. To accomplish this, it seeks above all else to destroy those aspects of the illusionistic theatre—especially identification and suspense—that encourage the loss of intellectual awareness and lulling of the critical sense. The devices created by Piscator and Brecht were many, but all had these same goals. In dramaturgy, the de-emphasis of plot (for its own sake) was sought; therefore, the well-made play could be seen as the antithesis of epic structure. Brecht himself, and others after him, have called epic theatre narrative rather than dramatic, meaning that epic theatre sought to present events in the cooler, more objective form of the narrative instead of the hot, subjective form of a drama where those events were given the illusion of really taking place. Where nonepic theatre might concentrate on events for their own sake, as effects, epic theatre would concentrate on the causes of events.

The particular devices used, especially by Brecht, were those associated with the theatre itself, rather than with representations of life: masks, signs and slogans, direct audience address, songs (used obviously as interpolations, not in the integrated fashion of the American musical), an acting area that is clearly that, and nonrepresentational scenery. It should be evident that these devices have much in common with other nonillusionistic theatres. Masks, slogans, and nonrepresentational scenery were common in the expressionistic theatre; the acting area as platform was essential to Copeau; songs commenting on the action were frequently found in agit-prop drama. As used by Brecht and Piscator, however, these techniques took on a different feeling and were made parts of a remarkably coherent whole. In the productions of Brecht's own plays, they were particularly successful.

Brecht's career in the theatre showed considerable change in style and attack from his youthful work, in the 1920s, to the mature productions of the Berliner Ensemble. Throughout virtually all of that career, however, ran a dominant concern with Marxism and a didactic, dialectic theatre. Although his early plays, such as *Baal* (1920) and *In the Swamp* (1922), were influenced by expressionism, the plays from the mid-1920s on were Marxist and didactic. *Saint Joan of the Stockyards* (1929), although it owes something to both Shaw's *Saint Joan* and the expressionists, is heading toward epic theatre in its structure and its use of such devices as a group chorus. *The Threepenny Opera* (1929), based loosely on the English *Beggar's Opera* by John Gay (1728), de-emphasizes plot, discourages emotional identification through the use of songs and a highly ironic tone, and ends with a frankly contrived, antirealistic resolution. Although in the 1930s Brecht wrote a few rigorously didactic—and colossally dull—pieces like *The Measures Taken*, the great plays of his maturity were written during those years and the 1940s: *Puntilla* (1941), *Mother Courage* (1939), *The Good Woman of Setzuan* (1940), *The Caucasian Chalk Circle* (1945), and *Galileo* (1938). Each of these plays is both Marxist dialectic and deeply affecting theatrical experience. Each accomplishes the double point of revealing for the audience's critical judgment an unjust social situation and of creating opportunities for the richest kind of epic theatre. In these best of Brechtian didactic plays, there is always a very specific Marxist message, but it coexists with brilliant theatre. The theatrical brilliance is not the sugar coating for the pill of dialectic, but the natural embodiment of dialectic in action.

One further aspect of Brechtian theory must be mentioned, if only because it has gained notoriety through excessive critical discussion. Brecht postulated a metaphor for the audience effect of his theatre— *Verfremdung*, translated into English as *alienation*—that sought to epitomize the goal of all epic techniques. This alienation effect, or A-effect, is not to be taken in the sense of something that will negatively alienate an audience, or turn it against the performance, but rather in the sense of something that will objectify the audience attitude (as a psychiatrist—an alienist, in England—helps one to objectify his attitude toward his own behavior). Thus, Brechtians may speak of alienation techniques when they discuss the epic devices in Brecht's own plays.

Brecht's theatre, the Berliner Ensemble, became to the mid-twentieth century what the Meiningers were to the nineteenth. They proved a revelation and an inspiration to theatre men throughout Europe (Eastern and Western) as well as in the United States. The troupe's visit to England in 1956 has been credited as the event from which the emergence of the new British theatre can be dated. American observers, perhaps because of their conditioning to the fairly naturalistic American style, have found the Ensemble equally inspiring, but many have commented that, within the epic techniques and the brilliant group performance, the basic acting approach seems to be very like that of Stanislavski. Although it is true that Brecht himself, at his death, was still trying to work out a definition and systematization of epic acting, it is doubtful that the great Brechtian actors like his widow, Helene Weigel, are as concerned with detailed inner life as Stanislavskian actors. It has proved true, in the United States at least, that the most devout practitioners of Stanislavskian acting have often failed in important Brechtian roles. One reason would seem to be the subjective truth of Stanislavskian acting, which does not jibe with the objective comment on the role—the alienation of the character from the actor— that epic theatre demands. Another reason would be the fundamental theatricalism of Brechtian theatre, a presentation of the performance for the audience's study and enjoyment that would be quite foreign to an actor with an obsessive internalism. Finally, Brecht's own expression for the dialectic effect of epic acting, "this, not that," or the externalizing of a character's decisions to show their causes and the choices involved, might not even occur to actors raised in a tradition of not "editorializing" a character and of not interpreting the *meaning* of a character's actions, but only the truthfulness of those actions.

The future influence of Brecht cannot, of course, be predicted. In the tradition of Reinhardt, he left models of his productions, expanded *Regiebuchs* with detailed photographs and drawings for other directors to use. His plays have been staged throughout the world and have been published in many languages, and his writings on the theatre have been widely read. Nevertheless, within a decade of his death, his influence in Eastern Europe waned, and there are indications that in England and the United States he now is as dated as the agit-prop plays of the 1930s. If a single reason can be found for this apparent decline, it may be that the basic ideas of alienation—of objectivity and critical judgment—from the audience were antipathetic to the 1960s. It was an age of involvement and of the union of performer and audience, rather than of their separation.

Still, Brecht's impact on the theatre of the 1950s and the early 1960s was tremendous. In England, the direct effects of his plays and his theories can be seen in such dramas as John Osborne's *Luther* (1961) and Robert Bolt's *A Man for All Seasons* (1960) and in the staging of directors like Peter Brook. In Germany, his epic style was adopted by Rolf Hochuth in *The Deputy* (1963) and in *The Soldiers* (1967) and by Peter Weiss in both the German version of *Marat-Sade* (1964) and in his *The Investigation* (1965). In Switzerland, the internationally important playwright Frederich Duerenmatt has shown Brechtian influence in such plays as *The Visit* (1956). In theatre design, the combined work of Brecht and Erwin Piscator can be felt in the now widespread use of projected scenery, of side stages or ramp stages that encircle the audience, and of such individual scenic elements as practical, miniature houses and cut-away buildings.

Pirandello, Giraudoux, and Anouilh

Of less general influence than Brecht, but of great importance in the nonillusionistic theatre of the twentieth century, are several playwrights whose plays have dominated their national theatres during their own lifetimes. Of them, the most outstanding was the Italian dramatist Luigi Pirandello (1867–1936), whose highly individual style represented one extreme of the avant-garde theatre almost until his death. Other Europeans whose work was neither epic, on the one hand, nor expressionist or surreal, on the other, include the French playwrights Jean Giraudoux (1882–1944) and Jean Anouilh (b. 1907), whereas in America the outstanding one has been Thornton Wilder (b. 1897).

Pirandello's exploitation of the theatre itself as the setting for action, and his parallel development of the theme of intermingled illusion and reality, gave rise to a school of imitative "pirandellism." During the 1920s and 1930s, a mannered imitation of the surface of Pirandello's dramaturgy characterized the plays of many other writers, and even today his copies can be found. The originals, however, had far more to them than the mere questioning of perceptual reality. In his greatest plays (as well as his novels) Pirandello set forth a world of suffering and of isolated individuals, and his use of the theatre as a place of illusion was largely a metaphor for the greater world, where suffering was reality and the questioning of perceptual phenomena was a kind of entertainment. This approach to experience was especially clear in *Right You Are (If You Think You Are)* (1918), whose very title suggests the standoff reached in any battle between beliefs. The play's action is the attempt by the gossipy members of a middle-class society to resolve the contradictions in their versions of the same experience between two newcomers. The play ends with the entrance of the veiled woman who supposedly reveals the truth, but she can say only that both versions are true and that she must suffer as a result. In *Henry IV* (also known as *The Emperor*, 1922) the same questions are raised concerning the conflicts between memory and fact, between madness and supposed sanity, and again the questions are not resolved but are merely confronted with each other and with the fact of violent death at the play's end. *Six Characters in Search of an Author* (1921) is one of several plays about the theatre itself, and along with *Tonight We Improvise* (1930), it represents the most searching use of the theatre itself as a mirror of illusions until the existential plays of the 1950s. In all, Pirandello's work is a brilliant use of the devices of the theatre of illusion to attack and anatomize the very foundation of that theatre itself, the representation of "reality." Although much of Pirandello's work has never been translated into English, he has been widely produced in the United States and, three decades after his death, seems still to command the attention that his plays did during his lifetime.

Jean Giraudoux was not the innovator that Pirandello was, but his position in the modern French theatre has importance because of the sense of responsibility with which he approached it. A professional diplomat as well as a writer, Giraudoux was deeply concerned with ethical questions, rationally analyzed. His importation of reason and ethics into a corrupted theatre concerned solely with light entertainment and titillation amounted to little less than a renascence for that theatre. His forms were old, even classical; his sense of seriousness was new.

Urbane, witty, and worldly, Giraudoux wrote plays whose generally fanciful (or fantastic) resolutions undercut the validity of the problem they seemed to solve. A bit reminiscent of Maeterlinck in his willingness to dramatize a world of magic and fantasy, he could, in a play like *The Madwoman of Chaillot* (1945), present a theatrical image of a corrupt and evil world that, for most of the play, is bitterly convincing and comically true. However, the impact of his conviction and his truth are frittered away in a closing scene where goodness and love prevail, without regard to the impotence of those qualities in the world the play purports to represent. Similarly, in *Tiger at the Gates* (also called *The Trojan War Will Not Take Place*, 1935) the real horrors of war become submerged in the horror of loss of reason, and the pessimistic conclusion of the play is not so much an ability to foresee the atrocities of the wars of the 1940s, 1950s, and 1960s as it is merely a cynical tongue-clucking over the fact that human beings are not always logical. Such plays as these were very effective at the time they were written; they may now seem too bound to that time, and too much without originality to speak freshly to a later day.

Jean Anouilh, like Giraudoux, writes in a traditional, and even classic, form that owes something to Molière, to French Romanticism, and to the elaborate farces of the late nineteenth century. Again, like Giraudoux, his plays suggest an urbane and slightly cynical author, brilliantly articulate and capable of inventing startling theatrical images. Anouilh himself is a very productive playwright, one whose work crosses generic categories and can range from the pageantlike sweep of *The Lark* (1953), a play about Joan of Arc that is strongly reminiscent of Shaw's *Saint Joan*, to romantic farce-fantasy in *Thieves' Carnival* (1932), to bitter comedy about missed opportunity and atrophied ideals in *Waltz of the Toreadors* (1952). Many of his plays have been staged in the United States, and a number have been commercial successes. If he now seems overshadowed by the French playwrights of the 1950s and 1960s it is probably because, despite the brilliance of his dialogue and the impressive versatility of his subjects, he, like Giraudoux, has never created a theatrical form of greater contemporary impact than the one that tradition gave him.

Thornton Wilder holds, among American playwrights, the position of having written the best known play of his time. *Our Town* (1938) has found its audience at every level from secondary schools to Broadway, as well as around the world in both Europe and Asia. It may be paradoxical that Wilder is a relatively unproductive playwright and that only one other play of his, *The Skin of Our Teeth* (1942), has claimed such wide attention. Nevertheless, for these two plays alone, Wilder had until recently the reputation of being the most innovative and experimental of American playwrights. Certainly the theatrical form of both these plays suggests a search for a new, nonillusionistic form. Both plays cut across time and space in their actions and both require a stage representation of spatial relations that is far from realistic. *Our Town* substitutes a bare stage and simple furniture for scenery, and for this reason it may seem deceptively simple to stage. *The Skin of Our Teeth* telescopes the history of man and substitutes literary and historical allusion for linear development of idea. (For example, Sabina, one of the principal characters, is both the maid in what seems to be a contemporary household and one of the Sabine women. Mr. Antrobus, the protagonist, is both head of the household and Adam. His son is Cain, a modern youth, and also the archetypal enemy of humanism. At one point in the play, Antrobus takes on the attributes of Noah before the flood, and again he gathers into his endangered suburban house such real and fictional figures as Homer, the Muses, and a dinosaur.) From Pirandello, Wilder seems to have adopted the use of the theatre itself as a partial locale for action, and in *The Skin of Our Teeth* the characters' action is interrupted by the supposed difficulties of the actors playing those characters. Wilder's plays keep the classical sense of action and of cause and effect, but they cast those familiar dramatic elements in a poetic and symbolic mold that seeks to give them universal importance. At worst, the direct statements about experience that arise in these plays occasionally seem pretentious; at best, Wilder's restless search for new ways to present human experience creates a refreshingly vivid theatrical moment.

Artaud, Cruelty, and the New Theatre

In the years during and immediately after World War II, many national theatres were relatively static or were in a transitional phase that was so slow to develop it could not immediately be seen. In the United States, Thornton Wilder's poetic theatre was not widely imitated, and the dominant tone continued to be illusionistic. In England, a brief flirtation with verse drama—especially that of T. S. Eliot (1888–1965) and Christopher Fry (b. 1907)—proved sterile and has seemed to have no recent proponents. The real postwar renascence of British theatre dates from Joan Littlewood's work of the early 1950s, and especially from John Osborne's "angry" play, *Look Back in Anger* (1956). In France, Jean Anouilh remained a prolific and successful writer. However, indications of a vigorous step away from his and Giraudoux' kind of theatre could be seen in the plays of Jean-Paul Sartre (b. 1905) and Albert Camus (1913–1960). Both of these existentialist writers sought to create a theatrical embodiment of the existential condition, and despite the thesis-play tone of much of Sartre's work, it is largely to him that we can credit the first postwar innovations in French drama. In Germany, as we have already pointed out, the influence of Brecht was dominant until recently and is still strong.

Nevertheless, by the middle 1950s a remarkable change could be seen in the French theatre, and that change had an only slightly delayed impact in England and the United States. This new theatre, called, with dubious accuracy, the "theatre of the absurd" by Martin Esslin in his book of that name, crystallized around new playwrights and new plays that challenged and virtually negated traditional dramatic values. It was absurd in that it sought to dramatize the absurdity of cold-war, atom-bomb, mass-media existence. Its method was sometimes absurd, as well, when it sought to be "antitheatrical"—illogical, nonsequential, and without motivated psychology or rationally comprehensible language. Still, the important point about this new theatre was not that it presented illogic, absurd psychology, or irrational language (after all, Oscar Wilde had done all those things), but that it rejected the concept that the theatre must mirror the surface reality of life.

Its philosophical base was existentialism. Its ideas of character and situation were metaphysical, not psychological or social. Its inspiring genius was a man already dead, Antonin Artaud (1896–1948).

More than Sartre and more than Camus, Artaud has given a voice to the impulses that mark such diverse theatre work as that of Jean Genet (b. 1910), Eugene Ionesco (b. 1912), Samuel Beckett (b. 1906), Harold Pinter (b. 1930), and Edward Albee (b. 1928). At one time a surrealist poet, then a film maker, an actor, and a playwright, Artaud ranged widely to find analogs for his own idea of the theatre, and he found those analogs in ceremonies and performances as different as those of American Indian tribes and the ritual dances of Bali. His mental balance was shaky, and most of the last decade of his life was spent in a mental institution. Even as a young man, his inability to accept logically structured language as a meaningful equivalent of phenomena was evident. For him words were not effective symbols of the things they were supposed to represent. Therefore, in his theatre some other means of symbolic discourse would have to be found. The playwright whose work most closely approximates Artaud's idea of theatre, Jean Genet, has spoken of the "profound web of active symbols" in which such a theatre must speak. With this rejection of language comes the rejection of logic and of causal sequence, or plot. In their places should come the continuing arousal and involvement of each member of the theatre audience, surrounded by the theatre performance and yet a part of it, recognizing the profound symbols with a part of one's consciousness that is beyond the intellectual.

The great bulk of Artaud's writing has not been translated into English, but the collection called *The Theater and Its Double* has had wide currency. It is, of course, contradictory that a man who trusted neither logic nor language should express himself in a more or less logical manner in written language. However, in that contradiction lies the essence of Artaud's concept and his personal torment. Out of his published work have come two important ideas, that of the theatre as a "double" of existence, and that of the "Theatre of Cruelty." The two are not really separable, for Artaud saw the universe as cruel (his word

Figure 2–50. Beckett's *Endgame* at the Hartford Stage Company, 1966, directed by Jacques Cartier, with Charles Cioffi (Hamm) and David Birney (Clov). (*Courtesy Hartford Stage Company.*)

for the mystery, the paradox, and the suffering that he seemed constantly to find), and any theatre that presented images of such a universe would itself become cruel. Yet, the word must not be taken literally to mean sadistic—that is, a theatre of horrors. The most famous Theatre of Cruelty production in the English-speaking world has been Peter Brook's *Marat-Sade* (1964–1965), admittedly a production that relied on shocking images (many of them verbal) of physical violation and torture. On the other hand, Artaud's love of such highly stylized theatre forms as the Balinese dance-drama clearly indicates that he could conceive of a theatre in which cruel events are themselves symbolized by abstract gestures. It is in this context that his metaphor of the theatre as a double (not, significantly, a mirror) is important. The mirror reflects surface flaws: a man finds a pimple on his nose; Arthur Miller finds Willy Loman in American society. The double creates images of cruelty: Doctor Frankenstein creates a monster-man; Samuel Beckett creates the situation of *Endgame*.

Like all the idealistic theoreticians we have seen, Artaud expressed most pointedly the theatre ideas of an entire period. For the time being, those ideas may be applied too literally, as were the ideas of Corneille, Zola, Craig, and Appia.

Samuel Beckett's *Endgame*

Of the contemporary playwrights whose work can be said to function within Artaud's idea of theatre, probably none has had such wide influence as Samuel Beckett. One of the triumvirate of dramatists writing in French in the 1950s who can truly be said to have constituted an avant garde (the others being Ionesco and Genet), Beckett's unsparing pictures of human isolation would seem to represent one extreme in the reduction of drama to its essentials. Where both Genet and Ionesco have developed an exotic rhetoric for their characters, Beckett has used a sparse vocabulary, a typically choppy rhythm of short, simple sentences, and above all, the highly charged silence— the void—that is created between disconnected statements. Where Ionesco and Genet have created bizarre situations—a world of men turning into beasts in Ionesco's *Rhinoceros* (1958), a brothel peopled by sexual fantasists in Genet's *The Balcony* (1956)—Beckett has turned increasingly to placelessness for his: a mound of sand in *Happy Days* (1961), a plain with a single tree in *Waiting for Godot* (1952), an old man's room in *Krapp's Last Tape* (1955). At the same time, he has concentrated on very small casts with very restricted physical circumstances: Winnie is buried to her waist, then to her neck, in *Happy Days*, and the only other character is seldom visible; Krapp is alone with his tape recorder in *Krapp's Last Tape*.

Beckett is not a notably prolific playwright. Early in his career he wrote several short novels. Like his friend James Joyce, he is Irish, and he seems to share Joyce's fascination with the malleable and interchangeable nature of words. His plays contain many puns, double meanings, and misunderstood variants of simple words. Although he usually writes in French, he translates his own plays into English. This practice suggests some of the care he gives to his dramatic language, although the apparent simplicity of that language might be misleading. It would be wrong to suggest that Beckett is opposed to the use of language in the theatre; rather, language is his most important tool— not because he uses it directly to express ideas (like, let us say, Shakespeare), but because it is in the very failure of that language to express anything but a painful questioning that his plays gain their greatest strength.

CHARACTER AND SITUATION. It would be useless to discuss plot in a play like *Endgame*, because the play has very little inner causality. (The term *endgame* is used in chess to describe the final moves leading to checkmate—as fitting a metaphor as any for the play's "plot.") Although there is progression and sequence, and although there is a discernible dramatic action, the end of the play is intentionally unresolved. Its situation, therefore, and its characters must have our first attention.

At the play's opening the audience is faced with an almost empty interior setting, later referred to as "the shelter." At the rear are two windows and on one side, a door. At the center a seated figure is covered with a cloth; near him two ashcans are also covered. The first character we see is Clov, a bestial, crippled man who apparently serves as caretaker and nurse of the others, whom he reveals as he pulls away the cloths: Hamm, a blind and crippled middle-aged man in the chair, center; and Nagg (an old man) and Nell (an old woman) each in his own ashcan. The situation in which these four find themselves seems to be unchanging and virtually unchangeable. The audience can see nothing through the two windows, and when Clov, with great difficulty because of his physical disability, climbs a ladder to look out, he reports that everything is "corpsed." One window, we learn, gives on the land, the other on the sea. Somewhere beyond the one door is Clov's kitchen, with a food cupboard that is locked with a lock to which only Hamm has the combination.

Of an outside world there is almost nothing to learn. In the past, it seems, Hamm had been a landowner, and he speaks of "Kov, beyond the gulf," but where that was we never know. Nagg and Nell, who are far older, slip into senile nostalgia about such recognizable places as Sedan, the Ardennes, and Lake Como, and Nagg tells a story about an Englishman, but these places have a fantastic quality and seem to have no real existence. Hamm speaks of going "south," but no destination is indicated. In short, the location of this strange room cannot be fixed in either place or time, except to say that its world overlaps ours and its time is close enough to ours so that telephones, combination locks, and guns are known.

The emotional relationships among the characters, however, are very clear. Hamm, who dominates the play both physically and verbally, is Nagg's son and is a kind of father to Clov. As he is the visual center of the play, so he is the center of a three-stage father-son sequence, and he has the same ambivalent, volatile relationship with each of the others. Nagg is, to him, the "accursed progenitor," the father despised for giving him existence; nevertheless, he needs his father as an intelligent listener to his lengthy stories. In the same way, Clov seems to hate Hamm, even to the point of wanting to kill him. The two men go on and on, attacking each other and appealing to each other, as they shift from hatred to emotional dependence. "Why this farce, day after day?" is a question asked in several forms throughout the play, and the tentative answer, "The dialogue," seems correct. In dialogue—the talking that requires two people—lies the salvation of each from solitude, isolation, and "infinite emptiness." The physical interdependencies of the three men reflect their emotional interdependencies, then, and Hamm's knowledge of the combination of the food cupboard needs Clov's eyes and Clov's legs if the cupboard is to open. Again, Nagg must have Hamm's permission if he is to get food, but Hamm must have Nagg's

Figure 2–51. Beckett's *Endgame* at the Cherry Lane Theater, New York. Directed by Alan Schneider. It is almost the end of the play, and Clov, loaded with his belongings, seems ready to depart. Of the skis, paddle, rope, and all the other gear Clov carries, the director said, "I wanted to suggest all kinds of transportation; I wanted to use snowshoes, too. As a kind of gag. . . . You could say that Beckett's *Waiting for Godot* is a play about an arrival that never takes place." The director's choice of Clov's props at this point underscores his last remark. Of the setting itself, which is the brick wall of the actual theatre with windows painted on it, Schneider said, "The bricks are real; the windows are painted. But they are *real* to Clov." He added, "I think those crumbling bricks have a texture that is better than any flat could possibly be. Not gloomy, but decaying, falling apart, yet still solid." It could be noted that this "texture" is carried through the robe on Hamm's lap, the props that Clov carries, and the ashcans of Nagg and Nell (reinforced, in their case, with careful painting). (*Photo, Miss Alix Jeffry.*)

listening ear if he is to tell the story that he seems so desperate to tell. The old woman, Nell, exists on the periphery of all this—physically and emotionally—no longer interested in eating, moribund, and almost totally lost in memories of things that may or may not have happened. She alone seems to be capable of joy, however fragile and however based on fantasy, and she alone seems to show a love (for Nagg) that requires nothing in return. But her love is impotent and she is totally passive, saying no to every question before she even understands what is being asked. Saying no to life, to everything around her, she dies in her ashcan with hardly a flicker of interest from Hamm and Clov. "The dead go fast," says Hamm.

There *is* forward momentum generated in the play. In a question so forthright that it is virtually a comment about the play itself, Hamm asks, "What's happening?" at important moments, and Clov's answer —"Something is taking its course"—is virtually a description of the play's action. That "something" is Clov's elaborate preparation to leave Hamm and the others. As it takes its course, other things happen as well: Nell dies; Nagg may die; Hamm invents an elaborate story that turns out to be an autobiographical account of his adoption of Clov as a little boy; and near the end of the play Clov thinks he sees another small boy standing outside. When, at the very end, Hamm delivers a lengthy and moving soliloquy on his solitude (his mother and father apparently dead, Clov standing in the door without a sound so that Hamm thinks him already gone), we are presented with a quandary: is this, indeed, the end of the game of relationships, or will Clov stay after all? Will Clov take in the new little boy (if he exists) and begin a new cycle, in which he will become Hamm and Hamm will take Nagg's place? What has happened? Something has taken—or is still taking—its course.

IDEA.   Beckett has resolutely refused to explain his plays, for the perfectly good reason that they have total life in performance. If they raise questions (as they certainly do.), they do not have to raise answers as well. If this theatre is a double of life, it is a double of a life in which, as we well know, we are surrounded with unanswered questions.

It is still possible, however, to see a perfectly concrete and comprehensible set of questions being created, and in that creation lies the idea of *Endgame*. It is not unfair to compare it with such other enigmatic dramas as *Hamlet* or *King Lear*, which also raise more questions than they can answer. As in those plays, we have a human situation and human beings of such devastating reality that we must not ask them to give us pat little explications of their own text. *Endgame* surely sets up the following ideas as the facts, or observations, that it has carried over from its real-world double: man is haunted by the fear of perpetual solitude, doomed to seek the comfort of his kind and then to suffer their rejection; human life is a partly funny, partly horrifying complex of physical disability, mental decay, inadequate verbal communication, and an aspiring mind that can never accomplish its own goals; God may very well exist, but in what manner and to what purpose is tantalizingly out of reach; mostly, adult existence is unrelenting suffering, relieved only by a selective memory of times that at least seem better than the present, and by sleep, dreams, and death.

As in all other matters in this play, Hamm is central to such ideas. His very name is emblematic, for he is both a ham actor, given to verbose set speeches and tear-jerking self-pity, and an after-image of Hamlet in his poetic creativeness and his introspection. (Indeed,

Beckett may be carrying the pun as far as the implication that a Hamlet is a little Hamm.) The others contribute, as well, and their names are equally emblematic: Clov is a clod and is a kind of cloven-hoofed devil to Hamm; Nagg is a broken-down old warhorse and a simple nag to his son; Nell, in her giving in to death, is the knell that sounds for everyone in the play. Such plays on the names are part of Beckett's careful manipulation of his language, as discussed earlier. Throughout the play the same multiple meanings are given to other words, most importantly to the bloody handkerchief that covers Hamm's face at the beginning of the play, and with which he covers it at the end. *Stancher* is his word for the handkerchief—it stanches the flow of his blood; it is a staunch friend; and it carries the stench of death. His final words are profoundly moving, the address of a solitary, terrified human being to the object that has soaked up his lifeblood: "Old stancher! (*Pause.*) You remain."

Other words occur again and again in this play, and all suggest the same field of interest: *emptiness, corpsed, zero, suffer, gray, hollow,*

Figure 2–52. Hamm in *Endgame* at the Cherry Lane Theatre, New York. Directed by Alan Schneider. Reaching toward the audience and ultimately dismissing them with this gesture, Hamm nears the end of his final soliloquy. He seems to accept Clov's leaving, in this play that the director says is about "a departure that never takes place. . . . It would be ideal to stage it both ways [that is, so that Clov's final action can be either a departure or a decision to stay]. The audience should be able to argue both sides with equal validity. That, I think, is Beckett's point." Lester Rawlins as Hamm. (*Photo, Miss Alix Jeffry.*)

pain, darkness, end. They all suggest the void in which Beckett's people live, the void of Hamm's blindness, the spatial void with which he is surrounded, the voids of miniature universes within the "hollow bricks" of which his walls are made, and the voids of pauses that exist between the words and the phrases of Beckett's dialogue. The play itself has been presented as having many external realities, including a recent nuclear war and an interpretation of the entire setting as the interior of a human head; but grafting on such realities is unnecessary. In *Endgame*, something is indeed taking its course, and we must follow that course and *not* ask superficial questions about the something. We are asked to join in an exploration of a void, and if all that such an exploration reveals is still more void, the exploration itself can still be theatrically compelling.

RECENT AMERICAN THEATRE

The importance of Artaud and Beckett to the European theatre was, as we have seen, very great; and the recent awarding of the Nobel Prize to Beckett was the supreme admission of the awareness of his importance. Yet, his position in the United States (much less Artaud's) throughout the 1950s seemed very minor. Plays like *Waiting for Godot* were greeted with open ridicule by many of the more entrenched commodity-theatre reviewers, and, despite a fairly rapid acceptance of Beckett (along with Ionesco, Genet, and others) in American universities, the visible impact on American theatre was very slight. Until about 1960, "avant-garde" in the United States meant European; there was, it seemed, no alternative to the commercial mainstream of New York theatre.

That theatre was still dominated, in serious drama, by Arthur Miller and Tennessee Williams; in comedy, the zany farceurs (particularly Moss Hart and George S. Kaufman) were mostly inactive, and in their places were a group of writers of "sophisticated" (that is, covertly sexual) comedies with an eye, if not both eyes, on sales to the movies. The musical comedy (America's only native theatrical form, according to her less kind critics) held to much the same sort of thing it had been doing since the Agnes de Mille-Oscar Hammerstein-Richard Rodgers innovative hit, *Oklahoma* (1942). The dominant acting techniques were those of Stanislavski, as proselytized by the Actors Studio. The dominant forms in stage design were exemplified by Jo Mielziner, designer of the New York setting for *Death of a Salesman*, and an artist of post-Appia realism.

The American theatre of 1949–1960 was not really a great deal different from the theatre of a decade or two before. Gone, it is true, were the Depression plays and the agit-prop plays, the Group Theatre and the Mercury Theatre; present, for the first time, were an "Off-Broadway" theatre with some style of its own and the beginnings of decentralization of the professional theatre. Nonetheless, there were signs of stagnation, as if the dominant theater aesthetics had held sway for too long. Change during the 1960s—and with it, new faces, new names, new "isms"—seemed inevitable.

1949–1962: The Aesthetic of Euphemism

The American theatre of the 1950s seemed to be grounded firmly in realism. The characteristics of its plays were very much the characteristics of earlier realistic drama—reliance on the three-act form (including the completion of the action and the answering of all questions before the final curtain), imitation of recognizable environments, peopled by recognizable types; and the use of symbols to extend the meanings of the play and to state by suggestion what apparently could not be stated openly.

For the theatre of the 1950s was a theatre of euphemism, a euphemism born of certain repressions within its society. It was a communal theatre in that it did embody the values of its audience, but that audience was no longer the total society and it was beginning to dwindle toward that homogeneous segment that it became in the 1960s. Its values were more or less the values of the well-to-do American living-room, still somewhat Puritanical, still unwilling to hear sounds from

Figure 2–53. Arthur Kopit's *Indians* at the Hilberry Classic Theatre of Wayne State University, 1972. Directed by Don Blakely, with settings by Russell Paquette, costumes by Vic Leverett, and lighting by Gary M. Witt.

the bedroom or the oddball house down the street or the ghetto a few miles away. And, confronted with the aesthetic imperative that it must still try to help its audience to "think the unthinkable," the American theatre of the period came to rely heavily on understatement and suggestive statement, through a set of conventions as useful as those practiced in the films of the same period. In the case of the more "daring" playwrights like Tennessee Williams, symbolic statement replaced overt statement. Broad areas of subject matter were taboo; some were legally so because of statutes concerning, for example, obscenity and nudity; some were traditionally so, as in the case of politics; and some existed because of sheer ignorance. In general, the taboos fell into the following four areas:

Overt Sexuality. The portrayal of sex on the stage was illegal in New York City, and still is in many parts of the United States. Social mores prohibited the public viewing of overt sexuality, which was traditionally the province of a thriving pornography industry. Nudity was also forbidden. (Predictably, of course, the near-presentation of nudity and sexuality were very profitable; strip shows prospered, dirty jokes abounded, and "girlie" magazines grew like the green bay tree.) Any open discussion in the theatre of divergent kinds of sexuality, especially homosexuality, was unthinkable. Where a sexually different character was implied—as, for example, in a number of Williams's plays—it was always as an outsider, a deviate, a curiosity. In comedy, sexuality provided a gold mine of *double entendre* gags, and the "will she or won't she?" plot sustained some otherwise thin work. In retrospect from the 1970s, one is inclined to wonder what was either funny or interesting about many of them.

Radical Politics. The American theatre has long had a tradition of not presenting an incumbent President on the stage, thus rather effectively denying a large area of political satire to the theatre. As well, the presentation of politics has always been something less than acute, the good humor and inoffensiveness of a musical like *Of Thee I Sing!* (1931) being an example. The play *Affairs of State* (1951) managed to feature a national political candidate without ever mentioning his party. Truly radical points of view were unknown, except for a few of the agit-prop plays of the 1930s. In the 1950s, radical points of view were relatively unknown throughout the whole society, for which some are inclined to blame Joseph McCarthy and others simply a national state of inertia. Whatever inheritance of political concern the theatre may have had from an earlier period, by the mid-1950s it was mostly rather nostalgic—idealistic, hopeful, and evolutionary, but not revolutionary.

Racial Honesty. As in politics, the social goals of the 1950s were, at least as publicly expressed, idealistic and optimistic. Racial integration, made a national goal by the 1954 Supreme Court decision, was given much lip service. Racial blindness seemed like a virtue; the celebration of racial identity, black or white, was taboo. The 1947 musical, *Finian's Rainbow*, was the theatre's idea of racial co-existence; in its lovely fantasy, a white Southern demagogue learns tolerance by being turned into a black—he becomes personally integrated. Yet the "happy ending" is a white happiness, and the very setting—the American South—was comfortably distant from the New York audience.

Language. The words that described the other taboos were themselves taboo. Virtually the entire language of sex, both vulgar and scientific, went unheard in the theatre (except in the lobby, the dressing rooms, and the work areas, of course); ethnic language was unknown, probably as much from ignorance as intent (although "black" and "nigger" were used for shock effects). The language of the stage, like the (supposed) language of the living room, was antiseptic.

The Alternative Theatre, 1950–1960

If the audience for the mainstream (Broadway) theatre was tending more and more to become a single, thin slice of an increasingly diversified society, there were still many people from other areas of that society with a hunger for theatre. An alternative theatre was needed for an alternative audience. When, then, Off-Broadway became not only a geographical area but also a kind of theatre in the early 1950s, that alternative audience was ready for it. Classics, European plays (especially from the new European avant-garde) and American plays in a new idiom made up the great bulk of Off-Broadway's offerings in its best years.

Although there had always been scattered, often nonprofessional productions beyond the limits of the Broadway (uptown) theatre district, the alternative theatre gained its identity in large part from recognition by Actors Equity (and, subsequently, others of the theatre unions) in the form of special contracts for the small theatres in which its plays were housed. The maximum number of seats (fewer than three hundred), salaries, number of Equity actors, and other conditions were spelled out. Requirements were economically generous enough to make the production of plays with smaller-than-Broadway potential stageable. With the smaller theatres and new plays came other innovations: increased use of thrust and in-the-round staging and a shift in emphasis in acting to an Americanized classic style and to a new, performance-geared use of improvisation. The former gave greater scope to young American actors appearing in the Off-Broadway revivals of Shaw, Shakespeare, Molière, and all the classics that Americans had neglected for a generation. The latter became popular with performing groups such as the Second City, from Chicago, and The Premise.

Despite the excitement generated by Off-Broadway (and it was truly exciting for new playwrights, for young actors, for audiences seeking an alternative to commodity theatre, and for critics seeking relief from Broadway), the new, smaller theatres did not substantially change the theatre's taboos. To be sure, shock waves ran through audiences in 1958 during Jean Genet's *The Balcony*. It offered a polymorphous view of sexuality that many audience members associated with the illicit and the illegal, and it was couched in a language to match. In 1961, Genet's *The Blacks* gave white audiences a preview of the coming racial mood of the 1960s. The effect on American writers, however, was more formal than contentual. In the early (Off-Broadway) plays of Edward Albee, the influence of Ionesco and even of Beckett can be seen in dialogue structure, in the use of a new, open-ended form that did not even pretend to answer the questions raised by the play, and in a comfortable acceptance of the short play as an artistically respectable form. And even when Albee established himself as the most important of the new playwrights with *Who's Afraid of Virginia Woolf?* (1962), the effects of the Europeans could be seen in the play's highly ambiguous game action and in its open ending. Nonetheless, much of the tons of paper devoted to that important play at the time noted that Albee had finally "graduated" to the uptown theatre and the "full-length" play. In effect, mainstream theatre values had not changed much. Off-Broadway and the European avant-garde would not bring about the collapse of the old taboos. (Indeed, Off-Broadway and the European avant-garde spawned a short-lived group of absurdist parodies, particularly by Murray Shisgal, whose play *Luv*—a pastiche of Beckett, Ionesco, Albee, and television gags—underscored the tenacity of the traditional forms: on Broadway, the same old Broadway audience chuckled at the follies of those far-out nuts.)

In 1959, critic Robert Brustein wrote an essay titled "Why American Drama Is Not Literature." The title itself is significant. Its negativism is typical of the period. Its emphasis on drama as literature (not theatre) shows where—perhaps mistakenly—the blame was being laid. And the date of the essay is significant, as well, for it marks a kind of turning point: The American theatre was to be revitalized by a sudden influx of talent at every level—acting, writing, producing, and directing —and the old taboos were to collapse. In 1959, the values of the theatre were still the values of the 1940s; the audience was Broadway's and the old repressions were stifling. By 1969, values could be defined only for the community that each kind of theatre was reaching; the taboos were greatly weakened, even moribund, and the audience for all levels of theatre seemed to be finding renewed life.

The Decline of Taboo: Underground and Off-Off

Even as Off-Broadway reached its most vigorous growth, attaining respect from critics, audiences, and actors in the late 1950s and early

1960s, an alternative to Off-Broadway appeared. (The turning point for Off-Broadway was marked by any or all of several events: the regular attendance by reviewers from the major New York newspapers; or the willingness, even eagerness, of established actors to appear Off-Broadway; or the announcement by a Broadway producer that he was going into Off-Broadway production.) Off-Broadway at its height was a wonderful institution: it featured theatres such as the Circle-in-the-Square and the Cherry Lane and The Phoenix; it presented new playwrights such as Edward Albee; and it gave opportunities to hundreds of talented new actors and directors and designers. Yet, it did not find its own community. When it was full-grown and its characteristics could be seen, it was clear that Off-Broadway had become a slightly more idealistic (or highbrow or advanced or artistic) version of Broadway.

But there was another community, another audience, even another kind of theatre making its appearance. The then "Beat Generation," whose more famous names were Jack Kerouac, Allan Ginsberg, and Laurence Ferlinghetti, were frequenting small coffee houses and cafes within the general geographical limits of Off-Broadway—"downtown." The Beat Generation went to hear poets read their work to the accompaniment of drums and guitars; they went to hear prerock folk singers and pre-electronic musical groups. And, in such generous premises as the cafes run by the late Joe Cino (the Cafe Cino) and Ellen Stewart (the Cafe LaMama) they could sometimes see plays. The theatres were minimal; the actors were mostly young, nonprofessional (or at least non-Equity); and sets and properties were spare. And the entire process was always in imminent danger of being stopped because of supposed violations of fire laws or building codes—although hindsight suggests that what was being violated was the traditional idea of what a theatre was and what kind of people should gather in it.

Two terms emerged for this new theatre, *underground* and *Off-Off-Broadway*. The first was probably taken over from films, for in the same years, the underground filmmakers—the Mekas brothers, Kenneth Anger, Stan Brakhage, Andy Warhol, and many others—were showing their work in cooperatives and in storefront theatres, and the old taboos were being thrown out like unusable snippets of film. Their open subject matter, sexual freedom, honesty of image and wholly nontraditional approach to the idea of performing art (film or otherwise) attracted violent criticism and much legal attention, but they were eventually to win the day. The live theatre, although lagging behind, was able to follow the path mapped by film.

Other underground and Off-Off-Broadway theatres appeared in the early 1960s to provide a meeting place for new playwrights, new actors, and new audiences. The Hardware Poets, the Judson Poets Theatre, the La Mama (evolved from the Cafe La Mama), and many others appeared. They showed audiences the valid, new, and sometimes startling work of writers like Sam Shepard, Marie Irene Fornes, Rochelle Owens,

Megan Terry, and Ronald Tavel, and of directors like Jacques Levy, Laurence Kornfeld, and Tom O'Horgan. It was no longer a question whether or not American drama was literature. By 1969, American drama, as it was represented by its underground, was theatre. And it was bursting out in all directions.

Each of the four areas of taboo was broken down. Often, changes in legal interpretation were necessary; however, the rapidly changing values of American society itself were most accountable for the sudden changes. (The entire process took no more than ten years; it can be argued that it took only five. It was overdue.)

Overt sexuality. The impact of underground film has already been noted. The 1965 production of Michael McClure's *The Beard* was innovative; later productions of The Living Theatre and The Performance Group (see pp. 207–210) also changed public attitudes. The 1969 production of the largely nude review, *Oh, Calcutta!*, however cynically intended, marked the end of any formal ban on nudity or the presentation of overt sexuality. Mart Crowley's *The Boys in the Band* (1968) gave American audiences (first Off-Broadway and later on film) their first widely publicized stage picture of homosexuality that was sympathetic and nonsensational. (The fact that there was a rash of quick-buck homosexual plays and nude plays after these does not detract from the fact that, however shocking they may have been, the pioneering works were honestly meant.)

Radical politics. Barbara Garson's skit-parody of *Macbeth*, *Macbird*, was one of the first theatre productions not only to deal cuttingly and brutally with a national issue, but also to extend its satire to all levels of politics. Significantly, the production (like that of *The Beard*) originated on the West Coast. Megan Terry's partly improvised theatre piece, *Viet Rock*, was also important. The most genuinely radical works were the Living Theatre's *Paradise Now* and the Performance Group's *Dionysus in 69*.

Racial honesty. See "Black Theatre," discussed subsequently.

Language. The collapse of the taboo on language paralleled the collapse of the other taboos, quite predictably. The works of the underground playwrights were studded with the once-famous four-letter words that took for granted a linguistic freedom that had become common in many segments of American society (including the high school-university age groups that were to make up a large part of the new theatre's audience). Art was catching up with nature. In racial matters, language was liberated by the Black Theatre itself.

The Black Theatre

The racial upheavals of the late 1950s and 1960s are an unsettling part of American history now—the early sit-ins and protests, the riots of

Figure 2–54. LeRoi Jones's *Dutchman* at the Cherry Lane Theatre, with Robert Hooks and Jennifer West. (*Photo, Miss Alix Jeffry.*)

Watts and Newark, the murders of Malcolm X and Martin Luther King —and the profound racial abrasion that they expressed found its own expression in the theatre. Thus, it was necessary to the destruction of theatrical racial taboos (as it was necessary to the destruction of the blindness—or ignorance, or indifference—in the society as a whole) that a powerful honesty and a sometimes strident militancy inform the early plays of what was to become a black theatre movement. Militancy alone, however, would not have given black theatre either a reason for continuing or an identity. From the early plays, which most often dramatized the black-white confrontation, black theatre has evolved into a profound concern with black life itself. In short, it has found its community in blackness.

As we have noted, Jean Genet's *The Blacks* (1961) was an early exploration of black-white enmity; yet, it has not been acknowledged by black playwrights as a starting point for them. Rather, the seminal figure most often noted in black theatre is LeRoi Jones (Imamu Amiri Baraka) whose *Dutchman* (1964) focused, with an abrupt and brutal authority, the attention of the white Off-Broadway audience on its own racial attitudes. The white world is represented by Lula, the subway-riding white female, the murderer of black manhood; the black world is Clay, her eventual victim, who nonetheless voices two important themes of the burgeoning black theatre: the privacy and separateness of a black community ("You don't know anything except what's there for you to see. An act. Lies. Device.") and the suffering, caused by white cruelty, that is at the heart of black art ("If I murdered you, then other white people would begin to understand. . . . If Bessie Smith had killed some white people she wouldn't have needed that music. She could have talked very straight about the world.") There are many such murders in the early plays of the black theatre, great outpourings of symbolic violence against the white world. And from it, evidently, came the ability to "talk very straight about the world"—especially the black world—to a black audience.

Yet, this is not to say by any means that either *The Blacks* or *Dutchman* was the first play about black life on the American stage. As a brief study of James Hatch's *Black Image on the American Stage* shows, black writers have been writing for the theatre for generations, from Will Marion Cook through Langston Hughes, Hall Johnston, Louis Peterson and many more. Rarely, however, had they been writing plays about black life that could reach black audiences. Like those white playwrights who tried to deal with black subject matter, they had to write largely for white audiences and to the standards of white criticism. One towering example of black theatrical artistry does predate LeRoi Jones—*A Raisin in the Sun*, by the late Lorraine Hansberry (1959). As critic Loften Mitchell said of the play, it "was monumental in terms of commitment, of 'standing up and being counted.'" It was a black play about black people, and, ironically (for Miss Hansberry died too early to see the black theatre flower fully), it anticipated the developments of the black theatre movement in the seventies.

Black theatre people insist that there is a difference between the white aesthetic of contemporary American theatre and a valid black aesthetic. In his introduction to the anthology called *The Black Aesthetic*, Addison Gayle writes, "To understand [the alleged participation of a black man in the My Lai massacre] and what must be done to correct it is to understand the Black Aesthetic. A critical methodology has no relevance to the black community unless it aids men in becoming better than they are." At another point, Gayle calls this aesthetic a "corrective." "The question for the black critic today is not how beautiful is a melody, a play, a poem, or a novel, but how much more beautiful has the poem, melody, or play made the life of a single black man?" This corrective, even moralistic, concept is fundamental—and considerably different from white theatre criticism. It marks a profound split. It accounts, in part, for the disdain, or at the very least the indifference, that many black artists feel for white critics. Moreover, it underlines the separation of the two theatres along racial lines. As Larry Neal said (in "The Black Arts Movement" in *The Black Aesthetic*) "Black Art is the aesthetic and spiritual sister of the Black Power concept. As such, it envisions an art that speaks directly to the needs and aspirations of Black America." Applying this idea specifically to the theatre, he added, "theatre is potentially the most social of all the arts. It is an integral part of the socializing process. It exists in direct relationship to the audience it claims to serve. The decadence and inanity of the contemporary American theatre is an accurate reflection of the state of American society. . . . [It] is a palliative prescribed to bourgeois patients who refuse to see the world as it is. . . ." The antidote is Black Theatre—by blacks and for blacks, what playwright Ron Milner calls "going home"—back to the values of the black community.

This condition of black theatre (separateness) is more than a little distasteful to many whites. It seems to negate the very ideas of integration, of oneness, that the civil rights movement of the 1950s was supposed to be about. Nonetheless, there is no denying that it has produced a theatre of great importance, a theatre that may be the most truly communal, even the most vital, in contemporary America. And it is a theatre that keeps its idea of community and vitality by *not* allowing itself to be absorbed into the (white) commercial mainstream. The (white) "tribal rock musical," *Hair*, for example, could move from the Off-Off-Broadway, semiunderground confines of the Public Theatre to a discotheque, and from there to a Broadway theatre, making piles of money (and, according to some of its early adherents, losing its communal identity) along the way; the plays of black theatre, by and large, do not experience the same metamorphosis.

To give their plays a home, black playwrights concerned with black community have turned to theatres of their own—the New Lafayette Theatre in Harlem, the Black Arts and Spirit House programs begun by LeRoi Jones in Harlem and Newark. Yet, many black playwrights have seen important first productions of their plays in theatres far removed (both geographically and communally) from blackness: Ed Bullins at the American Place Theatre (see p. 205); Charles Gordone at the Public Theatre; Ron Milner at the American Place; and a considerable number of writers at both the Chelsea Theater Center in Brooklyn and the Negro Ensemble Company. Their struggles to maintain an identity within the white theatre at the end of the 1960s was symptomatic of a problem faced by many black actors, writers and directors—how to maintain their identity and integrity without building a false separation between themselves and the larger society.

The struggle to satisfy the demands of a black aesthetic has led black playwrights to work in many forms, some very traditional and some innovative. In general, these fall into two types: one is realistic, detailed, and immediate, offering the joy of recognition of life in a black community, the form of Bullins and Milner; the other is poetic, sometimes heavy-handedly symbolic and didactic, sometimes lyrically beautiful, the form of Sonia Sanchez and the later plays of LeRoi Jones. Neither may offer easily accessible subject matter to white critics, but pleasing the established critics of the established theatre is not the goal. "A playwright writes to be understood by his community," said Ed Bullins. "My community is the black community."

Perhaps coincidentally, the year 1964 seems to have marked a number of new beginnings in the theatre. It was the year of Jones's *Dutchman*, the year of the New York production of the Theatre of Cruelty's *Marat-Sade*, and the year of the opening of the American Place Theatre with Robert Lowell's plays, *My Kinsman, Major Molyneux* and *Benito Cereno* (under the joint title, *The Old Glory*). The plays were hailed as a major contribution to American dramatic literature, a rennaissance. The American Place Theatre was hailed as an innovation in top-flight New York theatre production: a nonprofit theatre devoted to producing new works of the highest quality, with production standards as high as those of any theatre in the country. In the distinctly Off-Broadway setting of an old church in the Hell's Kitchen area of New York, under the direction of a veteran theatre man, Wynn Handman, the American Place thrived on a demanding schedule of new plays by both established writers from outside the theatre (Lowell, Anne Sexton, Paul Goodman, May Swenson, and Robert Coover), new writers (William Alfred, Ed Bullins, and Ron Milner), and established playwrights (Sam Shepard, Ronald Tavel, and Jack Gelber). In 1971, the American Place moved to a new location, a handsome, brand-new theatre built under a city-sponsored plan to encourage theatre construction within large business buildings.

Also in 1964, the first theatre company of The Lincoln Center for the Performing Arts was formed; initially under the guidance of Elia Kazan and Robert Whitehead (both established and highly respected men from the commercial theatre), the company has since undergone several changes of both leadership and membership. As a repertory theatre company, Lincoln Center has presented work of variable quality; its smaller, innovative theatre, however, the Forum, has with increasing frequency presented new plays by new playwrights such as Ron Cowan and John Ford Noonan.

After 1966–1967, the Public Theatre of the New York Shakespeare Festival, under the leadership of Joseph Papp, joined the American Place and the Forum as an outstanding producer of new plays. In actual fact, the Public Theatre is not a single stage, but several, all housed in the former Astor Library in lower Manhattan. From them have come important new writers and important new plays: David Rabe's *Sticks and Bones*, Charles Gordone's *No Place to be Somebody*, Jason Miller's *That Championship Season*, and many others. As well, the Public Theatre produces established plays and classics.

Many of the new names in playwriting in the 1960s and early 1970s came from these three pioneering theatres. However, the Off-Off-Broadway and underground movement, led by the early coffee-house theatre, also introduced new writers and even new kinds of theatre. Often, the companies and the producing organizations came and went with great

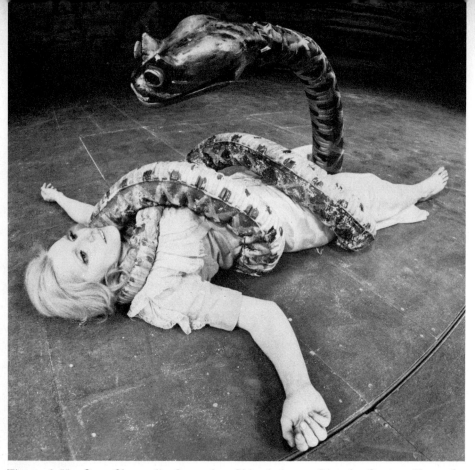

Figure 2–55. Sam Shepard's *Operation Sidewinder* at Lincoln Center. Here, the sidewinder (a runaway airforce computer) in action. Barbara eda-Young as Honey. (*Martha Swope photo.*)

suddenness; of them all, the La Mama and the Judson Poets Theatre maintained the most consistent and successful schedules. Some of the new playwrights moved across theatrical strata, to make their ultimate impact within both the underground and the mainstream theatre: Ronald Tavel began as a script writer for Andy Warhol, had his early plays produced by the Theatre of the Ridiculous ("beyond the absurd"), then by Judson, and saw *The Boy in the Straight-Backed Chair* produced at the American Place in 1969. Sam Shepard's plays were staged in a considerable number of cafe and Off-Off-Broadway theatres; his *La Turista* was produced at the American Place in 1967, and in 1970 *Operation Sidewinder* was a major production at Lincoln Center. Rochelle Owens' *Istanboul* (possibly the most-often produced play of the entire Off-Off-Broadway repertory) was a 1965 production at Judson; *Futz* was produced several times, including a staging at the prestigious Off-Broadway Theatre de Lys, directed by Tom O'Horgan (himself probably the period's foremost innovator in directing, who moved easily across theatrical lines himself, directing Off-Off-Broadway, on Broadway, and in cafe theatres). Rochelle Owens' *Bclech* was first presented at a regional repertory theatre, the Living Arts in Philadelphia, and later Off-Off-Broadway. In short, the ferment that was going on outside the confines of the commodity theatre saw a considerable number of highly talented new artists moving across established lines, expanding the communities of response to their own works, and finding a theatre environment in which they could work productively.

These noncommodity playwrights had several things in common, however different their ideas and their plays might be. They were militantly themselves, with little respect for tradition; their sense of theatre was far from realistic, and was often antirealistic and antiillusionistic; they were young; they were prolific; they wanted their plays staged, without going through the time-consuming, often deadening processes of the commodity theatre. And, whether knowingly or not, they found an audience that was itself an underground community.

A general division of the two principal lines of noncommodity theatre can be made, a division that is analogous to the split in American poetry in the 1950s and after. On the one side are the descendants of the Beats, on the other, the descendants of the "academics," the literary-renaissance people. The split between them is not a question of quality; it is a question of values, of community, and of theatre ideals.

Academic	Beat
Edward Albee	Sam Shepard
Robert Lowell	Rochelle Owens
Arthur Kopit	Ronald Tavel
Elia Kazan (director)	Tom O'Horgan (director)
The New York Times criticism	*Village Voice* criticism
Classical	Romantic
Carefulness	Carelessness
Time	Spontaneity
Authority	Individualism
Cultural sensitivity	Personal sensitivity
Stanislavski	Artaud
Method	Improvisation

This division still exists. The appearance of an entirely different theatrical strand in the late 1960s did not supplant existing ones; it merely offered a new, healthy alternative.

Environmental Theatre

The development in American theatre that came to be called environmental (meaning that the theatre event would become its audience's environment, satisfying Artaud's requirement in *The Theatre and its Double* of "a theatre of cruelty . . . surrounding the spectators"), group-created, physical, and antiliterary ("no more masterpieces") had its immediate theatrical precedents in the Happenings created in the 1950s and 1960s. The same influence was at work in music and in dance, where John Cage (probably the earliest to speak with some coherence of Happenings), Merce Cunningham, and Alwyn Nikolais were potent forces. Nonlinearity, chance structures, nonstory, and nonmeaning were characteristic goals of their work.

The great theatrical exemplar for the environmentalists of the American sixties, however (after Artaud, and such Europeans as Jerzy Grotowski—see pp. 282–283), were a small, militantly avant-garde group known as The Living Theatre. Under the leadership of Julian Beck and Judith Malina, this troupe, whose personnel changed throughout the period, evolved from a little-known performing unit in the late 1940s and early fifties into one of the most important of the Off-Broadway theatres in 1959–1961, when they presented the first productions of Jack Gelber's *The Connection*, William Carlos Williams' *Many Loves*, and Kenneth Brown's *The Brig*, as well as plays by Brecht, Pirandello, and others. Always political (in the sense, at least, that the leading members were actively antiwar, pro-individual, and humanist), The Living Theatre left the United States for political reasons in 1962; when it returned in 1968, it had been forged into a performing commune with an impressive European reputation for its presentation of three group-created works: *Frankenstein, Antigone,* and *Paradise Now.* Underlying all three was a profound belief in radical-revolutionary political action; the very means by which the works had been created suggested the direction of their radicalism—communal, ungoverned (even anarchic), benign humanism. Both in New York and on a national tour, the troupe was praised and damned; their theatricality was athletic and spare; their ability to communicate to an audience (so said their detractors) was muddy, their message mystical and private.

One of the early members of The Living Theatre company, Joseph Chaikin, did not accompany the group to Europe. Instead, beginning in 1963, he worked to create his own theatre. The result is the Open Theatre, a performing unit that is seemingly more dedicated to the exploration of acting as a means to human discovery than to the presentation of any one kind of play or idea, political or otherwise. One observer has called the Open Theatre "pastoral" in its attitude toward the audience (unlike The Living Theatre and other environmental theatres, in which the audience is not only made part of the theatrical event, but also sometimes is threatened or assaulted by the actors). The process by which Chaikin and the Open Theatre arrived at this condition, however, was not without experimentation in other directions, and the production for which it gained initial attention—Jean-Claude van Italie's *America, Hurrah*, in 1966—was neither entirely pastoral nor entirely nonpolitical. Later productions, however—*The Serpent*, 1968, and *Terminal*, 1970—have seen the Open Theatre leave such specifics as politics and move into the area of myth. The actor's work, achieved through long periods of search, meditation, and interaction with other actors, is partly ritual, partly a succession of disciplined "transformations" from role to role, figure to figure, and metaphor to metaphor. The Open Theatre style is related to dance; the playwrights who work with it are analagous to choreographers and composers, shaping, editing, and emphasizing—but not handing down the limiting, scripted structure of the traditional playwright.

Of the environmental theatre groups, none has been given more attention, nor achieved more notoriety, than the Performance Group, which presented *Dionysus in 69* in its Performing Garage in Manhattan in 1968. Since that time, some of the group's personnel have changed, but the over-all thrust and sense of the Performance Group have remained much the same. Youthful, dedicated, and sometimes seemingly mystical and too inner-oriented, it has, under the leadership of Richard Schechner, become one of the most important influences on contemporary American theatre. Its resemblances and its indebtedness to The Living Theatre are strong; it differs from Chaikin's Open Theatre in its sometimes abrasive, often radicalizing, attitude toward its audience. Schechner himself emerged from the educational theatre to found the group. Critic, editor, scholar, and teacher, he brought a formidable intellect and knowledge to his task. The Performance Group bears his stamp very strongly. As Dan Isaacs has pointed out in *Educational Theatre Journal*, "It is Schechner's political credo that explains [his use of the expression 'The Politics of Ecstasy']: theatre is a public art. To create *environmental* theatre is to liberate space and democratize the relationship between actor and audience." And it is Schechner's artistic credo (like Joseph Chaikin's) that there be no separation between the work of art and the life around it: art should integrate the individual and the society, communalize it. It was, perhaps, ironic that *Dionysus in 69* did more fragmenting than unifying; yet, the fragmentation that its audiences often showed (their reactions splitting harshly into enthusiastic acceptance or hostile rejection) can be viewed as a weeding-out process. In a fragmented society, it can be argued, the work of art must first identify the fragments and then unify within its own proper community.

It has been said that the environmental theatres are a healthy alternative to the more traditional forms of theatre. A comparison of those alternatives can be made (see p. 207):

Environmental
Joseph Chaikin, Open Theatre
Judith Malina and Julian Beck, The Living Theatre
Richard Schechner, The Performance Group

Every man is his own artist.
We, not I.

We perfect *our* rituals.
We evolve *our* techniques.
Communal sensitivity *is* cultural sensitivity.

Marshall McLuhan
R. Buckminster Fuller
Claude Levi-Strauss

The work of both The Performance Group and The Living Theatre has been both violently disliked and ardently admired. (The Open Theatre, by contrast, has aroused far less hostility, perhaps because it is less hostile to begin with.) The influence of both has given rise to innumerable imitations across the United States—groups hopefully united in a psychic, often private, sometimes noble and sometimes silly attempt to make the theatre a means of expressing, and discovering, meaningful truths that are absent in other activities. Such group-oriented, even tribal, theatre has been viewed as the product of the years that also produced the fashion for group therapy and group encounters, for sensitivity training, for touching and feeling rather than talking and thinking. It is, perhaps, a product of a widespread distrust (or disuse) of rational discourse. It is certainly, in its seeking after emotional and psychic wholeness, a product of that wretched decade that followed the assassination of John F. Kennedy. Perhaps, regrettably, there is a circularity to the work of most of the environmental theatre groups: like the religions they so often resemble, they have magic only for those who already believe. Many do not believe.

Arthur Kopit's *Indians*

In 1959, *Oh, Dad, Poor Dad, Mamma's Hung You in the Closet and I'm Feelin' So Sad* was performed Off-Broadway; productions in London, on tour, and in other countries followed. It was the work of a very young man, at that time a recent college graduate; it has since become one of the most widely performed of contemporary comedies. In a somewhat self-conscious way, it showed how European avant-garde theatre (especially the plays of Ionesco) could be incorporated by an American playwright.

Yet nothing in that early play—nor, for that matter, in the other plays that followed in the early 'sixties—foreshadowed *Indians*. Where Arthur Kopit's *Oh, Dad, Poor Dad* was facile and sometimes brainless, Arthur Kopit's *Indians* was deeply thoughtful; where his *Oh, Dad* seemed to play *at* theatre, his *Indians* was marvelously theatrical in an exciting way. It is sometimes difficult to believe that both plays are the work of the same writer, so different are they. Yet, in almost opposite ways, they show Kopit to be one of the outstanding younger talents in the American theatre.

Indians was first staged by the Royal Shakespeare Company in London in 1968; after some reworking, it appeared at the Arena Stage in Washington D. C., and later in New York, both in 1969.

PLOT. *Indians* revolves around Buffalo Bill, William Cody, the historical figure who made his reputation in the post-Civil War period as a buffalo hunter, and who later became world famous as the leading figure in his own Wild West Show. The real Cody was the stuff that legends are easily woven around—killer of thousands of buffalo, crack shot, hero to those who saw America's destiny in the conquering of the West and the spanning of the continent with railroads. Cody was, too, a myth figure who came almost ready-made, and who, in his suit of white buckskin, with a mane of silver hair and a big white horse, actually did tour the world with a troupe that included Annie Oakley and Sitting Bull, actually did play for Queen Victoria, and actually did make the winning of the West real to dreamers everywhere. And this Cody, both real and mythic, became part of the fiction of the American West when he was absorbed into the modern television and film mythos

Figure 2–56. *Indians* as staged by the University Players, the University of Michigan, directed by Bruce Levitt. Settings by William Davis, costumes by Bettie Seeman, lights by Alan Billings.

of the American West, along with Wild Bill Hickock, Daniel Boone, Bat Masterson, and all those others.

It is part of the originality of Kopit's play that its plot does not trace the life of Cody, nor even the myth of Cody, but the subtle process by which the life and the myth became intertwined, and the tragic process by which the end product became part of the modern American character. Within the play, it would seem that the immediate victims are the buffalo and the Indian; but the ultimate victims are Cody and all the American Codys who believe in a myth of an America that is founded in that expansionist, violence-happy, racist dream.

"I'm not ashamed of my life's bein' looked at," says Cody, appearing at the play's opening in a center ring that may be the ring of a Wild West show (although he has just come from "playin' two-a-day in a goddam ghost town," and around him, ragged hangings blow like curtains in the window of an abandoned house); he is controlled by an unseen Voice that both orders and coaxes him, and that is more powerful and more probing than the mere voice of his own conscience. It is, perhaps, the voice of a national conscience, of a might-have-been American ethic, and under its prodding, Buffalo Bill begins to act out a painful review of his own life.

This is the outer shell of the play, the skin of the onion: it is Buffalo Bill's confrontation with his past. Within that, and seemingly separate from it at first, is an investigation of the Sitting Rock Indian Reservation by a Senate committee in the late nineteenth century. They are Sitting Bull's Indians, the ones who killed General Custer ("one o' the great dumb-ass men in history," Bill calls Custer. Yet, there is a similarity between the two men in their dumb-assedness, their pursuit of glory). The investigation, with Buffalo Bill as would-be mediator, becomes increasingly hostile as it appears that the Indians do not want to be considered the children of the Great White Father in Washington, do not want to be turned into impoverished imitations of whites, do not want to be anything but what they were before the whites came—a free people, living in harmony with the land. And when Sitting Bull, magnificent in his anger, says this to the Senators, their hostility becomes implacable; contemptuously, they call for the "next Indian."

Within the shell of the investigation is the story of Buffalo Bill's own guilt, his own responsibility for bringing the Indians to their present condition by wiping out the buffalo. In trying to defend himself to the ghost of Sitting Bull, late in the play, Bill says, "You were very unrealistic . . . did you *really* believe the buffalo would return?" And Sitting Bull, tying together the ghastly conflict of life styles that has made the Indians and the whites such enemies, says, "It seemed no less likely than Christ's returning, and a great deal more useful. Though when I think of their reception here, I can't see why either would really want to come back."

Deeper even than the destruction of the buffalo, however, is the Wild

Figure 2–57. *Indians* in its Broadway production, with Stacey Keach as Buffalo Bill. (*Martha Swope photo.*)

West Show itself, the mythologizing, the glorification, of the destructive act. Cody becomes Buffalo Bill, "A GODDAM HERO!" as he proclaims himself; Geronimo becomes "THE MOST FEROCIOUS INDIAN ALIVE!" and is treated like a caged tiger in an animal act; Sitting Bull becomes a parody of himself, but confesses, "you allowed us to imitate our glory. . . . It was humiliating! For sometimes, we could almost imagine it was *real*."

At the end of the play, these several levels come together. The Senate investigation has ended much as it began, with misunderstanding and hostility; the Army has massacred Sitting Bull and his people; and the Wild West Show has become part of a way of life, an entertainment form in a cowboys-and-Indians America peopled by imitation Codys. Buffalo Bill has reviewed his life, and he ends by trying, pitifully, to expiate his guilt by hawking Indian trinkets to the audience. For an American audience, as for Bill himself, there is no satisfaction in this ending—neither resolution nor tragic recognition nor comic happiness —but only irony, the admission that things are as they are, unchangeably.

THEATRICALITY. *Indians* is as unabashedly spectacular in its use of the theatre as any musical extravaganza. Kopit has been quoted as calling it a "combination of Wild West Show, vaudeville, and circus. . . . There are dances; phony horses . . . it's a hallucinatory mosaic. . . ." In fact, it is the Wild West Show itself that opens up the theatrical possibilities of the play; itself a marvelously effective theatre event, the Wild West Show becomes both the controlling metaphor of the play (self-justification as heroic drama) and the permission for spectacle— Indians dancing, bands playing, and Annie Oakley shooting. And beyond this, the entire interplay of real show and false show has allowed Kopit (and his director and designer) to make free with reality. Time flows; space dissolves; the dead come back to life; the living die and leap up again—it is all show, like Cody's circus. Thus, the first appearance of Buffalo Bill is a *coup de théâtre*—a real actor enters astride an artificial horse that bucks and rears and prances. The theatrical joy of it is that we *know* that horse is artificial, and we admire the actor's skill in working it. Thus, too, the simple use of white cloths, upon which the now-dead Indians lie to symbolize the snow-covered graves after their massacre, is brilliant. The use of Indians wearing buffalo heads to represent the buffaloes that Bill massacres early in the play is also excellent.

Visually, theatrically, *Indians* is one of the most brilliant plays of modern times. It hardly matters whether individual bits of staging came from the playwright, the director, the designer, or the actor. The important point is that, in encapsulating the life of Buffalo Bill within the Wild West Show, Arthur Kopit made all of it possible.

IDEA. Like Robert Lowell in *The Old Glory* (1964) and *Endecott and the Red Cross* (1966), Arthur Kopit is trying to dig down to the roots of American behavior. Lowell found those roots in New England; Kopit finds them in the West. Lowell was concerned with the influence of Europe, particularly Puritan England; Kopit is concerned with an apparently native, home-grown hunger for glory at the price of a basic humanity.

One can argue that there are flaws in Kopit's thinking; certainly the weakest scenes in the play are the Senate-investigation episodes, which seem pat and hollow, pitting noble Indians against cardboard bureaucrats. However, it is not in these scenes that the enormous power of the play lies, but in the wilder, more visually exciting scenes of Buffalo Bill's life and his Wild West Show. (The investigation scenes are didactic, static, and just talk; the other scenes are impressionistic, vivid, and theatrical.) Perhaps, paradoxically, the idea of the play is contained in its nonverbal moments and its images far more tellingly than it is in its staged debates.

Buffalo Bill's prancing stallion is repeated (ironically) in a horse-shaped exercise machine ridden by the President of the United States while Bill tries to plead the Indians' cause with him. The dying buffalo of the play's third scene are repeated in Bill's name, then by a contemptuous reference to the nickel coin, and at last by a buffalo skin that Bill finds in his bag of trinkets and tries to hide from the audience (and from himself). Buffalo Bill, in his fringed finery, is repeated by a nightmare succession of figures who appear to him in a saloon, like portents of the dime-novel cowboys and movie heroes and TV bang-bang gunmen to come.

Perhaps most of all, the play's point is made by the recitation (twice) of the historical Chief Joseph's speech of surrender, when he and his Nez Percé Indians were finally captured. The speech is deeply moving. In its first context it is touching and ironic: the aged Chief Joseph in the Wild West ring, recites the surrender of an entire way of life to a white audience, "twice a day, three times on Sundays"—it is simple and heart-rending. In its second context, at the very end of the play, with only Bill's pathetic trinkets visible, it is shattering. In a sense, its repetition *is* the idea of the play.

3
The Critical
Analysis of Drama

The critical analysis of plays and performances can be a rewarding and enjoyable process, or it can be a destructive and dangerous one. That it is quite different from performance itself is obvious; criticism, for all its yearnings, is not the same kind of activity as acting or playwriting. Criticism has been called creative, particularly in the last twenty-five years, and the use of the word *creative* need not be withheld from it. However, no one should persuade himself that he is enriching the performance for the performer or the play for the playwright by analyzing it. He is engaged mostly in playing a rather complex game, for his own amusement and the amusement of people like him. With this attitude he can be assured that his game is every bit as ennobling as pure mathematics to the mathematician or theoretical physics to the physicist. Often the dramatic analyst's ideas will be of use and even of interest to theatre audiences.

In this chapter certain suggestions about plays are made—what they are made of, what they do, what they are about. Along the way, certain other attitudes have to be dealt with at some length, because theatrical criticism is burdened with a sizeable legacy of theories, rules, incorrect discoveries, and such, most of which stand in the way of criticism instead of helping it along. The conclusions reached, if any, are not intended to give criteria for judging a play's quality so much as to be tools for getting at its innards. Before you can answer the question, "How good was what you saw?" you must be able to answer a more difficult question, "What did you see?" This chapter indicates certain ways of analyzing what is seen or read, and ends with a few suggested questions that can be directed at a performance or a text. Its aim throughout is not prescriptive, but descriptive, analysis.

Text and Performance

There is a common and unfortunate tendency among literate human beings to prefer their own reading of a play to the performance of that play in a theatre. The attitude is probably harmless, unless it becomes part of a critical expression and thus becomes a comment on the theatre itself. Behind the attitude, of course, is the belief that the written text—the playwright's work, with its possibly unstageable stage directions, its often irrelevant physical character descriptions, and its sometimes private or unnecessary commentary and reference—*is* the play, and that what happens on the stage is merely a slavish fleshing out of this text. The playwright, in other words, is conceived as a novelist who happens to work heavily in dialogue.

As we tried to point out in Chapter One, there are far too many variables in the staging of any work for a single imagination, however skillful and however highly trained, to predict and comprehend them all in the isolation of the study. Moreover, the playwright's text is far from being the only work of theatre art. Nevertheless, an adequate understanding of that text is an important first step toward understanding both the performance of it and the means by which the performance is created. Therefore, certain literary techniques must make up the beginning of an approach to drama, and other, nonliterary, ones can then be added.

Narrative Form

Viewed somewhat narrowly (and, as we shall see later, such a view is ultimately *too* narrow, but useful here), what the dramatic "maker" makes is a narrative of a kind: typically, it contains incidents, beings who are usually meant to remind us of humans, and environments intended to remind us of our own environment, all arranged in an order that is, first of all, the order in which we perceive them, and, secondly, another order that is interpreted as causal and progressive. This product of the maker is a story (things happening to human beings in time). To define it thus, however, is immediately to categorize it further as fiction and to categorize the maker as an inventor of stories that, however closely they remind us of our own perceptible reality, are not of the same order, because the things in them are controlled, made, and arranged. (It should be noted, of course, that although these things are not of the same order of perceptible reality as our own, they become part of our perceptible reality *as they happen to us:* they have a reality, although they may be "untrue," just as any lie exists for both its inventor and the people to whom he chooses to tell it.) Aristotle, of whom more must be said shortly, chose to divide the maker's stories into three types, still useful for a rough pigeon-holing of dramas: (1) those that deal with things that never happened and never could happen (fantasy); (2) those that deal with things that have not happened but that could happen (fiction); (3) and those that deal with things that could happen and that have happened (history). Setting aside Aristotle's sense of propriety about the relative merits of these three categories, we should note in passing that the definition of each is highly variable, depending on the cultural sense of *could be* as opposed to *could not be.* Aristotle, for example, might well have found any story of space travel to be not fiction, but fantasy (he could not perceive how space travel could be made to happen), but we have seen space travel move from the realm of a Buck Rogers fantasy to history, to fiction based on historical events since 1958. As a critical tool, the designation of any given work as fantastic or historical or fictional is merely a rough beginning at definition of its content, its maker's attitude, and its tone. However, all too often such designations are made the final judgment of the work instead of the preliminary analysis. We might consider, for example, the number of plays that have been summarily dismissed because "things just don't happen that way." Such a judgment relies on a deep prejudice, not only about the nature of reality, but about the nature of theatre. It is, of course, a very popular means of judging theatre, probably because it is such an easy one.

Seen as narrative, then, the maker's work of art, as it is perceived by its audience, becomes part of that audience's experience. It becomes, as one aesthetician has put it, "virtual history" (Suzanne Langer, in *Feeling and Form*), information that can be called up from the audience's memory exactly as any other information can be. In this sense, it is a kind of *substitute memory* in which the discrete moments of the story are given to the members of the audience to form part of their own memories. However, unlike actual memory, the details of this substitute memory are perceived in a prearranged order, in a prearranged environment: in fact, perceived in a way that gives each detail a quality that perceptible reality only rarely has. It is a very important aspect of theatre as a narrative art, therefore, that it is the *donation of substitute memory*, and any criticism seeking to cope with drama as narrative must deal with such matters as the rate of donation, the order of donation, and what is being donated at any moment (words, gestures, objects; action, ideas, character).

The moment that we introduce ideas and character, we begin to enlarge our definition of narrative art, for we originally included only the barest essentials of what we called story. There is much more to theatre than stories, so our first idea of theatre as a narrative art is either wrong, or we must somehow be able to include more elements than story in the concept of narrative. It was pointed out at the beginning that the narrative concept was itself too narrow, and so we now need another, more inclusive one for the expanded elements of theatre. Suzanne Langer's "discursive form" (in *Feeling and Form*) is such a concept: that of a form that displays some of our first elements (things happening in time) and yet allows us to include things other than human beings or incidents (by which we now intend, most importantly, *meaning* as it can be communicated by all the elements of theatre, directly or symbolically, intrinsically or extrinsically). It is theatre as a discursive form, then, more than as mere narrative, that criticism must learn to describe.

Suspense in Discursive Form

Inherent in the human perception of any discursive form is an attitude best described for our purposes as suspense. The word is certainly a familiar one, albeit rather tarnished now because of its use in a single genre, the thriller. Suspense stories, meaning melodramatic ones whose primary, in fact only, appeal is to the intense curiosity aroused by a single plot question ("who did it?" or, sometimes, "how did who do it?") are perfectly valid examples of a very rigid, narrow, and usually inferior discursive form. They are not usually inferior because they rely so heavily on a single suspense, but because they fail to rely on other artistic elements (language, characterization, and ideas). Given high artistry in those other areas (which we have not yet considered), the suspense story can become a very superior product indeed. *Hamlet*, for example, although not exactly a whodunit, is certainly a how-will-he-do-it. It could be argued that the entire range of Elizabethan revenge plays are primarily suspense stories of this order.

But this raises an immediate question: suspense of what? It is easy enough to see that in the detective story our suspense does involve an answer to a question; suspense, in this case, seems to be nothing more than the tension surrounding our need to have a certain question answered. Any reader of detective stories should already have tried to point out, however, that the question is rarely a simple one, so that our anxiety, or suspense, is complex, not simple. Furthermore, it is not precisely the same as the suspense involved in getting the answer to a question, because it is usually spread over an entire narrative. Thus, the *maintenance* of suspense would appear to be part of the maker's artistry, just as the original creation of that suspense surely is.

But how does he create the suspense in the first place? Rarely does even the most straightforward whodunit begin with a question. (Who murdered Ashburnan Strether in his town house on August 29?) Typically, the question is implicit for a considerable part of the narrative; in fact, the question itself may be the answer to a prior question, itself implicit, about which we are to feel suspense.

If, then, discursive suspense is not adequately described in terms of question and answer, it can better be approached in terms of the elements of discursive form itself. Earlier, we outlined the theory of narrative as virtual history, in which the maker gives a substitute memory to the audience or perceiver. In that this memory is acquired over a period of time (discursively), it is evident that any part of the virtual history not yet reached by the perceiver will be part of *his own* future as well as part of the future of the history itself. All parts already perceived will be part of the substitute memory. Thus, at any point along the development of a discursive form, the perceiver is in the process of learning data that have previously been part of a *promised* future, are now part of an experienced present, and subsequently will be part of a rather special remembered past. That the future events are *promised* is inherent in the form itself, for discursiveness implies continuation until its own end is announced (often by purely arbitrary or conventional means—the back cover of a book, the lowering of a curtain, the words *The End* at the finish of a film). *This is not to say that any maker promises that events of a given kind will take place.* It means merely that the form promises its own, and its perceiver's, future. (It is possible, for example, to have a maker create his work by chance, as Merce Cunningham has created some dances. The form is at least in large part discursive, but Cunningham himself is not promising, *cannot* promise, his audience anything, because chance rules the order of events, even the nature of the events—body positions, movements, sounds. Rather, it is the form that promises something about its own future.)

Knowledge of this characteristic of discursive form in any art— theatre, dance, novel, or lyric poem—is part of the perception of that form. Therefore, although the maker does not promise specific futures, the perceiver (unless told not to) will compare given data with the data of the substitute memory, and often from this comparison he will make judgments about the probable nature of the future. Such behavior is typical in real life, where the variables are almost infinitely complex, the data often unreliable, and the memory blocked, prodded, or changed by psychological stress. In the perception of discursive form, the perceiver will indeed find that some of his same psychological stresses will block, prod, or change data in the substitute memory. However, the data itself is more reliable, having fewer variables, and is perceived in an environment that generally tries to reduce the possibilities of "wrong" perception. As a result, the perception of theatre by an audience (the communication of the information contained in performance) is partly this process of comparing all data, present and past, to predict possible futures.

Suspense, then, is merely a word used to describe this process. Given, however, the complex nature of that data (complex in presentation, primarily visual and aural; complex in content, dealing with different human beings, overt ideas, symbols, incidents), we must see that there is not *one* suspense, but many. Primary among these are the three areas of content that traditional criticism has most often dealt with: plot, character, and idea. It should be noted that formal suspenses are also possible (subintellectual predictions of visual or aural futures), but these are better described in terms of their main theatrical arts— directing, acting, and design.

Suspense of plot is the attempted prediction of future events or incidents. Simply, it is the attempt to answer the given question (who did it?) before the maker does. In more complex works (those having more than one plot), it is the attempt to connect apparently disconnected questions and give them a single answer. (Will Ralph save Cynthia from Herbert before the train goes through the tunnel and insane Harvey Belcher sets off the explosive?) Suspense of plot is typically disdained by most critics, because it is easily understood by a mass audience and is easily contrived or manipulated by its maker to give the greatest possible enjoyment to a puzzle-solving audience. It is a paradox, therefore, that the same critical attitude that will condemn plot-heavy works still relies almost totally on Aristotle, who stated very clearly that plot is the most important element in tragedy. In addition, the *lack* of plot suspense is reason enough to condemn a work from this point of view. Beckett's *Endgame,* for example, has been attacked because of its lack of plot, by which was meant, almost certainly, Beckett's refusal to create plot suspense in an audience. As a description of *Endgame,* a statement that it lacks suspense of plot is probably accurate enough. The conclusion, however, that it is, therefore, not a play, or even not a good play, is a *non sequitur.* Although it is generally true that most plays of the past have relied on some suspense of plot, and that Aristotelian criticism has considered suspense of plot necessary, to make suspense of plot the touchstone of theatre is ridiculous.

In this data comparison that is plot suspense, the point in the discursive work's development at which a comparison is made is of great importance. It is obvious, for example, that no substitute memory exists at the opening moment of any discursive work, and although an audience may bring with it certain prejudices about what *kinds* of suspense the work should create, that audience has no way of knowing what suspense will be created until the work is underway. The early stages of any work, then, put specific and peculiar demands on the maker: to load the substitute memory with data in such a way that the comparisons to be made at later stages will coincide with the kinds of suspense he is trying to create. In the case of suspense of plot, these data necessarily resemble what we call facts (Cynthia married Ralph last Tuesday; Harvey Belcher bought a keg of dynamite on Wednesday morning), none of which are known to the audience when the work begins. In the theatre the curtain goes up or the lights change or some announcement is made that the play is beginning. What happens onstage is perceived by the audience and stored as data. In many cases, however, the onstage "facts" are insufficient, and other "facts" must be narrated to the audience; that is, we may see the wedding scene of Cynthia's and Ralph's wedding, but we may have to learn through narration that Harvey bought his explosives the next morning (because there isn't time for another scene, or because the set would be too complicated, or for any of a vast number of reasons). Such secondary giving of data is generally called exposition. Typically, exposition is essential to an understanding of the entire play; the comparison to which it gives rise is made to lead, with more and more restriction (that is, there are fewer and fewer possible solutions to any comparison), to the so-called climax, the resolution of the suspense of plot. The movement toward the climax is often called development, rather a misnomer because of its implications of organic growth, enlargement, and enrichment. These three terms—*exposition, development,* and *climax*—mark the course of suspense of the plot. From the perceiver's point of view they mark three different processes: gathering of information, simultaneous gathering and comparison, and gathering of information as answers. Finally, the perceiver's use of, or reaction to, this information also falls into three stages: primary stasis, tension, and release (accompanied by surprise or self-congratulation). Where suspense of plot is aimed at as the primary artistic purpose of the maker (when, let us say, all intrinsic meanings are to be concentrated in suspense of plot), the end result is what has come to be known as the well-made play.

The Well-Made Play

When the promise made by discursive form (that it will have a future) becomes confused with the *use* of that form by the maker (when, that is, he promises that the future will take a certain shape), the result, in theatre, is the well-made play. Playwrights have not always entered into this kind of implied contract with their audiences, and their refusal to do so has meant a much richer use of dramatic form, because there is an immediate corollary to the contract that absolutely limits the playwright's field. That is, when he agrees to promise a certain future to his audience, he is implicitly promising that all acts, events, incidents, gestures, and words used in the performance of his play will lead to that same future. He is, in short, accepting the dogma of necessity of dramatic action. No word that is said, no gesture that is made, can any longer have merely intrinsic merit; it must contribute to the eventual future. The perceiver's work of comparison is thus greatly simplified, and his suspense, after a time, is lowered by the degree to which he learns to put together the pieces of the puzzle that the playwright is offering. The most capable of the dramatists who subscribed to this dogma was Eugene Scribe (1791–1861), whose plays were tight, beautifully controlled—in short, free of all matters that did not lead to the third-act climax. (Arthur Miller, although hardly an exponent of such playwriting, suffers some of its difficulties, and even in *Death of a Salesman* a student can find examples of the most careful planting of necessary, and avoidance of unnecessary, information.)

In the audience appreciation of the well-made play there is an assumed mode of perception. The audience must enter the theatre expecting the well-made play and nothing else. To give them any information that does not bear directly on the primary plot suspense is to confuse them, because they will not know what to do with it: it cannot be meaningfully compared to other data. *Hamlet* is a spectacular example of an ill-made play; if presented to Scribe's audience (if they could have avoided learning about the play's historical reputation), it would have puzzled, annoyed, and ultimately bored them. The opening scene is clear enough; we are to store data about the appearance of a ghost. The second is rather too diffuse, even in the beginning, to be really well made, but we can accept the king and his orders to his courtiers. The departure of Laertes is a bit much, because we have had no exposition about him and he appears to be hardly more important than Voltimand or Cornelius. (And what about that Fortinbras, who was mentioned briefly?) However, with the melancholy appearance of Hamlet himself we are completely lost; we have already been given too many variables—characters, scene locations, relationships, and attitudes—and we must conclude that Shakespeare, whoever he is, simply knows nothing about play construction. (Things do improve with the second Ghost scene, but as a first act, Shakespeare's simply cannot hold a candle to the worst of Scribe's.) The problem is not that Shakespeare's complex data is actually irrelevant, but that it will seem so to us if we have been conditioned by Scribe.

An analogy can be made with contemporary courtroom practice, in which the concept of admissible evidence is vital. Although it is true that the jury trial has an inherent theatrical quality (for a number of reasons, among them its intense ritualistic elements, its concentration, and its real discursive suspense), it is not itself an art form. The kind of "evidence" admissible in the courtroom is similar to the kind of data admissible in the well-made play. However, where the trial gains its tension from the contrast between the absolute limitations on this evidence and the highly variable and complex human qualities of its real participants, our perception of the equally strict limitations on the well-made play lessens the tension we feel toward its contrived and mimetic humans. In addition, the very limitations on data in the well-made play encourage contrivance, total control by the maker, and the reduction of human characters to puppets, slaves of the maker's rigid time scheme and the dogma of necessity.

So absolute, in fact, did the form of the well-made play become in the nineteenth century that one of its structural units was stressed over all others and was aimed at as the suspenseful climax. Thus, the *scène à faire* (the essential scene) became obligatory, a confrontation of individuals or an acting out of a stated thesis that the well-conditioned audience could not do without. To cite *Hamlet* again, we might say that the nineteenth-century audience could well have looked for a last-act *scène à faire* between Hamlet and Claudius, a confrontation based on some earlier promise made by the playwright. The play, of course, has no such scene, and we can see that no such promise exists. Yet it would be entirely possible to reconstruct *Hamlet* into a neat, well-made play in which such a confrontation was the climax, and we would have an oversimplified, easily understandable little work notable for its suspense of plot. That it would not be Shakespeare's *Hamlet*—that it would, in fact, be an awful play—is axiomatic.

If the well-made play and the *scène à faire* now seem artificial, even silly, to good contemporary critics, it should be remembered that many theatre reviewers still expect to see both on the stage. They may not use the same words, but they mean the same things when they say, for example, "The second act of M———'s new play is flawed by an irrelevant comic scene that detracts from the even flow of the story," or something like, "J———'s vicious satire is exciting moment by moment, but the whole is less than the sum of its parts." For the same reason a prominent American reviewer denigrated Arthur Miller's *Crucible* in its first production because the protagonist, John Proctor, did not deliver a heroic third-act speech—that is, the *scène à faire* was lacking.

It is historically interesting to judge plays written as well-made by their own standards. To apply the same standards to all dramas of all ages is to referee a hockey game using Roberts' *Rules of Order*.

Suspense of Character and Idea

Although suspense of plot is probably the most easily grasped of the discursive suspenses, suspense of idea and of character have traditionally been of greater importance, although not so frequently treated as fit matters for suspense. That is, although the word *suspense* has been applied narrowly to plot, words like *development, growth,* and *revelation* have typically been used for ideas and character. The reasons for this are not entirely clear, although there has been a continuing critical need to dignify character and ideas over plot by using other and more elevated words to describe them. Still, we should see that the data-comparison process we have described for the perception of a plot can equally well be applied to ideas or to characters.

Suspense of character can take three principal forms, any or all of which may be present in a given work. Most simply, there is the perceiver's suspense surrounding the "true" nature of a character. In the case of melodrama, for example, we are frequently confronted with clear cases of concealed identity, a rather crude but valid example of character suspense, as increasingly accurate data about the nature of villain and hero are fed to us. Such clear masking of identity is by no means rare, although it tends to limit such masked character to bold, black-and-white qualities. (Consider, for example, the traditional grade-B Western, with its rugged hero, about whom no suspense need be felt, and its villain, who lives in town as a respected banker, although he is really the leader of the vicious stagecoach band.)

A second, more complex character suspense lies in that felt by a character for himself. We may reduce such suspense to the "struggle for identity" that has become so fashionable in our own time, but it also exists in far richer forms in every period. Both *Hamlet* and *Oedipus Rex* concern themselves with just such suspense, although the terms in which the data of each protagonist's character is given to him are far different. For Hamlet, his personal suspense of character is couched in terms of doubt—of his own perceptions (the Ghost, madness, existence itself), of the validity of action, of his own good and his own evil—and is resolved in terms of assurance. For Oedipus, the contrary is true; personal suspense of character begins in assurance (the good king confidently seeking out the unknown polluter) and goes through a depth of doubt to a different assurance (the facts of his own history and their implications). For both, suspense of character can be used to describe the entire process, and it describes as well the process followed by the audience in perceiving them. The audience may perceive this suspense at a different rate from that of Hamlet or Oedipus, because often the audience gets far more data. The audience may even know ahead of time the final character resolution. Nevertheless, valid suspense is felt (valid comparison of information is made) because the added element of the character's own gathering of information poses new problems.

Finally, character suspense may surround the changing personality. Changed personalities are far rarer in both the theatre and in life than we should like to think. "He's a changed man" is a popular phrase, but usually this means no more than a change of environment or a change of minor mannerisms. It can be argued, too, that valid personality change is psychologically impossible, onstage or off. What is often mistaken for change (that of Hamlet or Oedipus, for example) proves, on examination, to be the gathering of information about the self. Finally, theatrical concepts of human psychology have tended more toward constancy of character than toward change. One may cite, for example, Molière's *commedia dell'arte*-based types, as in *The Miser*. One may, however, cite other dramatists—including Arthur Miller—for whom character change is possible. In these cases, audience perception of the change is suspenseful, involving readjustments to information originally given. In less believable cases (because they are obviously contrived for other purposes), character change ruptures character suspense instead of creating it. Much of the world's hack literature is heavily dependent on belated conversions of bad characters to good and last-act or last-chapter repentances or changes of heart. We have every right to suspect the lecherous villain who finally refuses to rape Little Nell after he has spent two acts trying to do just that. Our suspicion is justified not only by the abruptness of the change or even by its degree, but also by our sense that the maker has sacrificed character (about which, probably, little suspense has been generated) to suspense of plot, because in almost every case where such a late character change occurs we will find that the change satisfies some kind of plot suspense maintained throughout the work. Thus, any critical analysis that concentrates on character suspense through character change needs to be very sure of itself, for all too often it will find that the assumed character change is either a plot contrivance or, as in the case of much nineteenth-century English melodrama, wishful thinking. ("The vision of goodness can alter the most evil heart.")

If suspense of character can become complex in the theatre, then *suspense of idea* can become a complete tangle. The theatre is not the perfect medium for the communication of logical ideas, because its mode is not itself logical. As the contemporary playwright Eugene Ionesco has pointed out, one can find better logical ideas in books of

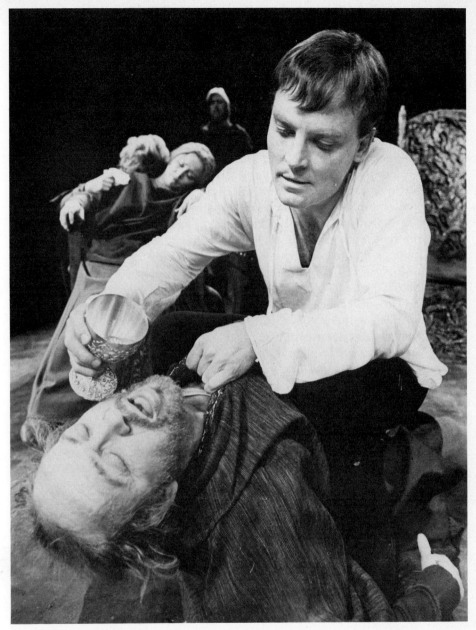

Figure 3–1. *Hamlet* at the Long Wharf Theatre, directed by Arvin Brown. Stacey Keach as Hamlet, Stefan Gierasch as Claudius. (*William L. Smith photo.*)

philosophy and better ideas about humanity in books of psychology. Still, we are faced with the rather disturbing facts that "The Idea of the Play" could be the title of at least one paragraph in traditional criticism of almost any play; that a first-rate American critic, Eric

Bentley, has written a book with the pointed title, *The Playwright As Thinker;* and that dramatic texts are the only source materials in some courses now being offered in the history of ideas at American universities. Aristotle, too, listed idea as one of the six elements of drama, but we can be grateful that his genius recognized the importance of the other five. In any case, we have to admit that the theatre has been and still is viewed as offering intellectual content in its performances.

Let us repeat: the theatre is not a logical form. The sequence of its discursive elements it not necessarily causal. A performance, therefore, need not pattern itself after the syllogism.

There is a logical example of discursive form: the essay. (We may overlook the suggestion that the essay is, in our time, the most fundamental unit of communication.) Suffice it to say that the philosophic essay, rigidly structured around the rational presentation of an idea, is different from anything that goes on in the theatre. Compare, for example, a Platonic dialogue with a dramatic text, whether *Oedipus Rex* or *Endgame.* Despite rather pathetic attempts in past ages to stage Plato's dialogues, there is every indication that they bear only superficial resemblance to anything that goes on in any theatre. Yet, they are filled with ideas; we can say, in fact, that they create, almost exclusively, a suspense of idea: the comparison of given intellectual data with data already planted in the substitute memory. Their data about character are few and are actually part of the idea, Plato's "characters" being rather single-minded spokesmen for intellectual attitudes. Their data about plot is more slight still. And, of course, they offer no aural or visual data that would intrude on the suspense of idea.

The theatre performance, on the other hand, already replete with aural and visual data, suspense of plot (sometimes), and suspense of character (often), resists most attempts to give it a logical structure (that is, to make suspense of idea the primary concern). Instead, it may offer brief essays—Hamlet's soliloquies, the lyrical outpourings of Sophocles' chorus on destiny—that, in the context of a performance, are absorbed into character and plot. In other words, "ideas," or "philosophy" ("What is Shakespeare's philosophy?" the final exam may ask) tend to disappear into the texture of the performance. Not surprisingly, one finds that ideas do the same thing in the everyday world, where what Mister Smith says is not so important as the fact that he says it, and how.

Does this mean that the theatre, then, is *not* a medium for ideas, or that the theatre, as a medium for ideas, works by indirection and cleverly buries its intellectual content in nonintellectual experience? The answer, of course, is no to both questions—but a no that is qualified by the awareness that no theatrical artist works with idea as his sole aim. Idea is not what is communicated. Ideas may be contained in the thing communicated. As such, they represent storable data; they can be compared, and a valid suspense of idea can be defined. Thus, as we shall see, ideas can be interpreted from performance, but never because the performance was first structured to serve logical suspense.

Conditioned Modes of Perception

It is plain from the discussion of the well-made play that audience response to a play is affected by the audience's real memory of former responses to similar plays. In a sense, then, any of the discursive suspenses is lessened by the theatrical experience of an audience, if the same means are used to create or maintain that suspense in subsequent works. In a rather crude way, this statement is true; in practice, however, it seems that the majority of audiences have been able to enjoy the specifics of any kind of suspense (the resolution of a specific plot, the self-discovery of a specific character) while enjoying quite separately the repetition of an experience they have already been through. The *scène à faire* is an obvious example of such enjoyed repetition, in which, in fact, the repetition itself of a given structural pattern became an obligation upon the maker. In every age of theatre activity, a tension is set up between just such experienced perception and the desire of some makers to violate the experienced expectation (*not* to create the *scène à faire*, for example). At stake in the tension between these two things—the audience's right to enjoy repetition, even to the point of ritual, and the artist's right to make the performance entirely suspenseful, without already experienced elements—is a considerable slice of critical concepts: the romantic idea of originality; the absolutist ideas of propriety, of "good" and "bad" ways of doing things in the theatre; the concept of style; and the question of such matters as didacticism, of entertainment, and of the relationship between the play and its audience. Clearly, too, the very existence of such conditioned modes of audience perception makes it necessary to understand the historical location of any given play, if only to discover what things in it were expected and what were truly suspenseful.

Consider, for example, the run-of-the-mill television series. Appearing once a week, the same characters run through the same general patterns again and again, sometimes for years. We are probably justified in guessing that it is the very sameness of such shows that assures their popularity—that, in fact, the virtual assurance of repetition gives comfort to the viewers (much as some primitive rituals give comfort to their participants). We are accustomed to seeing such words as *unoriginal* and *imitative* applied to such series. Apparently we should admit that these very qualities are part of their excellence *for their intended audiences*.

And so with all phases of the theatre. How relevant now is the question of Shakespeare's originality—that is, his refusal to do the expected thing at the expected time in a given place? The point of finding the historical source of *Hamlet* is not to prove or disprove Shakespeare's originality, but to try to understand some of its otherwise confusing elements in our own terms. Or again, the analysis of Molière's *The Miser* in terms of its *commedia dell'arte* antecedents is useless if all it allows us to do is prove that Molière gave his audience experiences they recognized and with which they felt comfortable. In the case of *Hamlet* and *The Miser* we find sizable areas of imitativeness, of catering to a conditioned audience, but we hardly write off the two plays for this reason. We can generalize, in fact, and say that the further one moves from his own time, the less important originality becomes in the qualitative judging of works, although it is helpful in analyzing the way in which these works were created.

In one's own time, on the other hand, originality—the fracturing of the practiced mode, the destruction of audience comfort—has great importance. We ordinarily say that original talents are pushing out the boundaries of theatre, although what they are probably doing is redefining the idea of suspense. The work of people like Alwyn Nikolais and John Cage in our own time would be of value if only because of its effect on audience perception. It is difficult to look at established forms with the same attitude after seeing a Nikolais or a Cage performance. (It is probably true, too, that such works are overpraised in some criticism because we happen to live in a romantic age: when, that is, novelty is valued for its own sake rather than for its relation to the theatre as a whole.)

Perhaps we can generalize again: it seems to be true that the great proportion of any theatrical audience values its comfort more than its pleasure in suspense, and that conditioned modes are most acceptable to the majority. Somewhat in reaction, smaller audiences, even coteries and claques, will overvalue the very opposite. Thus, there is a tension between the mass audience and the smaller audience (called, with varying degrees of accuracy, the educated, the aware, the tasteful, the avant-garde, or the thinking audience) that mirrors the tension felt by theatre artists in coping with the problems of suspense. It mirrors, too, the false tension created by many critics between entertainment and art—false because it is based in snobbery and ignores the evident facts that mass audience or coterie audience, the theatrical process is the same and that any worthwhile criticism should prize diversity.

Audience Identification and Objectivity

An audience's perception of a theatrical performance and its reaction to that perception are not the same thing; there is always an attitude *toward* the information taken in. In the main, two attitudes are identified in an audience, objectivity and identification. In the first, the audience observes the data (although the scientific implication of such language is unfair). In the other, it participates, or at least tries to participate. Children, for example, are marvelous participants in the theatre and often try to run onstage to take part in the performance. Children's plays are written to exploit this attitude, and they often turn the audience into an actual character in the play, asking it to sing songs, to answer questions about the play's action, and even to influence the play's action. (Tinkerbell, in *Peter Pan*, needs the audience's applause to survive.) Such an attitude seems on first glance to be very desirable in the theatre, because it obviously keeps its audience attentive and causes them to react often and violently. Many actors prefer such audiences at any performance; they speak of playing "sympathetic" roles, meaning roles that the audience will actively like.

On the other hand, the attitude has its drawbacks. Although human warmth and sympathy are desirable in society, they are not really desirable if the playwright or the director wants the audience to follow specific lines of information; particularly the so-called didactic theatre finds such audience identification repulsive because it interferes with learning. As a result, some playwrights, directors, and actors have developed techniques to encourage objectivity and discourage identification. The audience is cooled off repeatedly during the performance so that it can review its gathered data and, hopefully, make a decision on the basis of it. Probably the polarizing of the two attitudes is a mistake, and a mixture of them is inevitably present in every audience member. However, tendencies in one direction or the other can be encouraged by the makers. The devices used for this encouragement must be uncovered in the analysis of a performance, because, again, the understanding of the performance itself depends on knowing what the performance meant to do. Certain formal elements, particularly—the parabasis of Greek comedy, the rhetorical Elizabethan set speech, and some of the theatrical references in *Endgame*—are easily understood once they are seen as objectifying devices.

Similarly, the devices of identification are often revealing. The casting of actresses who look and talk like housewives in television commercials is intended to encourage audience identification, this leading it is hoped, to the buying of soap or floor wax. Slanting the social environment of a play's setting, its language, and its characters' jobs, to match that of the play's audience (possible only with a unified audience) may help the audience to identify. Some of the strength of Molière's *The Miser* certainly is the satirical reverse of this process: slanting his play toward his audience and trapping them into identification, so that their discovery of themselves will be sharp. As a general rule, one can say that reminders of the theatre itself—masks, speeches to the audience, houselights left up during a performance, and the use of the theatre building itself for the setting—will help an audience to objectify. Disguise of these elements—the darkened house, the naturalistic setting, the lack of formal or rhetorical language, and the naturalistic make-up—will encourage identification. Neither attitude is better *per se*, although we can note even at this point that identification belies the nature of the data taken in by the audience (trying to make it actual, not virtual, history), and that, historically, theatres that asked their audiences to identify often did so within the narrow range of strong sensations (thrills) and shallow emotions (sentimentality).

ARISTOTELIAN ANALYSIS

It is virtually impossible, at this late date in theatre history, to approach any performance critically without somehow encountering the influence of Aristotle. Most audience members of any experience whatever will have encountered him, often at second or third hand. All teachers of literature, drama, English, or aesthetics have studied him closely, and some still judge all works from his point of view. Even actors and directors whose own artistic approaches are deeply non-Aristotelian may find themselves discussing dramatic texts in strictly Aristotelian terms. For the theatre student, a firm knowledge of Aristotle is a necessary part of his critical equipment.

Aristotle was a late fourth-century B.C. philosopher whose comments on the theatre represent only a small part of his work. This theatre criticism, however, is in complete harmony with the rest of his work, in that it is founded on the same assumptions and prejudices about human beings and their environment. A student of Plato's, Aristotle shares Plato's reliance on logic as the prime function of the mind, the same tendency to identify levels of value with levels of logical thought. Thus, the theatre criticism contained in *The Poetics* is itself logical and seeks to find logical structure in the plays it analyzes. Naturally, it finds such structure, not because the structure is necessarily there but because Aristotle needs to find it there. For our purposes, we need to understand three aspects of the Aristotelian bias; that existence is logically progressive, and so a theatrical representation of existence must have progression and logic; that man is perfectible, and so "positive" theatrical characters (call them heroes, protagonists, or what we will) are reflections of the perfect (and any deviations from the idea of perfection will be viewed as errors or flaws); and that symmetry is an ideal aspect of existence, and so of the theatre (expressed typically as balance, proportion, propriety, or unity).

Most of Aristotle's important theatre ideas are contained in that section of the *Poetics* dealing with tragedy, but the ideas themselves have been used in judging the entire field of drama. The question of their relevance to tragedy itself can be delayed. One idea dominates, and to some extent explains, all others: the idea of dramatic unity. Unity, or wholeness, is the condition of a work that has *a beginning, a middle, and an end,* and in which the *component incidents must be so arranged that if one of them be altered or removed, the unity of the whole is disturbed and destroyed.* It is evident that Aristotle is concerned here principally with plot, which he views as being progressive

Figure 3–2. *Indians* at the University of Illinois, directed by Mary Arbenz. Settings by Don Llewellyn, costumes by Susan Benson.

and causal—that is, as a sequence of incidents that are a consequence of one another. Thus, the idea of unity is really an idea of causal (logical) progression, quite like the causal progression of a syllogism from premise to premise to conclusion.

Of only slightly less importance is the Aristotelian idea of *action*. *Tragedy is the representation of a whole action, whole meaning unified.* Again, we may guess (but only guess, because of the vagueness of much of the *Poetics*) that action means the same process we have already discussed—human beings working through a sequence in time. This process is often confused with plot in the *Poetics* (when, for example, the expression translated as *well-constructed plot* is substituted for *action* at the end of the passage on the wholeness of action). Recent commentators, however, have tended to enlarge the definition of action, partly to defend Aristotle against the attacks of twentieth-century criticism. A relevant definition of Gerald Else's, quoted by William Arrowsmith in "The Criticism of Greek Tragedy," views dramatic action as "a *transaction*," something taking place between human beings. This redefinition, of course, is quite different from plot, and it greatly strengthens Aristotle's view of drama as a whole. At any rate, the primacy of action in the *Poetics* reflects Aristotle's consciousness of drama as belonging to the narrative mode, and he apparently did understand drama in that sense. Drama in performance *is* pre-eminently active; when it stops being active it becomes something else. To say, however, as a consequence that drama in performance is *an action* is to make a partly critical judgment, not an entirely analytical description.

After the concepts of unity and of action, the most influential Aristotelian idea is his definition of character, and, most importantly, of the character of the protagonist, the principal dramatic figure in the action. Although not every detail of Aristotle's psychology is clear, it can certainly be said that he subscribed to some idea of motivated behavior in dramatic character and that he found the most important signs of motivated behavior in decisions made by these characters. Thus, from the Aristotelian point of view, any individual action can be explained as the result of a decision. (Oedipus *decides* to ignore the advice of Teiresias when confronted with the choice Teiresias offers.) Again, for Aristotle, all decisions must be consistent with each other; that is, one must be able to see the same powerful motivation behind all decisions. Character, in fact, can be defined as the sum total of the decisions contained in a play. Out of this theory of motivation and consistency comes one of the most disputed points of Aristotelian theory, the idea of *hamartia*. Badly translated as *tragic flaw*, the word is sometimes used to mean *error of judgment*—that is, a bad decision. (Again, we can cite Oedipus' apparently bad decision about Teiresias' advice.) The sense of tragic flaw is a terrible oversimplification of Aristotle's own discussion in the *Poetics;* even the idea behind it is founded, as we have seen, in a theory of perfection that many playwrights, actors, and directors have not believed. The *Phaedra* of Racine can well be discussed in terms of just such a tragic flaw, because Racine's dramaturgy is based on a very strict interpretation of Aristotle. On the other hand, Hamlet's behavior is frankly inconsistent and not flawed, because Elizabethan psychology could reject both the theory of perfection and the theory of consistency. The best that can be said for Aristotle's idea of character—perfectible, consistent, and flawed—is that when playwrights write *according to his concepts*, they occasionally produce works of great power. We should admit at the same time, however, that the very plays Aristotle used in formulating this theory (including *Oedipus Rex*) may have been written out of a different idea of human psychology. In our own time, certainly, the Aristotelian idea has proved inadequate for such theorists as the German playwright-director Berthold Brecht.

As we have said, a knowledge of Aristotle is necessary. A slavish use of Aristotle is not. As things now stand, a strict reading of the theory of tragedy contained in the *Poetics* is simply inadequate for the analysis of, let us say, *Hamlet*; the theory of character is inadequate for an analysis of Willy Loman in *Death of a Salesman*, of Harpagon in *The*

Miser, or even of Sophocles' *Oedipus*. We must always remember that a critical theory based on a belief in perfectibility, in logic, and in symmetry will not explain an artistic form that is neither logical nor symmetrical, and one that frequently seems to celebrate the imperfect instead of the perfect. As William Arrowsmith has pointed out, it is the very "turbulence" of Greek tragedies that gives them their greatness, yet it is the same turbulence (inconsistency of character, lack of unity, and shocked examination of a world in which perfection is impossible) from which Aristotle seems to have turned away.

Generic Criticism

Part of our Aristotelian heritage is our love of pigeonholing drama by genres. (Polonius' "tragedy, comedy, history, pastoral, pastoral-comical, historical-pastoral, tragical-historical, tragical-comical-historical-pastoral.") It is true, as we have already said, that rough divisions by types (fantasy, history, fiction) or by primary suspense (plot, character, idea) have a limited critical function; so, too, attention to a play's genre is fruitful because it sometimes allows us to understand better what an audience will do with the data given it. In actual practice, however, generic analysis has long since stopped being a mere analytical tool and has become an end in itself. The very classification of a play by genres has come to represent a value judgment in itself. Thus, Arthur Miller found it necessary to defend his own classification of *Death of a Salesman* as a tragedy, as if that classification could somehow improve the play itself or its performance. In the same way, a number of Molière's dramatic prefaces were devoted to defending comedy as a genre. In addition, the other principal genres (melodrama and farce) have often been considered inferior to tragedy and comedy, and the modifiers *melodramatic* and *farcical* have become pejorative critical terms. The reasons for such prescriptive use of descriptive terms is not always certain, but in general it appears to be true that social prejudice is at the root of the tragedy-comedy battle; an age-old critical tendency toward setting up absolute standards has led to the prescriptive use of genre. Most periods, of course, have borne quite happily with mixed genres (like those of Polonius), and there is a powerful urgency in contemporary plays toward the destruction not only of generic labels, but also of the "unified" tone that generic criticism has often demanded. *Endgame*, for example, moves from a laugh-getting vaudeville routine into a deeply serious presentation of cruelty, and out again, without even shifting gears. The play itself has intrinsic meanings of the utmost seriousness, presented in theatrical situations familiar from the music hall and burlesque.

The social basis for the tragedy-comedy division is suggested in the *Poetics*, but *only* suggested: "[Comedy] set out to represent people as worse than they are today, [tragedy] as better." "Comedy . . . is a representation of inferior people." "The laughable is a species of the base or ugly." Still, Aristotle never goes so far as to say that tragedy deals with a higher class of people, comedy with a lower class. His "inferior" category is largely a moral one, just as his tragic protagonist, as we have seen, is defined as morally superior (nearer the perfect). With the Latin poet Horace, however, the social application of this moral idea becomes overt, and the *Ars Poetica* of the Roman poet reflects the aristocratic bias of his age, the age of Vergil and Augustus Caesar. Thus, the moral elevation (even moral heroism) of Aristotle becomes a social elevation that encompasses moral heroism in Horace. (Caesar is both a political and a moral ideal.) In contrast, social inferiority belongs with moral inferiority, the designated field of comedy.

> Comedy rejects the poetry of tragedy;
> [A tragic scene] will not use
> Narration in everyday language of common people,
> The language that suits humble comedy.

In this sense, Horace can be used as a gloss on the vagueness of Aristotle, and he was so used in the Renaissance. The absolutist and aristocratic criticism of France in the seventeenth century, for example, depended heavily on social distinction, and elevated tragedy over comedy *because* of the social differences between the two (after defining the genres, to begin with, in partly social terms). Even with the destruction of the aristocratic bias in later democratic periods, the value distinction remained, and even today we often encounter an almost superstitious belief that tragedy is somehow better than comedy. It need not be. Frequently, talented playwrights have written what was called tragedy in their own times because of the reputation tragedy then enjoyed. As we can see with Molière, however, playwrights of gigantic talent have often turned to comedy or, as with Beckett, to indeterminate genres with equal success.

Setting aside generic analysis as a value judgment, the critic is still faced with the huge problem of defining the genres themselves. If we remove the social distinctions of Horace, the definition gets even harder. The world's critical literature is heavy with attempts to provide workable definitions, and none has yet proved satisfactory.

In a very general way, however, two or three definitions have been useful. One, represented by George Meredith's "Essay on Comedy," defines comedy (and tragedy by contrast) in terms of its subject matter, limiting comedy to the field of social behavior. Such a definition is to be expected from an English critic writing in a tradition that includes Jonson, the misnamed Restoration "comedy of manners," and such late comic examples as the operettas of Gilbert and Sullivan, the comedies of Pinero, and, to an extent, Shaw. Meredith's spirit of comedy is still rather aristocratic, and he finds in comedy a normative function rather than an expressive one; that is, comedy is a corrective that improves our social behavior by making us laugh at our foibles.

The French philosopher Henri Bergson set up another criterion for comedy, this one based on broader human, rather than narrow social, patterns of behavior. Taking Molière as his greatest example, Bergson postulated a theory of "the mechanical" that goes a good way toward explaining what is laughable about physical behavior (pratfalls, slapstick comedy, the custard pie, and the grotesque) as well as the more complex area of psychology (comic character as it is shown in Harpagon, for example). For Bergson, comic technique is the creation of nonhuman, or mechanical, patterns of action, behavior, and psychology: the mechanical is laughable to the human being. Bergson's theory is more useful than Meredith's, if only because it is more inclusive.

Still a third idea of dramatic comedy is based on the structure and kind of incidents in a play rather than on its subject matter or social area. Essentially anthropological, the theory is not so much a definition as a comparison with ancient comic forms. By finding certain kinds of incidents and certain kinds of character (nonfatal violence, ruses, sexual tricks and sexual references, real or mock weddings, final banquets or eating scenes, or intense concern with money), the critic can place a play within a line that begins with predramatic ritual and that can be shown to include most plays called comedies by other definitions.

Tragedy, too, has enjoyed many attempts at exact definition, none of them satisfying to everybody. Aristotle lies at the root of most of them; where he does not, an anthropological approach similar to that used for comedy has often been applied. The word *tragedy* itself has not always been used in the same way, of course. In the sixteenth century in England, for example, we find a play described as "a goodlie Tragedy, full of Mirth," and a reading of the play shows that it is indeed mirthful, but has a good deal of genuine bloodshed in it as well. In medieval and early Renaissance usage, *tragedy* often had a specifically Christian meaning, derived from an acute awareness of the importance of unrepentant death. Tragedy, thus, could be no more than a study of the life and death of a Christian who dies with all his sins still upon him (and *Hamlet* surely springs to mind here). Finally, tragedy was a word before it was a self-conscious theatrical form, and a fully fledged theatrical form before any attempt was made to set down rules for it.

Farce and melodrama are generally interpreted as subforms of comedy and tragedy. Farce (from a root meaning *to stuff*, probably because farce is "stuffed" with gag humor) is a time-honored kind of theatre and a most demanding one. It is very easily defined by its effect on an audience; if they don't laugh, you don't have a farce. In terms of textual analysis, of course, definition can be more difficult, because the farce of one period may be the comedy of another, and we have far too many instances (*The Miser, The Importance of Being Earnest*) of plays that are acceptably called both. If a distinction must be made between farce and comedy, however, it can probably best be made in terms of the presence or absence of intrinsic meaning. That is, comedy that seems to be more than farce is "more than farce" by its degree of intrinsic meaning. One might say that farce is the *mode* of comedy.

Similarly, melodrama is the mode of tragedy. Like farce, it typically lacks intrinsic meaning. Like farce, it can be partly identified by the presence of characteristic elements (surprise, extremes of tone, violence), but the same elements will identify any so-called tragedies. In fact, it is useful to think of *all* tragedies as melodramas because it helps to understand their impact on an audience. Although the word *melodrama* has come to have bad associations (the mustachioed villain, the old homestead, the railroad track), the mode itself retains its usefulness; it has simply been downgraded because of bad examples. If, on the other hand, we can think of tragedy as melodrama plus something else, we can see that melodrama itself is valid.

MYTH AND MEANING

We have already identified the "something else" of tragedy and comedy as intrinsic meaning. To attach such importance to any kind of meaning in the theatre, however, is an apparent contradiction of the earlier statement that the theatre is not a fit place for the communication of ideas. The contradiction is resolved, of course, by pointing out that ideas and meaning are simply not the same thing; ideas need logical structuring and verbal expression; meaning can be given logical structure at times, but not always, and finds verbal expression to be only one means of expression. In a sense, theatre follows Archibald MacLeish's dictum about poetry that "A poem must not mean, but be"; it has a self-justifying existence, like music and painting, as valid experience. However, the very richness of its means of expression, its symbols (language, human character, action, the visual effects of lighting, architecture, setting, costume, and make-up), and the fact of its temporal existence make it much more than sensuous experience. It is a symbolic discourse capable of complex, varied, and ultimately important meanings. The symbols by which these meanings are communicated are worth examining.

Language

"Words, words, words," Hamlet says, expressing a fatigue with language that seems paradoxical in such a wordy play. "Molière saved comedy from literature," said Fernandez, meaning somewhat the same thing about the usefulness of words in the theatre. Hamlet is only partly joking; Fernandez was very serious. French comedy before Molière's infusion of *commedia dell'arte* language was heavily verbal in the same way that a restoration English play like Wycherley's *Country Wife* is verbal, deriving much of its impact from word play and from overt comment. Then Molière came along and showed that intensely funny, intensely comic scenes could be created without word play or witty lines—showed, in fact, that language could have an important nonverbal function in the theatre. It was thus that he saved comedy from literature, and thus that his plays often seem so dead on the page when compared, for example, to those of Wycherley. An early scene from *The Country Wife* is almost totally verbal:

Enter Harcourt and Dorilant to Horner

HARCOURT. Come, your appearance at the play yesterday has, I hope, hardened you for the future against the women's contempt and the men's raillery; and now you'll abroad as you were wont.

HORNER. Did I not bear it bravely?

DORILANT. With a most theatrical impudence, nay, more than the orange-wenches show there, or a drunken vizard-mask, or a great-bellied actress; nay, or the most impudent of creatures, an ill poet; or what is yet more impudent, a second-hand critic.

HORNER. But what say the ladies? Have they no pity?

HARCOURT. What ladies? The vizard-masks, you know, never pity a man when all's gone, though in their service.

DORILANT. And for the women in the boxes, you'd never pity them when 'twas in your power.

HARCOURT. They say 'tis pity, but all that deal with common women should be served so.

DORILANT. Nay, I dare swear they won't admit you to play at cards with them, go to plays with 'em, or do the little duties which other shadows of men are wont to do for 'em.

HORNER. Who do you call shadows of men?

DORILANT. Half-men.

HORNER. What, boys?

DORILANT. Ay, your old boys, old *beaux garçons*, who, like superannuated stallions, are suffered to run, feed, and whinny with the mares as long as they live, though they can do nothing else.

HORNER. Well, a pox on love and wenching! Women serve but to keep a man from better company. Though I can't enjoy them, I shall you the more. Good fellowship and friendship are lasting, rational, and manly pleasures.

HARCOURT. For all that, give me some of those pleasures you call effeminate, too; they help to relish one another.

HORNER. They disturb one another.

HARCOURT. No, mistresses are like books. If you pore upon them too much, they doze you.

Act I, 1

And so on, with further similes, comparisons, and discussions. Compare the preceding scene with the following one from *The Miser:*

(*Maître Jacques enters to Harpagon and Cléante, who have been arguing*)

MAÎTRE JACQUES. Eh, eh, eh, Messieurs, what's this? What are you thinking of?

CLÉANTE. I defy him.

MAÎTRE JACQUES (*to Cléante*). Ah, Monsieur, gently!

HARPAGON. To speak to me with such insolence!

MAÎTRE JACQUES (*to Harpagon*). Ah, Monsieur, slowly.

CLÉANTE. I won't stand for it!

MAÎTRE JACQUES (*to Cléante*). What, what? To your father?

HARPAGON. Let me at him—!

MAÎTRE JACQUES (*to Harpagon*). What, what? To your son? Let me help, Monsieur.

HARPAGON. I want you, Maître Jacques, to be the judge of this yourself, to prove how right I am!

MAÎTRE JACQUES. I consent. (*to Cléante*). Remove yourself a bit, if you please.

HARPAGON. I love a girl, whom I want to marry; and that scoundrel has the insolence to love her along with me, and to go on doing it against my orders.

MAÎTRE JACQUES. Ah! he's very wrong.

HARPAGON. Isn't it a dreadful thing that a son will go into competition with his father? And shouldn't he, out of respect, get out of the way of my affection?

MAÎTRE JACQUES. You are so right! Let me speak to him, and you stay here. (*He crosses to Cléante, at the other side of the stage.*)

CLÉANTE (*to Maître Jacques as he approaches*). Very well! yes, since he wants to pick you as his judge, I'll tell you everything; I don't care who he is; and I must make you understand, Maître Jacques, what our battle is about.

MAÎTRE JACQUES. You honor me too much, Monsieur.

CLÉANTE. I adore a young woman, who loves me in return and who accepts gratefully my vows of love; and my father thinks he will disturb our love by the proposal he has made to her.

MAÎTRE JACQUES. He's quite wrong, obviously.

CLÉANTE. Has he no shame, at his age, to think of marrying? Can it be good for him to fall in love? And shouldn't he leave that occupation for younger men?

MAÎTRE JACQUES. You are absolutely right; he's making a fool of himself. Let me say a few words to him. (*He returns to Harpagon.*) Ah, well! your son is not so bizarre as you said, Monsieur, and he will submit to reason. He says that he knows the respect he owes to you, that he was carried away by the first flush of anger, and that he could hardly refuse to give in to whatever you desire.

(*And the scene goes on, with Maître Jacques moving from one to the other with increasing speed, until he leaves, and each discovers that he has been duped.*)

The first scene is almost totally expressed in its lines (although this is not true of the entire play); the second is expressed in movements that the lines command. The first restricts the theatrical experience to an auditory and intellectual one; the second expands it to a richly involved auditory and visual one. This quality of Molière's use of language has been the subject of much analysis; the term most often used for it is *choreographic*. It gives the scene not only its tone and its content, but its rhythm, the pattern of its movements, and the possibility of expanding the verbal content.

The comparison of the two scenes illustrates the first requisite of theatrical language: it must do more than simply communicate its own surface meaning. Considered as speech by the characters of a play, it must be part of a pattern of gestures that we associate with each of those characters, for speech is only one of many human gestures. Considered as part of the sensuous experience of a play, it must contribute to the sensuous patterns of the play's performance by demanding movement and rhythm. In all cultures where the theatre uses written texts as permanent records of the play's content, the playwright's language must require the richest possible use of the theatre's other symbols. When theatrical language does not make these demands—when, for example, it is impossible for an actor to enrich his speeches with movement, pauses, inflections, gestures; when visual patterns and auditory rhythms are merely imposed on the language rather than required by it—we have bad use of language. (And the "plays" of Byron can be cited here as examples of very bad use of language by a first-rate poet whose nontheatrical use of language was excellent.) It is tempting to jump to the conclusion that theatrical language should meet Mies van der Rohe's dictum, "Less is more"—that, somehow, merely leaving out certain data that language can convey will make for richer performance. Contemporary reviewers have, thus, spoken of leaving "holes" in the written text, the holes to be filled in by the actors' techniques. This kind of underwriting, however, is no more good theatrical writing than Byron's overwriting was, because all it generally means is dramaturgical laziness. In the rare case, however, where a playwright has so mastered his own language and its intricacies of connotative symbolic meanings, less *is* more. This is true not because the playwright has left holes for the actors, but because he uses language that is itself packed with meaning but unable to bear the full weight of the play's meaning—again demanding symbolic expansion in gesture, rhythm, movement, and spectacle. No modern playwright shows this more expressively than Samuel Beckett, and the dialogue of *Endgame* is excitingly theatrical. Beckett's language is spare, compressed, and intense. Like Molière's, it demands full theatrical expression in visual terms.

Given a use of language that satisfactorily demands other symbols and imposes gesture and rhythm, one must still expect other things from it. It is axiomatic that the use of language by a character must express that character. Similarly, we ordinarily expect vocabulary, idiom, and dialect to match what we are given of the character's circumstances. In illusionistic drama, we have a right to be puzzled by taxi drivers who talk like statesmen or children who talk like college presidents. On the other hand, we should not argue back from this and say that there is only one vocabulary or one idiom for any character. In the first place, historical shifts in language have made this impossible; in the second place, such general typing by language is partly a matter of prejudice and at least partly inaccurate; and finally, the dramatist and the actor must be allowed the freedom to create their own language and to define its limits as they see fit. *Endgame* shows a rare, nonillusionistic use of language, limited as it is in vocabulary and figures of speech. The soliloquies, or the Hamlet-Ghost scene, from *Hamlet*, on the other hand, are examples of a tremendously expanded and complex vocabulary, of a rich use of figures of speech, that are equally acceptable because they are harmonious with the terms the playwright has set. Probably the one use of language we will always be suspicious of is the one that tries to adapt vocabulary and figures of speech to the needs of the moment, rather than to the needs of character or the limits of the play itself. When, for example, the playwright reserves an elevated language—Latinate words, let us say, and elegant turns of phrase, and poetic figures of speech—for elevated moments (nobility of thought, heroism, moral resignation), he is misusing language. First, he is probably violating suspense of character, because there is a strong link between a character and his language. Secondly, and more important, he is violating the very limits he has apparently set throughout the play. The bulk of Arthur Miller's *Death of a Salesman* is illusionistic and the characters express themselves in a restricted but rich language whose vocabulary is that of a recognizable section of American society. The references are immediate, direct, known (Yankee Stadium, Yonkers, the refrigerator, shaving lotion), and Willy Loman and his family find no need for poetic figures of speech. When, however, the "Requiem" comes after Act II, Charley suddenly elevates his language to try to match the needed elevation of Willy as tragic protagonist:

CHARLEY. Nobody dast blame this man. You don't understand: Willy was a salesman. And for a salesman, there is no rock bottom to the life. He don't put a bolt to a nut, he don't tell you the law or give you medicine. He's a man way out there in the blue, riding on a smile and a shoeshine. And when they start not smiling back—that's an earthquake. And then you get yourself a couple of spots on your hat, and you're finished. Nobody dast blame this man. A salesman is got to dream, boy. It comes with the territory.

Although the speech is successful for its effect as a graveside eulogy, it is a departure from both the previous language of Charley and the language of the play itself. The vocabulary is the same, but the sudden poetic compression and the use of metaphor are a rather jarring shift.

When a playwright so enlarges his language and his use of it as to come within the borders of poetry, an analysis of his language must deal with its poetics as well as the aspects described previously. There is no requirement that a playwright approach the poetic, although T. S. Eliot and two millennia of critic-scholars have found it desirable. Poetry—whether in the limited sense of metrical verse, rhymed and unrhymed, or in the broader sense of rhythmic, nonmetrical contemporary poetry—is not always an ideal vehicle for theatre language. Its very formalism separates it from everyday speech, and so makes it of questionable use to the illusionistic theatre. The more restricted its meter, rhyme, and verse schemes become, the less leeway its playwright has in imposing other rhythms on the play's action. On the other hand, the richness that such poetic devices as metaphor, simile, personification, and illusion can bring to the theatre can be of great value, *if* they are fresh and vivid, *if* they can be taken in by the ear alone without repetition, and *if* they can lie within the limits of the playwright's over-all use of language. The simile used in *Death of a Salesman*, for example, of Willy as a "little boat looking for a harbor," besides being outside Miller's language limit, is not really a very good simile. It is far from fresh or new. The image it conjures up, particularly with the use of the word *little*, is pallid, even sentimental; and the comparison is so general as to lower, rather than raise, the subject of the simile, Willy Loman. In contrast, a single speech from *Hamlet* may compress several potent images into the same sentence, use a number of poetic devices in rapid succession, and all without any sense of violation because the language is that of the entire work and the devices themselves are vigorous:

> Witness this army, of such mass and charge,
> Led by a delicate and tender Prince
> Whose spirit with divine ambition puffed
> Makes mouths at the invisible event,
> Exposing what is mortal and unsure
> To all that fortune, death and danger dare,
> Even for an eggshell! Rightly to be great
> Is not to stir without great argument,
> But greatly to find quarrel in a straw
> When honor's at the stake. How stand I then,
> That have a father killed, a mother stained,
> Excitements of my reason and my blood,
> And let all sleep while to my shame I see
> The imminent death of twenty thousand men
> That for a fantasy and trick of fame
> Go to their graves like beds, fight for a plot
> Whereon the numbers cannot try the cause
> Which is not tomb enough and continent
> To hide the slain?

Hamlet, IV, 4

Immediately it should be noted that the images, like so many of Shakespeare's, are visual. Where Miller's image is general or fuzzy, Shakespeare's is simple but brilliantly clear—the army of "mass and charge," the "excitements of the reason and the blood," "imminent death," the complicated but finally clear vision of the small size of the ground to be fought over. There is, furthermore, the repeated use of doubles ("delicate and tender," "mortal and unsure," "fantasy and trick," "tomb enough and continent"), in which the second half of each double enlarges the visual picture by a partial contradiction of the first half. Moreover, the device of making the abstract visual through personification (the spirit, puffed, "makes mouths") heightens the visual impact of the entire passage.

Conversely it is well within Shakespeare's range to use language in nonpoetic ways. Besides the obvious prose of the gravediggers and the prosiness of Polonius, there are naturalistic passages such as the following, shorn of poetic devices:

GENTLEMAN. She speaks much of her father, says she hears
   There's tricks i' the world, and hems and beats her heart,
   Spurns enviously at straws, speaks things in doubt
   That carry but half-sense. Her speech is nothing,
   Yet the unshaped use of it doth move
   The hearers to collection. They aim at it,
   And botch the words up fit to their own thoughts,
   Which, as her winks and nods and gestures yield them,
   Indeed would make one think there might be thought,
   Though nothing sure, yet much unhappily.

Hamlet, IV, 5

The language here is sharply descriptive; it communicates, again, in vivid visual terms, but this time of a coherent picture that the messenger brings. It is not so much Ophelia's madness that we get as the impression that madness makes on her court audience. That picture, in turn, reflects back on Hamlet's madness and our interpretation of it. The vocabulary is relatively simple, relatively free of Latinate or lengthy words. (*Enviously* and *collection* are fairly simple exceptions.) The speech is punctuated with plosives, the hard sounds of *beats* and *botch*, the staccato of *tricks* and *yet*, *at it* and *thought*, and it ends in a succession of *th* sounds that suggests, and almost demands, a stammer: "Think there might be thought, Though nothing. . . ." Here, the language is brilliantly simple, tuned to its speaker, to his situation, and to the picture he must paint. (See p. 290 for further discussion of the speech.)

Language in drama, then, is the first and most important gesture among several; it is the playwright's most potent vehicle for meaning and his indication, as in a musical score, of tempo, rhythm, and choreography. It can be a precise clue to character, and character must be made to enlighten it. When, finally, language chooses to employ the techniques of poetry, it must perform its other tasks first.

Character and Character Psychology

If language is a partly limited means of communication in drama, certainly one of the primary limitations on understanding it is the character of the person speaking. Language, particularly language that is structured strangely or language used to convey complicated meanings, is hard enough to understand at best; when it must be interpreted in terms of its speaker, it becomes barely trustworthy. Sarcasm in everyday life is a common example of the difficulty; until we know someone fairly well, it is often hard to separate sarcasm from sincerity, and many friendships stumble on just such a rock. The simple statement, "You're very bright, aren't you!" takes on an easy tone of menace in one mouth, of flattery in another, and of sincere worship in still another.

The problem of interpreting such a line in a play is fairly difficult. Given the play itself, without critical glosses or playwright's introduction (and they are not always of value anyway), we rely on the data of the text itself to solve the language problem. In performance the problem is partly solved for us. We know a character generally by one of three ways: by what he says, by what is said about him, and by what he does. Contradiction among these three sources can cause great confusion. In Hamlet's soliloquy on Fortinbras (quoted on p. 245) our picture of Fortinbras is much colored by Hamlet's description, "tender and delicate." Is he, or isn't he? Seeing the actor playing Fortinbras would help us decide, and his name (suggesting strength of arms) suggests that he is neither tender nor delicate—but what if Hamlet is speaking of his spirit or his youth or his soul? Or what if Hamlet is mad? Or what if Hamlet is being heavily sarcastic? We have to know, because it is the presence of Fortinbras that sets Hamlet off on an important self-examination. The words about Fortinbras suddenly become limp balloons, visible only when filled with the character using them.

Some inevitable circularity appears. If we come to know a character partly through words, then we cannot know him, because we must know him, or other characters, to understand the words. Hence, the impressive ambiguity of Hamlet and the resonant mystery of Oedipus.

If, too, we accept the relativity of psychological theories, any contemporary interpretation of a classic character becomes something of a jerry-built fabrication. An age that demands consistency, as ours seems to, will be frankly puzzled by the product of an age that accepted inconsistency. Thus, an inconsistency that may have delighted the Elizabethan confounds us, and we tend to "interpret" Hamlet—often by cutting some of his inconsistencies out of the script. This is dirty·

pool, although the play will survive cutting. The answer to character confusion is not surgery, but research. If close acquaintance with the play's historical period shows certain types or certain patterns that explain the confusion, then part of the problem is solved; the other part is adapting that type or pattern to our own time. Thus, Hamlet's apparent contradictions can be partly understood through a knowledge of medieval morality heroes (which Hamlet is not), of earlier Elizabethan revenge figures (his situation fits, at least), of Elizabethan melancholy (which he often displays, particularly in a way then popular in the theatre), and of the conventional approaches to character presentation, which Shakespeare imitated (the rhetorical set speech and soliloquy, the self-examination, the witty putting down of dunderheaded courtiers, and so forth). The total effect of such research is not a presentable Hamlet, but a character at least conceived by his author and not put together by a committee.

But the ambiguity often remains. Research will not solve it fully. It is best solved not by approaching the play's meaning through the character, but by approaching the character through the play's meaning.

Figure 3–3. *The Three Sisters* at The Guthrie Theatre Company, 1965. Jessica Tandy as Olga, Hume Cronyn as Tchebutykin, Michael Levin as the Orderly, Ellen Geer as Irina. (*Courtesy of The Guthrie Theatre Company.*)

Ultimately, many complex plays are enlightened by nonverbal symbols. Any play so devoid of difficulty and ambiguity as to be completely clear in character, language, and total meaning, without the use of great supporting symbols, is overclear and oversimple. It is boulevard comedy, commodity drama; it is the totally expected product, without mystery of any kind, the ritual of comfort that is as artistic as a good back rub.

In the difficult play (the ambiguous play), on the other hand, nonverbal symbols expand the play beyond its own action into profundity. Sometimes such a symbol runs throughout a play and is pointed at again and again by the playwright—monstrosity, for example, in *Phaedra*. Sometimes it is the image on which a consistent metaphor rests—the unweeded garden of *Hamlet* (a poetic reference that is expanded beyond any verbal equivalent by its many uses in the play). Sometimes it is an action—Harpagon fearing his own hand in his pocket and accusing the audience of theft. Sometimes it is a visual effect, shocking in its clarity—the appearance of Teiresias in *Oedipus*, of Hamm in *Endgame*.

Teiresias is an excellent example. Sophocles, of course, attacks his dramatic problem from many directions, and the profundity of his meaning lies partly in his language, partly in his action and his characters, and partly in just such symbols. They are central to his plays: the appearance of Teiresias in *Oedipus Rex*, the omnipresent corpse in *Antigone*, and the mystical assumption of Oedipus in *Oedipus at Colonus*. But in Teiresias he found a quintessential symbol, both human being and image. The blind man who sees, the man who has been woman, the old man led by the boy—all these are clear to us with his entrance. The play's meanings are not spelled out by this gigantic symbol, but from it we understand that the play is about perception. When Oedipus blinds himself we have that understanding raised several degrees by a new visual symbol. One can reduce Sophocles' poetry by several degrees. (It is still powerful in translation, for example.) One can interpret the chorus' speeches in a number of ways, but the theatrical experience remains so long as the gigantic symbolic effects, with their supporting elements (the action itself, the metaphorical use of vision, and blindness) remain. Theatrical characters themselves rarely recognize the symbol for what it is. When they do, they come dangerously near spilling the beans and destroying the play. Hamlet does not immediately see the symbolic meaning of his own images, nor Harpagon of his own action.

Meaning As Myth

Drama is on the one hand an art that deals with man's search for perceptual certainty; at the same time, it is an example of that search.

When it is most doggedly pursuing that search, and gives over its other concerns for a time (the satisfactions of audience comfort or the presentation of simple verbal pyrotechnics or the glamorized indulgence of a charismatic personality, for example), its central meaning lies in its perceptual search, its myth. The search for certainty does not change much, because it is never successful for very long. The apparent solutions of one theatre (Sophocles' conclusions in *Oedipus at Colonus*, for example) are not satisfactory for another, and the process begins over again. Thus, the myth within the play takes different forms in different ages; the mythic protagonist changes (Oedipus to Hamlet to Harpagon to Hamm) and the details and the incidents of his activities change. The myth itself is capable of almost infinite expression, each play, at its best, adequate to the needs of its own culture. As a rule, the myth is contained within highly complex details of character, action, and verbally expressed ideas, and as a result it is often hard to find. Instead, critical attention is often given to surface ideas (the temporary expression of the myth), and those ideas are accepted as the drama's reason for being. They are not, at least not entirely.

The question arises, then, whether it is possible to have stageable theatre pieces that do *not* contain a profoundly meaningful myth. The answer, of course, is yes, just as it is possible to have graphic pieces that employ the tools of painting without being artistically satisfactory paintings or three-dimensional works that employ the tools of sculpture without being artistically satisfactory sculptures. It is perfectly possible, in fact disastrously easy, to work within the discursive, active mode of the theatre, employing the tools of theatre, without producing artistically satisfying theatre pieces. It is disastrously easy to learn delusive rules of structure, characterization, and plot; to practice economy and propriety; to use language fairly well; and to produce plays that have every appearance of being "about" something (race relations or castration or suburban anxiety or world piece). It is disastrously easy to have such plays accepted briefly. It is inevitable, however, that such plays will die an easy death if all that they are about is their superficial subject matter.

Extrinsic and Intrinsic Meaning

There are, thus, two kinds of meaning in any good play. One is on the surface, extrinsic; it is what the play is about in the sense that it occupies the energies and attentions of its characters, and it therefore will occupy the energies and attentions of its audience. *The Miser* is about bourgeois French avarice and romantic love; *Hamlet* is about Elizabethan English justice; *Endgame* is about modern anticipation. Extrinsic ideas have immediate interest for their audiences. They date easily. The closer they approach the particular interests of their first audience, the more easily dated they become. Thus, the many American activist labor plays of the 1930s are hopelessly dated now because their extrinsic concern has all but disappeared from the interests of the audience of the 1970s. Many of the plays of Henrik Ibsen seem very dated for the same reason; such extrinsic concerns as feminism, venereal disease, and religious hypocrisy have lost much of their nineteenth-century impact.

Yet, extrinsic ideas are essential to any play. To remove them completely is to cut off contact with the play's first audience. It is not enough to set up a performance that does nothing but give information; it must give information in which the audience has interest, to which it can react. Audiences are *analogous* to computers, but they are *not* computers; they have preferences. They are very inclined to mutter, "So what?" They must see that the play's extrinsic concerns are their own. Molière's *The Miser* will do for an example. Its extrinsic subject matter, avarice, was close to its first audience, made up as that audience was of nobility and upper bourgeoisie, all of whom understood usury, inheritances, and dowries very well. The matrix for this subject matter is partly romantic (the love affairs of Cléante-Mariane and Elise-Valère). Not all of the play, obviously, is concerned with the extrinsic subject; typically, Molièresque scenes of buffoonery and trickery have innate comic value and are merely self-justifying. (They are, in a sense, about themselves and nothing else. If such a remark sounds very much like the definition of drama itself, the similarity must be allowed: these comic scenes of trickery and ridicule are among Molière's most famous, and they explain in large part his durable reputation. It should not be at all surprising, as we shall see, to find that these scenes are fundamentally concerned with perception, the intrinsic subject matter of Molière's theatre.) Setting aside the self-justifying comic scenes, then, leaves a play with a fairly simple plot, an impressive and very active central character, and a number of secondary characters whose experiences are directly affected by the central character and his action. If we look for extrinsic meaning in the play, then, we will find it in the relationship between the central figure and those others—in their speeches to each other, in their actions toward each other, and, finally, in the value judgment put upon each by the playwright in the play's final outcome. Although rewarding one set of characters and punishing another is not by any means necessary, rewards and punishments are valid bases of judgment when we can be sure that the playwright means them as rewards and punishments—when, in other words, a workable value system is set up in the play and followed consistently.

It is perfectly possible, of course, for a playwright to alter the apparent value system as the play progresses; indeed, extrinsic meaning is often contained in the shifting attitudes of characters toward a value system. Thus, in Shakespeare's *Twelfth Night*, the play's outcome is not at all what many of the characters have desired through most

Figure 3–4. *Indians* in its original American production at the Arena Stage, Washington, D. C. Here, Ed Rombola as Geronimo. (*Ronald Freeman photo.*)

of the play (they are not rewarded in terms of their stated desires), but that outcome expresses some of the play's meaning because it is the adjustment of the value system that allows the characters to accept in the fifth act what they might, in the third, have seen as a punishment.

In *The Miser*, the gains and losses of the last act are more in line with the stated desires of the characters throughout the play. Harpagon loses his casket; Marianne and Cléante are united; Valère wins Elise; and Anselme finds his lost children. In the last moment, Harpagon is reunited with the casket—"my beloved casket," is his closing line—but the bulk of the last act is devoted to his suffering as a result of its loss. He is as surely undergoing a punishment as Anselme and the two pairs of young lovers are being rewarded.

If we look to the play for the question that is answered by these rewards and punishments, we can find it at the end of the first scene of the third act. Cléante, having discovered that the usurer from whom he would have borrowed money is his own father, exchanges angry insults with Harpagon. His last speech is a clear statement of the play's extrinsic problem: "Who is the greater sinner, the one who borrows money that he needs, or the one who steals money that he cannot use?" Behind the question, of course, is a definition of *need* that seems to be no more subtle than the requirement that one acquire money in order to spend it. Thus, Cléante "needs" money to dress well and to court Marianne, but Harpagon does not "need" money, because he only hoards it. The judgments of the last act, therefore, simply confirm the impression that the movement of comedy itself would give us: youth is more valuable than age, and generosity more valuable than miserliness. Cléante's question is answered clearly: he who takes money that he cannot spend is the greater sinner. Such an extrinsic meaning is to be expected from a play with an upper-bourgeois orientation like *The Miser*.

Intrinsically, however, the play does something else. The intrinsic meaning does not reverse the extrinsic; rather, it raises a question concerning the entire environment within which it operates. Intrinsically, the play's statement is not contained in direct speeches or in a clear reward or punishment; it is not defined by the happiness of the ending. On the contrary, it merely asks what is happy, after all, about an ending that sees irresponsible youth rewarded for no good reason and miserly age punished for a character trait it cannot help? At this level, Harpagon is not The Miser, but a man; Cléante is not The Young Lover, but merely a young man. Harpagon points out that Cléante is a spendthrift, that his clothes are extravagant. We have the evidence of the play itself that he is quite ready to bargain with his inheritance, even with his father's property, to get money. Ultimately he can condone theft to get what he wants. What he wants, of course, is love, but is such a creature really capable of love? The question must be answered by the actor or the director in terms of a specific production, and they will answer it by emphasizing the degree to which instrinsic, rather than extrinsic, meaning is important to them.

And what of Harpagon? Comic though he may be, he suffers. ("Nothing is funnier than unhappiness," says Nell in *Endgame*.) The object of *his* love is probably wrong, because it is inhuman; yet must he be punished for it? Is the emotion that he feels for money substantively worse than the emotion that Valère or Cléante feels? Yet all make him suffer. Isolated from the rest by his obsession, his perception of reality clouded, he desires fiercely what they desire only as a means, not an end. However, their treatment of him gives validity to Harpagon's position: trusting only himself, he lives in a world of people who trust each other. They must seem like madmen to him. Some of them are definitely not trustworthy, to be sure (his son, Cléante, who is something of a spendthrift and who is quite willing to borrow at high rates on the basis of a promised inheritance); some of them are openly hostile, and persecute him (La Flèche, Frosine). At best, they behave with a bewildering generosity that simply shows their own disregard of their best interests (Anselme).

It is all a bit confusing. To say that Harpagon is a sympathetic protagonist is too much. To say, on the other hand, that he is a vicious miser who can be dismissed as the negative exponent of the extrinsic meaning is also too much. The more we examine a play's intrinsic meaning, the more we may tend to change our own attitude toward its extrinsic meaning, although the extrinsic meaning remains the same. In short, the play's intrinsic meaning is a general, profound statement that often alters our understanding of the play's limited extrinsic meaning.

Ambiguity and Irony

That a play should have two different levels of meaning is itself a source of irony, for irony at its simplest is the comparison of two states of knowledge. We often discuss dramatic irony as if it had only one function, the comparison made by the audience between knowledge that it alone possesses and knowledge that an onstage character possesses. *Oedipus Rex*, for example, is often cited for its heavy ironies in the indifference of Oedipus to the facts of his past and present at a time when they are quite clear to the audience. His actions, as a result, are called ironic because they show his ignorance of the facts that the audience holds; his words are ironic because they so often are threats against a murderer whom we already know, or suspect, to be Oedipus himself. Certainly the role of this kind of irony is very important, particularly in Sophoclean tragedy. Irony is so important, in fact, that its actual limit in a Sophoclean play is hard to determine. Oedipus is seen (by the audience) ironically; Teiresias speaks ironically (he knows both levels of knowledge, that of Oedipus and of the audience). What of the chorus, whose speeches seem to carry so much of the extrinsic meaning of the play? What if the *playwright* is speaking ironically?

The playwright, of course, is always an ironist: that is, he carries both, or all, levels of knowledge. Thus, there is another kind of irony possible in drama, that created by a comparison of the audience's supposed knowledge and that held by the playwright or director or actor, the theatre artist who *knows* what the audience may only suspect, or not suspect at all. If, in fact, drama is symbolic discourse about symbolic discourse, then irony is essential to its understanding, for the states of knowledge being offered by performance are comparable in a way that can only be called ironic. In *Oedipus Rex*, then, we can almost say that the intrinsic meaning of the play *is* irony, or that existence is ironic (or, perhaps, that attempts to perceive actuality are ironic and that the theatre itself is, therefore, an irony).

Just as irony is essential to dramatic action and character, so ambiguity is essential to dramatic ideas. Intentional ambiguity, of course, is a waste of time and probably impossible, but the ambiguities present in the contrast and conflict of extrinsic and intrinsic meanings are rewarding and must be valued. They cannot be understood, except as ambiguities, or "resonances" as they have been called: the possible applications of certain ideas, or elements of them, to aspects of experience. That they are not universally exact or completely consistent in themselves is to their credit; Harpagon, for example, is a much more important figure because of the irreconcilable conflict between the extrinsic and intrinsic meanings of his actions than he would ever be as a consistent, shallow, straightforward miser. If, as we have suggested, the chorus of *Oedipus Rex* is conceived ironically, then its pious statements are not the basic truths of the play, and we must accept from Sophocles a massive ambiguity about the play and all its characters. If its meaning is not merely, "True wisdom is knowing the will of the gods," or "Suffering is valuable because it leads to wisdom," or even "Happy is the man who never has need of wisdom," but is more like an unanswered question, "What if there is no wisdom, and life itself is an irony?" then the play is ambiguous in the extreme, but right and valuable because it, with a few other plays in the classic canon, approaches the ambiguity of experience.

The Questions Analysis Ask

Play analysis is not simple, and it can be approached from many directions. Several traditional points, as we have tried to show, are self-limiting; generic criticism, neo-Aristotelian criticism, and structural analyses are probably best left for doctoral dissertations with a strong historical bent. A few questions, however, based on the ideas previously outlined, may help in at least making scripts and performances accessible. They should suggest many other questions and ideas:

1. What attitude is the audience to take toward the characters and the action, objective or involved? What devices are used to achieve this? Why?
2. What suspenses, if any, are emphasized in the text or the performance, and why?
3. What elements appear to digress from, or even damage, this suspense? Why are they there?
   (In *Hamlet*, for example, it is easy to see that the soliloquies are wide detours from plot suspense; similarly, a good deal of Claudius' plotting carries us away from character suspense. Historically, we can explain the soliloquies in terms of the Elizabethan taste for rhetoric, the villainous plots in terms of Claudius' type, the Machiavellian. Still, when we begin to cope with these apparent digressions in nonhistorical terms, we can see that the suspenses are merely the skeleton and the digressions the flesh of the entire work.)
4. What are the play's important nonverbal symbols, if any?
5. What myth underlies the play? How does it enforce or conflict with the play's extrinsic meanings?
6. What are the intrinsic and extrinsic meanings generated by answers to the preceding questions?

4 **Acting**

For many theatregoers, the actor *is* the theatre. He is the most visible of theatre artists and often the most personally accessible. Playwrights become famous, but they often remain remote; directors and designers are often only dimly noted names on the program. But the actor is always foremost, his modern presence reinforced by the machinery of advertising and popular-idol creation.

Although the social position of the actor has varied enormously from one historical period to another, his role as the immediate embodiment of the theatre has not. In fifth-century Greece, he had a quaisreligious function and was honored with special prizes; in the Renaissance, even though he was masked, he overshadowed his role in the *commedia dell'arte* performances and sometimes became internationally famous; and in modern Japan, he has in certain instances become a living national treasure for his artistry in classical Japanese theatre.

Since the mid-1960s, the American theatre has been in a great ferment, and the very definition of the word *theatre* has been changed. The place of the actor, however, has not been seriously questioned, and it might even be said that an important part of that ferment has come from an energetic attempt to make the actor even more important than he has been traditionally—to endow him with the creative functions of the playwright, the designer, and even the director. Thus, the contemporary American theatre is in the curious position of viewing the actor in two very different ways: the traditional one, in which the actor is part of a cohesive creative ensemble that is heavily dependent on the work of the playwright and the director; and the newer view that the actor is in large part the source of the theatrical event and that, either in solitude or in concert with other actors (and a coach, teacher, or director), he creates, often improvisationally, without an overwhelming dependence on the playwright. The first approach is oriented, in the United States, to a version of the acting theory of Konstantin Stanislavski (see pp. 148–149) and is still dominant in American commodity theatre, films, and television. The other is based on the example of such contemporary innovators as Jerzy Grotowski, Viola Spolin, Joseph Chaikin, and Richard Schechner and is dominant in much of the underground, avant-garde, and educational theatre (see pp. 207–210).

There is a measure of irony in this situation, for until the 1950s, Stanislavskian acting theories were still being widely argued about in the United States, and they were innovative even then. Rather abruptly, they have been thrust into an apparently traditional, conservative position, and by contrast the newer ideas may seem more radical— less rooted in the past—than they are. In actual fact, the split between the two ideas of acting may not be as profound as it has been made to seem; certainly, many younger actors have learned from both and can work with both. (In fact, if there is a distinguishing national quality to American acting and directing, it may well be this ability to assimilate methods and styles into an eclectic whole.)

The situation has its precedents. Indeed, the history of acting shows a constant replacement of one theory or system by another that is at first called radical or revolutionary and that, in its turn, becomes the traditional and the old fashioned. The earlier predecessor of Stanislavskian theory was the late-Romantic acting of Europe; Stanislavski and his contemporaries sought to correct what they saw as the excesses and the unnatural or untruthful exaggeration of the nineteenth century—although such acting had itself been a welcome corrective to the mannered and controlled performances of the eighteenth century.

Charles Marowitz noted the then-new acceptance of Stanislavskian acting in England with a list of "trad" and "mod" attitudes that was equally valid for the American theatre of the 1950s:

Trads	*Mods*
Let's get it blocked.	Let's get it analyzed.
Fix inflections and "readings."	Play for sense and let the inflections take care of themselves.
Block as soon as possible.	Final decisions as late as possible and always open to reversal.
It was a bad house.	It was a bad performance.
I take orders.	I give suggestions.
Am I being masked?	Am I important at this moment in the play?
Can I be heard?	Are my intentions clear?
I'm getting nothing from my partner.	I'm not getting what I expected, so I shall adjust.
Just as we rehearsed it.	As the immediacy of the performance dictates.
Let's get on with it and stop intellectualizing.	Let's apply what reason we have to the problems at hand.
More feeling.	More clarity of intention to produce more feeling.
Hold that pause.	Fill that pause.
Everything's in the lines.	Everything's in the subtext.
I'll play this role symbolically.	I can't play concepts, only actions.
I am the villain.	I refuse to pass moral judgments on my character.
My many years of professional experience convince me that	Nothing is ever the same.

From "Notes on the Theater of Cruelty," *Tulane Drama Review* (Winter 1966).

The so-called Stanislavski method did not become highly visible in the United States until the 1920s and 1930s, first when émigré Russians began teaching here and slightly later when the Group Theatre gained critical and popular acceptance throughout the decade of the 'thirties (see pp. 166–167). The Group Theatre's plays dealt with social issues, and its actors created characters who were socially and emotionally

Figure 4–1. The Actor's Studio production of *The Three Sisters*. Left to right, Robert Loggia, James Olson, Kim Stanley, Shirley Knight, Gerald Hiken, Luther Adler, Kevin McCarthy, and Geraldine Page. (*Courtesy Lee Strasberg.*)

truthful. From their example came the plays and films, and the acting approach, of the 1940s and 1950s—the deep social concerns of an Arthur Miller and the demanding emotional role of a Willy Loman.

Since the early 1960s, however, the Americanized Stanislavski approach to acting has come under attack. Although the theatrical ideas of Berthold Brecht (see p. 181) turned out to have little impact in the United States, the widespread publicizing of his rejection of Stanislavski did come at a time when Stanislavski was already being questioned. As well, the ideas of Artaud (see p. 187) were being widely discussed, especially in academic criticism and in drama classrooms. Finally, and perhaps most importantly, the distrust of established and traditional systems that characterized the decade of the 'sixties, particularly on American campuses, included a distrust of the by-then established and traditional acting approach of Stanislavski. In a sense, the community of the American theatre split into two communities, one based in New York City, traditional and professional; the other, based in colleges and universities, young, new, and committed to a life of involvement and activism rather than one of careers. Relevance and commitment were popular by-words, and there was much suspicion that an acting theory that served equally well to perform the plays of Anton Chekhov and Neil Simon was somehow unsuited to commitment and to relevance and could not be adequate to the demands of street and guerilla theatre. As the communities of audiences split after the mid-1960s, so, too, did the actors and those articulate spokesmen who set down what seemed to be the new systems and the new methods.

As has already been pointed out, the apparent split still exists (with the new having seemingly swept the old out of the acting classrooms at some universities), but an increasing number of young actors are taking the best from both and assimilating them into their own work.

The Psychology of the Actor

No matter what his approach to the art of acting, the personality of the actor has attracted concern for two reasons: (1) he uses his own self to create other persons; (2) his profession is such that his life differs from normal social habits. The actor's social personality attracts more popular interest. For 2,000 years actors have been treated as a minority, sometimes as outcasts; mistrusted, abused, patronized, even when they are lauded, rewarded, and emulated. The Roman theatre recruited actors from among the slaves. In medieval times, actors were at best household servants, at worst criminals, and often regarded by law as dangerous vagabonds. In Elizabethan times, some actors, such as Edward Alleyn, Richard Burbage, and William Shakespeare established themselves as gentlemen, but only after they acquired property by becoming producers. In the eighteenth century, some leading actors were admitted into polite society, although members of good families who entered acting were frowned upon. It was not until late in the nineteenth century, probably with the knighting of Henry Irving, that acting became recognized as a dignified profession.

By reputation the actor is emotionally unstable. He certainly leads a nervous life. Neither his working nor his social habits fit conventional patterns. Acting involves a prodigious expenditure of physical and emotional energy for concentrated periods. Whether an actor's basic motivation is exhibitionistic or not, he is required to exhibit himself in public, and frequently is asked to simulate behavior and emotions inimical to his personal values. He rarely enjoys steady employment. There is no graduated ladder of success in his career. Great financial reward may come suddenly or never, and when it does come the actor's private life ceases to be his own. His periods of inactivity hardly furnish rest, because he must remain near the sources of employment and suffer the anxiety of being evaluated for jobs by standards that often have little to do with his actual ability. When employed, his working hours make him a night person, unless the movies or television call him, in which case he is suddenly forced to adhere to a rigid daytime schedule.

Acting is punishing work, devastatingly competitive, sometimes destructive of personal equilibrium, an invasion of private life, and filled with anxiety. Its conditions are such that acting is seen clinically as a distinctive social behavior pattern in order to consider the extraordinary motivations that keep actors in acting. Such roots as exhibitionism, masochism, and compulsion toward perfection plausibly suggest themselves. Acting is also one of the strategies available to the nonconformist. One finds affluent, established actors lauding self-sacrifice and the nobility of giving one's genius to the world; one also finds unsuccessful young actors in a state of paranoia, bewailing the callous philistinism of the theatre and the incorrigible idiocy of audiences. Whether one sees it as a religion or a disease, an obsessive commitment to his profession characterizes the actor's personality, and the ability to summon great energy and discipline characterizes his working habits, whatever lack of such qualities may characterize his life outside the theatre.

Nevertheless, the theatre is filled with people who manage to lead fairly normal lives in spite of their profession's round-the-clock discipline, which demands of them an intensive exploitation of their own resources. The great binding element in their lives, of course, the factor that balances them and compensates for their work and discipline, is the successful creation of a demanding role. The life of the good and professionally satisfied actor is an enviable one, not for the sometimes immense salary he earns or for the immense popular attention he attracts, but for the kind of creativity he knows, using his full self, rewarding his full self.

"Artificial" and "Natural" Acting

The ideas of commitment and of discipline in acting suggest to some people a quality that smacks of artifice rather than of art. Such a suggestion, of course, gives rise to the false idea that *style* is a pejorative term. Obviously, it need not be when properly defined. Still, the idea of artificiality in acting as opposed to purely *natural* acting (an artificial style as opposed to a natural style) is almost inescapable, and the words *artificial* and *natural* have been used polemically for generations. Indeed, for as far back as at least the Restoration period, each dominant school of acting has defined itself as *natural* and the school it has displaced as *artificial;* our own "improvisational" versus "Stanislavskian" controversy is a manifestation of the same split. In every age, actors who cannot fully master physical and vocal techniques are inclined to label the work of those who can as artificial. Confusing their egos with their creative imaginations, they are inclined to call their own work natural—meaning, it would seem, that it is a manifestation of themselves rather than of an acquired set of gestures, rhythms, vocal patterns, and so on. Beneath this attitude, of course, is a misunderstanding of the nature of acting, a misunderstanding that has an equally limiting counterpart in the artificial or *technical* actor who has full control of his voice and body but little or no ability to exercise his imagination. Whereas the first actor, the "natural," confuses his own feelings, and his own ego, with creativity, the second actor confuses his own love of self-display, and his desire for public exposure, with artistic creation.

Figures 4–2 through 4–5. Four nineteenth-century Hamlets. (Above) Sir Henry Irving. (*Courtesy of the New York Public Library.*)

Figure 4–3. (Bottom right) Edwin Booth as Hamlet. (*Courtesy of the New York Public Library.*)

Figure 4–4. (Top right) The actor Mounet-Sully as Hamlet. (*Courtesy of the New York Public Library.*)

Figure 4–5. (Far right) Charles Kean as Hamlet. (*Courtesy of the New York Public Library.*)

Neither of the attitudes is possible for the actor who seeks to master his art, but in the division between them a considerable vocabulary of confusion has become popular. The term *real*, for example, is often used as the equivalent of *natural*, and so is *truthful*. ("Was it real?" a young actor may ask of his performance; the proper answer may well be another question: "Was what real?" Too often it will be found that the actor is asking about his own feelings, whereas the observer can talk only about the actor's outward manifestations of them.) On the other side of the coin, the words *classical* and *stylized* may be made synonymous with *artificial*, because of the misconception that great actors of the past were never given naturalistic or realistic roles to perform.

Classical philosophy, from which the terms *natural* and *artificial* spring, first made the distinction between organic creations of nature and man-created objects and activities. Nature was seen as governed by laws that man could understand through reason. Man's actions were "artificial," but, being subject to nature's laws, man was most worthwhile when he lived according to them. Stanislavski, who is sometimes regarded as anticlassical and highly naturalistic, was really quite neo-classical in using "creative organic nature" to describe acting. If acting is intended, to use another of his expressions, to communicate the "life of the human spirit," it must avoid dogmatic methods that commit it to only one view of nature.

Similarly, when Hamlet advises the players to "hold the mirror up to nature" he is not calling for exact reproduction of human behavior, but for honesty in the artistic reproduction of life—quite a different matter. His other instructions, although warning against various kinds of hammy excess (artificiality), do not assume that good acting is merely a reflection of the surface of life. For as both Shakespeare and Stanislavski were acutely aware, acting is founded in the same paradox as all other arts: it is "the lie that reveals the truth." In short, it is *both* artificial and natural.

Let anyone who thinks that acting is natural and no different from life try to be natural on any stage set, particularly an interior. Furniture is strangely angled. Dimensions seem compressed. Natural movements propel one into furniture or into paths that angle from stage center. One's steps become smaller and slower. One's normal voice seems hollow and weak and must be supported. The architecture of any stage is itself artificial. Even the most naturalistically minded designer does not operate as an interior decorator.

The very acoustic and optical conditions under which an actor appears before an audience demand that he learn artificial methods of speaking and moving, *even in order to appear natural.* In any hall, normal speech seems rapid and does not carry far. Articulation is blurred. In normal life, in order to speak more loudly one raises his pitch. But the traditionally trained actor learns to articulate consonants carefully, to control vowel lengths, to vary his tempos, and to use an artificial method of breathing in order to project his voice evenly at any desired pitch. By such control, and by minute variation in his phrasing, he achieves whatever style of delivery is desired (and speaks more rapidly than in real life into the bargain). The actor trained according to the ideas of Grotowski or Schechner may learn to use his voice as an expressive part of his physical and emotional self, as a musical instrument to be orchestrated with other voices. His physical movement, although not necessarily imitative of everyday life, will be carefully controlled and disciplined; his body will be the body of an athlete.

In moving, particularly on a proscenium stage, normal steps seem long; a straight diagonal line upstage seems to curve down; the same move downstage seems to curve up. The stage actor learns all over again how to move; executes all movements smoothly, even those meant to be awkward; restrains impulsive gestures; and takes unnatural positions in conversing with others—learns the whole range of artificial manipulation of the body called stage mechanics.

The final argument against the possibility of the purely natural in the theatre is the play or improvised act itself. The *fact* of the theatre makes real behavior impossible; one can see "real" acting, of course, which is real in the sense that it exists, but that is hardly what we mean. Occasionally, one can see real stagehands working or a real janitor sweeping a stage, but never in moments when the theatrical fact (the presence of the audience on a specific occasion) pertains. The playwright cannot supply the actor with perfectly real dialogue because real dialogue lacks structure, consistency, and movement forward; it is, except to those engaged in it (and sometimes for them as well), boring. (Consider, for example, the opening scene in Act II of *Death of a Salesman*. We have the illusion of real dialogue, real behavior, to be sure, but we most notice immediately how quickly Miller moves his action forward, how much information he gives us about Biff and Happy, and how little repetition or extraneous subject matter is included. The dialogue is far from real.)

Whatever the style, the structure, or the subject matter, the theatrical work of art is conceived of as an organism; anything that is extraneous or inconsistent betrays itself as inorganic, not alive. In this sense, then, theatre may very rightly be said to be "true to nature." In actual practice, the actor masters his craft so that its artificial methods become natural to him and permit him to communicate the truths of nature in his performance. Paradoxically, the actor who sets out to be natural without mastering his craft is certain to appear artificial because much that he does will be extraneous or inconsistent, inorganic, and dead.

Instrument and Imagination

Play analysis suggests that a text can be broken down into a series of units (scenes, French scenes, acts, rhythmic beats) each of which presents considerable variety of meanings. The problem of the actor, no matter what his approach to the art of acting, involves the ability to select a coherent series of meanings from among the many possibilities and to realize them on the stage. The faculty of making such choices, whether they are arrived at by pure instinct, cold analysis, or mere reaction to outside suggestion, might best be identified by the word that has served to describe the creative process in all the arts, *imagination*. The product of the imagination is communicated, in performance, through the actor's body (including the vocal apparatus), and, because the actor performs on it, it is often called the actor's *instrument.* In acting, instrument and imagination are linked indissolubly. No actor uses one without the other.

From age to age, however, the theatre seems to emphasize one at the expense of the other. The American emphasis on empathy and identification, which often leads us to judge the actor by the intensity of his feelings, the degree to which he "lives" the role, or even *is* the role, and that leads us to forgive a lack of external technique (perfection of the instrument), might be interpreted as an obsession with the imagination. The French theatre, on the other hand, with its tradition of inherited interpretations of classic roles and its concern for precise execution, might be accused of being obsessed with the instrument. Such degrees of emphasis, however, are a matter for objective historical discussion, and not for value judgment. Probably the greatest actors of all ages have had in common the *imagination* to make the finest discrimination among the choices offered by the plays of their time, as well as the *instruments* to communicate those choices most richly; lesser actors have simply had lesser ranges of either instrument or imagination. In this chapter we necessarily deal with the practices of our own day, but we should admit that a historical study of acting shows that the good actor must aim for the most profound exercise of the imagination and the most complete control of the acting instrument.

Approaches to Acting

When the various studies of acting of the past and present are examined, they are found invariably to take up two central aspects of the art: the technique, or process, of embodying the role in performance, and the actor's personal involvement in that process. Behind these two aspects, of course, lurk the basic terms discussed previously: the instrument and the imagination. Unfortunately, the two are often represented as separate and even antithetical, whereas even a cursory understanding of them suggests that they must be seen as compatible, even mutually dependent. Most theories of acting, however, either concern themselves narrowly with methods of disciplining the instrument or devote themselves to a metaphorical and occasionally mystical idealization of the imagination, isolating one to the exclusion of the other. Thus, we can learn that acting is expression, imitation, believing, reacting, analysis, and even sacrament; or that the source of acting is in the head, the heart, the viscera, or the pelvis; or that the actor thinks, feels, copies, metamorphoses, or alchemically transmutes the stuff of raw experience into theatrical gold. The odd thing is that one encounters the same range of contradictory theory in every age and in every country, and that the acting produced by the proponents of the same apparent theories differs greatly from age to age or country to country. For example, the American actors working in New York profess a wide variety of acting methods and styles, as do the French actors of Paris. However, the work of any American actor more closely resembles that of any other American actor than that of any French actor, even with the thorny question of different languages (with their different rhythms and intonations) aside. Because the kind of acting required in any age and place has a certain general unity, then, actors will tend to begin with the methods of acting most prevalent among the masters of their own society. They will imitate, probably study, learn by association with better actors, and, it is hoped, develop an approach to the acting process that will result in effective performances within their own theatre. (Still, actors are human beings, and each one will find his own particular method as he gains experience.) Out of insecurity, desire to educate others, or sheer intellectual compulsion, successful actors may finally attempt to codify their methods and will produce what may appear to be logical, coherent, and workable "theories" of acting. However, when the creator's actual stage work (in both rehearsal and performance) is compared with the written word, glaring contradictions may appear, leading to the wry conclusion that the best of artists is no better at analyzing his own processes than the rest of us.

Many excellent actors have refused to theorize and codify, contenting themselves with saying that there is no such thing as a right or wrong approach to acting, but only good and bad acting. In contemporary American practice, as we have already tried to point out, an eclectic use of elements from widely differing systems and theories is possible. Whether the result of such eclecticism is good or bad is an unresolvable problem, for it must be answered in part by the audience, in part by the ego of the actor, and in part by the artistic conscience of the actor.

Talent

Beyond the training of the instrument and the encouragement of the creative imagination, beyond the exercises, the games, and even the occasional breakthrough into understanding a given role, lies a large imponderable called talent. More often described metaphorically than defined empirically, it is a quality whose very existence has been questioned. Viola Spollin, certainly one of the most stimulating acting teachers in the United States, contends that anyone, everyone can act (*Improvisation for the Theatre*). (See p. 281.) At the opposite extreme, some entrenched professionals insist on a mystical requirement for the art of acting, God-given and self-discovering, that overrides all methodology, all chance, and all lack of opportunity. "There are no undiscovered actors," such a person will insist, believing that talent, the great intangible, always surfaces.

There is probably a given quality, perhaps the ability to combine imagination and trained instrument, perhaps a psychological drive toward both self-analysis and public display, that is inherent and that is required in the finest practice of the actor's art. However, no actor is merely born, nor born fully formed. Louis Jouvet (1887–1951), for example, was ugly, ungainly, had a stammer, and impressed no one as being particularly intelligent; he failed both of his entrance examinations at the *Comédie Française*, and yet he became one of the great modern actors. In 1804, at the age of 13, Master (William Henry) Betty (1791–1874) overwhelmed London with his performance in the great tragic roles and appeared to be the greatest natural actor of all times; yet, his career, like that of many successful child actors, came to nothing.

Talent is only potential. It must grow through training and experience, and to it must be added personal qualities necessary to a career in theatre: commitment, determination, discipline, and energy. Moreover, the intangibles demanded by a particular age may be needed: a certain physical appearance, or stage personality, or acting mannerisms.

When it comes to judging young talent, teachers and advisers can only assess the potential of imagination and instrument, within the context of contemporary theatre, and make some stab at weighing a candidate's personal drive. Quite possibly the most talented people in our society never think of entering the theatre. Many untalented people who do enter the theatre are stage-struck for personal reasons and believe they have talent because of their interest. However, it is possible for experienced professional judges to use a three- to six-minute audition to assess a young actor's potential, whatever his present state of development. A beginner's speech may be colloquial, slurred, even hesitant, and his voice badly placed; his body may be tense, his movement uncontrolled; or his interpretation may seem ridiculous. Yet, one can sense the range of his vocal instrument, note a flexible body, or perceive an instinctive involvement with the right problem, however wrong the interpretation. Similarly, a beginner with some training may read well, sound attractive, move gracefully, and produce a sound interpretation, but also betray his limitations: a bad dental structure, a "lazy tongue," a lack of internal energy, a satisfaction with superficial effects, or a lack of instinct for reaching beyond himself. The greatest achievements of acting are complex and reached only after long training and experience. The actor of great potential will continue to grow in his work, as did Jouvet, no matter how badly he begins. The actor whose potential is not so great will reach the bounds of his limitations, as did Master Betty, however impressive his initial facility.

In assessing the potential talent of young actors, experienced professionals also look for "a quality," which might be described as a presence, as inner energy, or as engagement with the moment. A quality stands out, sometimes with radiance, sometimes irritatingly, sometimes simply as a puzzle, but it commands attention and tells us that the actor belongs in the theatre. Looks may have something to do with it, although looks guarantee little, even in the movies. Few of the great actors have been conventionally attractive; many have been surprisingly plain offstage. Quality may only be the sign of an acting personality, another ambiguous notion. Some actors have succeeded by bending every note to their personality, others by infusing personality into many different roles. But however one defines talent, what one sees is an exceptional instrument, capable of producing effects of great variety, and an imagination that makes every moment vivid and exciting.

Style in Acting

Style is one of those charged words that is used in many different ways. It has great value in the theatre. Unfortunately, it cries out for definition in almost every context where it appears, for it has a number of loose usages (as in "His acting has style," or "He's playing style; that's all he knows how to do") that destroy precision. As in other uses of the word, *style* in reference to acting can have a historical connotation, and we can speak of the Elizabethan style or the Romantic style. We do not mean by this the style in which Elizabethan or Romantic plays are *now* acted, but the prevailing style of those periods, which, hopefully, we can discover through studying old books on acting, painting, and descriptions of performances.

In a still more general sense, which encompasses the historical, *style* in acting means *the whole use of the instrument to elicit a given response*. Both use of the instrument and its intent (the eliciting of response) are necessary, for without one or the other we are left with either a group of physical gestures or an audience reaction. In combination, the two can be understood as describing both a physical pattern (use of the instrument) and a reaction to it. Immediately, of course, we should sense that *a style* implies purpose, that the actor intends it and can control it. From this, we see further that mastery of any style requires training of the instrument (and of the imagination, as well). We should *not*, however, make the false assumption that a style, being purposeful and demanding training, is somehow false or wrong or inartistic. What is frequently mistaken for style (especially a national style) is not purposeful control of the instrument to gain a given response, but a partly unconscious reflection of the dominant (communal) vision of behavior. The actor, like the storyteller, builds upon archetypes; part of his communal style will be his presentation of such an archetype. Very probably this aspect of acting style is beyond individual control, arising from deeply buried emotional and psychological needs.

In popular usage, *style* may also connote two other things: the personal idiosyncrasies of a given actor ("his style") or the demands of a classic play. In the first sense, we are as often in the presence of lack of control as of purposeful control; each actor, like each other human being, has ineradicable *mannerisms* that set him apart and, in this very limited sense, give him a style. (But one might just as well say that a janitor has a personal style of mopping floors.) In the other sense, we often find plays of the past described as "stylized" or "needing style," meaning really that they were once part of a theatre whose acting style was different from that of the present, and that they demand some possible adjustment of the contemporary actor's use of his instrument if he is to elicit the desired response in a contemporary audience.

For example, probably no single period, at least in the English theatre, is so sadly "stylized" as the Restoration (roughly, 1660–1700). The great mistake of the contemporary actor, of course, is to think that his problem is to revive the acting style of the seventeenth century (an impossible and thankless feat). His job—not an easy one—is instead to use his creative imagination to find the ways in which Restoration characters can be embodied by his instrument, for his audience, as fully and vividly as they once were for the audience of the Restoration.

Intrinsically, no style of acting can be considered superior to another. As we have seen, every actor will have a personal style and will, as he perfects his craft, partake of a communal and a historical style. Occasionally, of course, an actor with no training and even no talent may appear to have great abilities (for a very brief time) because his personal style will exactly match the needs of a certain moment. But such a rarity is hardly an example of successful acting. It is the result of the accidental or automatic personal use of the instrument for a theatrical purpose, usually without any exercise of imagination. The "actor" in such a case is often a beginner, and he will be fortunate indeed if he comes out of the experience with an awareness of his own inadequacy. If in doubt, he can try honestly to answer a simple question: "Have I the imagination, and the trained instrument, to be equally effective in a vastly different role, in a vastly different play?"

TWO STRANDS IN MODERN ACTING

We have spoken of discipline, of control, of talent, and of style in acting. All of these terms are necessary to describe the actor's work; none, however, is adequate to describe the process by which he reaches the artistic level where both he and his audience are satisfied by that work. *Training* is usually used to describe the process, although its overtones of the classroom, of exercises, and of tedious repetition make it inadequate. *Preparation* may be a better term, so long as it is remembered that it is a demanding preparation and a never-ending one.

The actor is training and preparing until the day he leaves the theatre forever.

Such artistic preparation is part and parcel of any acting theory or system. Inherent in the formalizing of a theory of acting—that is, of the creation of the role on the stage—is the preparatory process by which the actor readies himself, the steps by which the instrument and the imagination are made more expressive and more sensitive.

The Contribution of Stanislavski

As stated earlier, until recently the most outstanding work in the American theatre was deeply influenced by Konstantin Stanislavski. Those who professed to reject his ideas had often absorbed them without acknowledgment; indeed, it can still be argued that Stanislavski's sense of what acting is and how the actor goes about his creative task goes far beyond the bounds of his so-called method or of his own time.

Many follies have been committed in Stanislavski's name, just as follies are always committed by the imitators of any original genius. (Contemporary innovators such as Grotowski and Chaikin are not exceptions.) Stanislavski's own writings on acting offer us the ideas of a gifted and humane man, one aware of the pitfalls in his own thinking. The work of his self-proclaimed disciples, however, especially in the United States in the 1940s and 1950s, sometimes bordered on the hysterical. Thus, it must be remembered that attacks on Stanislavski have often been attacks on the work of enthusiasts for whom he was hardly responsible. ("The Method," as the New York-based application of his ideas came to be known, eventually laid itself open to well-deserved criticism and easy parody. In its own way it became as guilty of excess and falseness as was the nineteenth-century acting that Stanislavski had sought to correct.)

Stanislavski was already a highly established actor when he began to examine the principles of acting seriously. The staleness that crept into his own acting and the failure of good, industrious actors to achieve their obvious potential puzzled him. He noticed three kinds of professional actors: creative, imitative, and hack. The creative actor, Stanislavski observed, brings to every performance a vitality, richness, and seemingly spontaneous invention that makes his ease of perfection seem to be achieved for the first time. The imitative actor imitates not others but himself, working in rehearsal to establish a performance that he attempts to repeat over and over, but which either becomes repetitiously stale or slowly loses its richness. The hack actor is efficient, enjoyable, and at times even inspired, but his performance is an anthology of previously mastered acting tricks. Stanislavski then set out to determine the qualities great creative actors naturally possess and to find acting processes to make them available to others. He did not contribute to the techniques of acting—although there is much to

Figure 4–6. Richard Burton as Hamlet. (*Springer/Bettman Film Archive.*)

be learned from him in this area, particularly in the teaching of acting —so much as to the extended use of the imagination. His work was designed not merely to train actors, but to make trained actors better.

Stanislavski isolated three performance qualities that distinguish the creative actor: *concentration*, *communication*, and *preparation*, to reduce them to single-word terms. They constitute the components of performance. The core of Stanislavski's "method" was formulated to achieve them. They sound like truisms. "How obvious!" one says, "Doesn't everybody?" The answer is that everybody takes these components for granted, and Stanislavski's originality consists in making us conscious of the obvious. He provided the sort of perspective that makes it possible to recast our approach to the subject, to assimilate the knowledge of the past into new ways of solving old problems. In reviewing previous acting theory, we find a consistent, if unconnected, concern with these qualities. Contemporary actors who reject "The Method" may emphasize them in discussing acting, even if they describe *concentration* as "professional discipline" or "doing justice to the performance," *communication* as "playing together," and *preparation* as "studying the part" or "coming on properly." Whatever method an actor employs he will do well to keep these three components of performance in mind.

In reflecting on what the three components of performance had in common, Stanislavski came up with his famous, if puzzling, term, *The Magic If*. To understand it, and its central place in his thought, is to wipe away most of the misunderstanding that the ideas of Stanislavski provoke. Logically, it converts acting from a series of conclusions into a series of propositions. Any dramatic moment is seen as dependent on the conditions which have led up to it. The actor considers those conditions before making his choice and operates along the lines of: if such is true, then *this* follows. Training and rehearsal consist of learning how to experiment with propositions. Performance is the enabling act that produces the exact conclusion, which in itself sets up the terms of the next proposition. The actor does not become truth; he establishes it. Both Stanislavski's detractors and his disciples have sometimes failed to grasp the distinction between *living* the part and *as if* living the part.

The Magic If provides the means for the actor to determine what the particular moment requires. It attempts to integrate the imagination and the instrument into the process of acting. It provides training exercises that force the student to understand the experience of characters in particular situations and to grasp the external results that situations demand. It provides rehearsal techniques for trying out the various possibilities of a character's response to particular situations. It provides means for the actor to concentrate, to respond fully, and to achieve consistent results from performance to performance. It is a way to approach acting. For Stanislavski, the actor who cultivates the use of *The Magic If* develops sound instinctive habits that coalesce into an effective acting method.

In developing his "system," which covers the range from beginning lessons to full performance, Stanislavski divided the acting process into two categories: (1) the actor's inner and outer work on himself, and (2) the actor's inner and outer work on his part. *Inner* has to do with the feelings, desires, and experiences of human beings; it demands the application of what we have called *the imagination*. *Outer* has to do with the external realization of human behavior through the use of what we have called *the instrument*. Inner work can be focused on the *motivation* of individual actions and on the *objective* that a character is trying to reach once an action is initiated. Such objectives must be made consistent with a character's *superobjective*, the "life goal" that often lies beyond the play. (The definition of the superobjective of a play's protagonist—Hamlet, let us say—can become a major determinant of the play's over-all thrust and meaning. If, for example, Hamlet's superobjective is stated simply as "to revenge my father," then the objectives of individual scenes must be dovetailed into this idea of revenge, and there is great danger of an almost ludicrous oversimplification of the play and the character. A superobjective such as "to set the world right" or "to restore harmony between the world of man and the world of the gods" may allow for a much richer development of a complex dramatic world. Such an inclusive superobjective, however, is counterproductive for a limited actor, for it can easily become a permission to be merely vague or contradictory.) Actions that the actor is tempted to perform that are not consistent with objectives and superobjectives are *tendencies*, disturbing and (for the audience) distracting zigzags across the line of the active life of the character.

For the Stanislavskian actor, all behavior is motivated and all life is active. Motivations and objectives are amoral; Claudius' sending Hamlet to England is not motivated by evil (the actor does not say, "I am doing this because I am the villain in this play,"), but by fear of discovery, or envy of Hamlet's relationship with his mother, or disgust with Hamlet's effect on the court. All motivations, all superobjectives, all scene objectives, are *active;* when the actor makes a note of them in his script or his notebook, he will note them actively, "I want to . . . ." Passivity is not an actable condition unless it is defined in terms of action—frustrated objectives, stasis motivated by fear or pride or grief or some other psychologically believable impetus. Hamlet's apparent passivity until he meets the ghost of his father *must* be made active; a generalized Elizabethan melancholy will not do. (It should be noted that there are several choices for his motivation, which are dependent on the definition of his superobjective and his *given circumstances*, those conditions outside his control that can determine his behavior: age, sex, state of health, his location in time and space, and the social conditions around him.)

For the Stanislavskian actor, character analysis is very complex, but such concepts as motivation, objective, and given circumstances make it workable. The dramatic text is the foundation of such work, and it is gradually interwoven with a *subtext* of the actor's creation, an active life "between the lines" of dialogue (a "network of criss-crossing objectives," as it has been called.)

Although it is easy to ridicule the excessive application of this approach to acting by discrediting the actor who finds it necessary to motivate every breath he takes, it is very difficult to define a coherent approach to the traditional dramatic text that is *not* concerned with motivations and objectives. Unmotivated action quickly becomes arbitrary; unmotivated behavior becomes unbelievable; and unmotivated dramatic character becomes so diffuse as to be incomprehensible. (A distinction must be made between productions of plays that offer behavior defined within the concept of motivation and those defined in some other way. Motivation is a psychological concept that was adequate for the nineteenth century and at least part of the twentieth, but it is a rational concept that does not easily include the quite arbitrary wit-play of the Restoration, the metaphysically-oriented action of some of the Theatre of the Absurd, or the irrational, "magical" behavior of the plays of the early 1970s.)

Stanislavskian Training

To sum up the ideas that are spread over several books in this brief space is impossible. For Stanislavski, training was a continuing and lifelong process. The Actors Studio, for example, which has been the nucleus of the best Stanislavskian work in the United States, is in large part a place for experienced actors, not beginners. Yet, the exercises and training methods that work for the veteran have also been shown to have application for the beginner.

An idea that is basic to Stanislavskian theory is that emotions can be stimulated within the actor, and that once they have been stimulated and experienced, *their manifestations* can be made part of the performance. Thus, the purpose of basic exercises in feeling (or of rehearsal work) is not to find ways to *imitate* emotion, but to find ways to stimulate the actor *as a means to external action;* he finds the subconscious by working back through the conscious. It is important for the beginning actor to learn that his own truthful inner responses are the source of his work as an actor; it is important for the veteran to refresh his own work by constantly returning to his inner, truthful self. In such internal work, there is a danger of being tempted into private psychological self-indulgence, of exploring the self as an end rather than a means. However, a studio environment, with coaching and positive criticism, is intended to guard against such a danger.

Stanislavski's achievement lay in returning the theatre to a working idealism that fit the concept of "total theatre" governing much twentieth-century theatrical theory. He committed actors to working with each other, and the ensemble to working with the play. The principal accusations made against his system—that it emphasizes character and plot over structure and idea; that it works only for naturalistic acting in naturalistic plays; that it commits the actor to a theory of motivational psychology that all ages and all playwrights have not shared; and that its search for narrative truth allows the ensemble to create subtext that can both exclude the audience and alter the basic nature of a play—are at least partly valid when leveled at his overzealous disciples. Only an indulgent and dogmatic use of his method justifies its detractors. Like all methods, it must be used in full consciousness of the fact that in any process as complex as acting, single-minded approaches will not solve all problems.

Stanislavski's idealism, passed on to another generation, risks vanity, dogma, and indolence, sins that his idolators have committed in his name, thinking that good intentions amount to great achievement. Stanislavski, being gifted with self-doubt and energy, tried to be guilty of none of them.

Beginning Inner Work

Obviously, much of what the beginning actor learns is not directly applicable to performance, and those beginning exercises also invite relaxation rather than tension.

The efficacy of immediate "being" exercises, in which one concentrates on converting one's complete feelings into either a pure stage of existence as another creature—the "be a tree," "be a troll," "be a primordial blob"—has been pretty much rejected. They have some use in life study for character work and can also serve as a private exercise in getting the sense of a scene or moment. Often a director will use imagery to describe a desired effect: "Float through like a cloud," "Your effect on people is like a machine gun," "This is the jungle." In these cases, creating the sense of what a cloud or a machine gun or a predator is like can be most helpful. But being exercises tend to separate the beginning actor forever from the real involvement of doing and to bury him in his own feelings. Beginning exercises should be designed to show the relation between externals and feeling, so that the actor learns to summon his emotional resources. A series of walking exercises—using such mechanical devices as short steps, long steps, short steps slow, long steps fast, arm stiff, any walk with one's center of gravity thrust forward, any walk with head held rigid, shoulders slumped, and so on—if each is kept going and then varied, will demonstrate that character and feeling automatically establish themselves once the actor relaxes into the exercise. From then on, one can deal with the actor's feelings.

Sense memory exercises are the first base of inner work. The idea is to concentrate on recalling exactly the response of one or all of the senses to some particular simple sense memory in one's own life. Tactile memory, of cloth, cold metal, castor oil, and such, is good to begin with. Next, tactile actions: reconstructing a hobby such as polishing a musical instrument, making a model airplane, kneading dough, the purpose being to make the exact re-enactment of the process evoke the sensations of the occasion. A visual description of stationary complex scenes recalled as fully as possible, say of a store window or an unusual room, sharpen one's ability to draw on the memory. Auditory recollections, of a silent room, a steam engine entering a station, or a sporting event, also help recreate atmosphere and mood.

Emotional memory, also known as emotional recall or affective memory, is perhaps the most controversial of Stanislavski's techniques. He borrowed the concept from the French psychologist Ribot, who was concerned with the ability of some people to recall past events of their life with total emotional context, whereas most people must intellectually reconstitute the event. As an acting device it has always been used by actors who wish to summon up the emotion requisite to a scene but cannot evoke it through concentration on the scene. One simply thinks of and acts out a significant personal event that provides parallel emotion to the required one. The device became incorporated into the Stanislavski approach to a point where actors used it as a matter of course in working on any scene, and in "preparing" to go on stage. Like being exercises, it led to such excessive internal reaction and concentration, and actor mysticism, that Stanislavski rejected it except when the actor had a block in working, and he declared that commitment to the action was the better course of preparation.

However, emotional memory as a beginning technique is extremely useful because it joins with feeling. As an exercise, the actor attempts to go through the actions of a remembered significant experience, carefully recreating the circumstances, sensations, and details of action, until the scene takes on a spontaneous emotional totality. Obviously, such exercises cannot be completely real. They are partly staged; they are forced. The actor pantomimes the action; that is, he recreates the exact motions, tries to handle the exact shape and texture of props (as opposed to mime, which involves an artistic reduction or abstraction of actions).

Spontaneous, improvised exercises follow: the teacher defines a situation and gently calls out changes: "You are rushing to the theatre. It is steaming hot. You look for the bus, it's not in sight. A thunder cloud cools the air. You cross the diagonal corner to look for another bus; no luck. Thunder, rain. You go under an awning. Chew gum to relax. Go look for bus." As the actor advances, improvisation becomes the key mode of all exercises. Improvisatory exercises establish the actor's receptivity and spontaneity. Even when the time comes to learn a part precisely, improvisational experience gives him an instinct for keeping his lines alive, for learning them not mechanically but within a living texture, and for finally learning the minute adjustments and responses that maintain the living integrity of a performance even when every line and move have been fixed.

Improvisational exercises really are games, in the best sense of that word. They involve concentrated imaginative free play, and many games of the charade variety (The Game, Twenty Questions, Detective, and so on) are good acting exercises.

Acting Exercises

The acting exercises that lead to actual performance are called communication work and are based on talking and doing. Many of the simple scenes from hack plays, for which we may justifiably have aesthetic contempt, present the needed problems in a direct form, and may be just what an individual needs.

Beginning communication exercises involve listening to create concentration in acting relationships. A good example of this involves one actor describing a very complex process with which he is familiar to another actor, so that the other understands it and can then explain the process back.

En route, the actor learns the concept of the objective, the ability to stick with a precise intention whatever response or circumstance changes the nature of the situation. Games of the "Button, button, who's got the button?" variety, with increasing participant permission to lie and deceive, can lead to actual personal improvisations among the class members. These can get very personal and require control, but they are worth some risk. Eventually these work into staged situational improvisations. For example, one actor wishes to buy gloves in a haberdashery shop; the other, as a salesman, tries to sell him a tie. The creation of conflicting objectives among different actors, the establishment of ingenious situations and effective ground rules, and the astuteness of the instructor in creating exercises that meet the needs of individual students are the keys to good improvisational work.

Improvisation As Acting

One of the clearest points of similarity between Stanislavskian and more recent approaches to acting is the use of improvisation. As already noted, its first use was confined to actor preparation; but it also had a place as a rehearsal technique in extending the action of a scene into an area not necessarily covered by the playwright (the so-called *étude*), in order to give the actors some insight into a scene with which they were having difficulty.

In the 1950s, however, improvisation as a valid performance technique began to surface, particularly in New York and Chicago. Michael V. Gazzo's play, *A Hatful of Rain,* was built in part around Actors Studio improvisations based, in turn, on ideas of the playwright's; in the final text, structure and language were controlled by the playwright. With such groups as the Second City and The Premise, however, structure and language passed into the hands of the actors, and a technique that had been confined to the rehearsal hall moved to the stage. It has since established itself and is now a widely accepted kind of theatre that includes scenes or brief "plays" constructed on premises offered by the audience; plays of varying degrees of formalization originally improvised by the actors; and the polished retelling of classic tales, as in the Story Theatre of Paul Sills.

Much of this use of improvisation was stimulated by Viola Spolin and by her book, *Improvisation for the Theatre* (1963), which was the keynote of much of the work of the 1960s. It describes exercises, games, and kinds of improvisatory situations, and it outlines the ground rules under which the improvisatory actor grows. In brief, these ground rules include the nonjudgmental posture of the coach (there is no bad or good, no rejection of the individual's sincere effort); the emphasis on group cooperation and communication; and the cooperative development of the improvised situation, not as a story with a beginning, middle, and end, but as an interaction carried only to the limit of its vitality. Developmental exercises might include

1. Simple communications games. (For example, "The Mirror," in which one actor tries to imitate precisely the facial movements of another; upon the direction of the coach, they switch roles back and forth until, quite literally, both are imitating and creating simultaneously.)
2. Cooperative pantomime games. (For example, volley ball or ping pong played without equipment.)
3. Sensory development exercises. (Moving through media of varying densities in pantomime; playing games in slow motion; handling imaginary objects whose weight doubles or halves.)
4. Group building games. (For example, one member of a group is asked to start pantomime construction of something with an imaginary material of his own choosing; as soon as another actor recognizes the material and the structure, he joins in and helps, until all are carrying the project through.)

Individual actor development is carried out along some of the same lines as for the Stanislavskian actor, although the improvisatory actor is frequently less bound to imitating reality. (The freedom of the improvisation, and its inclusion of pantomime, allows the actor to be an animal or a plant, a frog prince, or an astronaut in space.) He can develop vocal expressiveness by conceiving of his voice as a drum, or a trumpet, or a piccolo; he can develop physical expressiveness by playing an action with only his feet or his head, or with his face hidden. In improvising scenes with other actors, he may think in terms of something like motivation and objective, but the emphasis of Viola Spolin's work was primarily on the joint creation by the group and not on the individual; as a result, there is much less tendency to think of "my motivation." Instead, "our goals" is emphasized. Much of the work of the coach is devoted toward cautioning actors against noninvolvement, against denying another actor, against refusing to accept someone else's creation. (The reason for this should be obvious: the actor who holds rigidly to his own concept of how a scene should develop—who is story-telling—is destructive, not constructive, no matter how objectively good his idea may be. The effective improvisatory actor is always engaged in an elegant game that is somewhat like playing catch: the object is always to toss the ball back so the partner can catch it, not to keep the ball or throw it out of his reach. When both players are skilled, the ball can be thrown high or low or to the side, to give the partner the thrill of extending himself, but it is still thrown within the area of his ability.)

In the studio, the teacher or director or coach is always "side-coaching"—encouraging the actors, warning them away from blocks and pitfalls, urging them on. He may move unobtrusively around them, murmuring comments; his purpose is not to interfere or to tell them what to do, but only to make sure that they communicate, build, and develop.

The techniques developed by Spolin and others have made a very rich addition to the American theatrical scene. Improvisation has the great virtues of immediacy and spontaneity. It is highly responsive to shifts in its audience and in its audience's interests, and as a result it is an excellent form for topical comment. At its best, it is entirely without affection, and its actors have an ease that is rarely found elsewhere.

After Improvisation

The immediate impact of improvisatory theatre in the United States was to change the way in which acting was being taught, particularly in colleges and universities. With the realization that it was a performance technique, however, came an opening up of the very idea of what was theatrical. It also brought a considerable change in the way in which actors, particularly young actors far from New York City, satisfied the needs of their immediate communities. A possibly unpredicted effect was the widespread weakening of the actor's dependence on the spoken word and the dramatic text. This need was first seen in the Stanislavskian actor's use of a subtext, greatly increased in improvised theatre, and fully realized in the late 1960s by the nonverbalism found in productions of the Living Theatre, the Performance Group, and

Jerzy Grotowski's Polish Laboratory Theatre. Although this last-named group made only one visit to the United States (1968), it had been known here for at least five years before that, and it has had a world impact unequalled by the others.

There are differences among these theatres; indeed, their enthusiastic supporters are very outspoken about the uniqueness of each. What they have in common, however, is far more significant than their differences. They share a dedication to the sanctity of the theatre and to the rejection of commodity-theatre values; to the importance of the actor; and to the malleability of the dramatic text.

Grotowski deserves special attention for both his innovating influence and his international stature. Few directors have ever held the actor in the esteem that Grotowski does, and few have ever made such demands on the actor.

Again and again in Grotowski's conversations and interviews the same terms appear: *precision, clarity, discipline,* and *solitude.* It is Grotowski who has idealized the "holy actor," the actor whose life and work are as unified as an ascetic's. It is Grotowski who has defined the "poor theatre," a theatre that is both "total," and yet without obvious spectacle; without effects; and virtually without settings, properties, or technological devices. The actor is all. It is Grotowski who has given modern acting the goal of courage—the effort of the actor to surpass fatigue, pain, and superficial self-consciousness to enter into a state of daring in which voice and body combine to express the innermost psyche.

It has been said that Grotowski is mystical. Certainly many of his followers and imitators are. As with all acting systems that depend on intensive inner work, a certain element of faith must enter into its serious use, whether that system be Grotowski's or Stanislavski's. To say that such faith is irrational is to say very little about it, for when it helps the actor, it helps a great deal.

Basic to Grotowski's work with the actor is the idea of the *plastique,* a physical exercise that both conditions the body and also (at least in its advanced forms) demands the courage to surpass fatigue and normal physical limitations. In the *plastiques,* different parts of the body are brought into play, sometimes working together, sometimes working in opposition; there is a similarity to the American school of dance as it has developed since Martha Graham. As well, the Grotowski actor is trained in variations on the acting postures of François Delsarte (1811–1871), paradoxically a long-derided acting system of the late nineteenth century that has been almost universally rejected for its exaggeration and its rigidity. Nonetheless, aspects of it work for Grotowski, especially certain positive and negative body reactions to emotional stimuli.

Grotowski probably differs most from his American contemporaries in his rejection of the group as the focus of the actor. For Grotowski, the actor is a solitary figure, relying ultimately on himself. Grotowski has been openly contemptuous of the "warm bath of comfort" of group theatres. In a 1969 interview with Margaret Croydon in *The Drama Review*, he was quoted as dismissing the "American addiction to group-ism." For an American actor who developed in the 1960s, however—the decade of group therapy, sensitivity groups, groupies, the Woodstock generation, and all the rest—the idea of disciplined solitude may be incomprehensible. He may find more satisfaction in working with the commune-oriented theatres patterned after The Performance Group and the Living Theatre.

The coach or director of such a group, and the group itself, works intensively to create experiences and conditions that will lead to new theatrical expression. These include

1. Conditions and situations of trust within the group, extending into profound psychological and emotional rapport.

2. Exercises, like the *plastiques*, that will both develop the actor's body and cause him to make new connections between feelings and physical-vocal actions.

3. Group actions that arouse an intensity of feeling in the group equivalent to the individual's private, most powerful feelings. (One might say that historically this has been the function of the play itself. Contemporary groups most often use the word *ritual;* some have made wide use of rituals from other cultures. Thus, we have had the Papuan Birth Ritual as carried out by The Performance Group. The efficacy of an imported ritual is a touchstone of one's attitude toward the group: one either has faith or one has not.)

4. Searches for the immediate meaning, the direct relevance, of the dramatic text, if one is being used; or creation of a text out of the group's most vital concerns, by way of discussion, exercises, and rituals—the entire spectrum of the group's life together.

5. Devices aimed at keeping the actor's intensity high despite the repetition required by rehearsal and performance. For Stanislavski, this meant re-examining the self, but keeping the structure of the play and its dialogue intact; for the new theatre groups, this most often means keeping the self intact, but re-examining the structure and content of the performance. For Stanislavski, the real emotions of the actor are partly screened from the performance by the analytical process and by performance techniques; for the actor in the new theatre, real emotions are made the very stuff of the performance.

6. Techniques and devices that will insure the honesty and integrity of the event. Nudity and sexuality had their moment in the sun until it was found that even they become tarnished with repetition.

The actor in such a theatre group has the dangerous privilege of enjoying what has been called "self-exposure" in public. In the traditional theatre, it is the playwright's soul that is most on view; the actors are the servants of the playwright's self-exposure. The protection inherent in that arrangement has been reversed; in the new theatre, the playwright (when there is one) is the actor's servant, and it is the actor's soul that is publicly on display.

Certainly, there is much to be said for an actor who is unflinchingly honest, putting on the stage only those things that are truthful and important to him. Paradoxically, as our society has become more suspicious of itself, it has prized individual honesty and integrity more highly—particularly in public. There is the very real danger for the actor, however, of psychic damage. We shall always have the example of the final public appearances of Antonin Artaud in Paris after World War II—a madman performing himself.

Training the Instrument

The ultimate actor would be capable of making any required sound or movement with finite precision, which is what Gordon Craig meant when he called for the actor who was a perfect machine, or *uber marionette*. However, the director can command only the actor's imagination. The actor performs on his own instrument, which demands exercises in imagination on his part. But no amount of acting imagination compensates for a poor instrument, and every good actor does what he can to keep his instrument, which is his body and voice, tuned and in good shape.

The serious professional actor faces one incontrovertible fact: the deterioration of the body. The actor is an athlete, engaged in a particular sport, which demands its own physical regimen. Acting demands endurance, not brute strength; extraordinary breath control; adequate hearing; fair vision; a supple, flexible body capable of precise control of the limbs; instinctive response to the movement of other players; and the adroit handling of equipment. The time to begin training is middle adolescence. The best sports for actors do not overemphasize the development of particular parts of the body. Swimming is probably the best individual sport, basketball the best group sport. Contact sports are dangerous; a trick knee from football or a broken nose from boxing can be limiting. Actresses need to be especially careful. Muscle-bound legs and shoulders are most noticeable onstage, and the girl golfer or gymnast does not develop a very feminine figure.

Dance training for actors has been widely misunderstood. Ballet may teach rhythm and expressiveness, but the dancer's waddle is hard to eradicate, and although the ballet dancer's musculature is conducive to artificial movement, it inhibits the natural patterns of acting. Much modern dance, until mastered, invites forced movement and tension, which is the young actor's principal problem. Folk and ballroom dancing probably provide just as much coordination and rhythm sense to the young actor without risking muscular overdevelopment. Movement work in acting has four main purposes: body building, physical coordination, rhythmic comprehension, and adroit handling of props and costumes. Mime training, which has become popular through the work of Etienne Decroux and the theatre and teaching work of such famous pupils of his as Jean Louis Barrault, Marcel Marceau, and Jacque Lecoq, probably is the best foundation for today's actors.

Contrary to the conventional picture of the actor as a loose-living slob made presentable by makeup, personal hygiene becomes the good actor's obsession. Actors spend more on dental care than any one else and pay dearly for early neglect. Actresses must learn to care for their hair and dress it in a variety of ways; the same applies to actors more than is commonly acknowledged. Those who have weight problems had best master them while young. Body odor and bad breath should be avoided for practical, if not social, reasons. They may disturb those the actor works with and hinder his own acting, because acting is a group venture. Alcohol is an ancient theatre problem. Some medical authorities cite its relaxing effect after work. Anyone who has worked with actors who drink before work can testify to its dangers. It is an emotional stimulant, and can give one confidence. But it overrelaxes the voice, slows reactions, and upsets timing—conditions of which the drinking actor is not aware. It is hard to deny that some good actors drink, but they either abstain before a performance or else deteriorate.

The actor who continuously suffers sore throats, colds, or finds his voice constantly strained, hoarse, coarsened, or thinned after a performance is misusing it and needs expert, not amateur, help. In addition to proper voice training, he may need to consult a physician, because constant use of the vocal apparatus often causes physical ailments and structural difficulties (such as nodules or damaged or irritated tissues), similar to those bone-chip, cartilage, and ligament problems that strike athletes. Such normally unimportant matters as bad dental bite or a deviated septum can cause serious vocal problems. The actor who does not smoke obviously is taking better care of his voice than one who does, other risks aside.

Preopening-night sore throat is often a psychosomatic amateur experience. Knowing this does not help, however, even if the voice miraculously returns with the curtain. Moreover, lowered resistance from exhausting rehearsal invites health complications. Serious cases should be referred to a physician (who, if unfamiliar with theatre, will advise going to bed for a few days). Nonserious cases can be treated. The first rule is to stop talking (beginners usually go around volubly announcing their voice loss). Next, take care of cold symptoms with anticongestants, inhalers, and so on. A half hour of steam inhalation before the curtain often does the trick. Also, gargle every half hour with salt water. A few minutes before performance, a teaspoon of some anesthetizing medicine, such as elixir of terpin hydrate and codeine, will remove the tickle and torment. The student actor who has experienced a sore throat during performance can best resolve to learn to speak properly on stage.

Voice refers to the production of sound and speech to the shaping of sound. Some superbly endowed actors have managed without voice training, but most actors who lack it eventually strain the voice or discover their inability to use it effectively. During rehearsal with a good director, even the most inexperienced amateur will learn to project without shouting, to sustain lines, become articulate, enrich the quality of his voice, extend its range, and bring some variation into phrasing. However, the real difference between the imaginative amateur and the competent professional is in the use of voice and speech. The communication of meaning is almost a matter of music. Not that the "operatic" actor who treats each speech as an aria, or the pseudo-Shakespearean actor with his overly articulated trilling, should be the model for study. To the contrary—it is natural speech that must be achieved through training.

Emotion is expressed largely through voice. The actor finds a register within his vocal range that fits the character (and speech mannerisms and patterns that fit the character to the text). The feeling conveyed through every vocal response involves precise pitch. Intensity of emotion requires control of volume (while maintaining pitch). The shading of words comes from using resonance. Degrees of emphasis and reaction within lines demand controlled phrasing, the shaping of inflection and intonation, and the use of pauses that do not serve just to gulp air. Anyone who attends theatre in a foreign language is surprised how much exact meaning a master actor conveys vocally, how much undifferentiated general emotion comes from others.

VOICE PRODUCTION. The basis of vocal variation is the "supported" voice, which depends on the breath control necessary for stage delivery. In everyday life we take shallow gulps of air at regular intervals that cause the lower chest and abdomen to protrude. The actor who uses such normal breathing on stage may take deeper gulps of air and try to regulate the intervals between inhalation, but he then forces sound out with his muscles, which pitches his voice high, strains his vocal apparatus, and reduces his control of speech. Because he simultaneously tries to hold back air and to force it out, he wastes it and sounds breathy.

Good stage delivery requires that the actor store a supply of air without muscular constriction and that he direct it in spurts of various length and intensity at his vocal folds, which are in effect two reeds that produce sound according to how they are vibrated, pressured, and tensed by air. The actor keeps his abdomen contracted but relaxed. Contrary to some belief he also keeps his chest contracted, or rather subtly expands and contracts it as part of the process of exhaling and speaking. Above the abdomen, just below the center of the rib cage, is a group of muscles called the diaphragm that forms a sort of floor of

Figure 4–7. Katherine Cornell as Masha in *The Three Sisters*, 1942. (*The Theatre Collection of the New York Public Library.*)

the chest. As the actor inhales, he uses his intercostal muscles to raise his ribs upward and outward. His diaphragm curves convexly down to the supporting abdominal wall and the resulting cavity is filled with a good supply of air. (The process is related to deep breathing.) Air is forced out as needed by minute relaxing and tensing of the abdominal muscles.

Proper breath control is available to anyone who is willing to practice. It should be combined with movement, and in controlling and measuring exhalation the actor should practice counting, use nonsense syllables, and so on, being careful not to force himself into an endurance contest. If he fails to achieve relaxed contraction of the chest he will sense that he is only filling his upper lungs. If he cheats unconsciously by expanding his abdomen wall, he will at first get a good supply of air but will soon sense a hollow sound and fatigue in exhaling. The actress who unconsciously declines to use her intercostal muscles and inhales by gently thrusting back her shoulders (a habit with some figure-conscious beginners) will not get air and will sound breathy. This much can be learned through self-exercise, even instinctively, because many people accustomed to public speaking unconsciously master breath control and many sometimes wonder why, after speaking, their stomach aches slightly, whereas more strident speakers get sore throat. But the more refined techniques of voice control, and the solving of personal problems, are not to be learned from studying books. They require a professional teacher.

There is no correct way to pronounce language. Pronunciation varies from place to place, age to age, and language itself changes accordingly. The essential base of pronunciation in acting is standard speech, the consensus of well-spoken, educated speech in any country. The romance languages are standardized, probably because of the direct link between spelling and spoken sounds. The Germanic languages, of which English is one, are characterized by striking regional variation and have caused trouble in the theatre. The British universities appear to have homogenized southern and London speech into a standard English, which with modifications and through radio usage has been widely accepted. In America, the size of the country and immigration have created a variety of dialects (the pronunciation typical of a geographical area, such as "Southern," "down-east," "Brooklyn"), and accents (the pronunciation of English by those to whom it is not native or a first language: French, Jewish; or by those who speak a non-American English dialect: Irish, Scotch).

Nevertheless, through concern and practice, a standard of "Good American Speech" has evolved that many persons use naturally, that good actors master, and that good speech teachers have codified. In the theatre, we use it for classical and poetic drama, or in playing educated characters. The professional problem is that regional audiences are not fully accustomed to it and accept local variations of it or the horrors of "stage" or "summer stock British"—intonational affectations (dominated by a clipped nasality) and an absolute reliance on the broad *a* (in such words, for example, as *hand*)—which resemble no spoken or stage or British speech. Such habits pass at home, but when the actor tries to enter the professional theatre he does not fit in because his own speech either violates standard stage speech or conflicts with the New York regional variations audiences will tolerate, to say nothing of the falseness of such accents as Jewish, Italian, Irish, and of New York dialects, which actors born or trained in New York can learn accurately through first-hand imitation. Motion pictures and television have hindered rather than helped the use of good American speech because, by some unconscious audience agreement, the regional speech habits of the actor are accepted as individual character idiosyncrasy; a Midwesterner can play a New England farmer and get away with it, even in New England, if he speaks in a farmerlike manner. This makes it easier for the actor untrained in voice and speech to find employment in films. It also prevents the film and TV actor from succeeding on stage.

Voice and speech work are integral parts of acting training. It may help the actor only to master standard stage speech and to eliminate his regional habits, but he should first learn to use his vocal apparatus to support his voice and to deliver sounds. However, this technical achievement must be integrated with acting, because one learns voice to communicate emotion and speech to fit any necessary language the playwright has assigned a character. A singing teacher may improve the voice, a speech therapist pronunciation, but neither can help one's acting. Moreover, such teachers are useful to the actor only to the degree that their methods emphasize flexibility. Voice and speech are the primary means of communicating dramatic meaning. The director and acting teacher must know voice and speech, as the voice and speech teacher must know acting technique. The good actor should be capable of moving effortlessly from meaning to line delivery. He should also be capable of studying meaning through the voice and speech requirements of the text, particularly in classical drama.

As an example of the use of speech training in studying a part, take the speech of a Gentleman from *Hamlet*, Act IV, Scene 5 (attributed to Horatio in the Folio):

> She speaks much of her Father, says she hears
> There's tricks i' th' world, and hems, and beats her heart,
> Spurns enviously at straws, speaks things in doubt
> That carry but half sense. Her speech is nothing,
> Yet the unshaped use of it doth move
> The hearers to collection. They aim at it,
> And botch the words up fit to their own thoughts,
> Which, as her winks and nods and gestures yield them,
> Indeed would make one think there might be thought,
> Though nothing sure, yet much unhappily.

It is the only speech the Gentleman has in the play. There are no other means to deduce his character, which is certainly not outstanding: the speech is hardly Shakespeare at his best. It is uneven, and on first reading rather jerky. It takes off, then pulls up short. It seems to violate the iambic pentameter, containing extra beats. It is irregular in meter, but only lines 4 and 8 contain an extra syllable. What is strange is that there are sudden sequences of monosyllabic words, each of which takes strong emphasis, following flowing sequences of polysyllabic words, some of which contain difficult consonant clusters (cks, ct, tch, nks) and joined words ending and beginning with consonants (straws, speaks; botch, the), which obviously must be driven through, however ungainly they sound. The phrasing is very uneven; whole clauses pour out, run over line ends, and then stop short at the cesuras (which move from the beginning to the ends of lines in one speech, not a common habit of Shakespeare's). The grammatical construction toward the end is hard to hold. It winds up with a weakening piling on of dependent clauses and qualifications. Although the vowel sounds lack those dominant patterns that tell us much about poems, every time the speaker hits a long run of words the short vowels and flowing consonants take over, which invites a rising pitch, until he is brought up short by the long deep vowels and hard-voiced consonants that slow the tempo and lower the pitch.

To read the speech neutrally, emphasizing the sound and phrasing of speech analysis, without thought of characterization or dramatic situation, is to encounter a speaker who is alternately persistent and hesitant, who attempts the rhetoric of narrative description but pauses abruptly at odd moments to prolong a comment, and whose tone is one of urgency, fear, and insinuation. This is no lordly sentimental introduction of a lyrically mad Ophelia. It follows hard on Hamlet's resolution to let "My thoughts be bloody," although the Gentleman, who is loyal to Claudius, may know nothing of Hamlet's threat, or of Laertes' imminent rebellious arrival, Shakespeare means him to upset Gertrude by implying that Ophelia's madness is being interpreted in a dangerous way by others and requires close surveillance. The role is small, but the Gentleman is a member of the court; he may have been on stage through much of the play. The director who wishes to extend the life of the play into the court of Denmark may take his cue from this speech, with its implications of knowledge and suspicion beyond what may be admitted, in planning the use of his minor court characters, and the actor can construct upon it a character who is noticed and remembered.

Stage Mechanics

The "artificial" techniques of external action are called stage mechanics. Like voice and speech work, they should be taught concurrently with work on the actor's emotional resources, so that when the student moves into actual acting exercises he does them with an awareness of stage conditions.

Naturally, beginning actors have to master the simple vocabulary of stage placement (*upstage*, away from the audience in the proscenium theatre; *downstage*, toward the audience; *right* and *left* movements as seen from the actor's, not the audience's, point of view). In addition, the actor should be conscious of the relative values of stage positions and the strengths and weaknesses of movements up- or downstage (see p. 335 under "Directing"). An awareness of his own part in the stage picture and of his effect on other actors should make such movements as dressing (moving slightly down and in as another actor crosses below); giving stage (moving so that another actor will gain the principal focus); and taking stage (moving so as to gain the principal focus) almost automatic. Finally, of course, economy of movement, size and tempo of movement, and the proper direction of movement (as in, for example, the curved cross) must be learned.

All stage movement should be efficient and should avoid the busyness of everyday life—where movements are full of the irrelevant, the incongruous, or the inconsistent smaller physical actions that can be

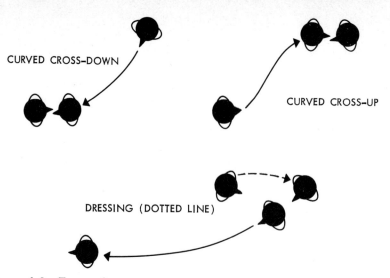

Figure 4-8. Types of stage movements.

related to what Stanislavski called "tendencies" (the emphasis of lines of character or action away from the spine of the play). Like character tendencies, irrelevant movements not only distract the audience but also create false ideas of the nature of the primary action. Even intentional minor physical actions, such as a facial tic or the outward signs of nervousness, need not be constantly in evidence. Moreover, although an actor should react when necessary, excessive reacting, the "living the life of the character" throughout the performance, diverts the audience's attention and creates problems for other actors, who must react to the reaction. No amount of arguing from a plea of "truthfulness" will excuse an actor who is unable or unwilling to practice economy of action and reaction.

When standing still, the actor has to stay alert, his body controlled and balanced with the weight on the balls of the feet, not the heels. The problem with hands is not where to put them but how to keep them from moving when they are not required for legitimate gesture and emphasis. "Don't just do something! *Stand there,*" a director reportedly told a fidgety young "method" actor. When in doubt, the beginner should keep the character involved and attentive, but should refrain from excessive movement.

The basic principle governing the actor's stage movement and action is to maintain easy visibility. One lets the audience see what needs to be seen; one moves so as to arrive at his next position easily, without distraction. Therefore, turns are generally made facing the audience, gestures and prop handling with the upstage hand, kneeling on the downstage knee. The actor learns to back into chairs, timing this sitting to the touch of the back of his leg, to cheat into an open sitting position, and to rise using his legs, one foot in front of the other. On a slanted couch, the downstage actor sits back, the upstage forward. Doors are closed with the downstage hand and opened with the upstage hand.

In approaching another actor on stage, if the approach is not parallel, a curved move is made, up when moving upstage, down for down. The purpose is partly visual, but mainly to arrive at one's destination in a good body position. In fact, all moves should be planned not from the impulse to move but according to the desired arrival position. The old adage about the purpose of stage movement being to avoid bumping into other actors or the furniture is essentially true, and is not at all inconsistent with honest or emotional acting. Once one's ability to maneuver becomes second nature, the apparent artificiality of stage mechanics becomes the means to greater reality for the audience, a help, not a hindrance, in realizing the important theatrical life of the character.

The Actor's Notebook

Many actors keep notebooks during rehearsal. Some fill them with an invented biography of the character—an outgrowth of Stanislavski's emphasis on given circumstances that has its merits until it leads to misplaced emphasis and keeps the actor from engaging in the real action of the play. The overliterate, conscientious actor may put his performance into his notebook, not on the stage. However, any note-taking system is worthwhile if it provides a good working review. Three main purposes might be suggested for note taking:

1. To keep clear the aims and meaning of the total production. In the minutiae of rehearsal they are often neglected, and reference to them often provides the clue to solving a knotty acting problem.
2. To extend and refine character concept. Any organic listing of traits, habits, facts, and acting devices employed, if revised as one goes along, serves as a short refresher.
3. To keep a diary of progress with each scene, listing its aims, problems, needs, and a step-by-step listing of difficulties encountered, particularly the director's comments.

After every rehearsal the actor should review for himself the things that need working on and go over the scene. Notebooks can grow voluminously.

Notes don't belong on the script, which has its own function. The script should be left as clean as possible, so that whatever markings are on it are incisive and up-to-date. Before rehearsal the actor underlines his character's name before every speech. During rehearsal, he carefully makes all line changes, cuts, and additions. He may use the margins of the script to list concisely what he is working for, as helps or warnings; but too much of this becomes meaningless. He may also use diagonal dashes to indicate phrasing and underline key words; he may write in phonetic pronunciation and draw in a stress over emphasized words. But he remembers that the script is for rehearsal, the notebook for rehearsal study.

Rehearsal is a process of discovery, not of learning by rote. A director may work minutely scene by scene, but the actor begins by establishing an outline and then fills it in. The real trick of acting is to try many readings and interpretations until one works, and then anchor it and use it to solve other problems. The actor who keeps changing his whole performance has failed to do his early rehearsal work and analysis thoroughly. One of the main problems of rehearsal is the order of things to work on. Scenes do provide a constant string of difficulties, but after a while the good actor recognizes that most stem from some central acting problem crucial to the role. An actor may sense and know instinctively that when he gets it right the rest of the performance will fall into place. Ophelia may be perplexed at how to sing the mad song; Creon's walk and carriage may need some significant, regal change after Oedipus' catastrophe; Clov's initial laughter upon looking into the ashcans may be difficult to get until late in the rehearsal period.

By and large, the solutions to acting problems grow out of rehearsal. The actor may suddenly realize that some simple thing the director has been criticizing, but about which he feels comfortable, contains the trouble that holds him back. Or the character who may be consistently but wrongly withdrawing from another character, may have been conceived as too fidgety; a set intonation may be wrong; a series of lesser objectives may really be what Stanislavski called "tendentious ideas," or tendencies leading away from the through line of action. Identifying one's problems may be difficult. Solving them may be excruciating. But the actor must go home and work on them himself, no matter how patient and perceptive the director is. It is then that the actor returns to beginning exercises, tries an emotional recall, and reworks the character's external gestures.

When the actor absorbs a sound outline of the part and then successfully deals with a number of small puzzling problems, and when he begins to communicate effectively with other actors making similar progress, he often hits a "breakthrough," a moment when everything falls together and a smooth, steadily growing process of work replaces the fits and starts and false successes of early rehearsal. Polishing then begins. He has made things happen, and his aim is to keep them happening. He discovers that he can drop excess movements, condense pauses, reduce the pressure of delivery on many lines, fix lines and moves, and let his energy and concentration flow more easily so that they take over his conscious control of scenes. Although he may find countless little additions, the final work of rehearsal is one of refinement, selection, and elimination, not embroidery.

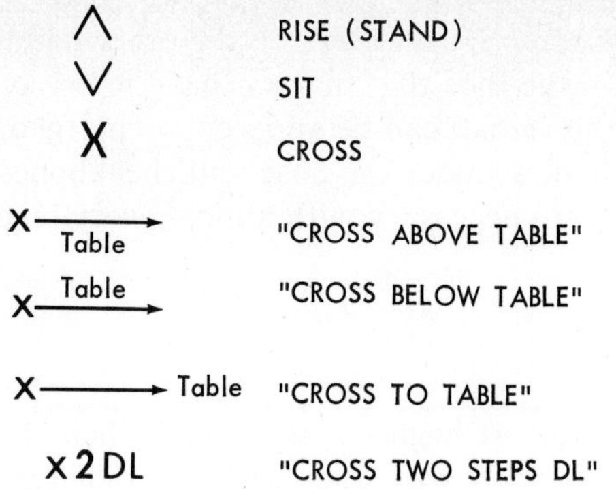

∧	RISE (STAND)
∨	SIT
X	CROSS
X——→ Table	"CROSS ABOVE TABLE"
X—Table—→	"CROSS BELOW TABLE"
X———→ Table	"CROSS TO TABLE"
X 2 DL	"CROSS TWO STEPS DL"

Figure 4–9. Examples of script notations used by both actor and director in indicating stage movement.

The Purpose of Makeup

The actor's face is part of his equipment. Like his voice, his hands, and his muscles, it is an expressive constant in his work—something that can be improved, even varied slightly, but not really changed. Unless he wears a mask, he will bring that face to each role he plays, using the face as the role requires.

Makeup helps the actor to use his face. Most simply, makeup helps his face to be visible under stage light; lighting colors wash out or bleach real skin colors, destroying contours where the actor and the audience need to have them emphasized. Makeup, then, not only compensates for the effects of stage lighting, but also capitalizes on lighting color to heighten the visibility and emphasize the molding of the face.

It also allows the actor to vary the face slightly to fit the given circumstances of a role for which he is not physically suited—age, race, state of health, even sex, where necessary. The use of prosthetic devices —artificial pieces to change the apparent structure of the face—will even allow the face to change its bone structure, although only within the rather strict limits of the materials available to the actor. In addition, the range of colors and the possibilities of treating areas of the face in many different ways allow the actor to suit it not only to the given circumstances of the role, but to the intent of the entire production. An actor may, for example, play a sick old man, adding to these given circumstances an interpretation of the character that is somewhat expressionistic, by using an over-all green for his base color. Makeup, it hardly need be said, is not only a device for making physical circumstances look real; it is a device that allows the actor to exploit circumstances theatrically.

Finally, makeup can be used as a corrective, as it is called. Corrective makeup is sometimes confused with so-called glamor makeup, the adaptation of the face to an ideal standard of good looks. Thus, a young girl playing a stock ingenue may be tempted to glamorize her face with falsely hollow cheeks and false eyelashes, just as she may be tempted to glamorize her bosom with a padded bra. As a rule, such glamorizing is dangerous because it tends toward a general type and away from particular character. Corrective makeup, on the other hand, is intended to modify problems in the face that make it hard to see or wrong for the role: eyes that are too small can be apparently enlarged; a mouth that disappears into a shadow under the nose and cheekbones can be outlined. Such corrections are necessary with almost every face that is going on a stage.

The Materials of Makeup

The raw material is the actor's skull. It begins with bones; when the actor knows where the bones are, how they interact, and how they cast shadows, then he can begin to apply makeup. Until he does know his underlying bone structure, little that he does will have any value. The face is like the painter's ground, and it must be studied closely and long so that it is really known.

Skin texture and skin color affect makeup. The skill will show through all but the most extreme shades; therefore, a given color of makeup will appear different on one actor, under identical lighting, than on another whose skin is darker or lighter.

Makeup itself is merely color in a handy, usable medium. In many ways the best medium is oil, and "grease paint" is still the most widely used kind of makeup. There are others, of course. Pancake is a dry solid makeup that is applied with a wet sponge; at least one major manufacturer has created a mixture of pancake and greasepaint that tries to preserve the advantages of both while overcoming their disadvantages. In general, the greatest disadvantages of greasepaint are its undeniable messiness (it is exactly as greasy as it sounds) and its harsh effects on sensitive skin. It has the important advantages, however, of not spotting or streaking when the actor perspires and of blending with other colors put over it. In that most completed makeups use several colors, the ability of grease to blend is its most important quality. Pancake, on the other hand, does not blend well, and it will streak and even disappear when the actor perspires.

Pancake is used mainly for the so-called *base*, the first, general color that goes on the face. Greasepaint is used both for a base and for *lining* colors, those applied over the base and blended with it to make shadows and highlights, to mold new lines and folds or to emphasize existing facial structure. In addition to base and liner, most finished makeups will use pencil colors (usually black, browns, or blues), semisoft dark colors in wood pencil form; rouges, either dry (a cake) or soft (merely a red or orange lining color); and powder over all oil-base paints. The custom of using colored powders to match the base color is gradually disappearing, and makeup manufacturers now offer excellent translucent powders that can be used on almost any color, allowing the color to show through while giving the face the necessary matte surface that prevents shiny reflections under stage lights.

A small, but important part of any makeup line is its special prosthetic materials. Of particular importance are nose putty (a hard material that becomes soft and sticky under heat), liquid latex, and various kinds of artificial hair, the best known of which, "crepe" hair, is lamb's wool. Many splendid effects are possible with these materials, and a good makeup book must devote pages to discussing them. Let us say here merely that nose putty has two disadvantages: it is hard to remove and it cannot be applied over any large area of moving facial muscles. These may sound contradictory, but nose putty sticks all too well to an unmoving surface (the bony part of the nose, for example), whereas a moving part—the cheek—quickly loosens it and causes it to fall off.

Liquid latex is an excellent material for building false wrinkles, for enlarging certain features, and for applying beards, moustaches, eyebrows, and other pieces. However, it has a rather strong solvent in it and can cause serious reactions on sensitive skin. Anyone intending to use it should try it out on a small area before using it in any quantity.

False hair, especially for men, is a time-honored material. Beards are easily built with it, in several pieces; a beard or moustache built on latex can be used several times. Ordinarily a beard that is applied a second time (and after) should be fastened with spirit gum, a quick-drying adhesive that holds better than latex but that lacks latex's advantages of elasticity and reusability. It must be removed with alcohol.

Color and Application

Makeup bases lie in a spectrum more or less like that of human skin tones. Makeup liners are not so limited and cover almost the complete visual range. Between the two, almost infinite variations are possible for a given character.

There are four principal makeup manufacturers whose products are generally available in the United States: Max Factor, Stein, Mehron, and the British Leichner. All are good and widely used. Regrettably, each uses a different number and name system for its makeup colors, so that a number 3 in one manufacturer's base may be totally different from the same number in another's. There is no rational system for resolving these differences, and the best that can be done is to consult the color charts in Richard Corson's excellent book, *Stage Makeup* (third edition), in which all manufacturers are keyed to a single color spectrum.

Within these limits, then, the actor chooses his colors and builds his character's face. In picking any color, he must know the lighting colors of the production, for his makeup will be seen by colored incident light. Incident light in a similar range will intensify a makeup color; incident light from the opposite side will darken, gray, or even blacken it. For example, many actors use a reddish-amber shade for healthy young

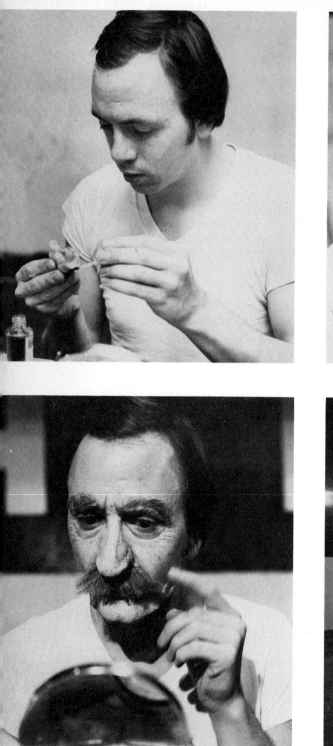
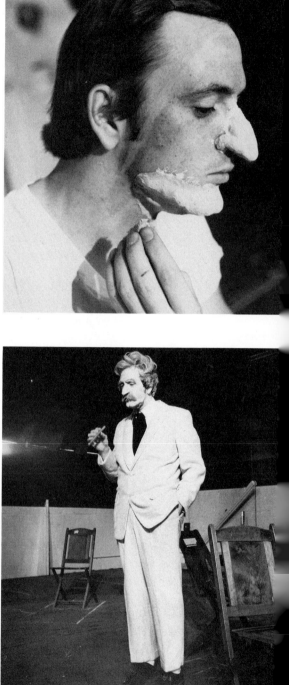

men. Similarly, many lighting men use amber as a dominant warm gel color for their lights. Such a base color under this light can be very good—intense, believable, and within the apparent skin-tone range. Such a base, however, in a night scene using greenish-blue gels would look gray, dark, and unnatural. The problem, then, of picking correct colors is very complicated, made even more so by the use of at least two colors (warm and cool) in most lighting designs, and by the use of at least three colors (warm base, cool shadow, and warm highlight) by the actor. Very generally, those choices will be based on the following tendencies:

1. Use of a warm base color, varied to suit the actor's own skin tone, and selected for the race, age, and state of health of the character in terms of the style of the production.
2. Use of one or more lining colors for shadows, chosen to blend with the base and to match its intensity under known theatre lighting. A red-brown shadow is excellent, particularly for older characters, because it picks up warm light and yet does not reflect cool. Blue and green shadow will look gray or black under warm light, but where there is much cool light, they will reflect and may appear their proper color.
3. Use of one or more lining colors for highlights, to emphasize or create planes that reflect incident light. Warm colors predominate, with white and yellow most common.
4. Use of pencil colors to match the shadows. Brown is most useful; black and blue often are too dark or look merely dirty.

In applying his makeup, the actor will use complicated techniques that demand experience and knowledge. A typical makeup application is summarized very briefly here:

1. The face is washed with soap and water to remove excess oil. Oil causes greasepaint to sink in, making it difficult to remove. Naturally, a male actor shaves before making up.
2. Base is dotted lightly all over the face, to look rather like measles.
3. The base is smoothed in until an even, light coat covers the face, neck, ears, back of the neck, and any exposed skin on the shoulders. The base should be even but not thick. (Some actors set the

Figures 4–10 through 4–13. The actor Chris Fazel preparing a Mark Twain makeup. 4–10. A latex nose piece is prepared for application. (The nose was built earlier, as were prosthetic jaw and neck lines and the moustache and eyebrows.) 4–11. The latex edges of the prosthetic pieces are blended into the skin with a sponge and adhesive, and then covered with a special makeup. 4–12. Moustache and eyebrows are applied and most of the makeup is complete. 4–13. Completed makeup and costume, with wig.

makeup by splashing on cold water at this point. The practice is questionable.)

4. Shadows are applied, usually with the finger where large areas are involved, with a small brush or "stomp" (a rolled paper pencil) where small areas or lines are needed. The actor's skull is used as a guide to application. For an aged character, such shadow will include the cheeks, the nasolabial folds, the jowls, temples, eye pouches, and forehead.

5. Primary and secondary highlights are applied. Primary highlights occur where light strikes directly on the top of a feature; secondary highlights are brightened by reflected light or light coming at an angle. Highlight is applied above most shadowed areas. In an aged character, these would include the brows, cheekbones, top of the nasolabial folds, the jawbone, and the knobs on the forehead. *Folds* are created, whether in the forehead, around the eyes, or next to the nose, by building up a contour with highlight, secondary highlight, shadow, and deep shadow (with pencil or very dark liner), from top to bottom. Secondary shadows are sometimes added *below* the fold, where such a feature would actually cast a shadow with light shining from above.

6. Corrective work is done with the pencil (as around the eyes) and rouge is added, where necessary. Beards and moustaches are added at this point; built-up features of nose putty or latex would have been put on before the base.

7. The face is powdered liberally, and the excess dusted off with a very soft brush.

When the makeup is finished, the face seen in the actor's mirror will hardly seem natural. The proper use of color and the correct application of it will have created a mask, transparent, it is true, but a mask whose colors seem excessive and obvious by ordinary light. Only on the stage will they interact correctly, under the light for which they were designed. If everything has been planned well, the face that the audience sees will be a readily visible, sharpened interpretation of the actor's face, altered to project his role.

5 Directing

If the central problem of the actor is to work so that a given role is projected to the audience in the most effective manner for that audience, then the great problem for the modern director is to combine many such roles with other elements into a theatrical whole. That artistic whole will, indeed, be the sum of its parts, but for the director the parts include not only the roles as they are performed, but the effects on those roles of setting, lighting, and the finest details of costume and makeup; in short, it is the director's intelligence that encourages the disparate elements of the theatre to become a totality, a coherence. With his creative impetus, the "thing to be communicated" that was discussed in Chapter One—the performance—becomes a whole having inner harmony.

This is not to say that the director is a fuller theatrical artist than the actor or the designer; rather, the director works with a different subject matter. His subject matter is the creative products of other artists. To the extent that he takes part in their creative acts (coaching an actor, working with the designer on the ground plan of each scene), he is able to help them prepare for their own artistic product, *but he never becomes an actor or a designer.* If he does, he is actually interfering with the total creative process, not aiding it. Thus, *to direct* does not mean to command; it means to encourage growth.

A cursory glance at theatre history shows, of course, that the director as a distinct individual is a fairly recent figure. Goethe, in his work at Weimar (1807–1820), can properly be called a director, albeit a dictatorial one, in that he was not an actor in the company he directed (as for example, the British actor-managers of the nineteenth century were). David Garrick (1717–1779) was an earlier example of an actor who was deeply concerned with the totality of his company's performance. However, in seeing Garrick in this light, we must probably admit that such earlier dominant actors as Thomas Betterton (c. 1635–1710) and Molière (1622–1673) took an interest in the totality of their companies' performances that we can call directorial. Nevertheless, the appearance of the director as a distinct figure really belongs to the late nineteenth century. Indeed, if any list of theatre "greats" of the first two thirds of the nineteenth century is compared with one drawn from the twentieth—say, for example, Kean, Booth, Talma, Capon; with Stanislavski, Copeau, Brecht, Meyerhold, Olivier, Craig—the first (excluding playwrights in each case) will be made up of actors and designers, and the second of directors, with actors and designers generally running a bit behind. The shaping of the twentieth-century theatre has, in fact, been done by men whose concerns were directorial. Even when those men concentrated on elements within the whole, as Gordon Craig did in much of his work, we will find that their real concern was with totality of performance, and even with new concepts of theatre itself.

In the contemporary theatre it is likely that some of the practical organizational work that might be performed by a director will be performed by a producer. This doubling of functions is sometimes unfortunate and is actually an economic rather than an artistic matter. The familiar situation of the Broadway-bound play's director leaving the show in Boston or Philadelphia is frequently the result of a conflict between producer and director over artistic matters. The conflict has no place in an *ideal* theatre situation, but in the practicalities of present-day professional theatre it is unavoidable.

The experienced director will work within the producer-director relationship, recognize its dangers, and usually head off deep conflicts before they happen. Like all other theatre artists, he will find that handling such human problems is part of his creative work, and in the case of the director the handling of human problems becomes of particular importance. Especially in his work with actors he will employ many devices (some so subtle or even unconscious that he will hardly think of them as devices) to create the totality for which he works. In the end, then, the director is an artist whose subject matter is not only the artistic products of other people, but those people themselves.

The Director Today

The modern concept of directing began with the European tours of the company of the Duke of Saxe-Meiningen in the late 1870s and 1880s (see pp. 146–147) and gained definition with the work of the leaders of the "free theatres" of France, Germany, and Russia. In each of these, individuals exerted artistic control over productions—Antoine in France, Brahm in Germany, and Stanislavski and Nemirovich-Danchenko in Russia. It was not an accident that all were breaking away from contemporary staging practices; it was not an accident that all were interested in the then-new theatres of the naturalists. To read, for example, Strindberg's notes for reforming the theatre along naturalistic lines is to see why an over-all artistic control of production was needed: Strindberg wanted radical changes in setting, in the way actors related to each other and to the audience, and in the groupings and movements of figures on the stage. He was far from alone.

With the widespread acceptance of naturalism, the new directors did not surrender the artistic control they had won, but maintained it. They had quickly become essential to the theatre, and their work easily was made to cover all kinds and styles of theatre—opera, musical comedy, experimental theatre, and the classics. As the educational theatre developed in the United States, it preserved the role of the strong director, perhaps even gave it more importance because of the student status of the actors. Too, as the "little-theatre" movement spread after World War I, amateur actors wanted the strength that a director could bring.

The Stanislavskian approach that dominated American professional

Figure 5-1. *Indians* at the Hilberry Classic Theatre, Wayne State University, 1972. Directed by Don Blakely, with settings by Russell Paquette, costumes by Vic Leverett, and lighting by Gary M. Witt.

acting in the 1940s and 1950s was geared toward work with a strong director. Actors, to be sure, were not to be treated like children, but they often welcomed paternal direction. Particularly in "inner" work, the director became more and more the adviser and confidant, and his success with actors depended greatly on his ability to set up close relationships with them, to engender trust, and to penetrate psychological defenses. By the late 1950s, the American director's role in the theatre had expanded from that of the organizer of staged actions to that of the teacher, guide, and stimulus for the actors. In those theatres where new plays were produced—notably in New York—the director achieved the position of master theatre craftsman. In working with the playwright, he both developed his own profound understanding of the play and altered the play according to that understanding by making suggestions to the playwright regarding his interpretation. In working with the actors, he both communicated his own understanding and amended it because of the actors' responses; in turn, the actors' responses often became new material for suggestions to the playwright.

The process was many-sided, a matter of constant feedback going in several directions simultaneously, with each new input changing all the others. At its best, it was very productive; at its worst, it caused intense bitterness, often directed against directors by playwrights who felt that their work had been so changed that it was no longer their own.

By 1960, then, the director was accepted as the defining figure in an American production. There would be no severe shock, as there had been in the 1880s, if a director seized total artistic control to redefine the theatre itself.

That is more or less what happened. It was happening in Europe as well as in America. Brecht, before his death in 1956, had defined his own theatre from the position of both playwright and director. Julian Beck and Judith Malina had increasingly radicalized their own concept of theatre in The Living Theatre. The early proponents of improvisatory theatre were on the scene well before 1960.

Behind the developments in acting in the 1960s (see pp. 282–285) were strong figures who functioned both as directors and as teachers of acting—Joseph Chaikin, Richard Schechner, and others. Jerzy Grotowski was doing the same thing with the Polish Laboratory Theatre. The new breed of director was doing what the earlier Stanislavksian directors had done, but he was working more closely with his actors than his predecessors ever had, sometimes living communally with them, erasing the lines between life and art, between the street and the theatre, and between rehearsal and performance.

Thus, by 1970, there were two rather different emphases in American directing. One was traditional, the emphasis of the commodity theatre and the classically oriented educational theatre, with a double interest in traditional staging and in actor-coaching along Stanislavskian lines. The other was innovative, the approach of the new theatres and of some university theatres, with interests in the new independence from the playwright and in methods of staging that were not based in proscenium-stage practice and in imitations of reality.

As with any innovation, directing in the new theatre has demanded the formation of new techniques. Each director has his own exercises and his own way of relating to his actors, often with great psychological intimacy. In those instances where dramatic texts have been used as the basis for production (The Performance Group's *Dionysus in 69*, The Living Theatre's *Antigone*) the directors have exerted a traditional influence as textual interpreters, although actors have been given great scope in changing lines and scenes. It would seem, however, that no matter how democratic each such group has been, a considerable amount of control has remained with the directors: one should never forget Alan Schneider's remark that "casting is style," and, in the new theatres, casting is still done by the directors—not, to be sure, according to traditional methods and not according to the rather brutal criteria of the "open call" and the audition, but by the very demanding criterion of whether or not the individual actor has the temperament, the commitment, and the beliefs to work in very close psychological proximity to this director.

It must be remembered, too, that despite the notoriety given the new directors and their theatres, the great bulk of work being done in the American theatre is still done along traditional lines: dramatic texts are still being staged with fidelity; actors still have individual personalities; and audiences still want to be delighted and even instructed. It is perhaps difficult to remember in an age of instant mass communication, when novelty is highly prized and instantly advertized, that a great proportion of theatre work is still being done as it was ten, twenty, and even two thousand years ago.

Directorial Approach

The creation of the actor is organic and personal. Nevertheless, it is a creation that comes into being within the difficult situation of rehearsals and discussions; it is, paradoxically, a very private act subject to and changed by many public pressures. Among the helpful public (or outside) influences on the actor, and probably the most important, is the work of the director in every phase of prerehearsal planning, in the rehearsal period itself, and often in the suggestions made during the performance period. In order for any director worthy of the name to begin his creative work with the actor, the director himself must first have done a great deal of private creation of his own in arriving at his approach to the play.

Directorial approach is a term that is loosely applied to several areas: to the written record of the director's ideas about a play; to the idiosyncratic use of stage techniques that distinguishes one director from another; and even to the concept of theatre that underlies a director's work. As used here, however, it means *the total sense of the play that can be translated into performance.* No director can arrive at his first rehearsal, or even his first casting session, without such an approach. It need not be written out in detail, but it may be; it need not be schematized in terms of blocking, ground plans, and character actions, but it often is. It need not be—cannot be, in fact—capable of being translated into verbal description, but it *must* be capable of being translated into performance.

In arriving at his approach, the director may consciously choose not to set down in precise detail everything that he wants to see in the final performance—first, because he could not possibly get everything he wants (unless he is a tyrant with underlings instead of actors), and second, because much of what he wants for the performance will come to him only during the production period (after, that is, the play is cast and discussions and rehearsal have begun). He will, however, have a firm sense of what the play is to him, in his own language (partly verbal). As an analog, we might use the Stanislavskian terms adopted by actors (see p. 276), *objective* and *superobjective*, but in an aesthetic instead of a psychological sense. The director will have, as it were, a firm idea of the aesthetic superobjective of the play (not "What is it about?" but "What will it do?"). He will also have for each scene or each important section of a scene, an aesthetic objective that explains how the scene contributes to the aesthetic superobjective; the two cannot conflict. The through-line of aesthetic objectives will give him his directorial spine—the line of primary development that he wants to see emphasized, dramatized. Finally, he must develop his own concept of the cumulative effect of the spine on his audience—the development of the performance and the shape of it in terms of high points and low points (climaxes and drop scenes).

Obviously such an approach is not always developed in strictly logical terms. Frank McMullan, in *The Directorial Image*, has emphasized the use of the visual image (to be carried out in the production's scenery and pictorial compositions). Such an image may, in fact, be the main impression in the director's consciousness after his first reading of the play. Such impressions are not to be ignored. With the heightened sensitivity of the creative director, the first encounter with a theatre piece may produce direct and fertile impressions that later experiences, clouded as they often are by the conscious search for specifics of character, action, and meaning, will not produce. A single image or a single statement, then, may be the guiding first reaction of the director, and out of it may grow his approach.

As an example, let us take *Endgame*. The play is filled with powerful images—the "shelter," the blind Hamm, the ashcans, the windows giving on a "corpsed" world. Yet, the reaction to the play may produce still another guiding impression. Alan Schneider, for example, has said, *"Waiting for Godot* is about an arrival that never takes place; *Endgame* is about a departure that never takes place." The statement was made long after he had directed the play, but the impression of a "departure that never takes place" could be used by a director as the aesthetic superobjective of his approach. Actors' objectives can be fitted to it; physical properties and costume can externalize it; and the meaning of the play can harmonize with it. Out of such a briefly stated, all-embracing statement can come the concept of the director's work: to make theatrically exciting the preparations for the departure that never takes place. (It is probably unnecessary to point out that this is far from the only view of the play.)

Thus, the director's approach may begin in a large and undefined image or idea. It must then move into specifics with more readings of the play: *What is the primary suspense, and how can it be made theatrically exciting?* (In *Endgame*, suspense of plot and suspense of idea are probably not to be used; suspense of character—both Clov's

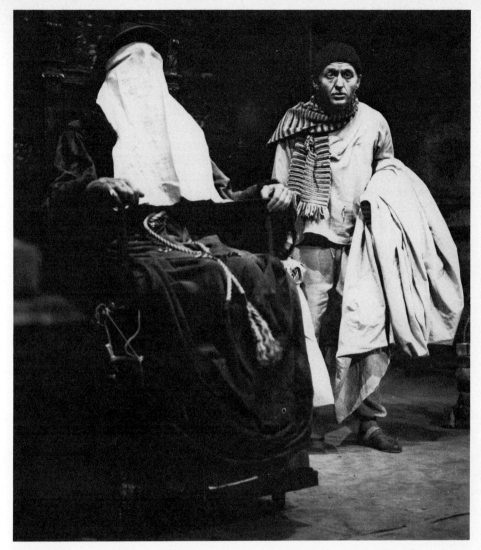

Figure 5–2. *Endgame* at the Cherry Lane Theatre, New York. Directed by Alan Schneider. In this photograph, Clov has just completed his opening pantomime. Speaking of the motivations for such actions in this kind of play, the director said, "We don't know for certain *why* Clov, for example, performs that opening pantomime. But we know *what* he does. That's given us. We can find valid reasons for the 'why' that won't invalidate the 'what.'" (*Photo, Miss Alix Jeffry.*)

and Hamm's—can be.) *What are the high points along the line of that suspense, and how will they be made theatrical?* (Hamm's narrative, broken into several pieces, is itself suspenseful and is a part of our suspense about Hamm and Clov; it must be heightened. How? In the same way, how can Clov's desperate final monologue be given maximum importance? And how will we balance Hamm's moving last soliloquy and Clov's passive listening to give theatrical excitement to the "departure that never takes place"?) *What is the contribution of each character to this line? What other values does each character bring to the play?* (Nagg and Nell are in danger of seeming irrelevant to the Hamm-Clov action. Yet they have many virtues; they are sometimes funny and sometimes touching; and their very physical appearance is an extension of the idea of departure. They extend in time—the past—what the spine of the play shows in action. How can this value be emphasized?) *What are the characters like, both physically and psychologically?* (Why is Nagg the "accursed progenitor"? Why doesn't Clov kill Hamm? Is Hamm the adopted father of Clov?) *What are the facts of the play?* (Where does this take place? When? How old is Clov? Is there a boy out there or isn't there? What produced this "corpsed" universe? How far away is Clov's kitchen?) These are questions that actors may ask in order to build a secure environment around their own sense of the characters; the director's answers to them need not be the author's so long as they are consistent and believable for the performance. They *must* be satisfying to the actors. Alan Schneider has said, "I don't worry about other realities—where the electricity comes from, whether the toilet flushes—which are irrelevant to *what is going on.*" Nevertheless, faced with an actor who had to have an answer to those questions, he could supply them.

The mechanics of setting down a directorial approach are unimportant. It is useful for student directors to make their approaches as specific as possible, often because by doing so they discover that they have overlooked many things. A mature director, however, may carry most of his approach in his head or on scraps of paper or in otherwise unintelligible jottings on his script. Directors trained in the American tradition of Stanislavski's theories may write out the objective, superobjective, and psychological gesture for each character at each important point in the play. Directors oriented toward the didactic theatre of someone like Brecht may concentrate on the idea of the play and the way in which that idea is to be communicated in each scene. Again, directors who are committed to the theories of Antonin Artaud or to environmental theatre, the theatre of cruelty, may fasten on a sense of the audience response they wish to arouse, and then create the actors' exercises that will finally arrive at such a point. In every case, however, the director's approach will include his own sense of the final impact of the performance, as well as his knowledge of how each actor can make that impact part of his own character.

The Director and the Actor

The director must be master of the vocabulary, the techniques, and the creative methods of his actors, and he must be constantly flexible in using them. Actors of different temperaments, different creative methods, and different rehearsal techniques will often work in the same production, and the director must be able to reach every actor on his own terms, without forcing that actor to change himself so radically as to lose the sense of creativity. The actor's playing of the role is the director's most important kind of subject matter, and he not only must bring the roles into balance with his own concept of the play and with the plastic elements of lighting and space, but he also must bring each actor's role into balance with all the others. The director need not be a brilliant actor, but he must have confidence in the many techniques that actors use.

Actors sometimes forget that the most important influence in creating a role is contributed by the director. The actor's character serves a particular function in a production that is attempting to realize the director's concept of the play. Too often, an actor studying a part commits himself so completely to an unwanted interpretation that he disturbs the rehearsal process. Ideally, the actor should study the role in the context of the entire script, so that he grasps its essential requirements but can visualize a number of solutions to the problem it raises. In auditioning, a good director, in turn, should look for an actor who can bring varied responses to the role. Unfortunately, many directors fix their own notion of the part before casting and then look for an actor whose approach fits that notion. Unless the director announces beforehand how he sees the part, the auditioning actor is handicapped. In such a case he is forced to develop a straight approach as imaginatively as he can and hope for the best.

In responding to directorial requests, the actor learns to know the part without committing himself to a fixed interpretation. The director's early blocking and his discussions at early rehearsals are then a great help. After that point the actor can try to provide a plausible character that fits the director's and his developed concept.

It is through preliminary readings, discussion, and early blocking that the director makes the actor aware of his approach and his expectations. He also gives each actor a chance to submit his own ideas and working habits during this period. The intelligent director will accommodate himself to his actors where possible, but in the long run the individual actor must assimilate the rehearsal approach of the director (length of rehearsals, the order in which different points—business, character, blocking, and given circumstances—are worked on).

It is essential that the director use the actor's vocabulary. The director will have his own idea of the spine or through-action of the play, and it will probably differ from each actor's idea, in that individual actors will relate the spine to their characters. In fact, it is usually best if the director does not insist on his own synthetic definitions of spine, superobjective, or motivation, for he is always in danger (particularly if he is inexperienced) of giving dramatic criticism rather than theatrical directon. It is no help to an actor, for example, to tell him that he is onstage as a foil for Hamlet, or to set the scene for the entrance of the king. The actor always needs to know why he is there as a human character (to tell Hamlet about the duel with Laertes, or to discuss the state of Denmark). In the same way, intellectual reasons ("You are a symbol of corruption") are worthless.

Probably for this reason, the tendency of many directors to use images is commendable. The image, concrete and exact, precludes critical or intellectual comment: "You're kind of like a butterfly or a hummingbird trying to get at Hamlet." A director has to learn to realize the difference between an actor who merely likes to talk about his role at great length and one who sincerely needs help in finding the right objective, the right given circumstances, the right image, but in either case he must be ready to deal with the actor in concrete language that is the actor's own.

Structuring the Scene

Even when a spine is defined for the entire production, the director will work with very small building blocks to put the entire work together. He may define these building blocks in different ways—as beats, scenes, motivational units—but he will find a workable small unit within which his actors can work most successfully. For many directors the motivational unit—the section between the initiation of a dominant character's motivation and his shift to another motivation, under the impetus of another character's behavior, an obstacle to his success, or his own exit from the stage—is the most easily handled rehearsal unit, for it has the natural shape of the evolution of the motivation itself. To a director who does not work strictly in motivational terms, however, the rhythmic beat—one pulse in the total rhythm of the performance—may be more useful. Yet again, the French scene— the section included between the entrance or exit of major characters —may be sufficient, although the typical French scene includes a number of motivational units and several beats, whose distinctive importance may be lost if the French scene itself is treated as the most basic unit in the play.

Whatever his basic unit, the director must have a sense of both the breakdown of the play into essential sections and its reassembly into a flowing whole. He may mark his own script by beats or units, even numbering them and giving each an emblematic title. At the opening of *Endgame*, for example, one unit breakdown might go as follows:

ONE. Starting another day like every other. (*Clov goes through the pantomime of the windows and the ladder.*)
TWO. The dead go slow. (*Clov uncovers and looks into the two ashcans.*)
THREE. Unveiling the monument. (*Clov uncovers Hamm.*)
FOUR. Whistling in the dark. (*Clov tells the audience that "it's finished," and he goes to his kitchen.*)

The four units, together, comprise a French scene. If the director conceives of the play opening in these terms, he can rehearse the units quite separately, exploring a different motivation for each, a different tempo, and then combining them into the scenic whole.

When working with the actors, the director must be prepared for constant challenges to his own sense of the play's structure and intent. It is almost inevitable that the director and the actor will see a role in different terms, at least at the beginning, and that the actor's acceptance of directorial suggestion be merely provisional for much of the rehearsal period. The director's request, "At least try it my way," and the actor's suggestion, "May I show you how I see it?" are significant of the director-actor relationship. Ideally (with enough rehearsal time, infinite patience on both sides, and respect for each other), they explore together all the possibilities of the role that lie within the particular actor's abilities. Many ideas may be rejected, and it is vital that the actor or the director not feel personally rejected along with his idea. The creation of one may replace the creation of the other, and it is equally vital that the director or actor whose creation becomes part of the performance not pretend a personal superiority. Again the director does not command; he gives.

Consider, for example, the following fictional interchanges among three different directors and their casts in rehearsing a brief unit from Act Two of *Death of a Salesman*. It is that revealing moment when, in a flashback, we see Biff's discovery of Willy and The Woman in Boston. Biff and his father have been discussing Biff's failure in school. Willy tries to ignore the sounds of The Woman from his hotel bathroom; Biff is increasingly puzzled by them. At last she bursts in, still undressed. Willy, in a futile attempt to justify himself, introduces her as "Miss Francis," a buyer whose room is being painted. He tries to get her out of the room before Biff guesses who she is:

WILLY. Go back, Miss Francis, go back. . . .
THE WOMAN. But my clothes, I can't go out naked in the hall!
WILLY (*pushing her offstage*). Get outa here! Go back, go back!
(*Biff slowly sits down on his suitcase as the argument continues offstage.*)

Three directors have arrived at the same idea: that Biff should collapse on the suitcase at the word *naked* and burst into tears. Director A has even written this direction into his script in ink; his rehearsal goes something like this:

DIRECTOR A. When she uses the word *naked*, Biff, I want you to sink down on the suitcase, to collapse, and start to cry.
ACTOR. But I don't start to cry for another half a page.
DIRECTOR A. I want you to cry here.
ACTOR. But why? I mean, Biff is a tough kind of guy—

DIRECTOR A (*parentally*). Would you just do as I ask, please? We have a dress rehearsal in eleven days.

The actor cries on cue. By opening night, he is giving a convincing portrayal of an actor crying on cue.

Director B has had the same idea; indeed he's rather proud of it. He has just had a run-through of Act Two and is giving the actors individual notes:

DIRECTOR B. Biff, there's something—I don't know, it's dead—in the hotel scene. We don't seem to have got to the right place fast enough. Let's try—when she uses—when Miss Francis says the word *naked*, Biff, that's got to *mean* something to him. She *is* naked, for him, especially—right then. *That's* when he understands. Pow! Recognition! I think that it crushes him, right then, and he just folds up on that suitcase like a little kid who's, well, Willy's *dead* for him suddenly— he folds up and bawls.

ACTOR. But I don't start to cry for another half a page.

DIRECTOR B. I know that's what the script says, that must have worked originally, but here, for us—we seem to be building the scene a little differently. Let's try it here.

ACTOR. But I don't feel like crying here.

DIRECTOR B. Of course you don't. How could you yet? But try it, see if you can't make it your own.

ACTOR. It won't work.

DIRECTOR B. All right, try it and *show* me it won't work.

He calls the other actors together and they try the scene the new way. After several sincere attempts, the actor playing Biff is clearly confused by the new demands put upon him; he likes the action of collapsing on the suitcase, but the weeping cannot be motivated. The director withdraws the second part of his idea, but still discontented with the emotional impact of the scene at this point, begins to re-examine it. The next day he has a new idea for the actress playing The Woman.

Director C, too, wants Biff to collapse and weep at the word *naked*. He has not yet had a run-through, and may postpone one for some weeks yet. Instead, he has been trying ideas with the actors, adapting them to their suggestions, and working out very slowly, beat by beat and moment by moment, the shape of each scene. There has been very little blocking done by the director except for the rudimentary planning of entrances and exits. Later he will adjust many positions and relationships to facilitate transition from one unit to another:

DIRECTOR C. Biff, I've got an idea. What happens if you *collapse* on the suitcase—not "slowly sit"—and start to bawl?

ACTOR. Let's find out.

(*They try it.*)

DIRECTOR C. It might work. I mean, it isn't yours yet, but I can see it working in the scene.

ACTOR. I have to change a lot of things, though. I mean, Biff is a tough guy.

DIRECTOR C. He's a tough *kid* at this point. *Seventeen.* Ever see a tough kid when the rug gets pulled out?"

ACTOR. All right, I see that part; I see how he does it and why he does it. You know, maybe I could build that football-hero-hey-pop tough stuff around this moment. *This* is Biff; the rest is a little—oh, not phoney, but it's like Biff's way of doing the same thing that Willy does. Putting on for the world. Suppose we went back and said that maybe that's *always* what he's doing: keep the world from making you cry. But here he fails.

DIRECTOR C. That means some changes earlier, but think about them and we'll try. Let's do it again.

SECOND ACTOR (*who plays Willy*). Yeah, but wait—I've got to change my reaction to him now. If he's going to cry, I'm left with egg all over my face. Here's my kid, the football hero, the man's man's kid or whatever—he's crying. Like *Bernard.* I can't just stand there.

DIRECTOR C. What do you want to do?

SECOND ACTOR. Get mad. Hit.

FIRST ACTOR. Hit me? That comes later, though, and it's good later.

DIRECTOR C. It's got to come later, but anger here is okay if it's directed differently. (*To second actor*) What really makes you mad?

SECOND ACTOR. Him. No, maybe not—I know my kid can cry; I've probably made him cry. It's what *makes* him cry that I get mad at.

DIRECTOR C. And that's . . . ?

SECOND ACTOR. Myself.

ACTRESS PLAYING THE WOMAN. No, me. I'm the thing that makes him cry. You'd get mad at me.

SECOND ACTOR. No, you're not doing enough for that.

DIRECTOR C. She could—suppose she giggled when Biff starts to cry.

SECOND ACTOR. I'd kill her.

ACTRESS. And *then* your line, "Get outa here! Go back, go back!" really means something. Really push me. Then I can play off that on the stocking business, I can be really mad.

The Actress and the Second Actor try this new action while the Director watches; later, when the action is clear, he will place it differently in the playing area. Meanwhile, the First Actor has begun to speak quietly to him:

FIRST ACTOR. You know, I can use this to build the difference, the things that are the same and different, between young Biff and old Biff. Like, at the end of Act One, when I'm all alone and I've found the gas tube behind the heater, suppose instead of going upstairs like it says, I do the same thing—I collapse, just for a second on something—I sit, and maybe I start to cry; just for a second the young Biff, the not-so-tough kid is there; then it's over, and *then* I go upstairs.

DIRECTOR C. That comes before this. To the audience, that may just be a guy who weeps.

FIRST ACTOR. I'll know what it is. And when we get to *this* scene, then they'll know.

DIRECTOR C. Let's try it.

And they do. And they may go on this way for weeks.

Intensity and Progression

In establishing the spine of the production, the director prescribes the rhythms, emotional content, intensities, and visual patterns of the production and sees the actor's scenes in relation to what has passed before. Only the director can bring *progressive* intensities from the totality of the performances, and it is with the help of the director that each actor finds the progression in his own role. The actor who neglects to attend the rehearsals of scenes in which he is not involved may find the director's instructions incomprehensible, and may even resist them. Too many actors work as if the play began with their first entrance, and they set about building their roles accordingly, out of step with the progressive intensity of each scene. The part of Bernard in *Death of a Salesman*, for example, is a small but vital one that must match the progression of the other roles. He does not appear until halfway through Act One and is onstage for barely a tenth of the play's length. The director should see immediately that Bernard enters as tension rises, and he returns at critical, explosive moments. There is no time to build Bernard's character. If the audience entered during one of his scenes, the stage action might seem forced and exaggerated. Thus, the director must help the actor playing Bernard to fit the intensity pattern of the entire production, to enter at that level of intensity, and to be in key with the actors already onstage—Biff, Happy, and Willy—who have built gradually to these peaks.

Intensity in a scene is sometimes confused with pace, the tempo at which a scene is played. Enforced pace will not work; the last-minute frenzy of the inexperienced director trying to force pace makes many actors sluggish, uncertain, and nervous at dress rehearsals and in performance. The real rhythm of a play becomes organically established through confident relaxation into the patterns established by rehearsal. The amateur director's urging to "pick up the pace" at final rehearsals reveals his failure to have established mood and intensity in rehearsal. Pace, as intended by amateurs, results in a forced delivery of lines in a monotonous tempo that actually makes a production seem even slower than it is. Real pace is achieved by ease of execution, by a shared sense of rhythm (actors and director), and by a controlled picking up of cues. Rhythm and tempo variations give a production the brilliance and life that command the audience's attention and permit even a long play to be performed without consciousness of time.

Style, as we have noted before, is simply the way in which theatre is done in a particular place at a particular time. In doing a period production, the director attempts an imaginative assimilation of the producing techniques of another place or time. Because each style really makes a particular use of one range of theatrical resources, the director and actor trained in any single style cannot easily make the adjustment. It is quite possible, even desirable, to apply our own contemporary approach to plays of the past, but unless the actor can deal with the particular qualities of the period and has an instrument equal to it, and the director can bring those qualities out in him, a classic is merely done as a contemporary play. (This often is dangerous because of the remaining period elements in text, psychology, structure, and so on.)

Without its own form, structure, and theatricality, a classic tends to disappear. If the iambic-based phrasing and line-run of Elizabethan verse are mastered, a good actor and director can produce most attractive variations on the verse, can even make it seem natural and modern; but to treat it as contemporary speech, without respecting its nature, is to destroy it. Similarly, one can easily motivate the long speeches, break them down to demonstrate their effect on the characters, and make them alive, direct, and part of human communication, but to try to make them casual is to lose their meaning. Shakespearean drama depends on scale. Its large scale can be transformed to other settings; it can assimilate detail (and may have been very detailed in its own time); but unless the scale is maintained, the play disappears. Restoration comedy obviously requires some sort of graceful, almost dancelike manners, and a most symmetrical pattern of blocking. If the actors are costumed in late seventeenth-century clothes, they must have "carriage." The lines require a fairly rapid delivery and a conscious concern for rhetorical turns of speech. Without the physical deportment—the ability to manipulate costume and to catch the cadences and pointed inflections of language—the play disappears. A play in the *commedia* tradition, particularly one of Molière's, requires an acrobatic agility, both with business and ideas. Contemporary knock-about farce will not suffice for the precise, agile routine of the comic characterizations, and the lovers require a lyrical lightness more demanding than any contemporary sophisticated comedy. Even the intense emotions of nineteenth-century melodrama require a control and ability to sketch in the large, chiaroscuro features that are alien to contemporary methods.

The director who attempts to stage a classic must examine his own sense of style honestly. In the first place, he must be able to cast actors who can do what is stylistically required; then, he must work in spatial terms that relate to the style of the play, and he must anticipate stage designs that will carry out that style. He must know the period not only of theatrical history, but also of social and cultural history. Finally, he must know what the play was in its own terms, what it is to him, and the difference between the two.

Yet this is not to say that every classic carries with it a predetermined style that defines directorial approach. On the contrary, it is by first understanding the stylistic boundaries of a given play *and then daring to surpass them* that many of the most important productions of recent years have been created. Shakespeare has been both the most rejuvenated and the most abused playwright in this sense. Charles Marowitz and Peter Brook directed a Theatre of Cruelty *Hamlet* that was startlingly different from the traditional, although the Shakespearean text was kept (much rearranged, cut, and re-emphasized). Joseph Papp's Public Theatre presented a *Hamlet* full of new and often shocking images, including one entrance made by Hamlet in a garbage can. The Royal Shakespeare Company presented an athletic, spare, and exciting *Midsummer Night's Dream* in a jungle-gym setting.

Merely thrusting a classical text into a different setting or period

Figure 5–3. *Hamlet* at the Cincinnati Playhouse in the Park, directed by Word Baker. (*Walt Burton photo.*)

may, of course, do unnecessary violence to it. The result may not be a stylistic innovation; it may be a mess. It is only when the director is willing to take on the responsibilities of the playwright—to create, in effect, a new text—that stylistic innovation with a classic can be productive. The object must always be to make the effects of time disappear, to give the classic the immediacy of a new play. In order to accomplish this, the contemporary director may need months of exploratory work with his actors; he may not even be able to say with any confidence that the result of their work will be a production. The process by which *The Bacchae* of Euripides became *Dionysus in 69* was a lengthy and difficult one in which not merely the style of the production, but the very techniques of acting, had to be gradually developed by the director and actors.

The Production Period

It is all too easy to lay down supposed rules about the conduct of casting, rehearsals, organization, and early performances, but the differences between experienced and inexperienced directors, and between professional and amateur actors, are so great that no common production schedule is possible for them. In general, it is probably true that a competent director with competent actors and an existing production staff can create a production in four weeks. Less than four weeks of rehearsal sometimes encourages cliché acting and machine directing. Considerably more than six weeks, except with creative actors of real experience and a first-rate director who is flexible, endlessly patient, and able to experiment, may lead to mere self-indulgence. Particularly with amateur actors who lack the training to try every possible variation and approach, and who do not have a method that will take them deeply into the role, rehearsals beyond six weeks sometimes bring tedium, boredom, and a steady decline in the quality of the production.

Any rehearsal period should bring its actors to a performance level of smoothness, ease, and relaxation several days before the opening. The excitement of those final days, with the complications of dress rehearsals, real instead of dummy properties, completed scenery, and the rigid schedule of technical cues, will not make them entirely useful for polishing performances.

Casting and Planning

Casting, of course, is done well in advance of the first rehearsal. In educational theatre, the period between casting and rehearsals may be determined by the academic calendar. In professional theatre, some cast members will be selected weeks ahead of the first rehearsal and others only after many auditions and very close to the beginning of the production.

The director's responsibility in an audition is very great. The process is rather an inhuman one, and professional actors become accustomed to people who enjoy making it more inhuman than it need be. The American actor William Redfield has mentioned the great pleasure of auditioning for Sir John Gielgud when he was directing *Hamlet* (*Letters from an Actor*): alone except for a single assistant far back in the house, Gielgud stood close to the stage in the empty theatre, spoke politely to the actor, and had ready two other actors (not a stage manager) to read with him if necessary. The lesson is clear: the object of an audition is to give the actor every chance to show his abilities, not to test his nerve or to prove the paternal power of the director.

Extremely brief auditions are unfair to all concerned. Many actors do not show well in sixty-second readings; on the other hand, some actors cannot produce improvised characterizations at the drop of a hat. The brief reading, without adequate preparation and without discussion from the director, encourages the "radio actor"—the hack who can read a laundry list so that it sounds like Shakespeare, but who cannot, after the first rehearsal, change that reading one iota. The brief improvisation, on the other hand, is of value only in showing how people react to new situations, and although it may reveal the potential of a nervous actor or a bad actor, it may also put off other actors whose own technique does not accept the improvisation as much other than a parlor game.

When possible, then, the director should do as much as he can to draw the best from each actor: make scripts available well before the audition, or explain the play in considerable detail; discuss the actor's concept of the role with him; let each actor read at least one role that he wants to play; find some means—walking a scene, improvising—of having each actor move onstage and react physically to the other actors.

After casting, the director can plan the production in terms of specific actors. Costume plans, the finished floor plan, and stage designs can be prepared. Meetings of the production staff, the director, and the technical and design staff should now settle all questions, however minute, of organization, authority, and over-all production concept. Decisions postponed until after rehearsals begin (selection of certain properties, details of the ground plan) should be clear to everyone. The actual preparation of sets, costumes, and properties should begin. By the first rehearsal, the director should feel that the production is already taking shape around the actors, and he may even want to use specific sets, costume accessories, and hand properties throughout the rehearsal period.

The temperament of the director has much to do with the prevailing tone of the rehearsals, but that does not mean that one kind of directorial temperament is better than others. The tyrant, familiar although he may be among amateurs, has no place on a professional stage; neither, on the other hand, has the mouse.

In scheduling rehearsals, the period devoted to any one activity must remain flexible. However, directors often find it convenient to think in terms of *preparatory* rehearsals, when much discussion is used; *blocking* rehearsals, when the mechanics of placement and movement are given; *building* rehearsals, when beats, scenes, or even acts are worked out in great detail; *polishing* rehearsals; *technical* rehearsals (scenery and lights); and *dress* rehearsals (costumes and make-up). A sample schedule, undoubtedly to be departed from in practice, is offered for a four-week rehearsal period in an amateur or educational situation:

First week:	first day:	read and discuss
	second day:	read and discuss
	third day:	actors walk, random ground plan
	fourth day:	actors walk, some rough blocking
	fifth day:	discussion, character work
Second week:	first days:	rough blocking
	end of week:	building rehearsals
Third week:	first day:	blocking completed, firm ground plan
	second or third day:	books down, run-through
	end of week:	building rehearsals, run-through
Fourth week:	first and second days:	polishing rehearsals
	third day:	technical rehearsal
	fourth day:	first dress
	fifth day:	final dress
	Performance	

During the preparation period and the early rehearsals, the director will probably keep his own book, a copy of the script with expanded margins, space for notes, and extensive comment on the play. His continuing work on this book constitutes a more developed approach to the play—the organic creation of his concept of the performance. It will contain not only his line-by-line blocking (in whatever system of symbols he finds convenient), but his rough ground plans, notes for certain acts, and, most importantly, his ideas on the play and the characters. Too much such preparation before casting can lead to errors, because it may force the director to cast according to a rigid concept rather than let actors show the possibilities of each role to him. However, after the casting period, the director cannot possibly think or know too much about his production. Only he can, and must, be ready to answer every question. His book is the basis of his answers; he may depart from its blocking, from its character descriptions, or from its ground plans before the first performance, but it is only because he has prepared himself so adequately that he is ever able to see the needs that lead to change.

THE DIRECTOR AS CREATIVE TECHNICIAN

The individual actor does not create his role in total isolation. Almost everything he does will be done partly in terms of what other actors are doing. His vocal tempi will relate to other voices; his movements will relate to the positions and movements of other actors, of furniture, of walls, and of empty space. Nevertheless, the interrelationship of actors will always be limited by the entirely admirable selfishness of each actor's need to create. Although there is considerable need for the actor to worry about how the *totality* of movements, of tempi, and of tableaux projects to the audience, he cannot from his single viewpoint gauge the success of these things alone. The director, then, works on these factors. Although the correlation of visual factors may not be the first thing done by the director (in terms of time), at some point he must come to grips with those visual needs.

Pictorialism

Since the late nineteenth century, *staging* has taken on the connotation of "picture making." The new directors are no more exceptions to holding this interpretation than were their forebears of the 1950s; Tom O'Horgan's staging of *Jesus Christ, Superstar* is probably as powerfully pictorial as the staging of any spectacle of the last several decades. The roots of pictorialism, however, are a century old.

In the United States, when directing has been a classroom subject, it has most often been treated pictorially. There are two sound reasons for this: first, pictorialism is a valid part of directing; and second, its rudiments can be systematized, whereas the more difficult nuances of psychology and human relationships cannot. In learning about pictorialism, the student encounters such terms as *emphasis, balance, composition,* and *picturization,* words that relate the stage picture to realistic painting. If the proscenium stage is seen as a framed picture, the analogy to painting makes sense; in open staging, which has no frame and which has so many viewing points, it is questionable.

The highest development of pictorial direction probably took place in silent films before the widespread use of the close-up. Medium shots in such films are strikingly handsome—the actors' positions are interesting and varied, the important actor is emphasized more than the others in a group. Such manipulation was necessary in a form where the audience saw, as it were, through the camera's eye, and where spoken dialog and sound could not provide information. Pictorial direction was a boon to such a form, especially to its story-telling needs. The close-up and sound greatly lessened the need for such a device; its preservation in the proscenium theatre attests to the need there for visual reinforcement of plot and language.

Insofar as every stage director must work with the pictures created

Figure 5–4. *Oedipus Rex* at the Missouri Repertory Theatre, University of Missouri, Kansas City. Directed by Alexis Minotis, with sets by J. Morton Walker, and costumes by Vincent Scassellati. Pictorial devices for emphasis and focus should be noted.

by actors and objects in space, his approach is pictorial. It is surely necessary that every director become aware at an early stage of development of the potency of pictorialism; it is probably also necessary that he later make it an unconscious part of his artistic work so that it does not become an end in itself. Particularly in theatre in the round and in environmental theatres, where the audience space is irregular and where, frequently, the audience is able to change its relation to the playing area during the performance, the practices of the proscenium stage become less and less important.

The conventional proscenium stage is usually divided into six major areas, both for planning subdivisions of the total playing space and for giving directions to actors. The pivotal point of these areas—stage center—is the intersection of the *centerline*, the perpendicular to the proscenium line halfway between the wings, and the *stage axis*, parallel to the proscenium line and halfway between it and the rear extremity of the playing space. Directions toward or away from the proscenium line are given as *downstage* or *upstage*, a terminology that derives from the Renaissance sloping stage. Despite the fact that the physical slope disappeared in the nineteenth century, the expressions up and down remain.

Directions parallel to the stage axis are given, in the United States, from the *actor's* point of view, meaning that the director reverses his own (and the audience's) left and right. (The opposite is true in some European theatres, and the difference has accounted for some of the confusion in translations of European plays.) With the directions away from stage center defined, then, as *up, down, left,* and *right,* the six basic stage areas in the proscenium theatre are *down right* (ideally, an area whose width is one third of the proscenium width and whose depth is one half of the stage depth, located at the audience's left); *up right* (the half of the stage depth above the stage axis, on the same side); *down center, up center, down left,* and *up left.* In actual practice, these areas seldom are of equal sizes, the outer edges of the left and right playing areas being squeezed in by the sight lines.

In practice, thirteen locations tend to get used by actors and directors: center, right center, up left center, and so on. It must be noted, however, that such terminology, and the visual theory that it defines (which will be discussed in more detail later), is true only of a proscenium stage. As the stage apron projects farther out into the audience, the forward orientation of this system begins to crumble, and on a thrust stage, with the audience on three sides of the playing area, the definition of such directions and such playing areas is largely a convenience. In theatre in the round, the terminology is useless, for there is no longer a forward line by which either stage axis or center-line can be defined, and *up, down, right,* and *left* have no common direction to which they can orient themselves. Thus, the breaking down of thrust and round stages into playing areas, although very helpful to the director in creating variety and limiting the physical dimensions of scenes, cannot be systematized. It should be immediately obvious that to move *down* in a proscenium stage really means to move *toward* the audience, and it is the movement *toward* that is really significant. On the other stages, movements toward the audience, if we were to term them moves downstage, would take on quite a different meaning. See Figure 5–6.

A cursory review of the origin of the proscenium stage shows why its terminology is restrictive. Oriented as such a stage is toward the single seat—one at the perspective focal point—it will find its strongest acting position as close to that seat as possible (downstage) and directly on the visual axis of that seat (center)—in short, at a point designated *down center.* Actors sense this; they will gravitate to down center for important speeches, big scenes, or, in fact, for any moment that they wish to emphasize. If, however, the single-seat focus of the proscenium stage is abandoned (as in a thrust or round stage), the single emphatic stage position disappears. As is shown in Figure 5–6, an actor who places himself at the middle of the forward edge of a thrust stage is in a down-center position for only part of his audience; another significant part of that audience will be looking at his profile or even his

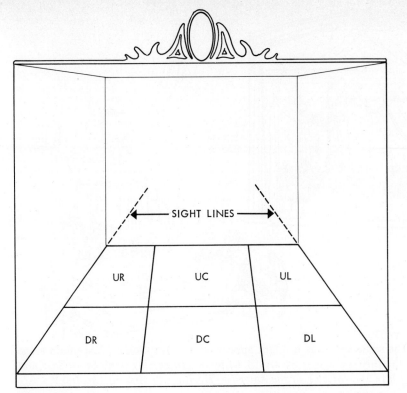

Figure 5–5. Basic areas of a proscenium stage; the terminology can be adapted to thrust stage use.

back, seeing him in a position that would be right center or left center in the proscenium theatre. However, because the wall from which the stage projects gives a linear orientation to that stage (that is, the actor moves *from* the back wall *into* the audience, and generally acts in front of scenic elements on the back wall), it is likely that the thrust-stage audience will still allow this down-center position to be very strong. Removal of the back wall, however, in the theatre in the round completely destroys the overpowering emphasis of any single location.

Just as downstage positions are dominant in the proscenium theatre, so certain lateral positions (left and right) are frequently thought to have special force. The most common explanation given for the supposed dominance of the right side of the stage is based on Western reading habits, the assumption being that a psychological emphasis is given to the left-hand side of the printed page. As a result, down right is thought to have greater strength than down left, up right to have greater strength than up left. Tenuous as this idea is, it is believed by many directors, some of whom even go so far as to ascribe particular *kinds* of emphasis (romantic, somber, ghostly, violent, and so forth) peculiar to each area. The virtue of such theorizing is not that it is

Figure 5–6. The same scene, as it might appear on a conventional proscenium stage (left) and on the thrust stage at Stratford, Ontario. (*Drawn by Arno Sternglass and reproduced with the permission of the American Heritage Publishing Co., Inc.*)

especially accurate—no controlled test in the psychology of perception has borne out the specific mood values of stage areas—but that it gives an insecure director a system within which he can work, while it gives even a secure director a short cut to three-dimensional variety in his physical blocking. Short cuts are rarely desirable as artistic devices, but in the practical world of one-week stock or an underrehearsed college production, they have some value.

The order of dominance generally given to stage areas in the proscenium theatre is down center, down right, down left, up center, up right, and up left. In the thrust stage, right and left are far less relevant, and in the theatre in the round, they are completely irrelevant. In the latter two theatres, then, the relative importance of acting areas will be determined by other means.

Level and Lighting

Of the remaining emphasizing devices, the most important is probably the use of scenic and property shapes to define and strengthen areas. Physically, the association of an actor with a scenic mass can be far more important than the location of the actor within the playing area. Similarly, the association of an actor with even so simple an object as a chair or a table will strengthen him, especially in the thrust and arena theatres. Such scenic considerations, however, are more appropriately discussed in connection with ground plans and the director's role in creating the stage design.

Level, the height of the actor above the stage floor, is an important device. All other things being equal, an actor on a level one or two feet above other actors will dominate the scene. By contrast, an actor sitting or lying down may dominate if everyone else stands. The use of platforms in upstage areas is very common in the proscenium theatre because it helps to counter the great de-emphasis of those areas. With a platform in the up-right area, for example, an entire scene can be played there and still be made to seem of equal importance with those played farther downstage. As a general rule, a director will need every area during the course of a full-length play, both for the variety he can gain thereby and for the added significance he can give the play through the scenic identification of different areas. (In *Death of a Salesman*, for example, many of the areas are clearly identified by their scenic demands: the kitchen, the boys' bedroom, and Linda's room. Others will be used for several different locations—the restaurant, the hotel room, Howard's office—but the significance of those areas must build as the play progresses, with subsequent uses of the same area for different locations maintaining the emotional tone of the area). The use of levels, particularly upstage, is very helpful to a director seeking to get maximum use out of his entire playing space.

With the creation of sophisticated lighting systems, of course, area emphasis and area identification became capable of very complex manipulation. The extreme selectivity of modern lighting allows single actors to become, as it were, the playing area: spotlighted on an otherwise dark stage, they *are* the stage. More subtly, area can be emphasized or de-emphasized by more or less light, or warmer or cooler light, and the reflectability of costume colors and materials can be exploited to give certain actors emphasis, no matter where they stand on the lighted stage. Such use of lighting for emphasis can be overdone, both because it tends to defeat the variety inherent in the other emphasizing devices and because selective lighting contains a message (its literal unreality) that is unsuitable for many plays. In the right play, however, in combination with level, three-dimensional mass and stage position, it can contribute richly to the production.

But Why Emphasize?

The very idea of emphasis in a production implies, of course, some standard by which degrees of difference can be judged. One might say that such a standard would be false, because a good playwright creates verbally all of the emphases and de-emphases he feels the play should need. For example, Shakespeare is sometimes staged without regard to

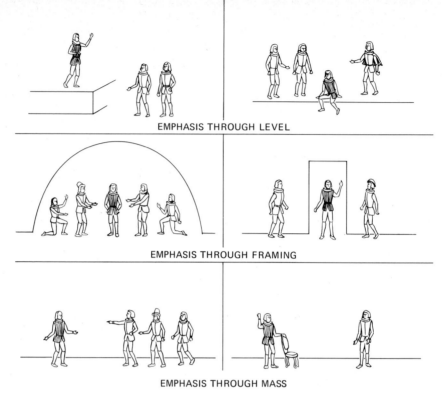

EMPHASIS THROUGH LEVEL

EMPHASIS THROUGH FRAMING

EMPHASIS THROUGH MASS

Figure 5–7. Ways of giving emphasis to one actor in a scene.

directorial emphasis—rather as if his plays were Platonic dialogues, all language and no action. "The poetry" is the excuse given for such productions, which are characterized by simple stage pictures, lengthy, static scenes, and very plain scenic structures. It is very true that Shakespeare, and almost every other playwright, does indeed write emphasis into his plays, and it is equally true that the production cannot safely ignore those emphases. However, the plain fact of staging (already discussed in Chapter One) is that the script is insufficient by itself, being not "the thing to be communicated" but a tributary to it. As soon as it is given the external solidity of production, it runs head-on into such problems as relative stage positions, levels, and so on. In short, one *cannot* choose to ignore visual emphasis: it exists as a condition of the theatre. One must, therefore, exploit it, use visual emphasis to underscore textual emphasis and use area identification to strengthen the "placeness" or the significance of a location in the text. And finally, of course, there is the very simple matter of audience perception; the audience must be led to see the right things, to hear the right actor, and to listen to the right word.

The director, then, at some time during the production period (not necessarily first) roughs out the area emphases of the entire play. Certain scenes that need strength, because they are strong—Hamlet and Gertrude, Willy Loman and Biff—will demand central or downstage areas. Certain others—Marcellus and Bernardo on the castle ramparts; Ben's entrance in *Salesman*—will tend to place themselves upstage because they have less emotional strength (their pacing is slower, their character intensity—the pursuit of objectives—less vital). In most full-length plays, however, the overlapping of scenes in the same areas will come very early, because there are simply not enough areas to play each scene separately. The director may then decide to give each area a title—"violence," "romantic love," "lust," "suspicion" —and play similar scenes in those areas. Such a practice seems at first glance to be naive and mechanical, but we should note that it is not quite the same as the earlier method of designating stage areas as *always* having the same qualities. Here, rather, the director uses the play itself to define the areas in its early scenes, and then redefines and deepens an area with each succeeding scene played in it. Consider, for example, the following breakdown of *Death of a Salesman:*

> Up Center: The Kitchen. Warm and symbolizing "home," it is both the background against which Willy's life is played and the haven to which he returns. To his wife, it also symbolizes home, but for her home means Willy. All scenes designated for the kitchen by Miller are of necessity played here.
> Up Right: Linda's bedroom. Her haven. She comforts Willy here; the apparent reunion between Biff and Willy (end of Act One) takes place here.
> Up Left: The boys' bedroom. Not a haven at all, but a way station. Used very sparingly by Miller.
> Down Center: The yard. The happy scenes with the boys are played here (the football game, the day that Biff played in Ebbetts Field, and so on). These scenes spill over into the left and right areas, with their increasingly sinister connotations. The center area is "invaded" by Ben when he trips Biff and threatens him with the umbrella.
> Down Right: Willy's illusions. The exit is made from this area to Ebbetts Field; Willy meets Bernard as a young man here; the Miss Francis scene is played here and in part of the up right area next to the house.
> Down Left: Disillusion and death. Howard's office, the restaurant, Willy's last scene with Ben (the planting of the garden) and the requiem take place here.
> Entrances: Ben always enters from up left (by the way station). Charlie always enters from up right (Linda's haven, Willy's comfort).

If this division seems arbitrary, we should consider what other choices a director might have. One, obviously, is to discount the idea of area significance altogether. When this is done, the use of areas tends to be accidental or organic: that is, to grow out of mere sequence, with no regard to overlap or contradiction between the scenes played in the same area. Again, controlled experiments in perception have not been used to test the idea of area significance, and an accidental selection of areas may be perfectly adequate (significance being, after all, little more than unconscious memory of prior uses of the area).

Body Positions

Just as the areas within which entire scenes are played can be varied and given degrees of emphasis, so the positions of individual actors are capable of a variety that has many meanings for the audience. On the proscenium stage, actors do not face each other precisely as in real life. For centuries, the most common body position was full front, facing the audience (or most of it, or the most influential part of it, depending on whether the actor was working in the Elizabethan, the Restoration thrust, or the proscenium stage), and lines and whole speeches were often "pointed" by the actor's turning *full front* (shoulders parallel to the proscenium line). One sound reason for such a position still exists: audibility. If the actor no longer looks into the audience unless the play dictates it, in all but a very intimate theatre he must still direct his voice, however obliquely, toward the audience. Beyond that practical need to orient himself toward the audience, theatre convention has established a number of body positions, based on theatrical principles and practices, that some directors follow slavishly and others follow only for convenience in talking to actors.

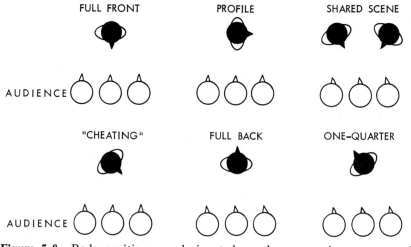

Figure 5–8. Body positions as designated on the proscenium stage, and adaptable to thrust stage use.

Various directions are used to bring actors to these positions: *open up*, means turn farther front (*turn out* means the same thing, although it generally is used for small adjustments); *turn in*, turn slightly upstage; *move up* (or *down*), move perpendicular to the apron; *forward* or *back* directions indicate moves along the actor's body axis and do not refer to stage axes at all. To *blend in* means to adjust the body position slightly in relation to other actors.

In taking these positions, the actor moves his whole body, including his feet. The head is often angled toward the audience ("cheated"), away from the body position.

Visual Symbolism

Thus far we have been talking about obvious and mechanical reasons for placing scenes on certain parts of the stage and for placing actors in certain positions. Nothing has yet been said about synthesis, the assimilation of these things. Yet the totality of actors' positions, their interrelations in terms of body position and stage location, is vastly more important than any of these things in isolation. This totality—the stage picture—is a visual interpretation of the play, shifting from moment to moment as the actors move, the lighting changes, the scenery shifts, and the discursive progression of the play gathers momentum.

It is not too much to say that the picture seen by the audience at any moment is a symbol of the play's content at that moment. In one sense, then, a performance is a succession of static tableaux, each one symbolizing something about the play. What is symbolized may be the subtext—that is, the human complexities that underlie what is said. It may be the intrinsic meaning of a scene, particularly when that intrinsic meaning negates the subtext. It may be a sudden revelation about an individual character. A director cannot ignore the symbolic effect of tableaux, because his audience is already accustomed to looking for visual symbolism in real-life tableaux. (Consider, for example, the common experience of seeing two people walking together. We can often read the subtext of their relationship by their body positions, their physical distance from each other and the direction of their heads. The subtext of two people strolling across a park with their heads together and their arms around each other is fairly clear; so is the subtext of the same two people walking quickly, one slightly ahead of the other, with six or eight feet of distance between them. If they separate even farther—thirty or forty feet, let's say—they are no longer together, but they still have a relationship that we can interpret.) The visual symbolism of the stage picture, then, is based in part on human behavior, just as acting is based on observation of behavior and playwriting is based on judgments about behavior.

The other deciding factor in the director's visual symbolism will be the emphases we have already discussed. That is, certain decisions about location and position will be based on simple matters of audibility and visibility; others will be made on the director's evaluation of who is dominant in a scene (not who must be heard, but who exercises power over the scene itself—the Ghost in Scene One of *Hamlet*, Uncle Ben in the fight with Biff in *Death of a Salesman*). Thus, the tableau will be created out of two needs: to show human values in the scene and to maintain theatrical values in the scene. As a general rule the second need can be used to supply a rough outline for the first; that is, the director's rough blocking of a scene should give it theatrical validity, whereas the work of the actors, and of the director with the actors, will fill in the details of the second. When, of course, the director's theatrical interpretation makes the human interrelationships difficult or even impossible, the blocking must be changed. Frequently, when actors sense that a scene is wrong but cannot explain why, the director will find that his emphases, although theatrically valid, are preventing the actors from establishing the human interrelationships that they need. He must change such a scene.

Three devices, based on the kinds of emphasis we have already discussed, can be used in setting up the theatrical symbolism of the tableau: relative position upstage or downstage, relative body position among the actors, and the visual focus from actor to actor (who is looking at whom). Thus, all things being equal (and they never are), the downstage actor symbolically will be the most powerful; the actor on the highest level symbolically will be the most powerful; the actor whose body position is farthest front or significantly different from the others will be the most powerful; the actor given the greatest amount of free space will be the most powerful; and the actor associated with scenic mass will be the most powerful. (Note that in this context *powerful* does not mean having social or political power, but having the most important effect on the nature of the scene.) *Endgame*, at first reading, would seem to be a play whose inherent physical patterns defy the director's attempts to shift emphasis from character to character. Hamm is center, facing full front, supported by the mass of his chair, and surrounded by free space. Nagg and Nell in their ashcans and Clov with his restricted movements are visually weaker in most scenes. Nevertheless, the play gains much of its theatrical force from this almost unchanging stage picture. If it is an exception to the practice of illusionistic directing, it is an exception that succeeds mightily, for it creates in its audience a visual hunger for variety, for a change of emphasis and power, and for an alteration of the stage picture that is an aesthetic counterpart of the metaphysical hunger of Beckett's characters themselves. To see this unusual and unchanging stage picture for over an hour is to yearn, as Hamm does, for the game's end.

It is virtually impossible in most productions to use emphasizing devices in isolation. Ideally, different devices should reinforce each other, although in practice they will often contradict each other. The director must try to get rid of the contradictions.

Human Relationships

Of the two bases of visual symbolism—theatrical dominance and human relationships—the second is unquestionably the more complex and varied. It is also more important. The first can be reduced to rough, pragmatic rules; the second, at least at present, cannot be reduced at all, although findings in psychology and sociology may help to sort out some patterns as being more easily recognizable to the audience than others. It is highly doubtful, therefore, that any director should begin by making decisions on a purely theatrical basis. In actual practice, of course, an experienced director will be thinking of human and theatrical meanings at the same time and will not be able to say precisely when or why he settled on a given stage picture. There is a degree of circular reasoning involved, at best, because actors often base their interpretations of a role on the blocking they are given, whereas directors are often reluctant to set a blocking pattern until the actors find that it is valid. A lengthy rehearsal period can, therefore, be immensely fruitful if a joint process of creating visual symbolism is carried out through the exploration of each scene and each character, with the director's synthesizing done day by day. He may then choose to impose a few patterns or tableaux *after* characters and relationships are firmly established.

All that can be said of the director's control of visual symbolism is that he must stay constantly aware of alternate possibilities for every important moment in his production. "What does it mean?" is a valid question to ask of every static picture, but "What else could it mean?" is an essential one. Consider, for example, a simple, two-person picture from *Hamlet:* Hamlet finds Claudius at prayer and considers killing him, at the moment when the king, finishing his prayers, speaks these lines:

> Help Angels, make assay:
> Bow stubborn knees, and heart with strings of steel,
> Be soft as sinews of the new-born Babe,
> All may be well.

Obviously, he is kneeling in silent prayer. Hamlet's first line is

> Now might I do it pat, now he is praying,
> And now I'll do't, and so he goes to Heaven,
> And so I am reveng'd.

Hamlet then reconsiders and, after a lengthy soliloquy, decides to kill Claudius in an act of evil rather than when he is praying. There is

Figure 5–9. A few of the possibilities for staging the prayer scene from *Hamlet*.

little human interrelationship on the surface of the scene. Claudius does not know that Hamlet is there; Hamlet's feeling toward the king is expressed to the audience, not to Claudius. Nevertheless, the relative positions of the two actors will symbolize a number of things about the scene and about Hamlet's real feelings. Is he psychologically hesitant? Is he almost unable to control himself? Is he pulled in two directions emotionally as well as intellectually? Is he afraid of Claudius? And whose scene is it? Hamlet's? In which case is it a progressive step toward the perception of his character? Or is it Claudius' scene? In that case his prayer and his own doubts, although an extrinsic digression from the Hamlet development, may help to present a larger and more potent totality. A decision as to what would be the best visual symbol could be made only on the basis of a given production, for it is only as a point in the progression toward the entire performance that any stage picture has meaning. The selection of what moments to reinforce by strong, symbolic static pictures (because the great part of any performance will be filled with movement, which has its own impact) will also depend on the director's interpretation of the play. His use of such pictures must have the same pattern, the same progression toward climactic moments, and the same sense of what is important and what can be understated, as his synthetic statement about the entire performance.

Movement

Unquestionably the single greatest fault with the blocking of beginning directors is an insufficiency of movement. Except in the rare cases of plays such as Beckett's *Endgame*, where economy of movement is essential to the play, movement is a vitally important means of conveying meaning to the audience. More than that, movement is the means to visual variety. Finally, of course, if static tableaux are created for high points of the performance, the kinetic means of going from tableau to tableau must also be created. That mere movement from static picture to static picture is bad would seem axiomatic. Movement, like static interrelationship, has its human meaning as well as its theatrical meaning, and it must first serve the human needs and then satisfy the necessity of getting the actor from point to point on the stage for reasons of emphasis, composition, or pictorial symbolism.

Much is said of motivated movement and of the director's need to find motivations for the movements that he gives to actors. If, however, a director has to hunt for a motivation, he might better ask himself if the movement is correct in the first place. If he feels, after real examination, that a movement is theatrically justified, he may then try to give an actor the reason for making it. All directors, however, are familiar with the situation in which an actor feels uncomfortable with a movement that the director has asked for, and most directors would admit that part of the time, at least, the actor is right to be uncomfortable, because the movement violates the human needs of his character.

Movement Meaning

Meaning itself is normally interpreted in the same way that body positions and the distance between bodies are interpreted as reflecting relationships. Consider, for example, the simple situation of two people being introduced and one of them saying, "How do you do?" Setting aside the possible inflections of those four words, we must see that in each of the following cases the relationships between the two people are radically different:

1. *A* approaches *B* and says, "How do you do?" while shaking his hand (conventional).
2. *A* backs away from *B*, saying, "How do you do?" (fear or repulsion).
3. *A* moves toward *B*, saying, "How do you do?" as *B* backs away (fear or repulsion on *B's* part).
4. *A* says, "How do you do?" turns, and walks away (anger or other negative emotion).

Basically, there are two simple moves possible on the part of either actor—toward or away from the other. These moves can be complicated by backing away, as opposed to turning and walking away. They can be intensified by the rate at which they are done; they can be given subtle shades of meaning by the relation of the move to the timing of the spoken line. For example, to say, "How do you do?" and then turn and walk away is quite different from first turning, walking away, and then saying, "How do you do?" If we further complicate the second example by having *B* (the person addressed) follow *A* and grasp his arm before he says, "How do you do?" we have a complete action, almost a story, involving two people who have very definite and quite different feelings about each other. Yet, we have not changed the sentence that is the sole textual statement, "How do you do?" Movement, then, is a powerful means of communicating subtext to the audience; it can, in fact, be the means by which a classic text is reinterpreted for a new audience.

Thus, movement must always validate the human (character) content of the scene. *When the text and the movement of a scene contradict each other, the audience will believe what it sees, not what it hears.*

Onstage Movement

Probably of less importance than the human value of movement, but still useful, is the stage effectiveness of movement. Movements toward the audience (downstage in the proscenium theatre), like positions near the audience, are strong; movements away are weak. As a result, a movement that seems valid in a rehearsal hall (without stage orientation) may suddenly seem wrong onstage, because it is made too weak or too strong. If, for example, *A* says, "How do you do?" turns, and moves downstage, he may seem to feel much more violently than he in fact should. A move parallel to the stage axis, or at an angle to it, may be preferable, whereas a move directly away from the audience may seem so weak as to deny the meaning of the move altogether. (However, in the case where *A* is weak or hesitant about such a show of feeling, an upstage move may be entirely correct.) A further consideration, of course, is that any move not only has value of its own but also brings the actor into new relationships with other actors and into a new stage position. Thus, for the greater part of a performance, a shifting of the stage picture is almost constant and unavoidable. Certain small moves, therefore, become almost automatic with many actors and are easily given by directors as requests to "dress" or "blend in"—in other words, to make slight corrections to re-establish both stage balance and the stage picture.

The actual movements made by actors will vary somewhat from the clear-cut movements of real life or even of the rehearsal studio. In the proscenium theatre, moves are usually curved so that the moving actor will wind up facing another actor and on a plane with that actor, if moving toward him. The director should, of course, be aware of the need for such moves.

Movement has the further and vitally important function of punctuating, or marking, units in lines, speeches, and scenes. The tempo of movement and the amount of movement will set off one scene from another; the point at which an actor moves will indicate a slight change in the progression of a lengthy speech. Very long speeches, therefore, are frequently treated as pacing scenes, during which the speaker paces back and forth, not so much to communicate nervousness or the intellectualizing of the pacer, but to break the speech into comprehensible building blocks. Hamlet's speech to the players ("Speak the speech, I pray you") can be treated somewhat this way, not by having Hamlet pace about, but by breaking the speech down into movements toward several different people.

Thus, movements must be precise and must begin and end at points that are in keeping with lines or with other movement. Nothing is less convincing than an actor who delivers his lines with great conviction but who moves sloppily. Not only will he fail to mark divisions in his speeches, but he will also blur over differences of intensity by beginning moves too early and carrying them on too late. His character will seem vague, no matter how convinced he is of its validity or how splendid his vocal delivery may be. Again the audience will believe what it sees, not what it hears. It is equally true, of course, that the director who fails to see the need for proper moves at precisely the proper times will be burdening his own production with vagueness, not to mention lack of visual variety.

The Director As Designer

Although the director will rarely be a professional designer of competence, his deep concern with the visual part of the production necessarily involves him in scenic design. No arbitrary separation between the director's and designer's work can be made, although as two extremes we can suggest the director, on the one hand, who gives his designer a scale ground plan of every scene and expects nothing more in return than a detailed elevation; and, on the other hand, the director who passively accepts the designer's decisions about everything from the size of the acting areas to the placement and style of ashtrays. A workable relationship obviously lies between these two possibilities. The director, aware that the designer is an artist in his own right with talents that the director does not possess, remains open to creative suggestions, expecting that the finished designs will parallel in style, period, mood, and progression his own and the actors' work. In return the designer must expect that a good part of the three-dimensional shaping of stage space will be done by the director. The director is not a designer, but his concern with pictures and with movements demands that he have partial control over the space in which those pictures and movements must exist.

In fact, a director cannot begin to work plastically with a scene without first outlining the areas within which the scene will be played —making a ground plan, in other words. It is a familiar rehearsal technique to shove furniture into random patterns on the stage or in

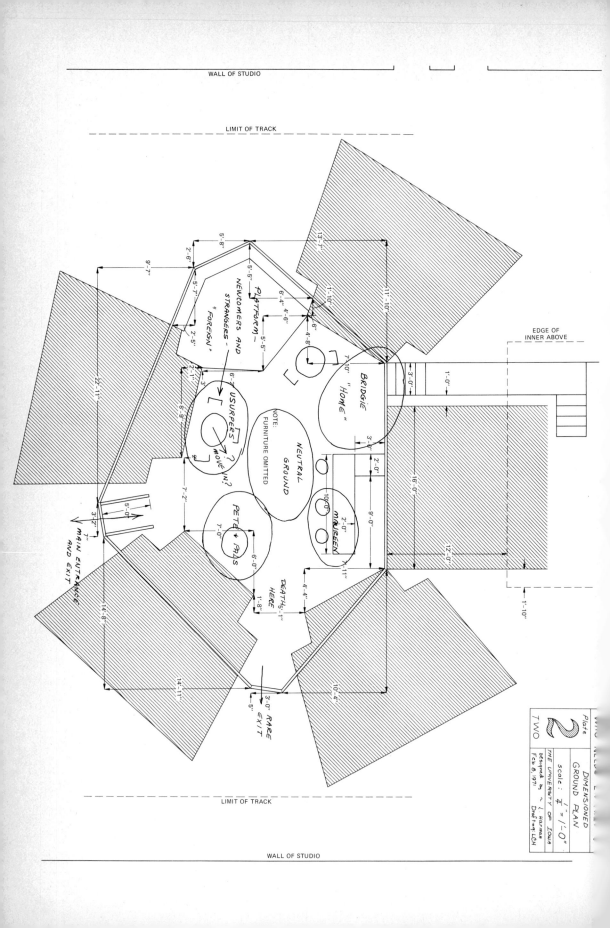

WALL OF STUDIO

LIMIT OF TRACK

EDGE OF
INNER ABOVE

PLATFORM —
NEWCOMERS AND
STRANGERS —
"FOREIGN"

USURPERS
"MOVE IN?"

NEUTRAL
GROUND

NOTE:
FURNITURE OMITTED

BRIDGIE
"HOME"

MAUREEN

PETE + PRIS

DEATHS
HERE

MAIN ENTRANCE
AND EXIT

3'-0" RARE
EXIT

LIMIT OF TRACK

WALL OF STUDIO

Plate

2

DIMENSIONED
GROUND PLAN

Scale: 1/4" = 1'-0"

THE UNIVERSITY OF IOWA

Designed by ~ L Harman
Feb 8, 1971
Drafting-LCH

TWO

the rehearsal studio and let the actors work with them. Such arrangements, however, although they may help the director and the actors to see the possibilities of a scene, are seldom the patterns that will ultimately be used. When they are—that is, the director chooses a random arrangement because it works—a decisive act has been made, and stage space has been given definition.

The Ground Plan

Such matters as area emphasis, strength of position for individual actors at high points of a scene, "placeness" of an area, and symbolizing potential of levels, areas, and props all affect the director's creation of a ground plan. Although precise scale and the exact location of each element may not be necessary, the director must be able to work with scale plans (which the designer will ultimately supply) and to ask for a specific placing of objects. If, after all, an actor's movement must be precise to be meaningful, it is clear that the objects and spaces among which he moves must be precise as well. Thus, the locations of furniture, of levels, and of all kinds of objects, are usually "set" during the rehearsal period, and they may even be marked on the stage floor with tape or paint so that they will not change, even slightly.

The director's original ground plan, however, will probably be imprecise, even impressionistic, because it reflects a first impression of the play as a whole. It may not even take audience orientation into account, but may be sketched (in plan) as a space that could face the audience from any of several angles. Its nature, however, will be determined by several factors: the mode of presentation (that is, with naturalistic or abstracted scenery, with areas determined largely by lighting or by level, use or rejection of symmetry, and so on); the number and nature of author-specified locations (the kitchen and two bedrooms of *Death of a Salesman*); association of areas with people or with emotional states (the multiple-use areas of *Death of a Salesman*); and the placing of exits and entrances. Although the last point may seem relatively unimportant, it often happens that the location of entrances (particularly in realistic interiors) will be decided on first, because entrances determine many movement patterns in the playing area. For example, it is almost axiomatic that in interiors, furniture defines playing areas. Furniture, however, has a very specific relationship to doorways, both because of the function of the furniture (tables are not placed across doorways, or chairs behind open doors) and be-

Figure 5–10. A director's working ground plan for early rehearsals. The notes are made here on a copy of the set designer's scale plan, but the areas are merely general indications of homes for characters or kinds of activity. Victor Power's *Who Needs Enemies* at the University of Iowa, directed by Kenneth Cameron. Designed by Len Harmon.

cause the distance from a piece of furniture to a doorway may be important in its direct bearing on the actor's exit.

Workable Ground Plans

No matter what the style or period of a given production, the director's ground plans for it must meet certain requirements. First, the ground plan must give definition to each acting area. Secondly, it must give variety. Thirdly, in illusionistic theatre, it must give verisimilitude to the placeness of the scene (a living room cannot have one chair and one table and no other furniture, even though those objects may be all that the director wants. Such an interior would not be a believable room; in a play such as *Endgame*, on the other hand, the very lack of furniture creates "place"). Finally, it should not, if possible, create acting areas that will not be used. For example, nothing is more confusing to an audience than a door that is never opened; its very disuse will create mystery about it.

The possibilities for creating ground plans for any good play are practically endless. At its best the director's ground plan should grow out of careful study of the play, a deep knowledge of the practicalities and the potential of his stage, and actual work with actors in early rehearsals.

6 Design

This chapter is not an aesthetic of theatre design. It is a brief survey of the problems that theatre designers must face, both those that affect designs as distinct works of art and those that affect the designer's role in the final nature of the performance. To this end, some little attention must be devoted to the place of the designer in the last century and at the present. Any real understanding of the subject, of course, must be based on a knowledge of the material in Chapter Two.

Theatre architecture is discussed along with design because the link between architecture and design is so strong that the two areas are interdependent.

Finally, some sample designs are discussed in detail to show the widely different approaches that can be made to the design problems raised by particular plays. None of the designs discussed here is suggested as an ultimate answer to all questions of stage design. Each is, instead, a successful illustration of a unique solution to a unique problem.

Although the technical means by which scenic designs and lighting are executed do not really fall within the scope of this book, a brief discussion of certain aspects of technical practice will be found on pp. 364–373.

THE DESIGNER AND THE THEATRE

The Evolution of Design

It is unlikely that anyone, at least in the United States, who has worked in, lived near, or regularly attended a live theatre—professional, community, or educational—would fail to recognize that somebody called a designer is part of the theatre's central creative constellation. Along with directors and business managers, designers are as much expected to be found in every theatre as seats and a box office. Even where actors are not paid, a designer often will be.

Things have not always been this way. In fact, in the centuries before our own, the word *designer* would probably not have meant much to a theatre-goer and would certainly not have meant what it does now. Audiences in the eighteenth and nineteenth centuries would certainly have expected some sample of what we consider the designer's art—onstage structures, painted to have some bearing on the play, usually intended to give an idea of the locale of the play's action. In the seventeenth century, the idea of resemblance would have been less explicit, and the sense of locale often irrelevant, but the decoration of the structures surrounding the action would have been recognizably the work of a graphic and plastic artist—a designer. If we were to continue our search to before the seventeenth century, we would find contradictions, although there were early and pre-Renaissance theatre artists who performed the modern designer's function.

Early designers were most often either architects, like Serlio and Inigo Jones, or painters, like the miniaturist Fouquet—although the very nature of Renaissance thinking would have made such rigid compartmentalization of the arts ridiculous. Theatrical design was largely an adjunct to other matters. Serlio, in designing his wooden theatre, also designed his cumbersome settings. Inigo Jones, in creating the lavish costumes, the machines, and the gorgeous set pieces for the court masques of James I, also was partly theatre architect and painter. These early designers were obsessed with two possibilities: movable scenery, which could be sensationally effective, and, far more importantly, the illusion of depth that could be created according to the principles of perspective. Space and distance were magical qualities; the creation of the *appearance* of great distances within the relatively small distance of the stage became a form of theatre in itself, so that the very word *perspective* was applied to a branch of spectacle. When Sir William Davenant began to give public performances at the end of the Cromwellian dictatorship in England (1658–1659), it was perspectives that he first displayed; we hear also of *prospects* and *shows* (of scenic views). The San Carlo Opera House in Naples, Italy (1737) was even built with a great door at the rear of the stage wall, so that the audience might look over the false distance of the onstage perspective to the real distance of the Bay of Naples beyond it—a spectacular scenic triumph for the painter-designer who could so manipulate the visual cues to depth perception (convergence of lines, diminution of objects, hazing or bluing of edges and colors, overlapping of objects) that the viewers could not distinguish the real from the man-made space.

This use of perspective (that is, the creation of three dimensions on the two dimensions of the scenic piece or drop—essentially a painter's vision) dominated scenic design until the late nineteenth century. Whether we consider the work of Giacomo Torrelli; of David Garrick's eighteenth-century designer, Loutherbourg; or of the nineteenth-century English painter-designer William Capon, we are still looking at perspectives. To be sure, the physical arrangement of flats, drops, and borders becomes more complex and more ingenious; the onstage edges become curved, cut, shaped, and "natural"; scenic structures include practical bridges, pieces at angles to the stage axis, pierced structures through which still farther distances can be glimpsed; and effects, from burning cities to volcanic eruptions, become ever more grandiose. But the fundamental principle remains the same.

But with the work of Adolphe Appia (see p. 174), a revolution began. Instead of painting in two dimensions, design shifted to plastic modeling in three dimensions, from the vision of the painter to the vision of the architect and sculptor. *Space* began to mean something quite different—not distance, but mass. With the then-new electric light, individual stage areas could be isolated, highlighted, and made to advance or recede visually; the very plasticity of onstage shapes could be made to change by lighting different surfaces or by changing the colors of surfaces. Before Appia, stage design was the realm of the painter, whose mind's eye saw by the directional, unchanging light of the sun. After Appia, stage design became the realm of the sculptor-architect, whose mind's eye saw by the flexible, multidirectional light of the new technology.

The Two Traditions

As we have already pointed out, there are two primary lines of theatre theory, which we have called presentational and representational. By *representational*, is meant what we have called illusionistic design; by *presentational*, is meant that kind of design that accepts the theatre as its environment. Representation is relatively recent; its architectural expression, the proscenium theatre, is more recent still; and its theoretical equivalent in drama (scientific naturalism) is not even a century old.

Representation began with perspective. With the turning outward of the artist's focus that accompanied early Renaissance thinking (from, as it were, inner metaphysical reality to outer physical reality), some means of expressing the new reality was sought. The contrast between the painter's flat surface and the real world in which he moved was spatial; no amount of detailed reproduction of texture, plane, or surface decoration would represent what he thought he saw of physical space. A philosophical concept that also lies at the root of Renaissance science gave the key to the two-dimensional reproduction of three-dimensional space: the individual would become the measure of reality. Thus, by selecting a single, individualistic point of view, the Renaissance artist could celebrate his new spatial reality:

> The whole picture or design [was] calculated to be valid for one station or observation point only. To the fifteenth century, the principle of perspective came as a complete revolution, involving an extreme and violent break with the medieval conception of space, and with the flat, floating arrangements which were its artistic expression.
>
> With the invention of perspective the modern notion of individualism found its artistic counterpart. Every element in a perspective representation is related to the unique point of view of the individual spectator.
>
> S. Giedion, *Space Time and Architecture*, p. 31

However, before we confuse this kind of individualism with social concepts, it must be emphasized that this is an individualism that is essentially aristocratic. In painting, the use of a single viewpoint seems natural, because the painter's eye looks from a chosen, and fixed, point; in the theatre, where perspective so quickly became dominant, the necessity of a single viewpoint remained, even though group viewing was essential. The contradiction was irreconcilable. As a result, there was a mental displacement performed habitually by anyone sitting far from the viewpoint (typically, the duke's or king's seat or box) in a perspective theatre; he literally put himself in the proper place, appreciating perspective illusion at second hand.

Whether imposed perspective is used or not in representational design, the idea of *spatial reality* is. The Renaissance artist saw three-dimensional space as the most demanding aspect of physical reality, and so does the representational scene designer.

The designer of a presentational setting, on the other hand, is concerned with *spatial relationships*, and the imitation of real distance is less important. The tendency to orient his setting to a single viewing point should be greatly lessened; multiple, even—as in theatre in the round—infinitely multiple viewing points may become possible. Space and distance to the presentational designer are relative concepts; where that relativity is threatened by concrete distance (as, for example, at the sides and the back of a proscenium stage), conventional or symbolic means must be found to suppress their concreteness—wrap-around cycloramas or plain drops. Within the playing area, selective lighting becomes supremely important.

The Realm of Stage Design

Theatre design has frequently been defined as the creation of stage environment. By this is usually meant either the actual environment of a play's action (locale) or the metaphorical environment of the play's meaning. Sometimes both are meant, the aim of stage design then being seen as the creation of localized environment whose visual effect —interrelations of mass and line, color, and light intensity—is an interpretation of the play's central moods and metaphors.

Mood is a potent word in design, and a highly subjective one; yet, we do associate mood values with visual phenomena (gloomy days, a threatening forest, and so on), and although there is a well-known artistic trap called the pathetic fallacy (the ascribing to inanimate nature of human feelings), the very act of creating in the theatre is not so very far from this fallacy itself: the theatre artist, after all, tries to focus audience perception in such a way that it *must* respond in a certain way. Mood, therefore, should be seen as the quality the designer wants an audience to perceive in a play's environment *because of the cues he has artificially put into it*.

A play's natural environment is, of course, the theatre itself (no matter what shape that theatre happens to take). At the same time, the play has another environment, the limited and altogether artificial surroundings of its characters, which may vary from the general "Another part of the forest" of Shakespeare, to the most specific of Ibsen's or Shaw's carefully described interiors. The first kind of environment depends on the definition of theatre itself; the second depends on historical, cultural, and social definitions of reality, definitions that can be called conventions. That the presentation of a play's locale can be merely conventional is clear from a study of theatre history. We should admit that there is no qualitative difference between conventions (Shakespeare's setting as compared to Ibsen's), but that *the conventional presentation of locale is always adequate for its own period.*

The Designer in the Theatre of Illusion

Any stage environment that tries to emphasize the reality, rather than the conventionality, of the secondary or artificial environment—that of the localized, specific habitat of the characters—is necessarily presentational, or illusionistic. Its theoretical basis, founded in scientific naturalism, demands that the *theatrical* environment be de-emphasized and that the localization be as accurate an imitation of the actual as technique can make it. At its extreme, illusionistic design is confounded by a paradox. The use of settings that are themselves actual (real living rooms, real butcher shops) is less convincing to the audience than imitations of the same thing made of wood and canvas and paint. The paradox is easily explained by the conditions under which the audience perceives the environment, which are themselves so different from perception of actual environments (because of real distance from the playing area, the use of intense and artificial lighting, the removal or distortion of some plane surfaces to keep sight lines clear, the entirely different scale required by large playing areas, and so on). Granted, however, that an illusionistic setting is often different from its actual counterpart, the fact remains that the primary purpose of the illusionistic setting's designer is to convey an exact imitation of the actual *under the conditions from which the audience perceives it.* As well, the illusionistic designer must honor the metaphorical environment of the play's action. His illusionism, then, must adapt itself to this other need. The use of symmetrical or asymmetrical constructions, the use of color, and the control of lighting, particularly, will be the result of this other need. The designer who creates settings for two widely different illusionistic plays will probably build convincingly real settings for both. In a sense, the two settings will be alike, for both will try to bear the same detailed resemblance to actual places, and probably the same detailed resemblance to historical periods. Both will try to show detailed correspondences between the environments and the play's characters. Yet, the two will differ widely. Both settings will be illusionistic, but each will adapt that illusion to three-dimensional patterns peculiar to the play itself.

Regrettably, designers for illusionistic plays have frequently sought to impose this theory on nonillusionistic plays. The problem of historical reconstruction is a complex one, but it should be obvious by now that a play of the past is not always best suited by matching it to the narrow habits of the present. A play from a highly conventionalized theatre (*Oedipus Rex*, for example) can suffer badly if given an archaeologically real setting. It might seem at first that this problem is merely a question of emphasis; that, for example, a detailed setting for *Oedipus* would be distracting but nothing more. On the contrary, the distraction is far less important than the question of theatricality that underlies the conflict between representation and presentation, between illusionism and convention. Even the briefest review of theatre history will suggest that there is more involved here than the comparative values of kinds of setting. Instead, we find that two quite different concepts of theatre are in conflict. As noted earlier, the matter of environment may be viewed illusionistically or conventionally, and the different attitudes toward environment have been expressed historically in terms of architecture.

The Designer As Architect

No matter what the play for which he is designing, no matter what the style of the actors or the methodology of the director, the designer inevitably finds himself concerned with architecture. If he is in an ideal position, he will be the architect who designs the theatre in which the production will be staged. However, because there are very few ideal positions, most designers find themselves working with an existing theatre's architecture; they must compensate for its faults and capitalize on its advantages for the production at hand. This does not remove from them the obligation to consider the architecture of the entire theatre; on the contrary, it complicates their task. If one accepts Richard Southern's conclusion, in *Seven Ages of the Theater*, that *no part of the theatre building can be changed without changing all its parts*, then it is clear that the designer must be concerned with the architectural whole, because he is engaged in changing an important part (the playing and scene areas). If he does not change them structurally, he changes the audience's perception of them, which is the same thing.

Traditional theatres encourage *habitual perception*, because they share common viewing distances, common stage heights, and common stage sizes; a member of the audience in one such theatre can move to another without changing his habits noticeably. Yet such habit is the enemy of the sharpened consciousness that the designer needs. Part of his work, therefore, lies in destroying the elements of habit—changing the shape and size of the playing area; changing, if he can, the viewing angle and the viewing distance; and changing totally his own approach to *spatial cuing* from production to production. He is always partly an architect.

Still another complicating factor is the perceptual isolation of each audience member. It too makes architectural demands on the designer, for it requires that he define exactly the relationship between each audience member and the designed environment for each production. To do so is to go much farther than the designer of a representational setting usually goes; it means defining, as Appia did, many viewing points (figuratively and literally) rather than only one. It means defining the exact extent of the environment—how much, that is, it is an environment for the action and how much an environment for the audience. It means defining exactly how much (and by what spatial means) the audience will be welded together or how much their essential individualism will be exploited so that each one will perceive in isolation. Any welding together, of course, will be only partial, for the nature of perception itself keeps the audience members separate.

Changes in the playing and scene areas spring from three concerns: physical problems of the structure (sight lines or storage space, for example); degree of inclusion of the audience in the action; and degree of extension of the designed environment to include the entire theatre. Sight-line problems (that is, blocking part of the playing area by structural members) play more havoc with, and have greater influence on, design for the proscenium theatre than any other single factor except the play itself. Side sight lines determine the depth of the stage environment, the usefulness of the side areas, and the over-all shape of the environment. The familiar trapezoidal shape of the box-set interior is a product of side sight lines, the side walls being built on, or almost on, the line of sight of the last seat in the first row on each side. Overhead sight lines (as from a balcony) also affect the depth of the environment and strictly limit the height of the playing area above the stage floor (in that heads will be cut off by the proscenium arch as the actors move upstage). Therefore, in any theatre where structural members frame the playing area, the shape of the designed environment will be determined by those architectural members. (The alternative is to ignore certain areas of the audience—side seats and the balcony—and design the environment according to other imperatives; the designer is then altering the architecture of the audience space, of course.)

Many designers struggle against such limitations on their work; in so doing, they become ever more the architect. The current tendency in the United States toward the use of the thrust stage (one whose principal playing area pushes out into the audience, unframed) is at least partly the result of design frustration in the proscenium theatre. Many designers have, at some time, tried to thrust the stage out in existing proscenium theatres; temporary aprons have been built outside the proscenium arch (as, for example, in Jo Mielziner's design for the Broadway production of *Death of a Salesman*); seats have been removed from parts of the audience area; and the proscenium arch itself has been hidden, disguised, or redecorated to blend into the playing area, in an attempt to bring the colors, surface textures, and masses of the design forward into the audience area.

The perfect solution to the spatial problems of the proscenium theatre has not been found. The thrust stage overcomes the problems of some sight lines, but creates another: no onstage structures can surround the playing area, because they will interfere between actor and audience, and actors may be forced into up-and-down routes to reach exits located, of necessity, in the proscenium wall. The theatre in the round suffers the same kind of difficulty, with the added one of limited masking and very limited entrances and exits. Each of these basic forms then—round, thrust, and proscenium—has its own advantages and disadvantages. The good designer sees the advantages and uses them.

It might seem that for the designer-architect, an ideal theatre would be one with built-in flexibility, one with infinitely variable audience-acting-area relationships and a completely flexible acting-area shape. Recent experience has shown, however, that this concept is more attractive on paper than in actuality; perhaps we must admit that ideal theatres, like ideal settings, do not exist. The flexible, multipurpose theatres that were designed—but seldom built—in the late 1950s and early 1960s were intended to satisfy all needs and, through ingenious technological innovations, to allow for the creation of virtually any audience-acting-area arrangement, within an architectural shell. Regrettably, they did not prove ideal; like the cafetoriums of some schools or the combined assembly halls-theatre-concert halls of other schools and towns, they satisfied nobody by trying to satisfy everybody.

It is hard enough, after all, to design a theatre that suits *one* purpose admirably, much less two or three or four.

The Designer and the Production

In actual practice, the designer could become so immersed in technical problems that the aesthetics of stage design would seem to disappear. Economics, for example, is a considerable factor, because the technical means of executing a design tend to be expensive. Physical considerations, as suggested earlier, are often limiting; the needs of actors and the desires of the director are of paramount importance. Finally, of course, there is the play itself. Yet, important as all these matters are, it must be remembered that none of them is the essential raw material of the stage designer. The raw material—the subject matter—of stage design is not the dramatic environment of the play, or the demands of the director, or the economic limitations of the production; the subject matter of stage design is three-dimensional space, for which the play provides a justification and a definition, and for which the other factors provide often sobering limitations. (When, of course, we say that the subject matter of stage design is three-dimensional space, we are being a little grandiose and almost impossibly idealistic. As one skeptic put it, "Have you ever had a really great time in the theatre because of somebody's use of three-dimensional space?" Indeed, when designers do allow themselves to explore *primarily* this spatial subject matter, they most often come up with ideal designs for unrealized productions, like some of Gordon Craig's—a designer's creative brainstormings, his stimulating dreams, on which he may draw for real productions at some other time. Three-dimensional space *is* the essential subject matter, but it is like a balloon that the designer must tie firmly to earth with practical considerations (the director's desires, actors' needs, economics, the play,) or else it will fly away and disappear.)

The Designer in the Theatre Organization

During production the designer is a powerful member of the production staff. Except in unusual situations—when he is a subordinate student in an academic theatre or when he is an unpaid volunteer in a community theatre—he is a practicing artist in his own right, and his effects on the ultimate quality of any production will be far-reaching. His definition of the acting space, if realized, will profoundly influence the actor's performance; his definition of the audience's environment will create the perceptual attitudes of that audience; and his interpretation of the locale of the action will affect the final meaning of the play.

The designer's work, although subject always to the director's approval, has an enormous effect on the production. He can change the over-all impact of a given play as no single actor can; but he cannot decide on what are the ultimate meanings of that play (unless he is a Gordon Craig). Ideally, he gives to the director the perfect visual and spatial equivalent of the director's image of the play—a particular and specific world that says, in spatial terms, what the actors and the script will say.

Let us assume that the perfect designer begins with a new script, neither a classic nor an impossibly bad play. He has been given the script because the producer trusts his artistry and because the director believes in his ability to create environments for the actors. He may then read the play many times, making new decisions on each reading; still, his final design may well be based on an image of the play formed in an early reading. This image will be spatial, probably a metaphor for the play's myth: perhaps a clearing in a jungle for *Death of a Salesman*, a cage for *Endgame*, an altar for *Oedipus Rex*. The final design will not look at all like a clearing, a cage, or an altar, but this guiding metaphor will have given the designer a firm starting point. It will suggest to him certain visual patterns that will be carried consistently through the design: vertical bars, threatening organic forms, and a central slab. It will give him a color range: dull metals and exotic, sickening greens and reds, the colors of blood and smoke. If his execution of this metaphor is too specific, his design will not be a metaphor of the play's action, but a self-aggrandizing (and self-defeating) object. If his final design has no guiding metaphor, it will be merely a superficial rendering of the play's locale, without important shape or color. As such, it may be pretty or ugly, realistic or fantastic, but it will be merely an arbitrary treatment of the visual possibilities of the acting space, quite irrelevant to the play under production. Such a design will be a disaster.

At its best the ideal design of the ideal designer will be a rendering of the play's metaphor that communicates all the nuances of that metaphor, without substituting the metaphorical shape for the theatrical reality of the play's locale. It will give the audience a complex symbol to work with, the actor a demanding environment in which to move and be, and the director a new theatre in which to stage his play.

The Designer and the Director

The director, like the designer, begins with an impression of the play that becomes a metaphor of the play. When the ideal designer and the ideal director come together, that metaphor will be the same. When they are at odds, the metaphors will be quite different and chaos will result. The audience will be caught between the designer's visual symbol and the director's action, and the play will become a mess.

This sometimes happens. Brilliant designers are sometimes wrong; brilliant directors sometimes go astray. Still, the collaboration of first-rate artists produces more agreement than contradiction, and at best the production organization permits the two to create productively together. It may work something like this: The director and designer discuss the play, its characters, and its theme. If it is a new play, they will discuss it in great detail with the author. The director will then form character concepts, a sense of the progression and meaning of the action. Often independently, the designer will form an idea of the play's environment that will be based on the scale of the setting in proportion to the actor, the effect of light and shade, and the big masses that represent his view of the play's metaphor. These may be expressed as preliminary sketches. Then, in consultation with the director, he will rough out the ground plan of each setting for which he has prepared the first rendering. (Many of these preliminary renderings rank among the best graphics of good designers, for they are very free and impressionistic; perhaps no thought has yet been given to materials, scene changes, or cost.) The first ground plan will probably be a mere approximation as to scale, and many areas may be left vague; for example, interior scenes may have many pieces marked merely "seating element," the actual chair or sofa or bench to be decided on later. The director too will have a ground plan, for his sense of the play's movement patterns will determine the location of entrances and exits, the localization of certain acting areas, and the need for variety. If the two rough ground plans are in severe disagreement, compromise or persuasion (or even arbitration) are needed. In the best case a final rough will be mutually acceptable and the designer will be free to go on to detailed drawings and renderings. (Such a procedure, of course, is necessary for each setting in a play.)

The Practicalities

Scenery is not designed in a vacuum. Some of Gordon Craig's designs, seminal though they may have been, were unworkable because they were not designed for any real production or any specific theatre. The practical designer, on the other hand, will find himself bending his desires to just such requirements in the case of each setting he creates.

He will prepare a set of detailed ground plans. They will represent the final decisions of both the designer and the director; drawn to scale, they will show every inch of the playing area for each setting. From them, working elevation drawings will be made, embellished in every instance with details or notations of texture, woodwork, foliage, and so on. Most importantly, a scale model is usually made, and both director and actors use the model profitably. Finally, color renderings will be made that will show each *stage* unit (flat or set piece or prop) in full color, to scale, down to the finest wood graining of a panel or the color values of an abstract construction. From these the technical staff will build and paint the actual setting.

Along the way practical details of the most mundane sort will concern the designer. Must the scenery be moved from theatre to theatre? (If so, certain kinds of construction will determine his choice of textures, shapes, and even colors.) How will the theatre building's problems (sight lines, insufficient fly space, and wing space being too small to store large pieces) affect the setting? Will the setting provide acoustical support for the actors? Is any detail of the setting too expensive to execute? Can scene changes be made quickly? The list of practical details is a long one. Suffice it to say that the good designer sees his creation through from the first impressionistic rendering to the installation of the last piece for the performance, adapting his design whenever necessary to inviolable practical facts.

The actual creation of designs can best be shown by discussing three successful designs in some detail. The three, for *Hamlet, The Miser,* and *Indians* represent highly varied approaches and solutions to design problems. All are the work of professionals working in American theatres in the twentieth century. They cover a range of styles, and taken together they present a picture of how designers work within special sets of conditions to create the settings for difficult plays.

It should be remembered, of course, in reading the designers' accounts of their work, that their verbal descriptions of their own creative processes are inadequate to those processes themselves—not because of any lack of literary ability, but simply because the written descriptions were made after the creative process was complete and because the creative process itself is not so logical as the accounts might make it seem. Claude Bragdon's descriptions of his creation of the *Hamlet* designs, for example, seem almost mathematical in their precision, but it is doubtful that his vision of the play was so precise or so rational in its early stages as it became in his memory of it.

Claude Bragdon's *Hamlet*

Claude Bragdon (1866–1946) was a successful architect who moved into the theatre for a second career as stage designer for the American actor Walter Hampden. A disciple of Louis Sullivan, the architect, Bragdon's ideas ranged widely across many areas of design; he was an articulate man who wrote several books on aspects of architecture, space, and decoration. Although not ranked usually with such great American theatre designers of his own period as Norman Bel Geddes, Lee Simonson, or Robert Edmond Jones, he was a highly capable professional who combined an architectural sense of space with great intelligence and a quick, poetic realization of the possibilities of the theatre. He saw very early in his theatre work, for example, the great importance of lighting in generating stage space.

His production of *Hamlet* for Walter Hampden in 1918 (see Figures 6–1 through 6–6) was called by one commentator a postage-stamp production of the play, for it was designed for a touring production, and both its economy of setting and its scale were dictated by the need to move it from city to city. In Bragdon's words, in his autobiography, *More Lives Than One*, it had to be "simple and inexpensive and would go in one baggage car with plenty of room to spare." Much of this economy was achieved by designing a single structure whose details could be changed.

A contemporary viewer, in the 1970s, accustomed to unit settings or "space" settings (abstract architectural forms whose various levels can be used as different locations, often with the aid of highly selective lighting) may find Bragdon's design overspecific in both its relative realism and its apparent historical evocation of medieval structures. But for Bragdon, in 1919, the burden of both realism and historical accuracy must have weighed heavily. Shakespearean production was just coming to the end of a period of meticulous, even fanatical, historical resurrection. Bragdon's abstraction from the real and the historical, then, was arrived at very carefully, as he points out in his autobiography:

> In attempting to provide the play of *Hamlet* with its appropriate *mise en scène* one is confronted with a number of possible alternatives, each soundly reasoned from a certain point of view, but mutually exclusive, so that at the very outset one is forced to determine upon what aspect of his masterpiece it is important to lay the most stress.
>
> In Shakespeare's day his plays were costumed in the then current fashion; the indications of scene were conventional and slight; archaeological accuracy was not even thought of, the imagination of the spectator, aided by descriptive passages in the play itself, being depended upon to provide the setting.

As the antithesis of this concept of doing *Hamlet* in settings (and costumes) contemporary with the spectators, Bragdon cites the pedantically accurate historical settings of late nineteenth-century productions. He concludes that "between the two alternatives of a contemporaneous and an archaeological presentation of the play, there is a third, which might be called *abstract* or (relatively) timeless. Its justification dwells in the fact that Hamlet is a known human type, and his story the dramatization of a perpetually recurring predicament: that of the introvert forced into action."

Bragdon's *Hamlet* designs, then, sought to create timelessness (to the 1919 audience) by a highly selective and economical use of decoration —motifs drawn from medieval decoration—and an equally selective use of architectural elements.

> All architecture, of whatever style or period, may be reduced to three elements, the column, the lintel and the arch, respectively represented by the vertical, the horizontal, and the curved line. In the words of Louis Sullivan, "These are the three, the only three letters from which has been expanded the architectural art." To make the architecture of Elsinore as abstract and archetypal as possible, these elements were employed in all their starkness, without mouldings, without ornament, without surface-decoration, or even the indication whether it be of one material or another, lest such things act as a snare to the mind and memory. [p. 227]

The simplicity of the designs, then, is grounded in the realities of architecture but lacks the specifics of either a structural material or decoration. The result is a fairly consistent design concept that carried through the entire production (although it is less evident in the properties and costumes; see pp. 383 *ff* and p. 357), a concept based on an idea of the primacy of the actor and the abstractness of the setting. The setting creates a world of space and time *for the play*, but that space and that time need not be identifiable by the audience.

In the last analysis, Bragdon was a self-effacing designer who saw his

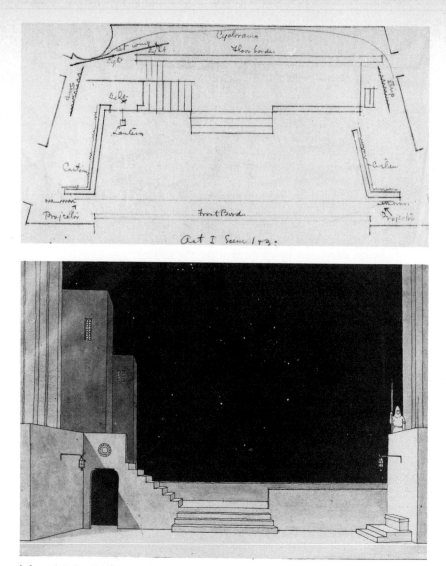

Figures 6–1 and 6–2. Designs by Claude Bragdon for the Walter Hampden production of *Hamlet* in 1919. Each scene is designed around the same basic architectural mass; for each of Bragdon's renderings, the appropriate sketch plan is shown. Describing his approach to these designs, Bragdon said,

> For the sake of poignancy of appeal and verisimilitude Hamlet should be shown as a man among men, in his habit as he might have lived, in an appropriate environment—that indicated by the dialogue. *But*, to bring out the play's mystical and symbolic aspect, there should be as little as possible to tie the imagination down to a particular place or a particular period. The archaeological sense, while being neither denied nor affronted, should be given nothing into which it might be able, so to speak, to set its teeth. In brief, there should be an effort toward abstraction, but never the abstraction of the play's essential human quality, thus relegating it to the limbo of the symbolist. *More Lives Than One*, p. 226. (*Designs reproduced with the permission of Henry W. Bragdon. Collection of the University of Rochester.*)

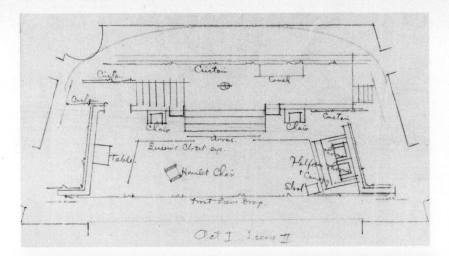

Figures 6–3 and 6–4. Claude Bragdon's *Hamlet.* (*Designs reproduced with the permission of Henry W. Bragdon. Collection of the University of Rochester.*)

own role as one of suppressing, rather than emphasizing, the visual effects created by stage design. He wrote,

> In order to establish a just relation between costumes, properties, scenery and lighting, it is necessary to determine their *relative importance*. Of *first* importance is the actor, that "mystical protagonist" who pre-empts both eye and ear. The thing of next importance is [costume]. . . . Next . . . the "hand props.". . . . Next in order of importance come the stage properties with which the actor comes

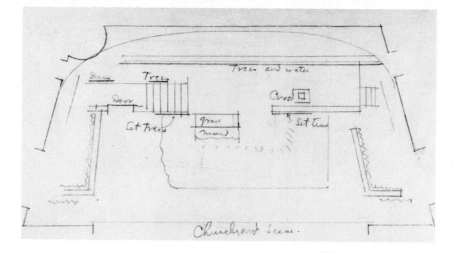

Figures 6–5 and 6–6. Claude Bragdon's *Hamlet*. (*Courtesy of Henry W. Bragdon. Collection of the University of Rochester.*)

> into occasional contact and relation, such as chairs and tables. . . . At the very foot of the list is the scenery itself: removed, static, but pervasive by reason of its spatial extension . . . for its function is to *accompany*, sounding always the right chord without attracting too much attention. [pp. 229–230]

These are very modest words. The designs are those of a modest man —not one who retreated from the design problem, but one who attacked the problem by simplifying and abstracting those elements that create the scene until they could "accompany" Hampden's actor-dominated production of *Hamlet*. The result is functional, practical, and aesthetically unified.

William D. Roberts' *The Miser*

After the Bragdon settings for *Hamlet*, at least two significant developments further affected design. One was the rapid growth, beginning in the early 1950s, of professional regional theatres, which more and more moved toward the use of arena or thrust stages, a strong movement away from the proscenium theatre that altered both the audience orientation to settings and the internal spatial relations of the acting area. The other important change was the use of new materials and an increased interest in the surface textures of scenic materials. (Claude Bragdon's "textureless" surfaces, although entirely right for his own time and for his *Hamlet*, would hardly be suggested as desirable for all, or even most, cases.) Metals, specially treated woods and plastics, allow designers to give an almost tactile element to many of their designs, especially when those surfaces are placed as close to the audience as they are in thrust or arena stages.

William D. Roberts' setting for *The Miser*, at the Charles Playhouse in Boston (1966), illustrates some of these changes. In addition, the special interpretation of the social environment of the play and of its style led to important decisions affecting the design. Roberts' own account of his creation follows:

> The major pitfall the director, Michael Murray and I wanted to avoid was over-decorative Molière: the cute, the pretty, the cheap. Although Molière wrote a number of frankly decorative *commedia* pieces (and too often, to my taste, these are given nauseatingly "styled" productions), "The Miser" is definitely not one of them. . . .
>
> We felt the atmosphere of "The Miser" is seedy, middle-class, very Paris Bourgeois of the late seventeenth century. The place, Harpagon's tatty but once elegant drawing room (probably in an old hotel around the Place des Vosges) seemed to us that it should be real in feeling: a sense of stained wood, heavy furniture, dusty hangings. . . . So the problem was to essentialize the period, but realistically, almost cinematically. These were "people," in a farce situation, to be sure, but also in a *room*, in a house, in a city.
>
> Molière designates [the location] simply: "The scene is Paris." And definitely the Paris of 1668, when the play was first performed. . . . Much is made of the fact that Harpagon is "old-fashioned"— the way he dresses, thinks, very measly and square. He is a widower, his wife probably dead for some years, and he spends not a penny on the house. *She* most likely saw to the decoration, some twenty years before, and with dowry furniture. That's why his desperately chic children hate the house; it is not the newly-fashionable high baroque so beloved by king and court, all swirling plaster and

Figures 6–7 and 6–8. William D. Robert's original sketch, and a photograph of the completed setting, for the Charles Playhouse, Boston, production of *The Miser* in 1965. See pp. 359–363 for a discussion by the designer. (*Courtesy of William D. Roberts.*)

Nature (tired) ceases garish exploitation in dream

Figure 6–9. The designer Kert Lundell's preliminary sketch for the first American production of *Indians* at the Arena Stage, Washington, D. C. The designer commented, "It is the first sketch I did, having read the script . . . I tried to incorporate all the visual elements I felt the play needed and through the weeks that followed we ended up using much of the look of the sketch. . . ." (*Courtesy of Kert Lundell.*)

gilded wood and mirrors, but heavy, old-hat, turned *wood*. Everything is *brown*, and to the teeny-boppers unutterably depressing. So, we came to the decision that the house was put together in about 1650 and hardly touched since. Threadbare, scratched. The servants are unbelievably dreadful, since Harpagon won't pay enough to get good ones. Therefore: dust, mess. I saw a *Comédie* production a couple of years ago in which the set was vast and cool, like something more suited to Racine. Molière, I hope, would have had some words to say about *that*.

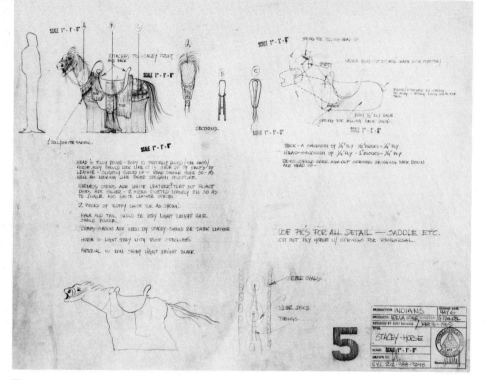

Figure 6–10. The designer Kert Lundell's working drawing for Buffalo Bill's horse in the Arena Stage production of *Indians*, 1969. (*Courtesy of Kert Lundell.*) See also Figure 7–4.

Since the Charles [Playhouse] is a three-quarter round theatre, with a sixteen-foot by sixteen-foot thrust, absolute proscenium realism was, of course, not practical (although I'd like to try it sometime with this play—an almost Chekhovian room). But everything was *wood*, carved, heavy, *brown*, with a giant walk-in stone fireplace (with no fire, of course) and heavy hangings. (I used scrim for these, both to facilitate our lighting and to help create a mood of dustiness.) The floor was treated in a parquet pattern (for financial reasons this had to be painted; it was the only non-wooden thing; I'd love to have had real parquet). The furniture were reproductions of heavy Jacobean pieces. If a cob-web machine had been practical (they wouldn't last for six weeks) I'd have used one.

Many arguments can be raised to such a strong-minded interpretation of the play—the nonfarcical emphasis on wood tones and brown, the young lovers as "teeny-boppers," the emphasis on reality—but what must be seen here is an utterly consistent design scheme, carried out with the director so that it would be consonant with his interpretation, with that of the actors, and with such other elements as costume (see p. 383). Moreover, the constant sense of the practical limitations—the

Figure 6–11. Stacey Keach as Buffalo Bill, with the Wild West Show horse, in the Arena Stage production of *Indians*. Compare with Figure 6–10. (*Roland L. Freeman photo.*)

size of the stage, the effect of the three-quarter thrust on the degree of realism, the cost of real parquet, the durability of artificial cobwebs, the use of scrim to aid the lighting—indicates the designer's real sense of responsibility to the realities of his situation. The result was a highly individualized production of *The Miser*, contemporary in its approach and exciting in its treatment of an established classic. (For a sketch of this design and a photograph of the production see Figures 6–7 and 6–8.)

TECHNICAL PRACTICE

When Lee Simonson wrote that "stagecraft at best is nothing more than the tail to the poet's kite," he was trying to put a very sensible check on the ambitions of stage design in the 1920s and early 1930s. The tendency of those ambitions was to see the theatre as defined by its architecture and its design, with playwrights accepting the definition and working within it. Simonson's practical reminder brought the relationship into a better focus; it also suggested that stage design itself is defined by the very realistic facts of construction, materials, and technology. Such a suggestion is not unlike Siegfried Giedion's view of technology as the "conscience" of design (*Space, Time and Architecture*). Theory is constantly tested by the practicalities of the strength of materials and durability. In the theatre, technology is a very strict conscience indeed, for it brings with it limitations of cost and time that are so severe as to seem impossible to some designers.

As a general statement, it is true that the technology of theatrical crafts is behind the technology of Western industry. In a society that gets its bills from a computer, its music from a plastic ribbon, and some of its news from an orbiting satellite, it may seem contradictory that much stage scenery is still being made exactly as Serlio and Inigo Jones made it. However, it can be pointed out with a good deal of logic that many painters are still using the same materials as Leonardo and getting quite acceptable results. If we turn to sculpture instead of painting, we find that modern technology has revolutionized that art, and as the lines between sculpture and painting crumble, the same thing becomes truer of painting. Welding, plastic bonding, the use of such new materials as stainless steel, concrete, and plastics have revitalized sculpture (and borne out Marshall McLuhan's contention that yesterday's technology is today's art). In most areas, however, the same technological change has been absent in stagecraft.

However, the situation is changing. The introduction of the electric light in the late nineteenth century was truly revolutionary, and neither stage design nor stagecraft could remain the same after it. Erwin Piscator's experiments with film in the 1930s opened the way for many uses of projected, rather than painted, backgrounds. George Izenour's imaginative use of electronic devices and computer techniques has, at least in theory, pointed the way to new uses of the acting space. In general, however, the theatre relies on traditional methods because change is expensive (innovations must usually be expressed in architecture, a costly investment), because the theatre lacks a unified drive toward new methods and new materials, and because the old ways still work.

Mere innovation, of course, is not change. Nor is mechanization alone either new or progressive. Except for the changes brought about by the electric light and electronics, the machinery of the theatre has not significantly benefited from the invention of new power sources: the

Japanese theatre used a revolving stage as early as the 1790s, and complicated systems for flying human beings and large properties were common in the Renaissance and, to an extent, in the medieval period. Shifting the source of power from human muscle to steam or electricity has changed little in the scenery imagined by the designer or seen by the audience. Change, when it comes, will probably come in the form of new materials and a new way of treating the surfaces of those materials. The discussion that follows, therefore, is not of the way things will, or even can be, done in the theatre, but of the way they are usually done in the theatre of the present.

SCENERY

Building and painting scenery are both complicated jobs. Despite the fact that construction methods may not have changed much since the days of Serlio and Jones, they have been refined and, as it were, codified, or at least regularized. A well-trained modern technician has a great many skills at his command and a great deal of knowledge in his head. He is a good carpenter, a fair sculptor, an excellent painter, and only slightly a mad scientist, for no matter how many problems of imitating real objects and producing effects he has solved in the past, some new one is bound to come along for which he will have to improvise a solution. It is impossible to set down even a fraction of this technical knowledge in a few pages; instead, some attempt will be made to show basic approaches to major problems.

Traditional Materials and Construction

The two most important materials for scene construction are wood and cloth. There are many others of course, but wood and cloth remain the essentials: they are cheap, light, readily available, and can be handled easily with fairly simple tools; also, wood and canvas scenery is easily handled and moved. In some theatres, painted cloth on a wood frame is not satisfactory for aesthetic reasons (Brecht, for example, wanted the real textures of natural surfaces, not a painted imitation on canvas); in a few theatres, painted cloth can be replaced by more expensive, but more durable, surfaces. Every scenery technician still grounds himself in a construction method that assumes canvas stretched over a wood frame—the stage flat.

The flat is the same as a painter's "ground"—a rigid surface that will take paint well. The wood frame is made of 1- by 3-inch or 1- by 4-inch stock, preferably without knots or warps. Its corners are joined with plywood triangles, usually screwed to the frame for rigidity; braces across two corners and a horizontal rail located somewhere about halfway up the sides make the frame strong without adding too much weight. Everything is attached, of course, to the frame's rear (upstage) side, so that no bulges will show in the completed flat.

With such a frame of, say, five feet in width by ten or twelve feet in height, put together and properly square at all four corners, we are ready for the cloth covering. Scene canvas comes in many weights and widths, preferably flame-proofed (if not, a flame-proofing compound can be mixed with the first coat of paint). Seams in the canvas will show, so a width of cloth at least equal to the frame is needed. Measured roughly to fit the frame, the cloth is then ripped (not cut) on all four sides, because the torn edges will blend into the frame where a cut edge would show a line. Ordinarily the cloth is measured to be slightly smaller than the outside dimension of the frame, because any cloth folded over the edge of the wood would fray against the stage floor, adjacent flats, or the stage ceiling. With the cloth ripped to the correct size, it is laid over the frame and a slight belly is allowed to form between the frame's members. When the canvas is painted, the cloth will shrink and the belly will disappear.

Canvas is best tacked or machine-stapled along the face of the frame, leaving an inch or two of the torn edges loose. These are glued down with scene glue later to insure a good bond of canvas and wood and to blend the torn edges in smoothly. With a coat of sizing (thin glue mixed with a neutral white powder called whiting), the canvas tightens and the flat is ready to be painted and then to join others in a setting.

Assembling Flats

The easiest way to join any two vertical wood surfaces is to nail them together. Nailing is rarely good on a stage, because scenery must often be separated quickly; therefore, a good deal of ingenious hardware has been devised.

For flats joining at right angles or edge-to-edge, "lash lines," are used; a line is attached to the top of one flat and laced down over short metal bars attached to the rear sides of the flats, rather as the vent of a turkey is laced up after stuffing. If tied with a half-hitch at the bottom, the lash line can be untied and unlaced with a single jerk, and the two flats taken apart. When tied, a lashed joint is thoroughly rigid.

Lashing works equally well for flats joined edge-to-edge to form a single straight wall; large clamps are also used for this, although they are slow to separate. Ordinarily such flush joints are not meant to be separated, however, and two flats are best joined side-by-side with fixed-pin hinges on the *front* (downstage) side. Hinge joining has the great advantage of allowing the two flats to be folded together (booked) so that they can be carried as a unit. When this is done, the hinges and the joint are covered on the downstage side by a strip of cloth called, rather oddly, dutchman. The painting of the joined flats is then completed, and the joint (if well done) is invisible from the audience.

Loose-pin hinges are sometimes used on the *upstage* side for flats joined at angles where quick separation is needed: the pins are pulled out, and the two flats fall apart. All these methods of joining may be present on a single setting, because all have advantages and disadvantages that make them useful under various conditions.

Shifting and Flying

Scenery moving, called shifting, is largely a matter of getting the greatest quantity of scenery moved by the smallest number of people. To accomplish this, most scenery is purposely built as light as possible; in addition, sliders or casters can be attached to the bottoms of large pieces, although heavier flats or books of flats may have a wheeled dolly permanently attached to their upstage side. Single flats or small books can be handled by one man. Two men can best move large flats or books by putting their upstage hands behind the flat, somewhere above the vertical balance point, and their downstage hands low down on the edge of the flat, one man on each side. The flat can then be easily carried with most of the weight on the downstage hand while the upstage hands balance it.

When scenery is not moved across a stage, it can be moved above it by flying—attaching it to long pipes (battens) that run parallel to the stage front and are supported by several ropes or cables (lines) running through pulleys far overhead. Curtains, drapes, drops, lighting instruments, and other equipment can also be flown in this way. Such batten systems are really typical only of proscenium theatre. Thrust-stage and round theatres are more likely to do without flying systems or to use single lines from ceiling ports. Where a flying batten system exists, however, it can be useful, although it must be remembered that such a system is potentially dangerous and easily misused. The weight on any batten is usually considerable and is balanced by counterweights —sandbags or metal bars—at the side of the stage. If a weight-carrying batten is not properly counterweighted, it will be very difficult to raise and will be dangerously likely to get out of control when lowered from on high. Conversely, if the weights on a batten (lights, let us say, or heavy drapes) are removed while the counterweights remain on the other end of the lines, the counterweights will plummet to the stage floor. Even a 25-pound sandbag is fatal when it drops 40 or 50 feet. Anyone not specifically connected with the flying system does well to stay far away from it whenever work is in progress.

Solid scenery to be flown is usually attached to the batten with lines and snaps for quick removal and attachment. Drapes are simply tied to the pipe with many short cords. Drops, scrims, and so on are tied on in the same way.

Other Materials

Because many scene pieces cannot be represented by flat surfaces, other units than the wood and canvas flat are often needed. Sensible carpentry will explain most stage construction; specific treatments of surfaces and shapes are too varied to discuss here. Papier-mâché over chicken wire, cloth soaked with glue over wood or wire frames, surgeon's plaster gauze, and many other materials are used. The only restrictions, again, are weight, strength, and cost.

More importantly, other materials are coming to be more and more widely used where their expense is not prohibitive. Of great interest are the many plastics that can be molded over forms in making both properties and scenic units. Fiberglass, of the type used in making and repairing small boats, is a very effective material whose use can be learned fairly quickly. Many other plastics, including a thermoplastic that becomes malleable after being dipped in hot water, have recently become available.

Metals, although usually too heavy and too expensive for theatre use, have begun to appear on some stages. A recent production used a permanent setting made out of crushed and baled automobile carcasses.

Figure 6–12. An artist's interpretation of the setting for Victor Power's *Who Needs Enemies?* designed by Len Harmon for theatre-in-the-round production. The setting was intended to thrust some of the audience into the Irish pub setting as delineated by the overhead beams, and to bring as much of the audience as possible close to the action. Compare with Figure 6–13.

Such "found-object" art is adaptable to stage design only within rigorous considerations of weight and where necessary, portability. Cheaper methods of welding, and the kind of metal joint that is made possible by the many inexpensive propane-gas units, promise an increased use of metals in stage design, and as the old antipathy for the highly reflective surface of polished metal lessens (probably under the impact of such eye-disturbing theatre forms as psychedelic light shows and happenings) its increased use can be expected.

One of the established lightweight scenic materials in wide use is corrugated cardboard, which can frequently replace the canvas and wood flat, with minimal framing. It has great strength along its face and makes very strong corners when folded. Although it takes paint well, it has the disadvantages of being hard to fireproof, of not being easily reusable, and of warping badly when painted if not properly framed or backed.

A newer and very light scenic material is provided by the group of expanded-foam plastics, including the liquid polyurethanes and the commercial material called Styrofoam, which is so light that the equivalent of six or eight flats could be carried by one man. Probably its greatest feature, however, is its use as a sculptural medium. It can be cut easily with a hot blade or current-carrying electric wire, much as cheese is cut with a stretched wire. Lacking any grain, it can be cut into any shape, and has already, in fact, become a commonplace with sculptors. For stage use, it has only two disadvantages, other than its cost: it cannot be joined quickly and easily, although glued joints can be made strong, and it dissolves under oil-base paints. Lacking the absorption of canvas, it demands much more drying time with the usual water-base stage paints; in the long run, modern latex paints are probably best for it.

There is not yet, and there probably never will be, a single ideal scene material. One would have to combine the cheapness and strength of wood, the paintable surface of canvas, the flexibility of cardboard, and the lightness and sculptural ease of Styrofoam to approach such a material. Perhaps a new plastic will provide it—a material that can be bent into any shape, but will be rigid and self-supporting; one whose surface will take paint but not decay; and one that will cost little to buy and will be endlessly reusable. Until it appears, scene technicians must continue to use the many and imperfect alternatives they have used for so many years.

Scene Painting

There was a time when any permanent paint was anathema to a scene painter, when, in fact, the *only* paint was that which came in cans and bags of powder and had to be mixed by hand. Stage paint still usually comes that way, but permanent paints now have their place in covering

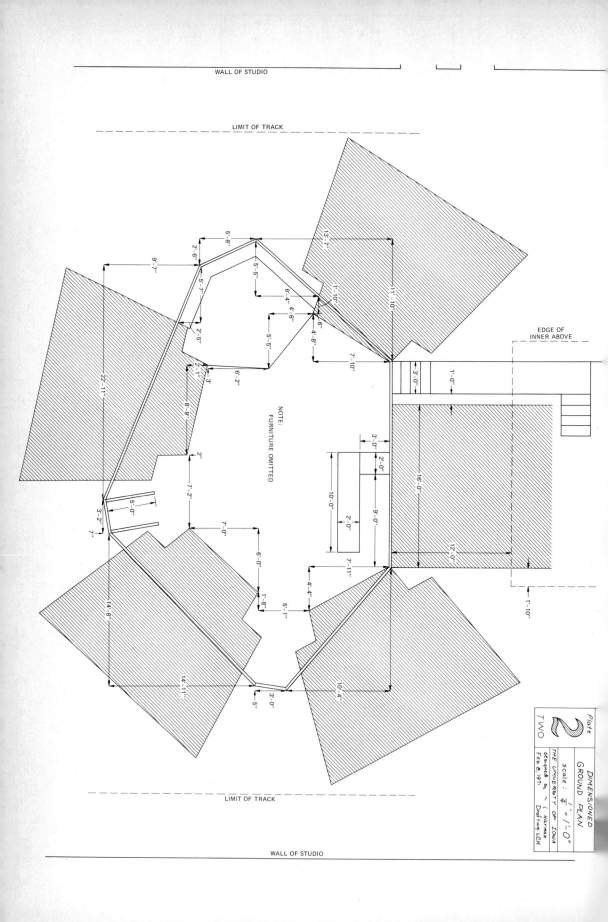

WALL OF STUDIO

LIMIT OF TRACK

EDGE OF
INNER ABOVE

NOTE:
FURNITURE OMITTED

LIMIT OF TRACK

WALL OF STUDIO

Plate
2
TWO

DIMENSIONED
GROUND PLAN

scale: ¼" = 1'-0"

THE UNIVERSITY OF IOWA
Designed by ~ L HALMER
Feb 8, 1971   Drafting LCH

some of the newer surfaces. Where cloth is the principal surface, however, scene paint will continue to be what it always has been.

It is messy. It is messy to use and messy to mix, although some old pros may work in shirt and tie and never have to wipe away a drop. It comes as a dry powder, a chemical or organic color; the range is wide, and the colors can be intermixed to make the complete spectrum. One of the disadvantages of stage paint is that it is a different color when mixed with water than when dry, and it may be a different color when the wet stuff dries. Experience is the best teacher with this paint. The safest thing is to assume that any dry color is an approximation, any wet color a lie; only a sample of the applied, dried product is the trustworthy article.

Scene paint has no matrix to fix it; therefore, glue is added to it, and when the glue and paint dry, the glue holds the paint and it does not rub off on passing actors or stagehands. The proper quantity of glue in stage paint is a matter of measurement, but a practical test will show that too much glue causes the painted surface to sparkle and too little lets it rub off on one's hand, rather like chalk from a blackboard. The glue itself comes from fish by a rather devious route, and it smells less sweet than most of us would like it to. Available, like the paint, in dry form, the glue is prepared by mixing it with water, soaking it, and cooking it in a double boiler (it will burn in a single pot). It will last, as a cold jelly, for some time after cooking, particularly if a disinfectant is added to it to prevent decay. At best, the smell of cooked fish glue is unattractive, and some painters add wintergreen or other strong odors to it in an attempt to protect themselves.

When the colors are chosen and mixed and the proper amount of glue is added, the wet paint is ready to be applied to the sized flat. Although scene paint can be applied over old paint, certain colors will not cover well, and others (called dye colors) will bleed through any amount of paint put over them. Washing flats between paintings, therefore, is economical and sensible, providing the painter with a fresh surface for each application. The paint covers better on fresh or washed canvas, and the "tooth" of the cloth is exposed for the painter's use.

Scene painting is almost an art. Its methods of imitating the many surfaces of natural or man-made things are difficult to master, and there are many of them. It should be evident that merely applying a coat of paint of the right color is only a beginning, whatever the scene

Figure 6–13. Designer Leonard Harmon's scale ground plan for the University of Iowa production of Victor Power's *Who Needs Enemies?*, directed by Kenneth Cameron. Note how playing areas and audience areas have been juxtaposed. The audience itself entered through the doors of the setting, and, in an improvised opening, sang with the performers and talked with them.

painter is imitating. The first color is only a base; over it will go other colors, applied with some or all of the following methods:

1. Spattering. Covering the surface with drops of paint by flicking a wet brush from a distance or by tapping the edge of the brush handle against the hand or arm. The size and spacing of the drops will depend on the distance and the force of the painter's arm. Useful for texturing and almost inevitable in breaking the too flat look of any surface that has no other surface detail.
2. Scumbling. Rolling a paint-moistened cloth or absorbent paper over the surface. Messy and given to leaving a distinct pattern on the surface, but useful at times as a substitute for a stencil when a repeated pattern is wanted.
3. Sponging. Using the pattern of air space in a natural or cellulose sponge to break up the surface. Although there is some danger of repeating the same discernible pattern in this way, the use of two sponges and shifting positions will avoid noticeable repeats. Useful for making bricks and cut stones with a sponge cut to size and shape.
4. Dry brushing. Stroking the surface with a barely wet brush to leave random streaks.
5. Stippling. Poking the bristles of a stiff brush directly at the surface, using only the tips to apply paint.
6. Painting a wet ground. With the surface (preferably cloth) still wet from the undercoat, other colors, usually two or three at a time, are blended across it with several brushes. The effect is subtle and can be very effective.

Specific surface features—wood molding, tree bark, wood graining, wallpaper, stone, brick, and so on—are imitated by combining the following methods:

1. Lining: painting in highlights and shadows with narrow brushes.
2. Stenciling: stippling through a pattern cut in an impervious material; useful, for example, for wallpaper.
3. Dry-brushing a pattern: for example, wood-graining with a light and dark color.
4. Painting detail: building up small features with light and shadow, such as cracks in plaster, ornamental carvings, swellings in the bole of a tree, and so on.

It should not be inferred from these examples that the imitation of realistic detail is the only use of the scene painter's techniques; it is true, however, that the techniques are most often called on to that end. They are, of course, equally useful in treating the surface in nonillusionistic ways. Although particular techniques may be useless for painting nonrepresentational scenery, it could hardly be said that the scene painter would be out of place. On the contrary, the demands of treating surfaces subtly, of painting reinforced structures, and, most importantly, of color itself test his ingenuity even further.

It is in color that the scene painter meets the ultimate problem. There are few successful accidents in the choice of stage color, for not only must a color balance be maintained across an entire setting (in fact, across an entire production), but the scene painter's colors must also be chosen to be seen under colored light. Individual colors change and the relationships of colors to each other change with the stage lighting; the scene painter can be said to be successful only when he is able to mix colors for specified lighting designs.

LIGHTING

Since Serlio's first experiments with onstage light and with colored lights, stage illumination has presented both a challenge and an inspiration to theatre artists. The relative lack of control over any light source other than an electric lamp made variations of either color or intensity almost impossible until the nineteenth century. Despite attempts like Loutherbourg's, through the use of colored translucent silks, colored glass, or bottles of colored fluid; despite ingenious attempts to shade or extinguish candles or lamps, found even as early as Sabbatini's *Prattica;* and despite even the much greater control that gaslight brought to the stage, it was not until the advent of electricity and the widespread use of electric lamps that stage lighting could be considered much more than a necessary evil and an intriguing, but frustrating, field for experiment.

With the pioneering work of practical theatre men, such as Steele Mackaye, and theoreticians like Adolphe Appia, however, lighting quickly caught up with spatial stage design. For a short time, early in the twentieth century, lighting itself virtually replaced three-dimensional design. Gordon Craig's drawings in *Toward a New Theater* illustrate his own well-founded belief that modern stage lighting could itself generate three-dimensional space, and that a single object could be spatially changed by altering the light falling on it. True as this theory is, and influential as it was on the design of unit settings or space stage settings, its single-minded use restricted both construction and painting unnecessarily. Ideally, then, modern stage lighting is a highly flexible *adjunct* to stage design, an over-all part of the visual production that, instead of merely illuminating the action (as in almost all pre-electric theatres), plays an important part in molding shapes, coloring and texturing surfaces, and emphasizing actors and actions. Basically, its flexibility has four elements: light intensity, color, direction, and size of the area lighted. These four elements are functions of the entire lighting system, not of any single part of that system. The system itself can be reduced to two parts, the instrument and the control, although it must be remembered that some means of coloring the light is a subsidiary part of the instrument, and some kind of electrical connection between control and instrument is obviously necessary.

The Lighting Instrument

Most of us are tempted to call it a light. At home, most light sources are called lights, unless they are called lamps, and sometimes we are tempted to call theatre instruments lamps also. The only trouble with this is that a stage lamp is what at home we call a bulb, whereas *a light* is too easily confused with *light*, and that term is probably best saved for the total effect of all the instruments in any given scene put together. Perhaps it is best, therefore, to accept a fairly simple vocabulary whose words have to mean something different from their non-theatrical meanings: the *instrument* is the total light-producing unit, consisting basically of a *lamp* and whatever other lenses, reflectors, and so on are necessary. Put several instruments together, aim them this way and that, shoot them the power, and we have stage *light*.

Stage instruments are designed for flexibility. Necessarily, there are several kinds of instruments, because it is not yet possible to build an instrument that will satisfy all lighting needs—that is, have maximum light output for its electrical input, allow either wide area (flood) lighting or pinpoint (spot) lighting, be cheap to operate, have long lamp life, and so on. In brief, the following things can be used in a variety of combinations to build several kinds of useful instruments:

THE LAMP. The lamp, the source of light, is a gas-filled glass envelope with a wire filament inside. When a current is passed through the filament, it heats and discharges energy particles in the visible spectrum. Many filament shapes and materials are used. Certain filament shapes are so-called point sources of light, meaning that they have the smallest possible practical discharging area. The size of the filament is very important, because it is the first variable in the instrument that affects the size and shape of the emanated light beam. For example, the simplest instrument is merely the lamp itself and its electrical connector. If the glass envelope is frosted, the light emanating from the filament is diffused and the lamp is a useful source of general illumination (the household light bulb, in fact). If the envelope is not frosted, light will be discharged in straight lines from the heated part of the filament; if the lamp has a point-source filament, the lines will run from the point, through the envelope, past any object held near the lamp, and will cast hard-edged shadows on a screen. Such a point-source lamp, with an electrical connector and a black box to absorb light emanating on the side away from the screen, is the simplest projector known and can be used to project silhouettes or colored shapes over very wide areas. In its refined form (the Linnebach Projector) it is much used for rear stage projections.

THE REFLECTOR. As with a household reading lamp, the addition of a shade over the light source both cuts out unwanted light and reflects the light in the direction in which it is wanted. The household lamp-shade is not very efficient, for it often allows a good deal of light to pass through it (if it is made of cloth or paper or frosted glass) or absorbs or diffuses light because its inner surface is not a good reflector. If, however, a highly polished opaque surface is substituted for the shade, almost all of the light striking it will be reflected. Highly polished metal is most frequently used in theatre instruments, not only because it is efficient and strong, but also because it can be shaped to surround the lamp in such a way as to reflect the light in a given direction with great accuracy. The commonest uses of such shaped reflectors are

1. *The flood or scoop.* Actual reflector shapes vary in such lamps, from a V-shape to a section of a sphere. The purpose of the reflector is merely to bounce as much light as possible back in the direction of the lamp; the purpose of the instrument is to give general, soft lighting that will not cast hard shadows. It is typically used for fill-in light or for lighting drops and cycloramas.

2. *Spherical reflectors.* Although some flood instruments use a spherical reflector, they use it in combination with a lamp whose filament is larger than a "point," with a diffusing surface on the reflector itself. When a spherical reflector with a highly polished surface is used in a housing with a point-source filament, the light emanating from the instrument is very definitely shaped into a beam. Such an instrument, using a point-source lamp and a spherical reflector, would lie somewhere between the simple flood and a spot. Under optimum use, a polished spherical reflector will reflect incident light rays according to very strict laws, so that if the lamp filament is placed at the center of the sphere (of which the reflector is only a section), all of the light striking the reflector will be reflected back through the filament. The result is a highly efficient instrument that behaves as if its filament discharges light in only one direction.

3. *Ellipsoidal reflectors.* An ellipse, if rotated on its long axis, generates a three-dimensional shape called an ellipsoid. If part of an ellipsoid is used as a reflector, and a point-source lamp is placed so far back in the reflector that almost all of the light coming from it strikes some part of the reflector, then the reflected light will (ideally, but not quite in practice) converge at a single point. Such convergence, in combination with a lens, produces the most sharply defined beam of any instrument.

THE LENS. Although the shaping of the beam that is done by spherical and ellipsoidal reflectors is a big step toward control of light, reflectors alone are not enough to shape the beam at the distances over which most stage light must be thrown. The use of a lens, therefore, is necessary whenever the width of the beam must be made narrower than the reflector alone can make it. Two principal lens types are now common:

1. *The planoconvex* (that is, having one flat side and one convex, spherical-section side). Such a lens gives the best definition of any in practical use, converging light rays to a degree that depends on the thickness and diameter of the lens. Using, as do all lenses, the principle of refraction, the planoconvex lens bends light coming from the reflector and the lamp. Typically, as in the most popular ellipsoidal spotlights, light rays emanating from the filament strike the reflector, are reflected through a single point between the lamp and the lens, strike the back of the lens at angles that are functions of the reflector design, and are converged by the lens into a beam whose sides are not quite parallel, so that at a distance of thirty feet from the instrument, the width of the beam may be eight or ten feet.

2. *The Fresnel lens.* Named for its inventor, this lens is a planoconvex whose spherical surface has been cut back into a series of steps, so that from the front it shows concentric rings and in cross section it looks like a rather choppy sea. Because glass absorbs light, the loss of light efficiency through a thick planoconvex lens is considerable; the reduction of the lens to a series of quarter-inch steps allows much more light to pass. However, the steps in the glass affect the pattern of the resulting beam, so the back side of the lens is usually pebbled to diffuse the light somewhat. The result is a more efficient lens, but one whose beam is both wider than a planoconvex of similar dimensions and a good deal less sharp along its edges.

THE HOUSING. A metal shell surrounds the optical system of every instrument, providing it with a shield and a convenient attachment for the mounting (the means of attaching it to a pipe batten or pole), the electrical connector, and a holder for the coloring medium. Different kinds of instruments have different minor adjustments built into their housings, but most will allow for some movement backward and forward of the lamp (to change its relationship to the light beams as focused by the reflector).

The Control System

Modern control systems are highly sophisticated and very complex. In essence, they allow the lighting designer to change the intensity of any instrument on command by changing the nature of the electrical impulse powering the instrument. At the moment three general types of controls (or dimmers, as they are commonly called) are used:

1. *The resistance dimmer* (rheostat). Without complicating matters with electrical theory, suffice it to say that a resistance (a current user) placed between a lamp and the power source will limit the current flowing to the lamp. If the resistance is variable, the current to the lamp can be controlled accordingly, from zero (if all the current is used by

the resistance) to full intensity (if the resistance is bypassed). Resistance dimmers are still very common and have the advantage of being relatively cheap. However, they heat up rapidly, making the area of the dimmers uncomfortable for the operator, and their capacities lie within rather narrow ranges for any given dimmer.

2. *The variable transformer* (variable voltage). If voltage is changed rather than current, the lamp can be dimmed or brightened with greater regularity, and more efficiently, than with a resistance dimmer. In addition, variable transformers have the great advantage of covering the entire range of loads up to their marked capacity (that is, from zero to 1,000 watts, for example), whereas the resistance dimmer has a lower as well as an upper limit. Variable transformers do not heat up and are more efficient; however, they are also slightly more expensive.

3. *Electronic dimmers.* Electronic dimmers are manufactured under several trade names, embody a number of principles, and represent the most recent development in lighting control. Using either tubes or transistors, electronic dimming devices function either by varying the voltage at the lamp or by actually providing the lamp with only part of the energy wave generated by an AC source. No matter what the actual name or type, however, electronic controls as developed by modern lighting companies have several advantages over other types: relative efficiency (little power loss through the dimmer); separation of the dimmer mechanism from the operator, who uses an easily portable control panel to send signals to the dimmer, which can be distant from him; a much improved lamp efficiency when getting only partial power; and, partly because of mechanical improvements in the control panel, more efficient and varied handling combinations of many lights at the same time. Such systems are expensive to install, but they promise to be more economical as time goes on.

Color

The use of colored light in the theatre is crucial in almost all areas of production; it is not enough to decide, on whatever basis, that light of a given color will be used, for it must be judged by its effects on the objects it lights. Only rarely does a lighting designer have a white surface to light; conversely, almost never can a scene designer, a costume designer, or an actor plan to work in white light. The inevitable result is communal decision, with the lighting designer's choice of colors influencing, and being influenced by, the color in the settings, the costumes, and the actors' make-up. The colors that the audience perceives are never the colors of the light alone or of the objects alone; rather, they are the net result of incident light of a given color being reflected by a surface that is also colored (a painted flat, a face, a piece of velvet). It is this resultant color that determines much of what the designers will do.

The reasons for using colored light, as opposed to the light as it comes from the lamp, are threefold: to convey facts and feelings about the locale of the action (sunlight or moonlight, cold melodrama or warm farce); to heighten colors chosen by the scene or costume designer; and to shape objects by using different-colored lights on different surfaces. Most often the last purpose is served by using a combination of warm and cool colors in different instruments, paired so that a cool light will fall one one surface and a warm light on a surface angled to it. Assuming that both *surfaces* are the same color, the difference in the incident light will emphasize their solidity. Such paired color combinations are often useful in emphasizing the actor's face, where a single color shining on it would wash it out. As a general rule, incident light directed from an angle of 45 degrees above the horizontal, from two instruments whose beams are 90 degrees apart, is supposed to provide optimum molding of onstage objects. Such a rule is a good starting point if only an optimum molding of objects is wanted, but most lighting people discover that other imperatives, particularly in thrust-stage or round theatres, make this arrangement oversimple. When it is possible, however—as in a very simple production in a proscenium theatre, where only good over-all lighting is wanted—the playing area can be split up into subareas of the size of the instrument beams, and each subarea will be lighted by properly paired instruments, one warm and one cool. Actual color of the light coming from such instruments is controlled by two factors:

1. *Incandescent color.* Light coming from the filament of an incandescent lamp is not white; it is yellowed at full intensity, and reddened progressively as the lamp is dimmed down to zero. Because of this, it is very hard to hold a color balance if lamps are held at partial intensity.

2. *Medium color.* Most stage instrument beams are further colored with a translucent medium, sometimes glass, but more often with a sheet plastic or gelatin. Gelatin is cheapest, but tends to fade; glass does not fade, but absorbs light and is fragile. No matter what the medium, the effect on the light is the same: to give it a color that, for a desired light intensity, will best fit the needs of the action. Unfortunately, in pairing warm and cool colors, an immediate imbalance is caused if the lamps are kept at the same intensity, for the warmed light coming from the filament will be partly blocked by a cool medium, passed by a warm one. As a result, less light is actually transmitted by a blue gelatin than by a pink or amber one, and the light loss can be severe if much dimming is done. Some lighting men get around this by cutting the centers from the blue gelatin or plastic; the light is less blue, but more intense, particularly because the lenses on most instruments pass more light through their centers than their edges. Typically, fairly pale colors are used on most lighting instruments, both to transmit as much light as possible and to keep incident stage light reasonably close to real light.

Companies manufacturing color media use varying systems of names and numbers. Descriptions of colors cannot be very meaningful, but it may be helpful to say that in most cases where natural lighting is wanted, color media in the range of amber, straw, and light pinks are widely used for warm colors; a true pale blue (that is, completely lacking red), a steel blue (very slightly green), or a blue that approaches a lavender are usually paired with them. True yellows, reds, and greens, or intense blues and purples, have only special uses, not only because of their higher color saturation, but because they cannot be balanced with existing make-up colors to produce anything like a natural effect on the actor.

Using the System

In mounting, aiming, and choosing color for the instruments, the lighting designer and his crew must make complex decisions based on the variables already discussed. In addition, account must be taken of several purely practical matters: the available location for instruments in the rigging—along the proscenium arch (if there is one), in ports over the audience, or along the front of a balcony; the number of available instruments; the kinds of available instruments; and the power available. It does no good, for example, to have forty 500-watt instruments if only 10,000 watts of power is available, unless the control panel has enough built-in flexibility so that twenty instruments can be used while the other twenty are switched out of the system. In addition, 500-watt soft-focus spotlights will be of little use in ports fifty feet from the playing area, and 2,000-watt ellipsoidal spotlights will usually be too powerful for a small stage whose greatest instrument-to-area throw is only twenty feet. Given the play, then, with the director's and set designer's ground plans, the lighting designer must make up his light plot for each scene by balancing the following variables for each important stage area:

1. Light intensity: a function of instrument-to-area distance, lamp wattage, instrument type, and power supplied from the dimmer. Color too can be a factor.
2. Light direction: a function of the location of the instrument, which is sometimes controlled arbitrarily by the architecture of the building; usually, however, the designer has considerable control over many locations.
3. Size of area lighted (pool) by each instrument: a function of instrument-to-area distance, size and type of instrument, and internal adjustments that can be made in the instrument itself (lamp-to-reflector distance and lens-to-lamp distance).
4. Color of each instrument: Largely a matter of the designer's choice of color medium, although it depends slightly on the dimmer setting of each lamp.

Figures 6–14 and 6–15. William D. Roberts' costume designs for the Charles Playhouse Production of *The Miser*. Attached to several of the sketches, with the designer's notes, is a swatch of sample fabric. (*Courtesy of William D. Roberts.*)

In balancing these variables against the practical problems cited earlier, the designer begins to shape the over-all design of the production. In practice, few lighting designers find themselves with all the proper

instruments they need and the infinitely flexible control system of which they dream. Instead, limited instrumentation, limited power, and limited control flexibility are the facts of life for most lighting men. Within those often strict limits, impressively creative effects are often made by lighting designers and technicians who double up on instruments, use color creatively, and know their system so well that each element in it is used to the fullest.

COSTUME DESIGN

Although costume designing is itself a distinct area of artistic practice, the regrettable truth is that except on Broadway, relatively few producing organizations can afford separate designers for costumes and for settings. At best, many regional, community, and educational theatres are able to find designers capable of working in both areas, and at worst they are forced to depend on the availability of costumes from either a limited stock of their own or the often distant and impersonal costume supply houses. In that the costume is worn by the actor, it is part of his working self and should become as much a part of his characterization as his make-up. On the other hand, in that costume, under light and in motion, is part of the over-all visual picture of the production, it is a potent design element. As Samuel Selden has put it, costume is "scenery worn by actors." He goes on to point out that the "most pronounced accents in the whole scene are often found in these bits of moving scenery" (*Stage Scenery and Lighting*, p. 15). In short, then, theatrical costume lies somewhere between make-up and setting in its relationship to the actor, on the one hand, and to the designer and director, on the other. Its practical aspects, therefore, are determined by both, and the costume maker and the costume designer must be concerned with both the totality of the production and such realities as comfort to the actor, fit, and durability.

The Bases of Costume Design

Like the actor and the director, the costume designer must begin with a profound knowledge of each character whose costumes he designs; and like the actor, rather than the stage designer, he will probably be more deeply concerned with individualities of character than with a play's total statement. This is not to say that all of his designs, taken together, should ever fail to have coherence and, depending on the production, either unity or progression in line, color, and style. The costume designer must always aim at a total design concept, expressed in detailed attention to each character. This concept, like the stage designer's, is based on an interpretation of the play itself, expressed as metaphor at times. However, because of the nature of clothing and its potent ability to communicate facts about a character (such as social class, historical period, nationality, and so on), the design concept may be much more directly a social, historical, or national comment than stage settings can usually be. Except in the case of fairly realistic interiors, settings are less liable to social interpretation than costume, both because they are less individualized and because they have to serve the quite different purpose of creating acting space. The old expression, "Clothes make the man," is as true on stage as on the street: as a result, costumes can be made to convey a great deal of information about the designer's view of the characters.

Consider, for example, William D. Roberts' designs for *The Miser* (see Figures 6–14 through 6–15). The design base for his costumes is itself an interpretation of Molière's play, which he sees not as one of Molière's "decorative *commedia* pieces," but as something "darker, more realistic, more a comedy of character. . . . The atmosphere of

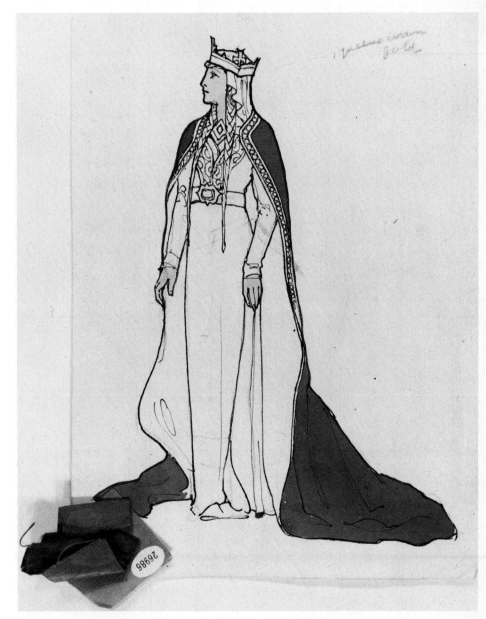

Figures 6–16 through 6–19. Four of Claude Bragdon's costume designs for the 1919 *Hamlet*. Sample fabric swatches are pinned to each sketch. (*Courtesy of Henry W. Bragdon, Collection of the University of Rochester.*)

The Miser is seedy, middle-class, very Paris bourgeois of the late 17th century. . . . The clothes [in his designs] were tangible, down to buttons missing from coat sleeves and stains on handkerchiefs. The fabrics were tweeds and heavy wools, real suitings, the palette neutral, bourgeois, clothes—believable. The period was essentialized, but realistically, almost cinematically" ("An Approach to Costuming *Love for Love*," *Theater Crafts*, March–April 1967). Although Roberts continually

uses the word *real* to describe his designs (including fabrics and colors), the sense of reality he aimed at is far more a social than a literary comment: he was not attempting to prove that Molière's play was realistic, in the literary sense, but that the greeds, frivolities, and follies of the play were real, in the social-historical sense. Another designer, attacking the play merely as a period comedy, might use quite a different approach—perhaps a triter one—and work in the more

conventional bright colors, light fabrics, and *unreality* often associated with farce comedy.

A different designer working on a different play may take a more metaphorical approach. Claude Bragdon's designs for *Hamlet*, for example (see Figures 6–16 through 6–19), are not a commentary on the play, but a poetic, almost symbolic, externalization of it. As Bragdon himself pointed out,

In *Hamlet* I did not myself have to decide upon the colours of the various costumes; *the characters settled that for me* [our italics]. Hamlet, of course, is garbed in his "customary suits of solemn black," a colour reserved for him alone—fate's executioner, a stalking nemesis. For Ophelia, the beginning of the description of her drowning, spoken by the Queen:

"There is a willow grows aslant a brook,"

gave me the hint I wanted: yellow-green, suggestive of spring, and cerulean blue, the colour of water and of the Virgin's robe. . . . Polonius I conceived of in a brown brocaded cloak, trimmed with grey fur, with a staff of office and a silver chain; for brown and grey are negative, noncommittal colours, and Polonius was a trimmer and a yes-man. For Horatio, the faithful friend, dark, rich green seemed the proper colour, because green corresponds to *sympathy* —even jealousy, "the green-eyed monster," is, in the last analysis, but the fear of the loss of sympathy.

The sense of a correspondence between color and certain human values should be noted—Polonius' "noncommittal" colors, and above all, the choices for Ophelia. Not only are these based on an idea of emotional values of color ("suggestive of spring"), but they also go deep into an interpretation of the character, and even answer some of the questions that director and actor must ask of the character of Ophelia: "Is she still a virgin?" ("cerulean blue, the colour of . . . the Virgin's robe") and "Is Ophelia's death to be pathetic?" answered very positively by the choice of the colors "suggestive of spring." In Charles Bragdon's designs, of course, color was the value he chose most to exploit, being limited partly by the date (1919) of the production, when some degree of historical verisimilitude still dominated both costume and set design. In William Roberts' *The Miser*, of course, it is both color and fabric that are exploited, as well as the minute attention to detail that he calls realistic. In both cases, as with all costume design schemes, the designers have chosen from among the *possible variables* of costume to arrive at a consistent and meaningful *style*.

The Variables in Costume Design

Before arriving at a discussion of style itself, the elements or variables possible within the costume design scheme should be noted. Briefly, they are historical period, social class, locality (both national and local, urban or rural), degree of formality (at-home clothes or clothes for a formal occasion), and the given circumstances of each character (age, state of health, taste, and such peculiarities as Harpagon's greed or Hamlet's black melancholy).

Yet, in discussing these variables, we really are coming close to another matter entirely—the process by which design decisions are made. The variables exist, to be sure; they represent a broad spectrum of possibilities. But they do not exist like articles of food in a cafeteria, to be selected whimsically—a little eighteenth-century outline for an appetizer, some bright color for a main course, a little upper-class fabric for dessert—but, rather, they are selections to be made because of decisions already reached. Those decisions are the basic stylistic determinants of the production, and they come from the director and the producer, with the collaboration of the scenic, lighting, and costume designers. It may have been the producer's long-treasured concept to do *The School for Scandal* in the settings and costumes of the Edwardian period (c. 1905). The reasons for this concept (and the tenacity of the producer's affection for it) may well be irrational—a dislike of the eighteenth century, a feeling that the play will be less dated in another period, a feeling that the play will be *more* dated in another period—but if he prevails, his director and his designers will have to accept the concept as a given of the production. One variable is thus already taken care of. Others (color and fabric) will depend on the desires of the director and producer and the designer's ideas of the production's mood, scene by scene. Silhouette, draping, and even fabric depend in part on the actor who will wear the costume, and the actors will have almost certainly been cast without any serious advice from the designers. This all sounds as if the costumer has no deciding voice in the production at all, and yet this is not true. Even if important stylistic decisions are made for him or her, there are yet important feedbacks into the production from the costume designer: into lighting design, which is crucial to the color and brilliance of the costumes; into the settings and their colors, for costume colors and fabrics must be seen against the right backgrounds to be effective; and into the director's work with the actors, so that carriage and posture and gesture enhance the costumes and are enhanced by them. It is, in short, a *process*, not a neat series of cut-and-dried steps. It is all process, all flux, with every artist's work, including the costume designer's, influencing all others and being influenced by them.

In the production of classics, the question of historical period becomes vitally important. It influences acting style, set design, and indeed the entire production concept. In costume, the problem is really a double one, for the designer must know not only the actual period of the play, but his audience's idea of the costumes of that period. This audience orientation may be based on quite inaccurate sources—museum paintings, caricatures or cartoons that featured only certain oddities of dress (for example, John Held's famous "flappers"), other theatrical interpretations, films, and musicals and plays—and it is tempered, as well, by the audience's idea of what is currently fashionable. Thus, a costume designer very rarely can aim at pure historical resurrection, for the paradoxical reasons that his audience may find his precision "inaccurate" (that is, not in line with their own impressions of the period) or unflattering to the point of being comical. As Claude Bragdon pointed out about his own *Hamlet*,

> The events portrayed . . . are supposed to have occurred in the eleventh century, for it was then that England was rendering tribute to Denmark, but the entire spirit of the play indicates a less rude

civilization. If it were correctly set in costumes for that period and place the result would be even more disturbing than if done in modern dress. . . . All of the characters would be blond in colouring, the men heavily bearded, and clothed for the most part in the skins of beasts. Without pursuing the subject further, it is clear that an archaeologically correct production of *Hamlet* would never do.

More Lives Than One, p. 225

Similarly, a *Hamlet* production that sought to revive exactly the dress of Shakespeare's England might find a number of characters (perhaps even Hamlet) in so-called pumpkin breeches—wide, often ballooned pantaloons that a twentieth-century audience would identify with bloomers and find ridiculous.

The costume designer seeking a historical base for his designs may select a period other than that of the play's action or its period of composition, and arrive at a design scheme that is right for his audience. The actual source materials for the period he finally selects must also be chosen with great care, for as Carl Kohler points out in his introduction to *A History of Costume,* "nothing but the original costume, if that be accessible, can be considered definitive for the conception we may legitimately entertain regarding the ideas about dress that prevailed in any period. We are far too ready to carry back to the costumes of bygone days our modern conception of what is becoming."

In descending order, then, the bare sources of historical costume available to the designer (from which he will abstract according to his other variables) are actual clothes of the period; accurate histories of dress; contemporary descriptions of the sort found in letters, diaries, and so on; and graphic works of the period itself (which are not often accurate, as Kohler points out, because of the tendency of the artists themselves to abstract or modify clothing for aesthetic purposes).

Within the historical period, the costume designer may emphasize social station in accordance with his interpretation of the play. (We might cite, for example, William Roberts' emphasis of the *bourgeois* quality of Harpagon's household.) The question of locality of costumes is not always important (the Danishness of *Hamlet* costuming hardly seems relevant), although, for example, in any American production, American clothes would certainly be wanted for *Death of a Salesman,* rather than the noticeably different English or Continental fashions of the same period.

Finally, individual costumes will be designed to express levels of formality (the Queen's costumes in the court scenes and in the closet scene might well be differentiated on this basis) and to show particular given circumstances of character (Harpagon's clothing should show his miserliness in patches, worn places, and out-of-date fashions). Taken together, all of these variables, with the added consideration of the level of realism of the entire scheme, can be said to constitute the *style* of the designer's production.

Realism—the imitation on the stage of actual clothing as we know it or think we know it—is an important and difficult factor in the designer's plan. As we have seen in the Roberts designs, it can become the dominant factor in making the design not only an element in producing a text, but a significant comment on the text itself. At a lesser remove, the level of realism, if consistent with the stage design, the acting style, and the director's concept, will go far toward expressing the mood, the values, and the final statement of the play.

Realism in this sense is a highly subjective product of the designer's imagination. In practice, however, it must be reduced to elements that can be worn or displayed by actors, and these elements are primarily color, line, surface decoration, and texture (fabric). Color is a predominant factor in costumes; this "moving scenery" will gain or lose focus, and set a somber or a buoyant mood, as its color values change. As a general rule, warm colors project an idea of gaiety and comedy, whereas cool or neutral colors withhold these values. In costume, the problem of how real any given color is as a clothing color can become very complicated, although a modern audience will certainly accept a greater range of colors, and stronger colors, as being more "real" for female costumes than for male. In the historical play, however, modern audiences tend to allow greater leeway in male colors as well, although certain preconditioned values will affect what colors, and their strength, will be allowed (see pages 383-386, Claude Bragdon's Hamlet costumes). The palette, or range of colors chosen by the costume designer, therefore, will be a powerful determinant of his style in the sense that it will both limit the mood possibilities of the production and express the total level of realism.

In line—or better, perhaps, outline—the costume designer finds the most tempting and most creative possibilities for abstracting from "real" dress. In large part, when we speak of a historical mode of dress —(historical in the sense that fashion, even from the recent past, is historical if it is perceptibly different from that of the present)—we are speaking of outline, or silhouette: the bustle, the short skirt of the 1920s, the tight-fitting men's clothing of the early Renaissance, the broad shouldered clothing of the 1940s. But, in addition to this, we mean both draping (the lines taken by a fabric as it follows the body) and the breaking up of the figure into horizontal segments by seams, belts, or other distinct breaks in the clothing. The smooth flow from shoulder to feet of Egyptian female garments is distinctly different from the Empire style, in which the garment is pulled in under the breasts, creating a horizontal line there, with a free flow from the breasts to the feet. In contrast to both of these, the female dress of the early 1930s and of the medieval period are broken horizontally at the hips, in the first case by a belt or sash that all too easily becomes ugly

Figures 6–20 and 6–21. Molière's *Doctor in Spite of Himself* and *The Versailles Impromptu* on a double bill at the University of Iowa, directed by Kenneth Cameron. The same actors were used in both plays. In *The Doctor in Spite of Himself*, the costumes by Sandra Tappan were made of felt in bright colors and large motifs; the play was presented against a painted setting by Arnold Gillette. In *The Versailles Impromptu*, the costumes by Margaret Hall were of light fabrics in muted colors; the play was presented against the neutral background of a bare stage.

or comic, and in the second by a line of drapery (sometimes a girdle) that follows the pelvic line in front, flowing more smoothly into an easy fall to the feet. The designer, having chosen his silhouette, can still manipulate that silhouette somewhat by emphasizing or supressing certain features, either to enhance the costume (to make it more flattering) or to make it the opposite. In addition, he can control the surface decoration of each costume. Fabrics can be chosen for their unadorned simplicity (large areas of one color) or their high degree of decoration (brocaded, embroidered, or printed patterns). They can be added to with decorative bands, jewels, edging, or fringe. Here, of course, the earlier considerations of social standing, formality, and given circumstances of the character may determine *why* the character wears such a costume, but within the designer's over-all scheme his own decision to break or enhance the silhouette with pattern or decoration will be determined by his sense of style.

It cannot be emphasized too strongly that the costume designer must work throughout the production period with the set designer and the lighting designer. Such apparently simple matters as the width of doorways or the distance between pieces of furniture may have much to do with the silhouettes of costumes. The choice of lighting colors (on the acting areas, not the background) may dictate certain modifications in costume color, or the costume designer's needs may require modification in the lighting. As Hunton D. Sellman has observed, "Generalizing, one can say that light of a complementary hue will make a costume appear gray, but light of a similar hue will enhance the beauty of a piece of fabric and make it more prominent. Blue light on blue velvet or satin makes it seem to glow from within." Control, then, of the delicate variables of costume design must come in cooperation with the other designing artists.

Working with the actors, the costume designer may find that the addition of certain accessories will enhance his designs and help the actor. A considerable change in silhouette can be gained, for example, by adding a parasol to a female costume or a walking stick or sword to a male costume, when other considerations allow it. Often such an accessory will help the actor as well as the costume, giving him a sense of period movement through the demands of handling an accessory proper to that period. With the cooperation of the director, therefore, the designer can extend his sense of costume out from clothing alone, and create stage pictures with added excitement.

Mood and Progression

The costumes created by the designer can be made to add up to a significant whole that contributes greatly in externalizing the play. More than a symbol of individual characters, more than a creator of style, the costume scheme can have sequence and progression—of color, of picturization, and of meaning. Color control, for example (limiting the costume palette for a given scene), can be used progressively throughout a production until the entire spectrum is reached, or until the entire palette chosen by the designer is reached. One of Claude Bragdon's early devices was to use black and white throughout a scene, leaving the appearance of a primary color until the entrance of a dominant character, creating an aesthetic hunger for that color. Less obviously, fabric, pattern, and silhouette can be used in the same sequential way.

Costumes create mood in three ways, through color, through line, and through mass. Just as line, mass, and color create mood in a setting (with the help of lighting), so the same elements can create mood with costume. The massing of similarly colored costumes, the isolation of one color among a group of widely different colors, and the design of a smoothly flowing drapery among vertical, undraped figures can parallel the dramatic action and emphasize the important elements of each scene. They give the costume designer great importance in the staging of any play in the contemporary theatre.

Conversely, any play staged without creative costume design will lack these elements to the point of defeating the attempts of other theatrical artists to produce it successfully. The wrong color, the inappropriate historical period, the lack of a governing style, a bad silhouette where a becoming one is needed, any of these, being so close to the actor and so vitally before the audience's eye, can spoil a production. With the stage designer and the director, the costume designer in the modern theatre is an essential contributor to the total production.

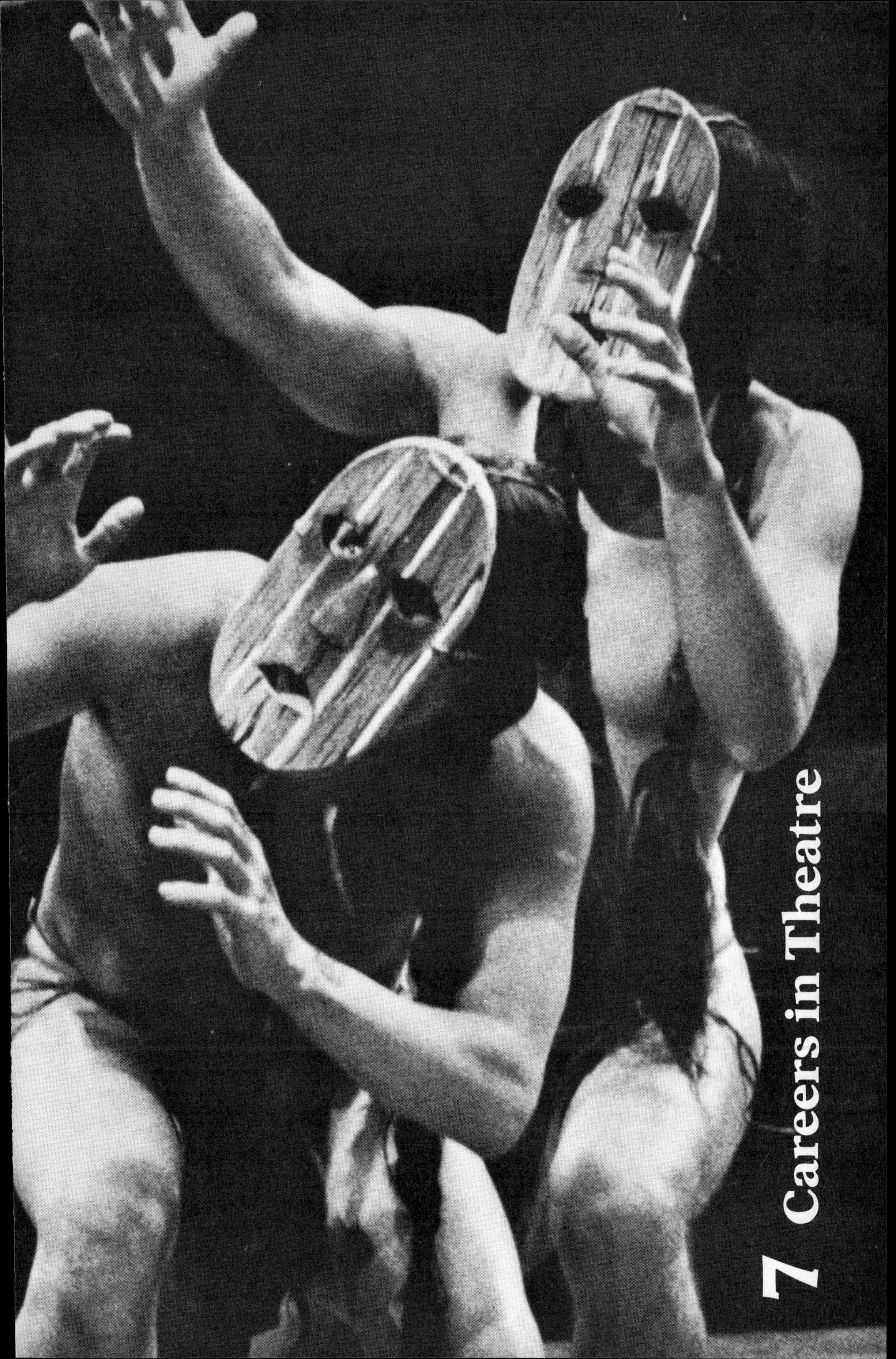

7 Careers in Theatre

The most commonly asked questions that teachers of theatre are likely to be confronted with are, "Should I pursue a career in the theatre?" and "How do I go about it?"

The first is often unanswerable, demanding not only the tact of a master diplomat but also the judgment of a Solomon; and the second, although answerable in a general fashion, is so dependent on geography, field of interest, and special needs and abilities that different answers must be found for different people.

To the first question, however—in spite of whatever else he may find to say—the teacher can answer affirmatively *only* if, disabused of his ideas of glamor and fun, the student can be seen to have a powerful determination, strong inner resources to enable him to withstand repeated rejection, and a very real desire. Particularly in the performing side of theatre, sheer ability to work hard and to persevere are toweringly important, and, sad although it may seem, the ability to endure may often be more important than the ability to act or sing or direct or dance. Theatre is a very wonderful, but very hard profession.

The Professional Theatre

Despite the growth of professional repertory theatres in the United States in the 1960s, and despite the relative health of connected forms (television and films, particularly), the professional theatre at present is even riskier than it traditionally has been. Actors Equity, for example, has more than sixteen thousand members—more than enough to staff every professional production in the country several times over. Although all of these sixteen thousand actors are "professionals," only a fraction of them make a decent living as actors. The same is true, of course, of directors, designers, and all other theatre artists, although conditions differ widely from field to field. The various theatre artists' unions, for example, are not parallel in either structure or membership, so that comparisons between the situation of Actors Equity and the designers' unions cannot profitably be made. It can be said that, because of the nature of their work (full-time involvement in a production over a long period of time), actors probably find it hardest to use their talents profitably in other related fields, except in the immediate area of acting employment (New York or Los Angeles). Many actors still are reluctant to leave New York, where the great bulk of hiring is done, lest they miss an important audition or call. A designer, on the other hand, is able to move about geographically and to send a portfolio of his work to interested theatres. He can even design two or more widely separated productions on overlapping schedules. The same is not exactly true of a director, but a director's association with a production is of shorter duration than an actor's, and a director does not have to tie himself so rigidly to the geographical center of hiring.

In general, it can be said of all areas of the professional theatre in the United States that it is New York-oriented (with certain regional exceptions); that membership in an art or craft union is usually not merely advisable, but most often a requisite to continued employment; that initial employment and initial union membership are very difficult, with certain craft unions having such rigid requirements and limited membership as to make them virtually closed; and that, with the exception of the very lucky and the very gifted, continued employment is not a matter of finding easier and easier access to jobs, but of continually proving oneself over and over and over.

Training is essential and never-ending. A college or university degree is almost meaningless in some areas (in acting, for example; that is, the kind of training that the best university programs give is valuable, but the degree itself means nothing to many casting directors). In other areas (technical practice, for example) the degrees of certain institutions are highly respected. Without exceptions, contacts—knowing somebody, having an initial introduction—are a very large part of the beginner's entry into the theatre.

Educational Theatre

The United States is not unique in having degree programs at the university level in theatre, but it is certainly alone in the number and breadth of programs offered (more than two thousand across the country). As a result, there is a large market for teachers of theatre, perhaps a less active one than in the early 1960s, but one that is still vigorous. To be sure, the field of educational theatre (including a rapidly expanding secondary school field) has been affected by the national surplus of teachers in all fields, but this is hardly the same as saying that hiring has ceased.

Historically, American educational theatre began as a stepchild of other academic programs—usually either English or speech and rhetoric. However, degree-granting departments were already in existence in several major universities by the 1920s, and the field has seen almost constant growth since that time. A general trend away from sponsorship by other academic areas has led to the separate department of theatre or department of drama. Some departments, however, still operate under the aegis of, or in cooperation with, such fields as speech, communications, and other performing arts. As well, the educational goals of various departments differ widely. As a very general observation, it can be said that on the two coasts, large universities have tended toward an increasingly "preprofessional" training, especially at the undergraduate and masters' level, whereas in the central states, the emphasis has traditionally been on teacher training and community theatre training (quite natural goals in areas where the university is often the only theatre center in a vast geographical area). Since the 1960s, however, there has been an increasing tendency toward preprofessional programs.

Careers in educational theatre, as in professional theatre, differ from one area of specialty to another. Experts in technical theatre, for example, have long been in demand. Directors, on the other hand, are plentiful, and playwrights generally find so few positions that they must be able to offer a strong second specialization to find a job.

Unlike the professional theatre, the educational theatre has no specialized unions and no stated limitations for entry into the profession. The two largest national organizations—the American Educational Theatre Association and the Speech Communications Association—perform multiple functions for their members by publishing

Figure 7–1. The first appearance of his father's ghost to Hamlet, from the 1957 production at the Stratford Shakespearean Festival, Stratford, Ontario. The period of the costumes is approximately that of the play; this should be compared with Figure 2–23. (*Courtesy of the Stratford Shakespearean Festival.*)

journals; providing lines of communication; holding annual conventions; sponsoring area conferences in secondary school and community and children's theatre; and offering well-organized and very effective job-placement services. Although they do not function as employment agencies, they do bring applicants and employers together in an efficient fashion.

Formal education is, of course, essential in any career in educational theatre. Increasingly, the doctorate (Ph.D.) is necessary, even in such areas as directing and design. To a lesser degree, the Master of Fine Arts (MFA) and the Master of Arts (MA) may suffice in performance-related areas such as acting, vocal production, and theatre speech. However, anyone considering such a career must bear in mind that theatre departments are units within colleges and universities, where continued employment and advancement depend on teaching performance and, more and more, on scholarly or artistic performance. Some specialized areas (notably voice and speech, and, to an extent, acting) offer very limited opportunities for artistic performance, and many qualified and effective teachers in these fields are not inclined toward scholarship. Thus, the problem of progressing within a university community in these fields may sometimes be more difficult than finding a position in the first place.

At present, artistic standards in educational theatre are high and are going higher. No longer can a sharp division be made between professional and educational theatre on the basis of production quality. In part, a continuing interchange of talents between professional and educational theatre has brought this about. In part, a self-generated attempt to raise its own standards has helped the educational theatre—particularly in such national programs as the annual American Theatre Festival performances in Washington, D. C., when selected colleges and universities from across the country subject their productions to demanding public and critical scrutiny.

A student planning to enter a career in educational theatre can be confident that he will be engaging in a worthwhile artistic and educational enterprise. He must be certain, however, that he has the proper intellectual and educational preparation, and that he is intellectually and professionally capable of quality teaching, scholarship, and, where appropriate, artistry.

Community Theatre

With the spread of the regional professional theatres in the United States, it was feared that community theatres might suffer—organized and funded theatres with, as a rule, nonprofessional actors drawn from the community of their audience. Often, however, the reverse has been true, and community theatre audiences have actually grown. Typically, interest in one theatre has been good for all theatre, and many community theatres seem to have profited from the situation, just as earlier community theatres sprang up in many of the very cities that were played by the road productions of the 1920s.

Essentially, the community theatre is an amateur's theatre with professional intentions. Except in very small communities or in very special circumstances, the theatre depends on a subscription audience and other box-office income for the money to keep going. As a result, front personnel—theatre managers, organizers, and public relations people—are in demand in community theatre. They are the heart of such an operation's survival. (To an extent, of course, this is true of all theatres; however, it is futile to speak of planning a similar career in such high-powered operations as Broadway productions.) Although a community theatre's over-all direction, including play selection, is normally decided by a committee of members, the presence of a trained director is the norm. In addition, many community theatres employ technicians and designers (although frequently the same man or woman will do both jobs); the presence of professional actors is uncommon, however, except on very special occasions.

Thus, there are career opportunities for theatre management personnel, for directors, designers, and technicians in community theatre. There is virtually no regular employment there for actors or playwrights, and very little opportunity for specialists in speech, movement, or voice—except where a school is associated with a community theatre. People interested in children's theatre may find employment here, however, as more community theatres set up an adjunct for children and young people.

In general, there is an overlap in interests and opportunities between community theatre and educational theatre. The latter, however, with its increasing emphasis on advanced degrees, scholarship, and association with the professional theatre and its standards, may be widening the gap from community theatre. For the student who likes working with nonprofessionals, however, in a somewhat more relaxed situation (often for less money), the community theatre can offer an enjoyable and satisfying career.

Career: The Actor

As we have already pointed out, the number of actors earning a living in the professional theatre is only a small percentage of the membership of Actors Equity. In addition, there are thousands more non-Equity actors who earn some money each year in theatres that can hire nonunion actors (theatres far from New York or Los Angeles; summer, and a few winter, stock theatres that are non-Equity; and theatres with an Equity contract that allows for the hiring of a small number of nonunion actors). Equity or not, however, the actor finds that competition in the field is fierce and never-ending.

Figure 7-2. *The School for Scandal* at the Dallas Theatre Center, 1971. Directed by Campbell Thomas, with settings by Lynn Lester and costumes by Carolyn Frost. (*Andy Hanson photo.*)

Nevertheless, the young actor at least has the consolation that his youth is not in itself a bar to employment and that acting is a field in which genuine talent sometimes appears early. Thus, it is possible and advisable for him to train his instrument from an early age, either in one of the many good college and university programs, or in one of the private studios that exist, mostly on both coasts (although a good one must be chosen with care). As well, the young actor, even while training, may find experience in summer stock, in college productions, in community theatre productions, and so on. It is impossible to say at what age a young actor or actress is ready to compete on a professional level, because this will differ for each individual. Certainly, the completion of a formal period of training (four years of college, or a lengthy course of private study) is no sign of such readiness; it merely signifies that the institution feels it has completed its teaching obligation. In actual fact, every actor must continue studying and training for as long as he is in the profession, and organizations such as the Actors Studio came into being in large part to provide such training for mature actors.

The beginner, however, can feel some confidence that he is ready to reach out when he has mastered the basics of his craft: movement and voice; the interpretation of roles; new techniques in rehearsal; improvisation; role creation; makeup; and the handling of costumes and props—the lot. Not, that is, when he has finished a course in each of these with a grade of C or better, but when he has *mastered* them. Then, if he can show experience in a range of roles, perhaps he is ready to apply to one of the regional repertory theatres, or to a quality summer stock theatre, for a job.

Membership in Actors Equity for a beginning actor is of arguable value. Excellent experience can be acquired in non-Equity theatres, and most of the underground and showcase theatres in New York are more accessible to a non-Equity actor. As well, the initial cost of Equity membership is high. And joining Equity is not a simple matter of making application; rather, the actor or actress must have a job with an Equity producer waiting, or a stated amount of experience as an apprentice with Equity producers, before application can be made.

The actor who chooses to enter the professional theatre must have stamina, enormous patience, and great self-confidence. Normally, he must have an agent, as well. (The theatre's *Catch-22* is that it can be as difficult to acquire the services of a good agent as it is to get a job.) Although it is easy to be dazzled by the glamor—or what seems to be glamor—of the public side of the successful actor's life, we must recognize that most working actors are not stars and never will be; furthermore, the few genuine stars who do exist are generally in their forties or older. A ten- to twenty-year period of making rounds (going at least once a week from producer to producer, agent to agent, leaving photographs and résumés of experience), of seeking jobs, of auditioning, and of finding minor roles may lie ahead of even an enormously talented beginner before he or she can become established—that is, known to casting directors and producers and agents as a certain kind of actor, with talent, experience, and proven reliability. One hears of "overnight" successes: as a rule, they come on a night that has been preceded by years of work.

For many actors, the educational theatre, or some combination of educational and professional theatre, is more advisable than the rigors of pure professionalism. People with a natural bent for teaching, people who are comfortable in an academic atmosphere, and people with the intelligence and the fortitude to earn an advanced degree may well be better off in educational theatre. The rewards of teaching are great, and in a field like acting, where promising students make enormous progress under a good teacher, it can be particularly gratifying. With the growing tendency for colleges and universities to sponsor theatre companies whose actors are faculty members, the chances for an actor to find the best of both the educational and the professional worlds are increasing.

The great problem for the actor, in whatever segment of the theatre he chooses, is stagnation. Partly because of geographical isolation, the actor who is not close to high-quality productions and quality training may stagnate without even knowing it. He can allow himself to go on practicing, and teaching, techniques that have become mannerisms and methods that have become habits. Therefore, constant exposure to new techniques, by working with a wide variety of other actors and directors, and by studying at the best possible places, is essential to the actor's career, whether that career lies in the professional or in the educational theatre.

Career: The Playwright

The playwright Robert Anderson is reported to have said that the trouble with Broadway is that a writer can't make a living there; all he can make is a killing. He was speaking as a man of experience, and he was, regrettably, speaking accurately. It appears that even the killings are getting fewer, and it now seems, to be brutal about it, as if only a lunatic would say that he was choosing a *career* as a playwright. To write plays, of course, is something else again; but in writing plays, one must admit that there is no longer any necessary connection between creating the play and entering a profession. Nor is it really possible to prepare to be a playwright; there are courses in many schools, to be sure, and there are even advanced degrees to be earned in playwriting, but the correspondence between such degrees and the subsequent writing of plays that find their place in the theatre is discouragingly small.

For playwrights, who certainly are not born, are not really made, either. They are simply people who write plays. Historical data suggest that broad theatre experience is more important than literary training. Conversely, successful writers from nontheatre fields have sometimes become important innovators in playwriting. The most valuable quality, of course, is creative ability: the sensitivity to the historical moment and to the communal values one's society celebrates, and the talent to mold these to dramatic shapes. But this cannot be taught.

Given native ability, however, and perceptiveness, and given the fact that he has used these requirements to create a play, the contemporary playwright is still far from earning a living (much less making a killing) in the theatre. Of all theatrical artists, his may be the most difficult task: to penetrate the complex and often illogical structure that separates him from production. And even then, once the play is produced, if it is to have continuing life (further productions), it must somehow

Figure 7–3. *The Three Sisters* at The Guthrie Theatre Company, 1963, directed by Tyrone Guthrie and designed by Tanya Moiseiwitsch. Far left, Rita Gam as Masha; kneeling, Ellen Geer as Irina, and Jessica Tandy as Olga. (*Courtesy of The Guthrie Theatre Company.*)

be put into broad circulation. The Broadway hit has no problem with this; indeed, individuals and companies will be bidding for the right to represent it. It is the playwrights of the nonsmash hit and the non-Broadway play—the underground playwright and the playwright of the educational theatre—who must work to achieve broader recognition.

A number of institutions exist to help him. In the educational theatre, the American Educational Theatre Association once sponsored, through its Playwrights Conference, a widely circulated catalog of educational theatre plays. It was not successful. Closer to the Broadway scene, the American Playwrights Theatre has been successful in organizing educational and community theatre productions of new plays, but the number of writers so represented is necessarily small. Two other institutions, Samuel French, Incorporated and the Dramatists Play Service, care for the amateur rights of thousands of plays and publish thick catalogs to describe their playwrights' work; they collect amateur and semiprofessional royalties that can often mean more in the way of a "living" for the writer than a professional production can. (Stuart Little and Arthur Cantor, in *The Playmakers*, cite the case of a play that ran only a few weeks on Broadway, but earned hundreds of thousands of dollars thereafter.) Still, the underground or educational theatre playwright who has not achieved widespread attention in the media will have a hard time placing his play with one of the play services. Of late, the paperback publication of a few such plays in anthologies has offered an opportunity for non-commodity playwrights to reach a wider public—but the chance of their collecting royalties for productions of such published plays is questionable, without the help of an aggressive agent or a play service.

In the great majority of cases, the playwright needs an agent. With the exception of one-time educational theatre productions, initial contact between play and producer will normally be made by a "writer's representative" (who will take ten per cent of the writer's income from the play—usually a bargain for the writer, who gets not only the agent's initial work, but also his business and legal expertise at contract time). Young playwrights should certainly solicit the help of an agent, but should not expect any agent, however enthusiastic, to "carry" them, psychologically or financially. Nor are most agents play doctors or instructors in playwriting.

The beginning playwright should seek production, virtually any production. In some cases, amateur productions of new plays (both community and educational theatres) may not be notably helpful to him, but they will give him confidence and possibly help him to become known. If he chooses then to commit himself to the theatre as a writer, he can usually do no better than to join with a performing group or with a director who likes his work. If he insists on going for that rare "killing," then he must find an agent and be prepared to have his patience, and his courage, tested. Every aspiring playwright must bear in mind the sobering fact that of the thousands of play scripts received in agents' and producers' offices each year, fewer than a hundred—perhaps only half that many—are optioned (that is, reserved for possible production with the payment of a renewable fee). And of all those optioned, fewer than one in four are ever produced.

Career: The Director

Until recently, the American and English theatres were called directors' theatres (the American perhaps more so that the English); the feeling, the tone, and the style of an entire production bore the director's stamp. Recent developments, of course, have pushed the director slightly into the background and emphasized the creative group. Nevertheless, the director remains a figure of great importance; and if his powers and his function appear to have changed somewhat, and he seems to have become a combination of guru, playwright, and guiding genius, he is still very much with us.

As with actors, the competition among directors in the professional theatre is intense. Positions at the regional repertory theatres are hard to come by, but more opportunities exist there for young directors with ability than in New York. Still, it is in the underground and in the peripheral theatres that young directors find their best opportunities, particularly those directors who have an original vision of the theatre and the ability to translate it into theatre work. A director whose strength lies in commendably traditional productions of Shakespeare and Molière, on the other hand, will be better off seeking work elsewhere. Whatever one may say of the professional theatre (particularly in New York), one must admit that it is at its best with new work—the direction of new plays with highly gifted actors.

A young director who honestly finds that he does not show a very real ability to stage new plays will be better off in the more traditional regional theatres or in the educational theatre, where a much higher premium is put on the production of classics. If the young director is happy directing classics, but miserable on those occasions when a living playwright sits at his elbow, his way should be clear.

To be sure, there are more jobs for directors in the educational and the community theatre than in the professional; on the other hand, in recent years the market in even these areas has become more difficult. As with the playwright, the director who wants to teach must have a good second string to his bow; he almost certainly needs an advanced degree, and he must plan to keep up his awareness of developments in the theatre both by scholarly study and by creative work outside his own college or university.

The ability to perform the mechanics of traditional directing (traffic directing, as it has been called) are not sufficient for any director planning to make the theatre his life. Above all, he must be sensitive to other people's feelings and needs if he is to communicate with them and get them to perform up to their own potentials, whether they are students (for the educational theatre director is always teaching); or amateurs in a community theatre (when the director's tact and his sense of human dynamics will sometimes be sorely tested); or the most experienced professionals (whose performances will be the result of very delicate transactions with the director and with other actors, under the director's sensitive guidance). Unless, therefore, an aspiring director is confident of his ability to work with people, he must think very seriously of his chances in the theatre.

Career: The Designer-Technician

Perhaps because of the great amount of training needed, perhaps because of the difficulties in the way of employment in the professional theatre (the designers' and stagehands' union is more than slightly difficult to enter), or perhaps because of the relative anonymity of designers and technical people in our glamorized theatre, this field shows less apparent competition than the others. Capable people in the

THE DUKE'S HORSE

Figure 7–4. The Duke's horse in the Arena Stage production of *Indians*, as designed by Kert Lundell. "It was meant to suggest the opposite of the wild look of [Buffalo Bill's] horse—hence the wheels and well padded look," the designer commented concerning this sketch. (*Courtesy of Kert Lundell.*)

technical areas have always been in demand, especially in educational theatre; indeed, there typically have been more job openings than applicants. Yet, it is no more advisable for a young designer to expect early success than it is for an actor or a director; the sheer numerical opportunities are simply too few. Fortunately, there is no real incompatibility between educational theatre and professional or community theatre in this area, and anyone preparing for it is well advised to ready himself to work in both.

Where the beginning designer or technician insists on trying to enter the professional theatre, he can probably do no better than to try to work for an established designer or an established craft workshop, in whatever capacity he can find. When, on the other hand, he wishes to work in educational theatre, he must be prepared to teach within the general subject areas and to work regularly on theatre productions. For either of these choices, educational preparation is of the utmost importance; it is no accident that one of the strongest areas offered by theatre departments over the last half century has been in design and technical practice, just as it is no accident that some of the foremost designers in our theatre now teach in educational theatre departments. Advanced degrees, to at least the master's level, are advisable. There is so much to be learned, and so much new material is constantly appearing, that programs at the doctoral level are common.

Career: Front of the House

The field of theatre management has come late to the course offerings in most American departments, and as a major within such departments it is still fairly new. Nonetheless, the field offers exciting career possibilities for men and women who combine an interest in the theatre with organizational ability and business sense. Under the impetus of such programs as the Ford Foundation's Management Internship Program in the 1960s, increased interest in the field has been aroused, and it has become better known and more attractive to people going into the theatre. The field has the considerable advantage, as well, of offering potentially higher salaries and more regular employment than many others. Although the term *theatre manager* implies a static position as the businessman-mediator between the commercial and the artistic sides of community and professional theatres, there can be far more to it—not merely the business management of such theatres, but also the expansion into production at the highest levels of the commercial theatre. As well, there is an increasing demand for artistically aware managers for university and urban cultural complexes. Even though the field is young as an academic subject, it offers broad possibilities.

Related areas such as public relations and artistic management are also possibilities. Again, the combination of theatrical knowledge and special skill is required; and, although actual education in theatre public relations is rare, there are ample opportunities for study in more general public relations and business areas. As with so many fields within the theatre, to prepare rigidly for one limited career is a mistake; but to prepare broadly, with emphasis on those areas of one's own interest and aptitude, is to be recommended greatly.

In no area of theatre, in fact, can narrowness be recommended. It is simply impossible to predict where any individual's experience will take him. The young man who sets out to become an actor may find himself, ten years later, as a successful teacher of directing; the young woman who plans to be a playwright may ultimately become a producer. A would-be theatre manager with experience in law may end up as a top agent. Nor is it to be considered in any way a failure to allow a career to undergo such change. Although there are ugly clichés about each area (critics are failed playwrights, stage managers are failed directors, technicians are failed designers, and so on), the achievement of success in any theatrical field, whether in the professional, the educational or the community theatre, is reason for great self-congratulation. The beginner does well by knowing something of each field and its demands, so that his choices can be made wisely when opportunities come.

The main thing, in the beginning, is to find a place in the theatre. Any place. There are all manner of jobs, from being a gopher (the one who has to "go for" everybody else's coffee), to walking on in miniscule roles, to typing subscription appeals in the front office. None should be overlooked. The theatre's organizational structure is a curious one, and the routes through it can be very devious. Like a maze in an Alice-in-Wonderland puzzle, it can be entered at many points, all of which, through ingenuity and endurance, open to routes to the center.

Glossary of Terms

Agit-prop. Strongly propagandistic ideological drama, typically of the 1930s.

Alexandrine. A six-foot, twelve-syllable line of verse, the typical line of neoclassic French tragedy.

Anagnorisis. The tragic vision, or understanding, of the protagonist as the result of his suffering.

Apron. That part of a proscenium stage extending beyond the proscenium arch toward the audience. An *apron stage* is one having an extended apron and, frequently, correspondingly less depth behind the proscenium, if any at all.

Arena stage. A stage completely surrounded by the audience, with no proscenium or other structure to separate audience and playing area.

Autos sacramentales. Spanish religious dramas, played both inside the church and out.

Batten. Pipe or rod located over and around the playing area, from which lights, scenery, and curtains can be hung. Proscenium stages frequently have complete batten systems, consisting of counter-weighted battens on pulley systems, so they can be raised or lowered to any height, over the entire stage area.

Beat. A basic scene unit in the total rhythm of the play. Often used as synonymous with *motivational unit*. The word is also used to designate the length of pauses between speeches or actions, as, for example, in "one beat" or "two beats" in the established tempo of the scene.

Blocking. The movements and locations of actors within a set.

Book. (1) The play script, especially the copy containing the director's or stage manager's blocking diagrams, directions, and notes. (2) A hinged scenic piece made of two flats that can be folded together for shifting.

Choregus. In fifth-century Athens, the wealthy citizen chosen to underwrite one playwright and chorus of the City Dionysia.

Chorus. In fifth-century Athens, the group of from fifteen to fifty male actor-dancers who performed, usually as a unit and in the *orkestra*, in tragedies and comedies. More loosely, any figure who takes little or no part in the dramatic action, but introduces and comments on it.

Climax. The moment of highest intensity in any discursive form.

Comedy of manners. Comic or satirical drama focusing on the supposedly laughable interplay of an upper class with inferior classes, especially the newly rich bourgeoisie, written from the upper-class point of view.

Commedia dell'arte. Popular professional Italian comedy that reached its peak between the late sixteenth and the early eighteenth centuries. Partly improvisational in nature, it is contrasted to the *commedia erudita*, the theatre of classic plays and their imitations.

Convention. Any element in the theatre that is established, with both artists and audience, by long usage.

Corpus Christi plays. Generic term for medieval cycle plays, derived from their association with the Feast of Corpus Christi.

Cycle plays. Medieval plays dealing with the history of the world from its creation to Doomsday, based on scripture, the Apocrypha, and religious legend.

Counterweights. Weights attached to one end of a pulley system to balance whatever is suspended from the other end (drapes, scenery, lights, and so on).

Deus ex machina. The "god from the machine," literally the god who sometimes intervened at the end of classical tragedy to resolve the action; used more generally for any solution of a dramatic problem that does not grow out of the drama itself, but is imposed by the playwright.

Deuteragonist. The second actor of Greek tragedy; also applied loosely to the kind of role such an actor might play, the confidant or supporter of the principal character (for example, Horatio).

Development. That part of a dramatic action when, after initial exposition, action becomes increasingly complex and points with growing intensity to the climax.

Didactic theatre. Any theatre that insists on impressing a specific lesson or message on its audience.

Dionysia. In fifth-century Greece, the religious celebrations associated with the god Dionysus; the festivals at which plays were normally staged.

Dimmer. Any device for the graduated control of light.

Discursive form. Artistic form that must be sensed over a period of time and in the sequence determined by the artist.

Dithyramb. A poetic form performed by a chorus at the Dionysian festivals; narrative and lyric rather than dramatic.

Doubling. The playing of more than one character in the same play by a single actor.

Downstage. In a proscenium theatre, the area toward the audience.

Dress rehearsal. A rehearsal under full performance conditions, with performance properties, costumes, settings, and lighting.

Dry-brushing. A scene-painting method using a brush almost free of paint. The brush is stroked lightly over the surface, leaving parallel streaks created by individual bristles or small groups of bristles.

Dutchman. Material used to cover an exposed joint in the scenery.

Ekkyklema. Mechanical device in classical Greek theatre for bringing actors or objects from inside the *skene* to the stage; probably a wagon brought out through the central doors.

Emotional recall. The actor's re-creation of emotion (analogous to the emotional response needed in a role) by re-creating the environment, circumstances, and actions surrounding the emotion in his own past.

Environmental theatre. Spatially democratized theatre of the 1960s that tries to satisfy Artaud's requirement for a theatre that surrounds the spectators.

Epic theatre. Term used by Piscator and Brecht for a theatre that would be narrative rather than dramatic, didactic rather than aesthetic.

Episode. In classical Greek tragedy, the action between odes.

Erudite theatre. Any theatre whose audience is limited by class and intellect, whose organization is not primarily professional, and whose aim is, at least in part, the re-creation or imitation of a prior form—for example, the court theatre in England after 1603; the Oxford-Cambridge neoclassical theatre of the mid-sixteenth century.

Exodos. Final exit of the chorus in classical Greek tragedy.

Exposition. Giving of necessary information about characters, prior events, or the situation, directly through the narrative rather than through dramatic action.

Extrinsic idea. First-level statement made by a play, especially in terms of final conclusions drawn by characters or a chorus.

Farce. "Stuffed" comedy (from a Latin root meaning to *stuff*), whose sole aim is to cause laughter.

Floodlight. Any light having a wide-angle beam and a soft edge. The characteristics of beam width, hardness of edge, and length of throw can be controlled by lenses or reflectors or both.

Flying. Hanging scenery over its stage location in a storage area (fly space) above the stage; vertical movement is controlled by a variety of counterweighted batten systems or even individual, motor-driven winches.

Form. The fundamental nature of a creation, as it can be defined by its peculiar characteristics. Thus, discursive form can be distinguished from presentational; theatrical form can be distinguished from novelistic; and the form of revenge tragedy can be distinguished from the form of Molièresque comedy.

Fresnel lens. A lens used in stage lights, essentially planoconvex, but with the convex side reduced to concentric rings whose cross sections are arcs of the entire convex face, dropped to the same plane to reduce the thickness of the lens.

Genre. An aesthetic category distinguished by form and purpose.

Grip. A stagehand, especially one responsible for moving scenery.

Ground plan. Drawing of a setting, showing all acting areas, furniture, entrances, and variations of level.

Guilds. In medieval Europe, social and economic organizations by craft, by geographical area or by patron saint, always with a religious affiliation.

Happening. A public event aimed at audience involvement, largely nonverbal in nature and seeking to be nonsequential or nondiscursive.

Hubris or hybris. An Aristotelian concept carried over into neoclassical criticism: the defiance of divine will shown by a tragic character.

Humor. In medieval medicine, one of four fluids—blood, phlegm, black bile, yellow bile—whose balance determined personality traits. In

1599, Ben Jonson's *Every Man in His Humour* exploited the idea of the excess of one humor as a comic theory of psychology, the comedy of humor. In Elizabethan tragedy, melancholy humor in its several forms was associated with introspection, pessimism, and isolation.

Illusionistic theatre. Any theatre whose action, characters, language, and *mise en scène* seek to match the audience's idea of actual experience.

Improvisation. Invention by actors of characters, dialogue, environment, and/or action around a so-called premise, such as an idea, a situation, a prop. Although most useful as a rehearsal technique and a learning experience, the improvisation can be repeated, changed, shaped, and turned into a performable theatre piece.

Incident light. Light falling on a surface directly from the light source.

Intrinsic idea. Meaning communicated by a performance below the primary level of direct statement or apparent judgments contained in the action; the cultural attitudes reflected or rejected, often unconsciously, by a playwright.

Introit. The opening section of the mass.

Lash lines. Ropes used to fasten together two flats, usually by tightening them over staggered cleats on the backs of the flats.

Ludi. Medieval term for any theatrical events.

Magic If. Stanislavskian term for imaginative invention of circumstances surrounding an action to help the actor in finding his externalization of it.

Masque. Renaissance dramatic form, usually associated with the erudite theatre of the nobility, relying heavily on spectacle, scenic effects, and dance, with little or no intrinsic idea.

Mekane. The machine, in classical and Hellenistic Greek theatre, for lowering actors into the playing area from above (see *Deus ex machina*).

Melodrama. Originally (early nineteenth century) a form of musical drama exploited in England to circumvent legal restrictions on staging plays; later, a form of serious drama relying on gross effects and frequent sentimentality. More generally, any serious form that seeks to arouse audience identification, fear, and anxiety.

Mime. Nonverbal performer or performance seeking to represent or imitate actual experience (but without subordinating actions and rhythms to music, as in dance).

Mimesis. Aristotelian term for *imitation* in its largest sense: not the narrow copying of behavior by an actor, but the representation of meaningful experience by a drama.

Mise en scène. Physical staging, including the use and concept of scenery, movement, composition, and visual effects.

Mood. The mental or emotional state generated in an audience by a theatrical event or some aspect of it; used often to denote (usually through metaphor) the theatrical elements that generate such states, as in the mood values of a specific setting or of a part of the text. In general, mood values are highly subjective (that is, they are defined as much by the nature of the response as by the element that seeks to generate it).

Morality play. Allegorical drama, especially in the late medieval period, in which most or all characters are personified religious or moral abstractions.

Motivational unit. A scene unit defined by the initiation and completion (or alteration) of motivation in the dominant character.

Myth. Stories of archetypal figures whose nature is a projection of widespread cultural beliefs, hopes, or fears.

Nativity play. That part of a medieval cycle concerned with the birth of Christ (usually including the stories of Herod, the Magi, and the Shepherds; sometimes including the Conception and related matters).

Neoclassic. Imitative of Greek and Roman models (usually with a narrower critical interpretation of those models than they were subjected to in their own day).

Objective. A dramatic character's goal within a motivational unit.

Orkestra. "Dancing-floor"; the (usually) circular, flat area occupied by the chorus in the fifth-century Greek theatre, surrounded on three sides by the audience and tangent to the proskenion.

Pace. Literally, the tempo of any performance or unit within it; often used to mean "effective speed," as in "The show lacks pace."

Pageant wagons. Wheeled settings for parts of medieval cycles. The *pageant* may refer to either the play's subject matter ("The Pageant of the Creation") or to the physical embodiment of it; the *wagon* need not have been merely a farm wagon or cart, but may have been any of a variety of wheeled objects (for example, Noah's ship).

Parados. In the fifth-century Greek theatre, one of the two symmetrically placed chorus entrances; in the drama of the period, the song with which the chorus entered.

Passion play. Christian religious play, or that part of a cycle dealing with the life of Christ from the entrance into Jerusalem through the ascension.

Pathos. That part of tragedy dealing with the physical and emotional suffering of the hero.

Periaktos. A three-sided prism pivoted at each end so it will revolve and show different faces; in the Hellenistic theatre, pairs of *periaktoi* were used as changeable scenic units.

Planoconvex lens. A lens having one flat face and one that is part of a sphere.

Plastique. Bodily exercise developed by Jerzy Grotowski.

Platea or place. In medieval terminology, the acting area (sometimes used as an audience area as well) between, or in the center of, localizing structures (scaffolds, mansions, sedes).

Plot. Progressive sequence of incidents, causally linked, and limited to the subject matter common to all the incidents.

Poor theatre. Jerzy Grotowski's term for a theatre that emphasizes the actor and de-emphasizes technology and spectacle.

Presentational. Not restricted to an imitation of actual environment or actual experience; interpretive as well as imitative; using the devices of the theatre for themselves.

Prologos. In fifth-century Greek tragedy, the short scene (usually limited to one or two characters) before the choral *parados*.

Props, properties. Any objects used by actors in a performance, somewhat arbitrarily distinguished from scenery and costumes in terms of who has responsibility for creating and caring for them.

Proscenium. The opening that serves as frame for the stage, in a wall that masks the offstage areas from the audience, in any theatre where the audience is on one side of the playing area and that playing area is largely behind the plane of the masking wall.

Proskenion. In the Greek theatre, the area immediately in front of the skene.

Protagonist. In the Greek theatre, the first actor; used more generally for the kind of role he would play—the principal figure in the principal action.

Psychological gesture. The physical equivalent of a psychological reaction; the expressive, truthful gesture found by the actor to externalize emotion.

Quem quaeritis trope. Interpolated protodramatic section in the early medieval mass, beginning *Quem quaeritis*, "Whom do you seek?"

Raisonneur. A character at or close to the ideological center of a play; frequently a spokesman for the author's point of view.

Récit. In classical French drama, a lengthy set speech devoted to the recounting of past action.

Reflector. Surface behind a theatrical light source, specially shaped and with any of several surface finishes, to direct reflected light back toward the playing area.

Representational. Imitative of actual experience, with little or no exploitation of theatrical devices or conventions for their own sakes.

Restoration. The period in England after the return of Charles II (1660), usually understood as continuing until about 1700 (although Charles died in 1685).

Return. A scene surface angled from a wing.

Revenge play. Especially in Elizabethan and Jacobean England, a serious play whose plot is organized around the impulse for an otherwise good man to revenge himself on a villain for atrocities against his family; typical elements are the revenger's uncertainty about the villain, the revenger's madness during a period of stress, and the deaths of both revenger and villain when the villain's final trick goes awry.

Revolve, revolving stage. A large, circular portion of the playing area that can revolve in either direction through 360 degrees.

Rigging. Ropes, blocks, and associated equipment in a fly system.

Ritual. Any much-repeated act with a specific goal; in religion, a ceremony whose form is fixed by long usage and whose goal is contact with, or the influence of, a god.

Satire. Revelation or degradation of error, folly, or vice by making it the object of laughter.

Scaffold. In the medieval theatre, a localizing structure in a fixed location in, or on the edge of, the playing area.

Scaena ductilis. In the Roman theatre, a moving scenic background, probably a painted canvas on rollers (imitated, in other forms, in the Renaissance).

Scenario. In the *commedia dell'arte*, the written outline of plot and characters; more generally, the prose description of any play, film, or theatre piece.

Scène à faire. The obligatory scene in the well-made play, pointed toward and foreshadowed by rigid plot development through the developmental section of the play.

Scrim. Coarse-weave cloth that is transparent when lighted from behind and more or less opaque when lighted from in front.

Sentimental comedy. An eighteenth-century dramatic type that substituted moral behavior for upper-class amorality as the comic focus; at its center was the man of sentiment, the naturally good, often nonwitty moral man.

Sequential staging. In the medieval period, use of localized settings (usually wagons or movable pageants) singly and in sequence, rather than simultaneously.

Serlian wing. Permanent scene piece approximately parallel to the major stage axis, usually used in opposed pairs for false perspective effects; first described by Sebastiano Serlio. Combined with a return.

Simultaneous staging. Principally in the medieval period, but used as a design principle in some contemporary "space" stages; the use of several localized settings within the same playing area at the same time; some or all may actually be included in the action at the same time.

Sight lines. Imaginary lines from the extremes of the audience area through the major masking or blocking element in the playing area (for example, the proscenium arch) to indicate the limits of the playing area that can be seen by the entire audience.

Sizing. Any material for treating a painting ground, normally to fill the fabric, to prevent excessive absorption of paint.

Skene. In the fifth-century Greek theatre, the scene building, located across the *orkestra* from the center point of the audience.

Soliloquy. A form of set speech in which the speaking character is alone with the audience; normally, it takes the form of an interior monologue.

Shifting (of scenery). Moving of scenery with grips.

Spine. The "line of through action" of a role (Stanislavski). Consistent line connecting common elements of motivations and objectives in all scenes.

Spotlight. Hard-edged light with focusing devices, usually both shaped reflector and condensing lens system.

Stations. Locations for playing or for showing pageant wagons in sequentially staged medieval drama.

Structure. Descriptive analysis of the sequence and intensities of impact of a performance on its audience.

Subtext. Following Stanislavski's work, this term has been used to describe the interaction of objectives taking place between characters in any given scene; the text is only a surface appearance of such interaction.

Super-objective. In Stanislavskian acting, the over-all life goal of a character that embraces all objectives.

Symbol. One thing that can be seen to stand for or to represent another.

Tableau. Static scene using live figures.

Tendencies. In Stanislavskian acting, digressions from the pursuit of an objective by the actor.

Theatre in the round. Arena staging, with the audience completely surrounding the playing area.

Theatre of cruelty. A phrase first associated with Artaud; in his sense, it implied a theatre that would reflect the metaphysical cruelty of existence. As used by later practitioners, it describes a theatre of intense audience involvement, often (but not necessarily) one characterized by shock and violence.

Thesis play. A play written to illustrate an idea that can be reduced to logical statement.

Thrust stage. A playing area with an extended apron or tongue and sometimes lacking any proscenium, surrounded on approximately three sides by the audience.

Tirade. In the French neoclassic tradition, a set speech of connected, impassioned Alexandrines, delivered in a virtually operatic manner like an aria.

Tritagonist. In fifth-century Greece, the third actor of tragedy.

Typology. The medieval view of certain events as antecedents, or "types" of others.

Ubermarionette. Gordon Craig's superpuppet, the articulated figure that would replace the living actor in his ideal theatre.

Unit set. A three-dimensional construction that can be used for an entire play, different scenes being individually lighted and the unit itself rotated, shifted, and superficially changed through the addition of minor elements.

Well-made play. An expression most often connected with the French playwright Sardou, but used for any play in which meticulous attention to three-act structure, to the inclusion of only the most narrowly relevant material, and to the symmetrical knitting-up of every plot element takes precedence over originality, character, idea, and so on.

Wing. Any two-dimensional scenic piece placed more or less parallel to the proscenium line on a proscenium stage, and located at the sides of the playing area (hence "in the wings" to describe the general offstage areas at the sides of many proscenium stages).

Bibliography

Adams, John C. *The Globe Playhouse.* 2nd ed. (New York: Barnes & Noble, 1961).

Adams, J. Q. *Chief Pre-Shakespearean Dramas* (Boston: Houghton-Mifflin, 1929).

Appia, Adolphe. *Music and the Art of the Theatre,* trans. by Robert W. Corrigan and Mary Douglas Dirks (Miami, Fla.: University of Miami Press, 1962).

———. *The Work of Living Art,* trans. by H. D. Albright (Miami, Fla.: University of Miami Press, 1960).

Arnott, Peter D. *Greek Scenic Convention in the Fifth Century,* B.C. (New York: Oxford University Press, 1962).

———, *An Introduction to the Greek Theatre.* (London: Macmillan and Co., Ltd., 1959).

Arrowsmith, William. "The Criticism of Greek Tragedy" (first published in *Tulane Drama Review*).

Artaud, Antonin. *The Theatre and its Double,* trans. by Mary C. Richards (New York: Grove Press, 1958).

Barton, Lucy. *Historic Costume for the Stage.* Baker's Plays, 1935.

Beare, W. *The Roman Stage.* 3rd ed. (New York: Barnes & Noble).

Bentley, Eric. *The Life of the Drama.* (New York: Atheneum Press, 1964).

Bieber, Margarete. *The History of the Greek and Roman Theatre.* 2nd ed. (Princeton, N. J.: Princeton University Press, 1961).

Chekhov, Michael. *To the Actor.* (New York: Harper & Row, 1953).

Clurman, Harold. *The Fervent Years.* (New York: Hill and Wang, 1957).

Cook, Albert S. *The Dark Voyage and the Golden Mean.* (Cambridge, Mass.: Harvard University Press, 1949).

Corson, Richard. *Stage Makeup.* 3rd ed. (New York: Appleton-Century-Crofts, 1960).

Craig, Edward Gordon. *The Theatre—Advancing.* (New York: Little, Brown, and Company, 1919).

———. *Towards a New Theatre,* (J. M. Dent and Sons, 1913).

Craig, Hardin. *English Religious Drama of the Middle Ages.* (New York: Oxford University Press, 1960). Reprint edition.

Dean, Alexander. *Fundamentals of Play Directing,* rev. by Lawrence Carra. (New York: Holt, Rinehart and Winston, 1965).

Descotes, Maurice. *Les grands rôles du théâtre de Jean Racine.* (Paris: Presses Universitaires de France, 1957).

Duchartre, Pierre-Louis. *La Commedia dell'arte et ses Enfants.* Paris: Editions d'art et d'Industrie (*n.d.*)

Else, Gerald F. *Aristotle's Poetics.* (Cambridge, Mass.: Harvard University Press, 1953).

———. *The Origin and Early Form of Greek Tragedy.* (Cambridge, Mass.: Harvard University Press, 1965).

Enciclopedia dello Spettacolo. Unione editoriale. (Rome: 1954).

Esslin, Martin. *The Theatre of the Absurd.* (New York: Doubleday & Company, 1961).

Ferguson, Francis. *The Idea of a Theater.* (Princeton, N. J.: Princeton University Press, 1949).

Fernandez, Ramon. *Molière—The Man Seen Through the Plays,* trans. by Wilson Follett. (New York: Hill and Wang, 1958).

Frye, Northrop. *Anatomy of Criticism.* (Princeton, N. J.: Princeton University Press, 1957).

Gayle, Addison, Jr., ed. *The Black Aesthetic.* (New York: Doubleday & Company, 1971).

Gibbs, Lewis (Joseph Walter Cove). *Sheridan, His Life and His Theatre.* (New York: William Morrow and Company, 1948).

Giedion, Siegfried. *Time, Space and Architecture.* (Cambridge, Mass.: Harvard University Press, 1954).

Gillette, A. S. *Stage Scenery: Its Construction and Rigging.* (2nd edition) (New York: Harper and Row, 1972).

Granger, Frank, ed. *Vitruvius on Architecture.* (New York: Putnam, & Company, 1931).

Hall, Edward. *The Hidden Dimension.* (New York: Doubleday & Company, 1966).

Hapgood, Elizabeth Reynolds, ed. *Stanislavski's Legacy.* (New York: Theatre Arts Books, 1958).

Hardison, O. B. *Christian Rite and Christian Drama in the Middle Ages.* (Baltimore, Md.: Johns Hopkins University Press, 1965).

Hodges, C. W. *The Globe Restored.* (London: Ernest Benn, Ltd. 1953).

Hotson, Leslie. *Shakespeare's Wooden O.* (New York: Macmillan Inc., 1960).

Houghton, Norris. *Moscow Rehearsals.* (New York: Harcourt Brace Jovanovich, Inc., 1936).

Kernodle, George. *From Art to Theatre.* (Chicago: University of Chicago Press, 1944).

Kerr, Walter. *How Not to Write a Play.* (New York: Simon and Shuster, 1955).

Kitto, H. D. F. *Greek Tragedy.* 2d ed. (London: Methuen & Co., Ltd., 1950).

Kohler, Carl. *A History of Costume,* trans. by Alexander Dallas. (New York: Dover Publications, 1963). Reprint of the George G. Harrap and Co. edition, London: 1928.

Kolve, V. A. *The Play Called Corpus Christi.* (Stanford, Calif.: Stanford University Press, 1966).

Komisarjevsky, Theodor. *The Theatre.* (London: The Bodley Head, Ltd. (Century Library), 1935).

Kott, Jan. *Shakespeare, Our Contemporary,* trans. by Boleslaw Taborski. (New York: Doubleday & Company, 1964).

Lancaster, Henry Carrington. *A History of French Dramatic Literature in the Seventeenth Century.* (Baltimore: Johns Hopkins University Press, 1929–1942).

————, ed. *Le Mémoire de Mahelot, Laurent, et d'autres Décorateurs.* (Paris: Champion, 1920).

Lahr, John. *Up Against the Fourth Wall.* (New York: Grove Press, 1970).

Langer, Susanne. *Feeling and Form.* (New York: Charles Scribner's Sons, 1953).

Lewis, Robert. *Method—or Madness?* (London: William Heinemann, Ltd., 1960).

Little, Stuart W. *Off-Broadway.* (New York: Coward, McCann and Geohegan, Inc., 1972).

Little, Stuart W., and Cantor, Arthur. *The Playmakers.* (New York: E. P. Dutton & Co., 1971).

Lynch, James, J. *Box, Pit and Gallery.* (Berkeley: University of California Press, 1953).

Marowitz, Charles. "Notes on the Theatre of Cruelty." *Tulane Drama Review* (Winter, 1966).

McCandless, Stanley. *A Method of Lighting the Stage.* 4th ed. (New York: Theatre Arts Books, 1958).

McLuhan, Marshall. *Understanding Media.* (New York: McGraw-Hill, 1964).

McMullan, Frank. *The Directorial Image.* (The Shoestring Press, 1962).

Moore, Will Grayburn. *Molière.* 2nd ed. (New York: Oxford University Press, 1964).

Munk, Erika, ed. *Stanislavski and America.* (New York: Hill and Wang, 1966).

Neff, Renfreu. *The Living Theatre: USA.* (New York: Bobbs-Merrill Company, 1970).

Nemirovitch-Dantchenko, Vladimir. *My Life in the Russian Theatre.* (Theatre Arts Books, 1936).

The New York Times

Nicoll, Allardyce. *The Development of the Theatre.* 3rd ed. (New York: Harcourt Brace Jovanovich, Inc., 1946).

————. *The World of Harlequin.* (New York: Cambridge University Press, 1963).

Olson, Elder, ed. *Aristotle's Poetics and English Literature.* (Chicago: University of Chicago Press, 1965).

————. *Tragedy and the Theory of the Drama.* (Detroit: Wayne State University Press, 1961).

Palmer, John, *Molière,* (Brewer and Warren, 1930.)

Performance Group. *Dionysus in 69.* Richard Schechner, ed. (New York: Farrar, Straus and Giroux, 1970).

Pickard-Cambridge, A. W. *The Dramatic Festivals of Athens.* (Oxford: Oxford University Press, 1953).

Prosser, Eleanor. *Hamlet and Revenge.* (Stanford, Calif.: Stanford University Press, 1967).

————. *Drama and Religion in the English Mystery Plays.* (Stanford, Calif.: Stanford University Press, 1961).

Selden, Samuel, and Hunton D. Selman. *Stage Scenery and Lighting.* 3rd ed. (New York: Appleton-Century-Crofts, 1959).

Shaw, George Bernard. *Shaw on Theatre.* E. J. West, ed. (New York: Hill and Wang, 1958).

Simonson, Lee. *The Art of Scenic Design.* (New York: Harper & Row, 1950).

——. *The Stage Is Set.* (New York: Dover, 1932).

Southern, Richard. *The Medieval Theatre in the Round.* (London: Faber and Faber, Ltd., 1957).

——. *Seven Ages of the Theatre.* (New York: Hill and Wang, 1957).

Spivack, Bernard. *Shakespeare and the Allegory of Evil.* (New York: Cambridge University Press, 1958).

Spolin, Viola. *Improvisation in the Theatre.* (Evanston, Ill.: Northwestern University Press, 1963).

Stanislavski, Konstantin. *An Actor Prepares.* trans. by Elizabeth Reynolds Hapgood. (New York: Theatre Arts Books, 1963).

——. *Building a Character*, trans. by Elizabeth Reynolds Hapgood. (New York: Theatre Arts Books 1949).

——. *My Life in Art*, trans. by J. J. Robbins. (New York: Theatre Arts Books, 1948).

Styan, J. L. *Chekhov in Performance* (New York: Cambridge University Press, 1971).

TDR (Formerly *Tulane Drama Review* and *Carleton College Drama Review.*)

Turnell, Martin. *The Classical Moment: Studies in Corneille, Molière and Racine.* (New York: New Directions, 1948).

Village Voice, New York.

Waxman, S. M. *Antoine and the Théatre Libre.* (Cambridge, Mass.: Harvard University Press, 1926).

Wickham, Glynne. *Early English Stages, 1300–1660.* (New York: Columbia University Press, 1959–1963).

Williams, Arnold. *The Drama of Medieval England.* (Ann Arbor: Michigan State University Press, 1961).

Williams, Raymond. *Drama from Ibsen to Eliot.* (London: Chatto and Windus Ltd., 1952).

Note: References to illustrations are in italics.

Capon, William, 143, 303, 344
Career
　as actor, 401–404
　　See also Actor
　as designer-technician, 407–409
　as director, 406–407
　in educational theatre, 399–400, 403
　as playwright, 404–406
Carey, Helen, *129, 133*
Carnovsky, Morris, 167
Cartier, Jacques, *189*
Casting, 319–321
Castle of Perseverance, The, 61
Central staging, 324
Chaikin, Joseph, 208, 209, 259, 306
Character
　Aristotle on, 236
　character psychology and, 247–248
　in *commedia dell'arte*, 114–116
　in *Hamlet*, 86–88
　suspense of, 227–228
　See also Acting techniques
Charles II, 124, 126
Charles Playhouse, 359, *360, 381*
Chekhov, Anton, 15, 167
　The Cherry Orchard, 157, 161
　The Seagull, 156–158
　Shaw and, 155
　The Three Sisters, 149, 153, 154, 155, 157–162
　Uncle Vanya, 157, 161
　The Wood Demon, 157
Chelsea Theater Center, 204
Cherry Lane Theatre, *192, 194*, 200, *202, 309*
Children's plays, 232–233
Chinoy, Helen Krich, 164
Choral elaboration in medieval drama, 55, 56, 58
Chorus, Greek, 27–28, 32, 41, 42, 44
Church
　influence of, 54–56, 90
　medieval staging and, 58, 60, 62–65
　See also Religion
Cincinnati Playhouse in the Park, *318*
Cino, Joe, 200
Cioffi, Charles, *189*
Circle-in-the-Square, 200
City Dionysia, 24, 28, 29
Civic Repertory Theatre, *153*
Classicism of Molière, 106–111, 116–122
Classics, 11, 20–215
　staging of, 317–318

Clowns, 69
Clurman, Harold, 167
Cobb, Lee J., 167
Collier, Jeremy, 133
Color
　of costumes, 392–393
　in lighting, 377–380
　in makeup, 296–300
　of scenery, 369, 371–373
Comédie-ballet, 108
Comédie Française, 107, 113
Comédie Italienne, 113
Comedy
　black, 157–158
　in *Death of a Salesman*, 172–173
　English, 125, 131, 134–136
　of Molière, 108–111, 116–123
　musical, 195
　Restoration, 131–132
　Roman, 49–51
　sentimental English, 134–136
　tragedy and, 237–240
Comedy of manners, 132, 133
Comic scene, Serlio's, *95*
Commedia dell'arte, 49, 107–116
　The Miser and, 119, 120
Commedia erudita, 110, 114
Community theatre, 11–17, 400–401
Communication
　exercises in, 280
　theatre as, 4–7
Companies, acting, 6
　Shakespearean, 68–69
　See also Actors
Competition in Greek theatre, 24–25, 28, 30, 31
Concordia Regularis, 56, 58
Congreve, William, 132
　The Way of the World, 137
Connelly, Marc, 177
Constructivism, 180
Control system for lights, 376–377
Copeau, Jacques, 179, 180, 303
Corneille, Pierre, 94–96
　Le Cid, 94, 104
Cornell, Katherine, *288*
Corson, Richard, *Stage Makeup*, 297
Costumes
　design of, 380–393
　mood and progression through, 392–393
Covent Garden Opera House, 128
Cowan, Ron, 205
Craig, Gordon, 174–176, 179, 285, 351, 353
　The Art of the Theater, 175

　as director, 303
　expressionism and, 178
　The Theater—Advancing, 175
　Toward a New Theater, 175, 373
　ubermarionettes of, 175, 285
Creon, 26, *43*, 44–46
Criticism
　of Aristotle, 21, 234–240
　French, 94
　generic, 237–240
　methods of, 5–7
　neoclassic, 93–97
　neoclassical plays and, 93–97
　role of, 219
Cromwell, Oliver, 126, 344
Cronyn, Hume, *248*
Crowley, Mart, *The Boys in the Band*, 201
Croydon, Margaret, 284
Cruelty, Theatre of, 188–189, 205, 318
Cunningham, Merce, 208, 222–223
Curtain, The, 67, 70

Dallas Theater Center, 17, *402*
Dance training and acting, 285
Darwinism, 144
D'Avenant, William, 126, 128, 344
Davis, Owen, 163
Davis, William, *211*
Death of a Salesman (Miller), 168–172, 178, 195, 225, 237, 261
　acting in, 267
　design for, 350
　directing of, 316
　ground plans and, 340
　language of, 244–246
　scene from, 313–316, 327, 329
Decroux, Etienne, 179
Delsarte, François, 164, 283
Design, 343–393
　costume, 380–393
　director and, 352–353
　evolution of, 343–345
　stage, 93, 346; *See also* Staging
　three examples of, 354–365
Designer
　as architect, 348–350
　director as, 337–340
　ground plans of, 339–343
　production and, 350–351
　in theatre organization, 351–352
Designer-technician, career as, 407–409
Deus ex machina, 35

Shepard, Sam (*Continued*)
Operation Sidewinder, 10, 206
Sheridan, Richard Brinsley, *The School for Scandal*, 125, *127*, 128, *129*, *130*, *133*, 135–142, *402*
Sherwood, Robert E., *The Petrified Forest*, 168
Shifting of scenery, 367
Shisgal, Murray, *Luv*, 199
Shostokovitch, Dmitri, 181
Sicily, remains of Greek theatre in, *23*
Siddons, Sarah, 130
Sills, Paul, 281
Simonson, Lee, *177*, 354, 364
Skelton, Thomas, 13
Skene, 32–35
Slaiman, Marjorie, 13
Smith, Oliver, 13
Smith, Russ, *162*
Social aspects of theatre, 11–17
  in America, 167, 168
  criticism and, 238
  epic theatre, 181, 182
  in Ibsen's plays, 150, 151
  Shaw and Chekhov and, 155
  in Strindberg's work, 152
  in Zola's work, 144–146
Socrates, Plato on trial of, 40–41
Soliloquy, 121
Sophocles, 25, 28, 29
  ambiguity and irony of, 254–255
  Antigone, 41, 249
  Oedipus at Colonus, 41, 47, 249, 250
  Oedipus Rex, see Oedipus Rex
  symbols of, 249
Southern, Richard, 65, 79
  The Medieval Theatre in the Round, 61, 64
  Seven Ages of the Theatre, 34, 77, 348
Spatial reality and design, 345–346
Spear, Richard D., 7, *38*
Spectator papers, 133
Speech, 289–290
  See also Acting techniques; Voice
Speech Communications Association, 399
Spenser, Edmund, *Fairie Queen*, 66
Spirit House, 204
Spollin, Viola, 259, 269, 281, 282
Stage(s)
  early English, 61–62
  Elizabethan, 75
  of Molière, *111*

realism in, *151*
Roman, *94*
in Serlio's theatre, *89*, *91*
thrust, 324, *325*, 326, *330*, 349–350, 362
  See also Staging; Theatre architecture
Stage areas, 323, 324, 329–330
Stage design, 93, 346
  See also Design
Stage mechanics of actor, 291–293
  See also Acting techniques
Stage movement, notes on, *295*
  See also Staging
Staging
  central, 324
  for emphasis, 327–328
  in expressionism, 178, 179
  human relationships and, 333–334
  inside and outside churches, 58, 60–61
  level of, and lighting, 326–327
  medieval, 62–65
  movement in, 334–337
  neoclassical, 99–100
  outdoor, church and, 62–65
  pictorialism in, 322–326
  in Shakespeare's theatre, 73, 78, 79
  for social drama, 181
  visual symbolism and, 331–333
  See also Designers; Presentation; Scenery
Stanislavski, Konstantin, 148–149, 175, 180, 195, 207
  actor's notebook and, 293, 294
  Chekhov and, 156, 157
  contribution of, 273–277
  as director, 303
  influence of
    in America, 166, 167, 259–261, 263, 266, 304–305, 310
    by 1960s, 306
  on stage mechanics, 292
Stanislavskian system, 154, 155, 183
  American directors and, 310
  Brecht and, 183–184
  on directorial approach, 308
  training in, 277–282, 284
Stanley, Kim, *261*
Steele, Richard, 134
Stewart, Ellen, 200
Stoerker, Lewis, 5
Stories, 221

Story Theatre, 281
Strasberg, Lee, 167
Stratford Shakespearean Festival Theatre, 3, 29, *43*, *83*, *129*, *133*, *326*, 399
Strindberg, Auguste, 151–153
  To Damascus, 153, 176
  The Dance of Death, 152
  The Dream Play, 153, 176
  The Father, 152
  The Ghost Sonata, 153, 176
  Miss Julie, 152
  O'Neill and, 165
  Reinhardt directs, 178
  There Are Crimes and Crimes, 152–153
Strollers, 70
Style
  in acting, 271–272
  colors and, in costume design, 390–392
  in directing, 317–318
Substitute memory, 221, 222, 224
Sullivan, Louis, 354, 355
Suspense
  of character, 227–228
  in discursive form, 221–225
  of idea, 228–231
  of plot, 223–225
Swan drawing, *68*, *75*, *76*, *78*, *79*, *81*
Symbolic discourse, 8, 9
Symbolism, 176–178
  nonverbal, 249
  visual, in staging, 331–333

Taboos in theatre, 197–201
Talent, 269–271
Talma, François, 303
Tandy, Jessica, *86*, *248*, *405*
Tappan, Sandra, *391*
Tarleton, Richard, 69
Tavel, Ronald, 201, 205–207
Teatro Olimpico, 92
Tempo of scene, 316
Tendencies, Stanislavski on, 292, 294
Terence, 50, 51, 54, 90, *94*, 114, 134, 135
Terry, Megan, *Viet Rock*, 201
Text
  in communication, 4–6
  performance and, 219–220
  units in, 267
Theater, The, 67, 70
Theatre
  absurd, 188
  academic and Beat, 207
  alternative, 198–199
  black, 201–204
  careers in, *see* Careers
  coffee-house, 200, 205

as communication, 4–7
community and, 11–17, 400–401
companies, 126–128
    See also Actors; Staging
of cruelty, 188–189, 205, 318
education required in, 398–400
educational, 398–400
Elizabethan, *see* Elizabethan
environmental, 207–210
epic, 181–184
"free," 147, 148
group, 284
of illusion, 163–168, 173–174, 347–348
as industry, 14–16, 69–70
laws on, 124, 128
management of, 409–410
as motion, 92–102
mythos of, 8–11
nature of, 3–17
nineteenth-century, 142–162
noncommercial, 205–210
professionalism in, 69–70, 110, 397–398, 403
Renaissance, 89
Shakespearean, 67–89
taboos in, 197–201
technical practice in, 364–365
See also Acting techniques
theory of
    Horace on, 53
    presentational and representational, 345–346
three elements of, 4
traditional and modern attitudes in, 260
underground, 16–17, 199–201, 205–206
    See also Avant-garde theatre
See also Broadway; Theatre architecture; individual countries
Theatre architecture
architects and, in design, 354
of Beat Generation, 200
design and, 343, 344
design of, 3
designer and, 348–350
eighteenth-century, late, 125
Elizabethan, 75–78
English, about 1596, *68*
fifteenth-century, *57*
French drama and, 179
French neoclassical, 98–101
Greek, *23*, *30*, 32–34, *52*, *53*

improvisation and, 281
London, 1660 to 1777, 126–127
medieval, *61*, *62*
of Molière's time, *111*
nineteenth-century, 143
for noncommercial theatre, 205
outdoor, 62–66
recent, *3*
Renaissance interpretation of, *54*, 90–92
Roman, 47, 48, *89*, *91*
round, *368*
Shakespeare's, *73*, *76*
Vitruvius on, 51–53
Theatre of Dionysus, 31–34, *52*
Theatre Guild, 165–167
Théâtre Libre, 147, 173
Théâtre de l'Oeuvre, 176
Theatre Royal, 126, 127, 136
    at Drury Lane, 127–129, 134, 137
Thespis, 28, 39, 41
Thomas, Campbell, *402*
Three Sisters, The (Chekhov), *15*, *149*, 153–155, 157–162, *248*, *261*, *288*, *405*
Thrust stage, 324, *325*, 326, *330*, 349–350
Thymele, 32
Tirade, 97, 121, 122
Toller, Ernst, 176
    Man and the Masses, 177
Torelli, Giacomo, 93, 344
Tragedy
    in ancient Greece, 21–27
    Aristotle on, 235
    comedy and, 237–240
    Miller, Arthur, on, 172
    Molière and, 108
    neoclassicism and, 94–96
    origins of, 36–47
    Renaissance, 105, 106
    Roman, 49
    Serlio's scene for, *98*
    theory of, 236
Tragic flaw, 236
Transformers in lighting, 377
Tribalism, 11
Trilling, Lionel, 12
Trilogy, 29–30
Trinity Square Repertory Company, *15*
Tritagonist, 25, 26, 40
Trope, 56
Troupes, *commedia dell'arte*, 111, *112*
    See also Actors
Turgenyev, Ivan, 157
Turnell, Martin, 102

Ubermarionette, 175, 285
Underground theatre, 16–17, 199–201, 205–206

Unity
    Aristotle on, 235, 236
    neoclassical, 96, 102, 103
University of Illinois, *103*, *235*
University of Iowa, *339*, *371*, *391*
University of Missouri, 5, *323*
University Players, University of Michigan, *211*

van Italie, Jean-Claude, *America, Hurrah*, 208
Vanbrugh, John, 128
Vergil, 102
Victor, Dee, *137*
Le Vieux Colombier, 179
Village Voice, The, 207
Vitruvius, 22, 51–53
    De Architectura, 51, 90–92
Voice, 26–27
    use of, 287–291
        in neoclassical theatre, 97–98

Wagner, Richard, 173, 174
Walker, J. Morton, *323*
Warhol, Andy, 200, 206
Wayne State University, 7, *38*, *80*, *117*, *162*, *196*, *305*
Weigel, Helene, 183
Weiss, Peter
    The Investigation, 184
    Marat-Sade, 184
West, Jennifer, *202*
Whitehead, Robert, 205
Wickham, Glynn, 58, 61, 70
Wilde, Oscar, 155, 188
Wilder, Thornton, 185–187
    Our Town, 186, 187
    Skin of Our Teeth, The, 186
    Woman of Andros, 50
Williams, Tennessee, 166, 168, 169, 195, 197
    Streetcar Named Desire, 168
Williams, William Carlos, *Many Loves*, 208
Witt, Gary M., *38*, *80*, *196*, *305*
Woffington, Peg, 130
Woods, Richard, *137*
Wordsworth, William, "Preface to *Lyrical Ballads*," 143
Workers theatres, 181
WPA Theater Project, 181
Wycherley, William, *The Country Wife*, 50, 132, 241

Zola, Emile, 144–146, 149, 152–154
    Thérèse Racquin, 154